WORDSWORTH CLASSICS
OF WORLD LITERATURE

General Editor: Tom Griffith MA, MPhil

FIVE HISTORY PLAYS

William Shakespeare
Five History Plays

Richard III
Richard II
Henry IV Part 1
Henry IV Part 2
Henry V

❖

With Introductions by Emma Smith

WORDSWORTH CLASSICS
OF WORLD LITERATURE

This edition published 2000 by Wordsworth Editions Limited
Cumberland House, Crib Street, Ware, Hertfordshire SG12 9ET

ISBN 1 84022 101 1

Typeset by Antony Gray
Printed and bound in Great Britain by
Mackays of Chatham, Chatham, Kent

CONTENTS

INTRODUCTION

History as a storehouse of dramatic incident and character seems to have appealed to Shakespeare throughout his career, from his earliest plays on the reign of Henry VI to his account of Henry VIII, possibly his last play, some twenty years later. However, plays based on events and periods of English history were an especially prominent part of Shakespeare's output during the 1590s – the last decade of Elizabeth I's long reign. Indeed, history as a genre, in prose accounts such as Raphael Holinshed's *Chronicles . . . of England, Scotland and Ireland* (1587), poetic renditions such as the 'antique registers' of Alma's House of Temperance in Spenser's epic *The Faerie Queene* (1590), and plays by Shakespeare and others, was a preoccupation of Elizabethan culture. History provided a means of relating the present to the past and future, it was an important element in the establishment of English national and religious identity, and it allowed for the veiled discussion of current political issues. For the Renaissance, an age which defined itself by its self-conscious relation to the past, history was everywhere. Thus the exiled Jesuit priest Robert Parsons adduced examples from history to illustrate his argument[1] that the line of royal succession might be altered by the people in certain circumstances; for John Foxe history proved the inevitable justness of the Protestant faith[2]; for the Florentine political philosopher Niccolo Machiavelli (1469–1527), history showed how politics was the result of human, rather than divine, actions[3];

1 *A Conference about the Next Succession* (1594).
2 *Actes and Monuments* (first published in 1563 and frequently reprinted).
3 *The Prince* (1517).

examples from history gave John Stubbs the misguided confidence to advise Queen Elizabeth against marrying a French nobleman.[4] Late sixteenth-century England was fascinated by versions of its own ancestry.

History, however, was never firmly in the past, but instead offered a curious temporal amalgam, with its moral exemplars and warnings and its cycles of repetition, echo, prophecy, prefiguring, expiation, and the extended, sometimes mysterious, mechanisms of cause and effect. The writing of history was topical and immediate – sometimes explicitly, as in the references to Ireland in Henry V which have little to do with the historical situation and everything to do with England in 1599, and sometimes more obliquely, as in the plays' fascination with rebellion and with the transfer of power, which may owe something to contemporary concerns with the ageing and childless Elizabeth's unknown successor.

Ideas of history and the writing of history – historiography – were undergoing considerable change during the sixteenth century. The medieval model of a providential history, in which divine will alone motivated events, was being superseded by a version of the past in which human will was a prominent causal factor. An example from Holinshed's *Chronicles* may indicate how these two visions of the past could coexist. When he describes the rebellion of the Earl of Huntingdon against Henry IV, Holinshed spends some time detailing the material disadvantages and the tactical errors made by the Earl: his men were outnumbered, they were wrongly positioned, they set fire to some houses and were blinded by the smoke. The failure of the rebellion, therefore, had explicable human causes, and its history is viewed as the result of human actions. Holinshed ends his account, however, with a quite different attribution. The ultimate authority in the matter of Huntingdon's rebellion against his sovereign is divine: 'such was the ordinance of the mighty Lord of hosts, who disposeth all things at his pleasure.' If the rebellion fails because God wills it, there is little need to spend time on the human errors which confounded the Earl's uprising. Holinshed's account registers an overlap of providential and humanist ideas of history, and a similar overlap can be found in Shakespeare's plays.

4 *The Discovery of a Gaping Gulf* (1579).

There is no single view of history to be found in the plays grouped as 'histories' in the first collected edition of Shakespeare, the Folio of 1623: *Richard II* and *Richard III* have claims to be what *Hamlet*'s Polonius pedantically called 'tragical-historical'; the chorus structure of *Henry V* gives it an epic quality and the ending is straight out of comedy; and both parts of *Henry IV* employ comic devices and episodes, in particular the character of Falstaff who does indeed reappear in his own comedy, *The Merry Wives of Windsor* (1597). Similarly, some plays which are now identified as belonging to the rarefied category of tragedy have at their core historical sources: both *Macbeth* and *King Lear* take their plot and characters from the same historical chronicles used by Shakespeare for his history plays, and can be seen to share their concerns with succession, authority, rebellion and kingship. Just as different ideas of history can be discerned in the period, so too can different types of historical play, as Shakespeare's histories exist as a genre in the interstices of comedy and tragedy, borrowing freely from their repertoire of dramatic conventions and devices.

When Shakespeare's history plays came to be gathered together for collected publication after his death, they were printed in order of historical sequence. This is not, however, the order in which they were written: if Shakespeare conceived them as a serial historical epic, he certainly did not begin at the beginning and work through to the end. Plays dealing with the reign of Henry VI were written first, followed by *Richard III*, and then the run of plays historically preceding these: *Richard II*, both parts of *Henry IV*, and *Henry V*. In the present edition, the plays are printed in the order in which they were written. History is always subject to dramatic irony: we know what its protagonists can never know – what happened next. The order in which Shakespeare wrote his history plays compounds this irony. When the Epilogue to *Henry V*, for example, prophesies the collapse of Henry's magnificent victory during the reign of his son, this would not have been news to the play's first audiences, who would have already had the opportunity to see this part of the saga. On one level, the history plays exist as individual and complete pieces and were originally performed as such. The tradition of performing them in sequence, as the English Shakespeare Company did on tour in Britain during the 1980s, is a modern one, and may reflect our ideas of historical continuity rather than Elizabethan ones. The plays do, however, form a composite aesthetic experience, with shared imagery and a structure of recollection and prophecy which looks forward and backwards, within both the chronology of historical events and the chronology of Shakespearean composition.

By the end of the sixteenth century, the writing of English history had become restricted and censored. Its facility for debating current events and for alluding to contemporary personages was too dangerous to be left uncontrolled, and like many nervous political regimes before and since, the Privy Council asserted its authority over the present through its control of accounts of the past. History's capacity to affect the present was confirmed by this action. Shakespeare's history plays are, above all, topical and political, then as now. From Elizabeth I's supposed identification of herself with Richard II, to satirical cartoons of the eighteenth century which pictured the Prince Regent as a dissolute Hal, to Laurence Olivier's stirringly patriotic wartime *Henry V* in the cinema, the history plays have been used to comment on different political regimes and situations. Just as the historical material was used by Shakespeare with an eye to the political context of the late sixteenth century, so the plays have been variously refashioned by readers, critics and theatre practitioners to speak to their own particular context. As for the Elizabethans, so for us: history is never finished and never over, hence the perennial fascination of these intensely and humanly political plays.

EMMA SMITH
Hertford College
Oxford

NOTE ON THE TEXT

None of Shakespeare's plays exists in an original manuscript. Ever since the earliest sixteenth- and seventeenth-century editions, therefore, the plays have been shaped, in small but significant ways, by publication. There is no 'original' – except a printed one – to revert to. Different editors see their role in different ways, but most modern editions try to balance authenticity with accessibility. Thus, most modern editions, like this one, have modernised spelling and punctuation, *dramatis personae*, and additional stage directions. Where two early texts of a play exist, the editor must adjudicate between their competing claims in order to draw up his or her own text.

This edition is derived from the New Shakespeare series produced under the general editorship of Sir Arthur Quiller-Couch and John Dover Wilson. In it the following typographical conventions have been adopted to indicate editorial intervention:

Original stage directions are indicated between two single quotation marks; all other stage directions are editorial.

Where two differing versions of the play exist, passages which are not found in both are enclosed in square brackets.

Readers who would like to find out more about the early texts of Shakespeare's plays and the issues involved in editing are referred to Stanley Wells and Gary Taylor, *William Shakespeare: A Textual Companion* (Oxford, 1987).

The Houses of Lancaster and York

EDWARD III (1327–1377) *m.* Philippa of Hainault (d.1369)

EDWARD Prince of Wales (Black Prince) (d.1376)

LIONEL Duke of Clarence (d.1368)

JOHN of Gaunt Duke of Lancaster (d.1399) *m.* (1) Blanche of Lancaster (d.1369)

EDMUND Duke of York (d.1402) *m.* Isabella of Castile (d.1369)

JOAN of Kent (d.1385) *m.* **EDWARD** Prince of Wales (Black Prince) (d.1376)

RICHARD II (1377–1399)

HENRY IV (of Bolingbroke) (1399–1413) *m.* Mary de Bohun (d.1394)

RICHARD Earl of Cambridge (ex.1415) *m.* ANNE MORTIMER

EDWARD Duke of York (d.1415)

HENRY V (1413–1422) *m.* Katherine of Valois (d.1437)

RICHARD PLANTAGENET Duke of York, Protector of England (1411–1460) *m.* CECILY NEVILLE (Granddaughter of John of Gaunt and Katherine Swynford)

HENRY VI (1422–1461) (1470–1471) *m.* Margaret of Anjou (d.1482)

EDWARD IV (1461–1483) *m.* Elizabeth Woodville (d.1492)

GEORGE Duke of Clarence (d.1478)

RICHARD III (1483–1485) *m.* Anne Neville (d.1485)

EDWARD Prince of Wales (d.1471)

ELIZABETH of York (d.1503) *m.* **HENRY VII** (1485–1509)

EDWARD V (never crowned) (1483)

EDWARD Prince of Wales (d.1484)

RICHARD III

INTRODUCTION

Written and performed around 1592–93, *Richard III* was printed in
1597. In it, Shakespeare draws on existing accounts of Richard of
Gloucester, especially those provided by Raphael Holinshed and by
Sir Thomas More, but he deals freely with historical sequence in
order to focus attention on his protagonist. *Richard III* was described
as a tragedy at its earliest publication, and while its moral character
may not fit our expectations that a tragic hero be a noble figure
fatally but sympathetically flawed, the play's dramatic emphasis on
Richard corresponds to the individualistic aesthetic of tragedy.

Richard opens the play, in a speech which does much to remind
audiences of the events of Henry VI's reign as told in three plays
performed between 1590 and 1592. Part 3 of *Henry VI*, the play
which immediately precedes *Richard III* in narrative sequence, ended
with Richard Duke of Gloucester's ambition to become king, and it is
this bloody ambition which motivates the first half of Richard's own
play. Introducing the play with a soliloquy by its eponymous 'hero' is
unique in Shakespeare, and this opening emphasises Richard's domi-
nation of the play. The famous opening lines, 'Now is the winter of
our discontent Made glorious summer by this sun of York' (1.1.1–2),
and the description of the smoothing of 'grim-visaged war' (9), reveal
that Richard is not a man suited to the leisurely pursuits of peacetime.
He seems consciously to take up wickedness: 'I am determinéd to
prove a villain And hate the idle pleasures of these days' (30–31). This
extended use of soliloquy also makes the audience immediately
sympathetic with him: unlike Richard's victims, we are in on the plot
from the beginning, and while we may scruple at his methods and his
lack of conscience, we cannot help but be attracted by this ironic,
intelligent, unscrupulous, self-revelatory villain.

Richard's characterisation is extreme but it is not two-dimensional, and, as one of Shakespeare's longest roles, it has attracted tragic actors of the highest calibre. His cool awareness of his own turpitude and his self-delight are infectious, and his sardonic wit is beguiling. When he wonders at his success in wooing Lady Anne over the corpse of the husband he has murdered, his sense of achievement is palpable: 'Was ever woman in this humour wooed? Was ever woman in this humour won?' (1.2.227–28). Some of his remarks and his asides are addressed directly to an audience – 'here Clarence comes' (1.1.41) – and we are complicit in his wickedness. Ian McKellen, in a recent film version of the play directed by Richard Loncraine, looked directly and unflinchingly at the camera in his opening speech, urging it to follow him with a jerk of his head, and thus demonstrating his control of it, and by extension, the audience.

Richard's terrible attractiveness is experienced by characters within the play. While his physical person is deformed and there is a litany of abusive terms for him which reduce him to the level of a beast – 'hedgehog' (1.2.102), 'toad' (1.2.147), 'elvish-marked, abortive, rooting hog!' (1.3.228), 'bottled spider' (1.3.242) – he has a very real, but almost indefinable, seductive quality. He is able to persuade Lady Anne of his repentance, and to sow dissension among the royal family. The same wit and intelligence which appeal to an audience, even as we deplore the ends to which these qualities are put, are able to manipulate Richard onto the throne. He is a consummate stage-manager, first staging the scene in which Buckingham and the mayor beg him to take on the crown and then staging his own reluctance. Richard voices a truth: 'I am unfit for state and majesty' (3.7.205), and he so directs the scene that he seems to have been forced, against his will, to take the crown. Even his eventual, well-timed acceptance is conditional on their reporting his unwillingness. There is heavy dramatic irony in his pious statement: 'For God doth know, and you may partly see, How far I am from the desire of this' (3.7.235–36).

For much of the play, Richard's rise seems unstoppable. One effect of his predominant stage-presence is that no other character is able to challenge him – morally or dramatically. Only the women in the play, in their formalised rituals of cursing, memory and prophecy, offer any resistance to his plotting, and in the end their maledictions are fulfilled. They have no means of action save language, and thus the women's roles present some of the most noticeable examples of the play's formal rhetorical style, almost as if the moral chaos around them can be contained through artificial, highly wrought utterance. Queen Margaret, widow of Henry VI, gives form to her grief through the liturgical rhythms of repetition: 'I had an Edward, till a Richard killed him; I had a Harry, till a Richard killed him: Thou hadst an Edward, till a Richard killed him; Thou hadst a Richard, till a Richard killed him' (4.4.40–43)

Richard's energies are considerable. As the king surrounded by his enemies at the decisive battle of Bosworth, he delivers a powerful address to his soldiers and his country: 'Fight, gentlemen of England! Fight, bold yeomen!' (5.3.338). The echo of this call to arms will be heard in *Henry V*. Richmond's summary of his adversary, 'A bloody tyrant and a homicide: One raised in blood, and one in blood established' (5.3.246–47) may tell the facts, but it does not convey the character of the man. Richard's soliloquy before the battle articulates a painfully isolated sense of self: 'There is no creature loves me; And if I die, no soul will pity me: Nay, wherefore should they, since that I myself Find in myself no pity to myself' (5.3.200–03). The procession of ghosts which haunt him can be seen as a representation of an inner, conscience-stricken state rather than the sensational irruption of the supernatural. There is no nod towards conventional morality even at the end, as Richard dies without repentance. Having controlled his own destiny through the supreme effort of will, he surrenders to chance rather than to heaven: 'I will stand the hazard of the die' (5.4.10). And for all that Shakespeare's extreme representation of Richard's character may be attributed to the need, under the Tudor monarch Elizabeth, to present her ancestor Richmond as the saviour of his beleaguered country, Richmond himself is pale and uninteresting compared to the dramatic vigour of his adversary. 'Abate the edge of traitors, gracious Lord', prays the godly Richmond, as he predicts that his descendants will 'Enrich the time to come with smooth-faced peace, With smiling plenty and fair prosperous days' (5.5.33–34). But while this may be a worthy political aspiration, it is not a very dramatic one. For all his wickedness, Richard's vitality ensured his place as hero and dramatic centre of his play, and for all its disturbance, his bloody reign made for good drama. No wonder, then, that it is not 'smooth-faced peace', but rather 'grim-visaged war' which is to preoccupy Shakespeare's next historical plays.

The scene: London and elsewhere in England

CHARACTERS IN THE PLAY

KING EDWARD THE FOURTH
EDWARD, PRINCE OF WALES,
   afterwards King Edward V } *sons to the King*
RICHARD, *Duke of York*
GEORGE, *Duke of Clarence*
RICHARD, *Duke of Gloucester,* } *brothers to King Edward*
   afterwards King Richard III
A young son of Clarence [Edward Plantagenet]
HENRY, *Earl of Richmond, afterwards King Henry VII*
CARDINAL [*Thomas Bourchier, Archbishop of Canterbury*]
ARCHBISHOP OF YORK [*Thomas Rotherham*]
BISHOP OF ELY [*John Morton*]
DUKE OF BUCKINGHAM
DUKE OF NORFOLK
EARL OF SURREY, *his son*
ANTHONY WOODVILLE, EARL RIVERS, *brother to Elizabeth*
MARQUIS OF DORSET *and* LORD GREY, *sons to Elizabeth*
EARL OF OXFORD
LORD HASTINGS
LORD STANLEY, EARL OF DERBY
LORD LOVEL
SIR THOMAS VAUGHAN
SIR RICHARD RATCLIFFE
SIR WILLIAM CATESBY
SIR JAMES TYRREL
SIR JAMES BLOUNT
SIR WALTER HERBERT
SIR ROBERT BRAKENBURY, *Lieutenant of the Tower*
SIR WILLIAM BRANDON
CHRISTOPHER URSWICK, *a priest*
Another Priest
TRESSEL *and* BERKELEY, *gentlemen attending on the*
   Lady Anne

Lord Mayor of London
Sheriff of Wiltshire

ELIZABETH, *queen to King Edward IV*
MARGARET, *widow of King Henry VI*
DUCHESS OF YORK, *mother to King Edward IV*
LADY ANNE, *widow of Edward Prince of Wales, the son of
    King Henry VI; afterwards married to Richard*
A young daughter of Clarence [*Margaret Plantagenet*]

*Ghosts of those murdered by Richard III, Lords and other
Attendants; a Pursuivant, Scrivener, Citizens, Murderers,
Messengers, Soldiers, etc.*

THE TRAGEDY OF RICHARD III

ACT I SCENE I

London. A street

'*Enter* RICHARD, DUKE OF GLOUCESTER, *solus*'

RICHARD   Now is the winter of our discontent
Made glorious summer by this sun of York;
And all the clouds that loured upon our house
In the deep bosom of the ocean buried.
Now are our brows bound with victorious wreaths,
Our bruiséd arms hung up for monuments,
Our stern alarums changed to merry meetings,
Our dreadful marches to delightful measures.
Grim-visaged war hath smoothed his wrinkléd front;
And now, instead of mounting barbéd steeds   10
To fright the souls of fearful adversaries,
He capers nimbly in a lady's chamber
To the lascivious pleasing of a lute.
But I, that am not shaped for sportive tricks,
Nor made to court an amorous looking-glass;
I, that am rudely stamped, and want love's majesty
To strut before a wanton ambling nymph;
I, that am curtailed of this fair proportion,
Cheated of feature by dissembling Nature,
Deformed, unfinished, sent before my time   20
Into this breathing world, scarce half made up,
And that so lamely and unfashionable
That dogs bark at me as I halt by them;
Why, I, in this weak piping time of peace,
Have no delight to pass away the time,
Unless to spy my shadow in the sun
And descant on mine own deformity:
And therefore, since I cannot prove a lover,
To entertain these fair well-spoken days,
I am determinéd to prove a villain   30
And hate the idle pleasures of these days.
Plots have I laid, inductions dangerous,

By drunken prophecies, libels and dreams,
To set my brother Clarence and the king
In deadly hate the one against the other:
And if King Edward be as true and just
As I am subtle, false and treacherous,
This day should Clarence closely be mewed up,
About a prophecy, which says that G
Of Edward's heirs the murderer shall be.   40
Dive, thoughts, down to my soul – here Clarence
                             comes.

Enter CLARENCE, *guarded, and*
BRAKENBURY, *Lieutenant of the Tower*

Brother, good day: what means this arméd guard
That waits upon your grace?
CLARENCE   His majesty,
Tend'ring my person's safety, hath appointed
This conduct to convey me to the Tower.
RICHARD   Upon what cause?
CLARENCE   Because my name is George.
RICHARD   Alack, my lord, that fault is none of yours;
He should, for that, commit your godfathers:
Belike his majesty hath some intent
That you should be new-christ'ned in the Tower.   50
But what's the matter, Clarence? May I know?
CLARENCE Yea, Richard, when I know; for I protest
As yet I do not: but, as I can learn,
He hearkens after prophecies and dreams;
And from the cross-row plucks the letter G,
And says a wizard told him that by G
His issue disinherited should be;
And, for my name of George begins with G,
It follows in his thought that I am he.
These, as I learn, and such like toys as these   60
Hath moved his highness to commit me now.
RICHARD   Why, this it is, when men are ruled by women:
'Tis not the king that sends you to the Tower;
My Lady Grey his wife, Clarence, 'tis she
That tempers him to this extremity.
Was it not she, and that good man of worship,

Anthony Woodville, her brother there,
That made him send Lord Hastings to the Tower,
From whence this present day he is delivered?
We are not safe, Clarence, we are not safe.   70

CLARENCE By heaven, I think there's no man is secure
But the queen's kindred, and night-walking heralds
That trudge betwixt the king and Mistress Shore.
Heard you not what an humble suppliant
Lord Hastings was for his delivery?

RICHARD Humbly complaining to her deity
Got my Lord Chamberlain his liberty.
I'll tell you what, I think it is our way
If we will keep in favour with the king,
To be her men and wear her livery.   80
The jealous o'erworn widow and herself,
Since that our brother dubbed them gentlewomen,
Are mighty gossips in our monarchy.

BRAKEN. Beseech your graces both to pardon me;
His majesty hath straitly given in charge
That no man shall have private conference
(Of what degree soever) with his brother.

RICHARD Even so; an't please your worship, Brakenbury,
You may partake of anything we say:
We speak no treason, man: we say the king   90
Is wise and virtuous, and his noble queen
Well struck in years, fair, and not jealous;
We say that Shore's wife hath a pretty foot,
A cherry lip, a bonny eye, a passing pleasing tongue;
And that the queen's kin are made gentlefolks:
How say you, sir? Can you deny all this?

BRAKEN. With this, my lord, myself have nought to do.

RICHARD Naught to do with Mistress Shore! I tell thee, fellow,
He that doth naught with her (excepting one)
Were best to do it secretly, alone.   100

BRAKEN. What one, my lord?

RICHARD Her husband, knave: wouldst thou betray me?

BRAKEN. I do beseech your grace to pardon me:
Forbear your conference with the noble duke.

CLARENCE We know thy charge, Brakenbury, and will obey.

RICHARD   We are the queen's abjects, and must obey.
          Brother, farewell: I will unto the king;
          And whatsoe'er you will employ me in,
          Were it to call King Edward's widow sister,
          I will perform it to enfranchise you.   110
          Meantime, this deep disgrace in brotherhood
          Touches me nearer than you can imagine.
CLARENCE I know it pleaseth neither of us well.
RICHARD   Well, your imprisonment shall not be long;
          I will deliver you, or else lie for you:
          Meantime, have patience.
CLARENCE   I must perforce. Farewell.
              [Clarence, Brakenbury, and the Guard pass on
RICHARD   Go, tread the path that thou shalt ne'er return:
          Simple, plain Clarence, I do love thee so,
          That I will shortly send thy soul to heaven,
          If heaven will take the present at our hands.   120
          But who comes here? The new-delivered Hastings?

                  'Enter LORD HASTINGS'

HASTINGS Good time of day unto my gracious lord!
RICHARD   As much unto my good Lord Chamberlain!
          Well are you welcome to the open air.
          How hath your lordship brooked imprisonment?
HASTINGS With patience, noble lord, as prisoners must:
          But I shall live, my lord, to give them thanks
          That were the cause of my imprisonment.
RICHARD   No doubt, no doubt; and so shall Clarence too;
          For they that were your enemies are his,   130
          And have prevailed as much on him as you.
HASTINGS More pity that the eagles should be mewed,
          Whiles kites and buzzards prey at liberty.
RICHARD   What news abroad?
HASTINGS No news so bad abroad as this at home:
          The king is sickly, weak, and melancholy,
          And his physicians fear him mightily.
RICHARD   Now, by Saint John, that news is bad indeed.
          O, he hath kept an evil diet long,
          And overmuch consumed his royal person: 140

'Tis very grievous to be thought upon.
Where is he, in his bed?

HASTINGS He is.

RICHARD   Go you before, and I will follow you. [*Hastings departs*
He cannot live, I hope; and must not die
Till George be packed with post-horse up to heaven.
I'll in, to urge his hatred more to Clarence
With lies well steeled with weighty arguments;
And, if I fail not in my deep intent,
Clarence hath not another day to live: 150
Which done, God take King Edward to his mercy,
And leave the world for me to bustle in!
For then I'll marry Warwick's youngest daughter.
What though I killed her husband and her father?
The readiest way to make the wench amends
Is to become her husband and her father:
The which will I; not all so much for love
As for another secret close intent
By marrying her which I must reach unto.
But yet I run before my horse to market: 160
Clarence still breathes, Edward still lives and reigns;
When they are gone, then must I count my gains.
                                              [*he goes*

SCENE 2

'Enter the corpse of Henry the Sixth, with halberds to guard it;
LADY ANNE *being the mourner', attended by* TRESSEL *and* BERKELEY

ANNE   Set down, set down your honourable load,
If honour may be shrouded in a hearse,
Whilst I awhile obsequiously lament
Th'untimely fall of virtuous Lancaster.
Poor key-cold figure of a holy king!
Pale ashes of the house of Lancaster!
Thou bloodless remnant of that royal blood!
Be it lawful that I invocate thy ghost,
To hear the lamentations of poor Anne,
Wife to thy Edward, to thy slaught'red son,   10

Stabbed by the selfsame hand that made these wounds!
Lo, in these windows that let forth thy life
I pour the helpless balm of my poor eyes.
O curséd be the hand that made these holes!
Curséd the blood that let this blood from hence!
Curséd the heart that had the heart to do it!
More direful hap betide that hated wretch
That makes us wretched by the death of thee
Than I can wish to adders, spiders, toads,
Or any creeping venomed thing that lives!   20
If ever he have child, abortive be it,
Prodigious, and untimely brought to light,
Whose ugly and unnatural aspect
May fright the hopeful mother at the view;
And that be heir to his unhappiness!
If ever he have wife, let her be made
More miserable by the life of him
Than I am by my young lord's death and thee!
Come, now towards Chertsey with your holy load,
Taken from Paul's to be interréd there;   30
And still, as you are weary of this weight,
Rest you, whiles I lament King Henry's corse.

'Enter RICHARD, DUKE OF GLOUCESTER*'*

RICHARD   Stay, you that bear the corse, and set it down.
ANNE   What black magician conjures up this fiend,
            To stop devoted charitable deeds?
RICHARD   Villains, set down the corse; or, by Saint Paul,
            I'll make a corse of him that disobeys.
HALBERD   My lord, stand back, and let the coffin pass.
RICHARD   Unmannered dog! Stand thou, when I command:
            Advance thy halberd higher than my breast,   40
            Or, by Saint Paul, I'll strike thee to my foot,
            And spurn upon thee, beggar, for thy boldness.
ANNE   What, do you tremble? Are you all afraid?
            Alas, I blame you not, for you are mortal,
            And mortal eyes cannot endure the devil.
            Avaunt, thou dreadful minister of hell!
            Thou hadst but power over his mortal body,
            His soul thou canst not have; therefore, be gone.

RICHARD	Sweet saint, for charity, be not so curst.
ANNE	Foul devil, for God's sake, hence, and trouble us not, 50
	For thou hast made the happy earth thy hell,
	Filled it with cursing cries and deep exclaims.
	If thou delight to view thy heinous deeds,
	Behold this pattern of thy butcheries.
	O, gentlemen, see, see! Dead Henry's wounds
	Open their congealed mouths and bleed afresh.
	Blush, blush, thou lump of foul deformity;
	For 'tis thy presence that exhales this blood
	From cold and empty veins, where no blood dwells;
	Thy deeds, inhuman and unnatural, 60
	Provokes this deluge most unnatural.
	O God, which this blood mad'st, revenge his death!
	O earth, which this blood drink'st, revenge his death!
	Either heaven, with lightning strike the murd'rer dead,
	Or earth, gape open wide and eat him quick,
	As thou dost swallow up this good king's blood,
	Which his hell-governed arm hath butcheréd!
RICHARD	Lady, you know no rules of charity,
	Which renders good for bad, blessings for curses.
ANNE	Villain, thou know'st no law of God nor man: 70
	No beast so fierce but knows some touch of pity.
RICHARD	But I know none, and therefore am no beast.
ANNE	O wonderful, when devils tell the truth!
RICHARD	More wonderful, when angels are so angry.
	Vouchsafe, divine perfection of a woman,
	Of these supposéd crimes to give me leave,
	By circumstance, but to acquit myself.
ANNE	Vouchsafe, diffused infection of a man,
	Of these known evils but to give me leave,
	By circumstance, to accuse thy curséd self. 80
RICHARD	Fairer than tongue can name thee, let me have
	Some patient leisure to excuse myself.
ANNE	Fouler than heart can think thee, thou canst make
	No excuse current but to hang thyself.
RICHARD	By such despair, I should accuse myself.
ANNE	And, by despairing, shalt thou stand excused
	For doing worthy vengeance on thyself

	That didst unworthy slaughter upon others.
RICHARD	Say that I slew them not?
ANNE	Then say they were not slain:
	But dead they are, and, devilish slave, by thee. 90
RICHARD	I did not kill your husband.
ANNE	Why, then he is alive.
RICHARD	Nay, he is dead; and slain by Edward's hands.
ANNE	In thy foul throat thou liest: Queen Margaret saw
	Thy murd'rous falchion smoking in his blood;
	The which thou once didst bend against her breast,
	But that thy brothers beat aside the point.
RICHARD	I was provokéd by her sland'rous tongue,
	That laid their guilt upon my guiltless shoulders.
ANNE	Thou wast provokéd by thy bloody mind,
	That never dream'st on aught but butcheries. 100
	Didst thou not kill this king?
RICHARD	I grant ye.
ANNE	Dost grant me, hedgehog? Then, God grant me too
	Thou mayst be damnéd for that wicked deed!
	O, he was gentle, mild, and virtuous!
RICHARD	The better for the King of heaven, that hath him.
ANNE	He is in heaven, where thou shalt never come.
RICHARD	Let him thank me, that holp to send him thither;
	For he was fitter for that place than earth.
ANNE	And thou unfit for any place but hell.
RICHARD	Yes, one place else, if you will hear me name it. 110
ANNE	Some dungeon.
RICHARD	Your bed-chamber.
ANNE	Ill rest betide the chamber where thou liest!
RICHARD	So will it, madam, till I lie with you.
ANNE	I hope so.
RICHARD	I know so. But, gentle Lady Anne,
	To leave this keen encounter of our wits,
	And fall something into a slower method,
	Is not the causer of the timeless deaths
	Of these Plantagenets, Henry and Edward,
	As blameful as the executioner?
ANNE	Thou wast the cause of that accursed effect. 120
RICHARD	Your beauty was the cause of that effect;

            Your beauty, that did haunt me in my sleep
            To undertake the death of all the world,
            So I might live one hour in your sweet bosom.

ANNE   If I thought that, I tell thee, homicide,
            These nails should rend that beauty from my cheeks.

RICHARD   These eyes could not endure that beauty's wrack;
            You should not blemish it, if I stood by:
            As all the world is cheeréd by the sun,
            So I by that; it is my day, my life.   130

ANNE   Black night o'ershade thy day, and death thy life!

RICHARD   Curse not thyself, fair creature; thou art both.

ANNE   I would I were, to be revenged on thee.

RICHARD   It is a quarrel most unnatural,
            To be revenged on him that loveth thee.

ANNE   It is a quarrel just and reasonable,
            To be revenged on him that killed my husband.

RICHARD   He that bereft thee, lady, of thy husband,
            Did it to help thee to a better husband.

ANNE   His better doth not breathe upon the earth.   140

RICHARD   He lives that loves thee better than he could.

ANNE   Name him.

RICHARD   Plantagenet.

ANNE   Why, that was he,

RICHARD   The selfsame name, but one of better nature.

ANNE   Where is he?

RICHARD   Here.   [*she 'spits at him'*
                 Why dost thou spit at me?

ANNE   Would it were mortal poison, for thy sake!

RICHARD   Never came poison from so sweet a place.

ANNE   Never hung poison on a fouler toad.
            Out of my sight! Thou dost infect mine eyes.

RICHARD   Thine eyes, sweet lady, have infected mine.

ANNE   Would they were basilisks to strike thee dead!   150

RICHARD   I would they were, that I might die at once;
            For now they kill me with a living death.
            Those eyes of thine from mine have drawn salt tears,
            Shamed their aspects with store of childish drops:
            These eyes, which never shed remorseful tear,
            No, when my father York and Edward wept,

To hear the piteous moan that Rutland made
When black-faced Clifford shook his sword at him;
Nor when thy warlike father, like a child,
Told the sad story of my father's death,   160
And twenty times made pause to sob and weep
That all the standers-by had wet their cheeks
Like trees bedashed with rain – in that sad time
My manly eyes did scorn an humble tear;
And what these sorrows could not thence exhale
Thy beauty hath, and made them blind with weeping.
I never sued to friend nor enemy;
My tongue could never learn sweet smoothing word;
But, now thy beauty is proposed my fee,
My proud heart sues, and prompts my tongue to speak.   170
                        [*'she looks scornfully at him'*
Teach not thy lip such scorn, for it was made
For kissing, lady, not for such contempt.
If thy revengeful heart cannot forgive,
Lo, here I lend thee this sharp-pointed sword;
Which if thou please to hide in this true breast,
And let the soul forth that adoreth thee,
I lay it naked to the deadly stroke,
And humbly beg the death upon my knee.
        [*'he lays his breast open: she offers at it with his sword'*
Nay, do not pause; for I did kill King Henry,
But 'twas thy beauty that provokéd me.   180
Nay, now dispatch; 'twas I that stabbed young Edward,
But 'twas thy heavenly face that set me on.
                            [*'she falls the sword'*
Take up the sword again, or take up me.

ANNE   Arise, dissembler: though I wish thy death,
            I will not be thy executioner.
RICHARD   Then bid me kill myself, and I will do it.
ANNE   I have already.
RICHARD   That was in thy rage:
            Speak it again, and even with the word
            This hand, which, for thy love, did kill thy love,
            Shall, for thy love, kill a far truer love;   190
            To both their deaths shalt thou be accessary.

ANNE   I would I knew thy heart.

RICHARD   'Tis figured in my tongue.

ANNE   I fear me both are false.

RICHARD   Then never was man true.

ANNE   Well, well, put up your sword.

RICHARD   Say, then, my peace is made.

ANNE   That shalt thou know hereafter.

RICHARD   But shall I live in hope?

ANNE   All men, I hope, live so.   200

RICHARD   Vouchsafe to wear this ring.

ANNE   To take is not to give.   [*she puts on the ring*

RICHARD   Look how my ring encompasseth thy finger,
           Even so thy breast encloseth my poor heart;
           Wear both of them, for both of them are thine.
           And if thy poor devoted servant may
           But beg one favour at thy gracious hand,
           Thou dost confirm his happiness for ever.

ANNE   What is it?

RICHARD   That it may please you leave these sad designs   210
           To him that hath most cause to be a mourner,
           And presently repair to Crosby House;
           Where, after I have solemnly interred
           At Chertsey monast'ry this noble king,
           And wet his grave with my repentant tears,
           I will with all expedient duty see you:
           For divers unknown reasons, I beseech you,
           Grant me this boon.

ANNE   With all my heart; and much it joys me too,
           To see you are become so penitent.   220
           Tressel and Berkeley, go along with me.

RICHARD   Bid me farewell.

ANNE   'Tis more than you deserve;
           But since you teach me how to flatter you,
           Imagine I have said farewell already.
                  [*she goes, followed by two of the halberds*

RICHARD   Sirs, take up the corse.

HALBERD   Towards Chertsey, noble lord?

RICHARD   No, to Whitefriars; there attend my coming.
                [*they carry away the corpse*

Was ever woman in this humour wooed?
Was ever woman in this humour won?
I'll have her; but I will not keep her long.
What! I, that killed her husband and his father,   230
To take her in her heart's extremest hate,
With curses in her mouth, tears in her eyes,
The bleeding witness of my hatred by;
Having God, her conscience, and these bars against me,
And I no friends to back my suit at all,
But the plain devil and dissembling looks,
And yet to win her! All the world to nothing!
Ha?
Hath she forgot already that brave prince,
Edward, her lord, whom I, some three months since,   240
Stabbed in my angry mood at Tewkesbury?
A sweeter and a lovelier gentleman –
Framed in the prodigality of nature,
Young, valiant, wise, and, no doubt, right royal –
The spacious world cannot again afford:
And will she yet abase her eyes on me,
That cropped the golden prime of this sweet prince,
And made her widow to a woeful bed?
On me, whose all not equals Edward's moiety?
On me, that halts and am misshapen thus?   250
My dukedom to a beggarly denier,
I do mistake my person all this while:
Upon my life, she finds, although I cannot,
Myself to be a marv'llous proper man.
I'll be at charges for a looking-glass,
And entertain a score or two of tailors,
To study fashions to adorn my body:
Since I am crept in favour with myself,
I will maintain it with some little cost.
But first I'll turn yon fellow in his grave;   260
And then return lamenting to my love.
Shine out, fair sun, till I have bought a glass,
That I may see my shadow as I pass.

                                             [he goes

SCENE 3

London. The palace

Enter QUEEN ELIZABETH, LORD RIVERS, *and* LORD GREY

RIVERS   Have patience, madam: there's no doubt his majesty
           Will soon recover his accustomed health.

GREY   In that you brook it ill, it makes him worse:
           Therefore, for God's sake, entertain good comfort,
           And cheer his grace with quick and merry eyes.

Q. ELIZAB. If he were dead, what would betide on me?

GREY   No other harm but loss of such a lord.

Q. ELIZAB. The loss of such a lord includes all harms.

GREY   The heavens have blessed you with a goodly son,
           To be your comforter when he is gone.   10

Q. ELIZAB. Ah, he is young, and his minority
           Is put unto the trust of Richard Gloucester,
           A man that loves not me, nor none of you.

RIVERS   Is it concluded he shall be Protector?

Q. ELIZAB. It is determined, not concluded yet:
           But so it must be, if the king miscarry.

Enter BUCKINGHAM *and* STANLEY, EARL OF DERBY

GREY   Here come the lords of Buckingham and Derby.

BUCK'HAM Good time of day unto your royal grace!

STANLEY God make your majesty joyful as you have been!

Q. ELIZAB. The Countess Richmond, good my Lord of Derby,   20
           To your good prayer will scarcely say amen.
           Yet, Derby, notwithstanding she's your wife,
           And loves not me, be you, good lord, assured
           I hate not you for her proud arrogance.

STANLEY I do beseech you, either not believe
           The envious slanders of her false accusers,
           Or if she be accused on true report,
           Bear with her weakness, which I think proceeds
           From wayward sickness, and no grounded malice.

Q. ELIZAB. Saw you the king today, my Lord of Derby?   30

STANLEY But now the Duke of Buckingham and I
           Are come from visiting his majesty.

Q. ELIZAB. What likelihood of his amendment, lords?

BUCK'HAM Madam, good hope; his grace speaks cheerfully.

Q. ELIZAB. God grant him health! Did you confer with him?

BUCK'HAM Ay, madam: he desires to make atonement
Between the Duke of Gloucester and your brothers,
And between them and my Lord Chamberlain;
And sent to warn them to his royal presence.

Q. ELIZAB. Would all were well! But that will never be: 40
I fear our happiness is at the height.

Enter RICHARD, HASTINGS, *and* DORSET

RICHARD They do me wrong, and I will not endure it.
Who is it that complains unto the king,
That I, forsooth, am stern and love them not?
By holy Paul, they love his grace but lightly
That fill his ears with such dissentious rumours.
Because I cannot flatter and look fair,
Smile in men's faces, smooth, deceive and cog,
Duck with French nods and apish courtesy,
I must be held a rancorous enemy.   50
Cannot a plain man live and think no harm,
But thus his simple truth must be abused
With silken, sly, insinuating Jacks?

GREY To whom in all this presence speaks your grace?

RICHARD To thee, that hast nor honesty nor grace.
When have I injured thee? When done thee wrong?
Or thee? Or thee? Or any of your faction?
A plague upon you all! His royal grace
(Whom God preserve better than you would wish!)
Cannot be quiet scarce a breathing while,   60
But you must trouble him with lewd complaints.

Q. ELIZAB. Brother of Gloucester, you mistake the matter.
The king, on his own royal disposition,
And not provoked by any suitor else,
Aiming, belike, at your interior hatred,
That in your outward action shows itself
Against my children, brothers, and myself,
Makes him to send, that he may learn the ground
Of your ill-will, and thereby to remove it.

RICHARD	I cannot tell; the world is grown so bad, 70
	That wrens make prey where eagles dare not perch:
	Since every Jack became a gentleman,
	There's many a gentle person made a Jack.
Q. ELIZAB.	Come, come, we know your meaning, brother
	Gloucester;
	You envy my advancement and my friends'.
	God grant we never may have need of you!
RICHARD	Meantime, God grants that I have need of you:
	Our brother is imprisoned by your means,
	Myself disgraced, and the nobility
	Held in contempt, while great promotions 80
	Are daily given to ennoble those
	That scarce some two days since were worth a noble.
Q. ELIZAB.	By Him that raised me to this careful height
	From that contented hap which I enjoyed,
	I never did incense his majesty
	Against the Duke of Clarence, but have been
	An earnest advocate to plead for him.
	My lord, you do me shameful injury,
	Falsely to draw me in these vile suspects.
RICHARD	You may deny that you were not the mean 90
	Of my Lord Hastings' late imprisonment.
RIVERS	She may, my lord, for –
RICHARD	She may, Lord Rivers! Why, who knows not so?
	She may do more, sir, than denying that:
	She may help you to many fair preferments
	And then deny her aiding hand therein,
	And lay those honours on your high desert.
	What may she not? She may – ay, marry, may she –
RIVERS	What, marry, may she?
RICHARD	What, marry, may she! Marry with a king, 100
	A bachelor, and a handsome stripling too:
	Iwis your grandam had a worser match.
Q. ELIZAB.	My Lord of Gloucester, I have too long borne
	Your blunt upbraidings and your bitter scoffs:
	By heaven, I will acquaint his majesty
	Of those gross taunts that oft I have endured.
	I had rather be a country servant-maid

Than a great queen, with this condition,
To be so baited, scorned, and storméd at.

'Enter old QUEEN MARGARET*', behind*

	Small joy have I in being England's queen.	110
Q. MARG.	And less'néd be that small, God I beseech him!
	Thy honour, state, and seat is due to me.
RICHARD	What! Threat you me with telling of the king?
	Tell him, and spare not: look what I have said
	I will avouch't in presence of the king:
	I dare adventure to be sent to th'Tower.
	'Tis time to speak; my pains are quite forgot.
Q. MARG.	Out, devil! I do remember them too well:
	Thou kill'dst my husband Henry in the Tower,
	And Edward, my poor son, at Tewkesbury.	120
RICHARD	Ere you were queen, ay, or your husband king,
	I was a pack-horse in his great affairs;
	A weeder-out of his proud adversaries,
	A liberal rewarder of his friends:
	To royalise his blood I spent mine own.
Q. MARG.	Ay, and much better blood than his or thine.
RICHARD	In all which time you and your husband Grey
	Were factious for the house of Lancaster;
	And, Rivers, so were you. Was not your husband
	In Margaret's battle at Saint Albans slain?	130
	Let me put in your minds, if you forget,
	What you have been ere this, and what you are;
	Withal, what I have been, and what I am.
Q. MARG.	A murd'rous villain, and so still thou art.
RICHARD	Poor Clarence did forsake his father, Warwick;
	Ay, and forswore himself – which Jesu pardon! –
Q. MARG.	Which God revenge!
RICHARD	To fight on Edward's party for the crown;
	And for his meed, poor lord, he is mewed up.
	I would to God my heart were flint, like Edward's,	140
	Or Edward's soft and pitiful, like mine:
	I am too childish-foolish for this world.
Q. MARG.	Hie thee to hell for shame and leave this world,
	Thou cacodemon! There thy kingdom is.
RIVERS	My Lord of Gloucester, in those busy days

Which here you urge to prove us enemies,
We followed then our lord, our sovereign king:
So should we you, if you should be our king.

RICHARD   If I should be! I had rather be a pedlar:
Far be it from my heart, the thought thereof!   150

Q. ELIZAB. As little joy, my lord, as you suppose
You should enjoy, were you this country's king,
As little joy you may suppose in me
That I enjoy, being the queen thereof.

Q. MARG.   As little joy enjoys the queen thereof;
For I am she, and altogether joyless
I can no longer hold me patient.

                                        [aloud, advancing

Hear me, you wrangling pirates, that fall out
In sharing that which you have pilled from me!
Which of you trembles not that looks on me?   160
If not that, I am queen, you bow like subjects,
Yet that, by you deposed, you quake like rebels?
Ah, gentle villain, do not turn away!

RICHARD   Foul wrinklèd witch, what mak'st thou in my sight?

Q. MARG.   But repetition of what thou hast marred;
That will I make before I let thee go.

RICHARD   Wert thou not banishèd on pain of death?

Q. MARG.   I was; but I do find more pain in banishment
Than death can yield me here by my abode.
A husband and a son thou ow'st to me;   170
And thou a kingdom; all of you allegiance:
This sorrow that I have, by right is yours,
And all the pleasures you usurp are mine.

RICHARD   The curse my noble father laid on thee,
When thou didst crown his warlike brows with paper
And with thy scorns drew'st rivers from his eyes,
And then, to dry them, gav'st the duke a clout
Steeped in the faultless blood of pretty Rutland —
His curses, then from bitterness of soul
Denounced against thee, are all fall'n upon thee;   180
And God, not we, hath plagued thy bloody deed.

Q. ELIZAB. So just is God to right the innocent.

HASTINGS   O, 'twas the foulest deed to slay that babe,

	And the most merciless that e'er was heard of!
RIVERS	Tyrants themselves wept when it was reported.
DORSET	No man but prophesied revenge for it.
BUCK'HAM	Northumberland, then present, wept to see it.
Q. MARG.	What! Were you snarling all before I came,

And the most merciless that e'er was heard of!

RIVERS Tyrants themselves wept when it was reported.

DORSET No man but prophesied revenge for it.

BUCK'HAM Northumberland, then present, wept to see it.

Q. MARG. What! Were you snarling all before I came,
Ready to catch each other by the throat,
And turn you all your hatred now on me?   190
Did York's dread curse prevail so much with heaven
That Henry's death, my lovely Edward's death,
Their kingdom's loss, my woeful banishment,
Should all but answer for that peevish brat?
Can curses pierce the clouds and enter heaven?
Why, then, give way, dull clouds, to my quick curses!
Though not by war, by surfeit die your king,
As ours, by murder, to make him a king!
Edward thy son, that now is Prince of Wales,
For Edward our son, that was Prince of Wales,   200
Die in his youth by like untimely violence!
Thyself a queen, for me that was a queen,
Outlive thy glory, like my wretched self!
Long mayst thou live to wail thy children's death;
And see another, as I see thee now,
Decked in thy rights, as thou art stalled in mine!
Long die thy happy days before thy death;
And, after many length'ned hours of grief,
Die neither mother, wife, nor England's queen!
Rivers and Dorset, you were standers by,   210
And so wast thou, Lord Hastings, when my son
Was stabbed with bloody daggers: God I pray him,
That none of you may live his natural age,
But by some unlooked accident cut off!

RICHARD Have done thy charm, thou hateful withered hag!

Q. MARG. And leave out thee? Stay, dog, for thou shalt hear me.
If heaven have any grievous plague in store
Exceeding those that I can wish upon thee,
O, let them keep it till thy sins be ripe,
And then hurl down their indignation   220
On thee, the troubler of the poor world's peace!
The worm of conscience still begnaw thy soul!

Thy friends suspect for traitors while thou liv'st,
And take deep traitors for thy dearest friends!
No sleep close up that deadly eye of thine,
Unless it be while some tormenting dream
Affrights thee with a hell of ugly devils!
Thou elvish-marked, abortive, rooting hog!
Thou that wast sealed in thy nativity
The slave of nature and the son of hell!   230
Thou slander of thy heavy mother's womb!
Thou loathéd issue of thy father's loins!
Thou rag of honour! Thou detested —

RICHARD   Margaret.
Q. MARG.   Richard!
RICHARD   Ha?
Q. MARG.   I call thee not.
RICHARD   I cry thee mercy then, for I did think
That thou hadst called me all these bitter names.
Q. MARG.   Why, so I did, but looked for no reply.
O, let me make the period to my curse!
RICHARD   'Tis done by me, and ends in 'Margaret'.
Q. ELIZAB. Thus have you breathed your curse against yourself.   240
Q. MARG.   Poor painted queen, vain flourish of my fortune!
Why strew'st thou sugar on that bottled spider,
Whose deadly web ensnareth thee about?
Fool, fool! Thou whet'st a knife to kill thyself.
The day will come that thou shalt wish for me
To help thee curse this poisonous bunch-backed toad.
HASTINGS False-boding woman, end thy frantic curse,
Lest to thy harm thou move our patience.
Q. MARG.   Foul shame upon you! You have all moved mine.
RIVERS   Were you well served, you would be taught your duty.   250
Q. MARG.   To serve me well, you all should do me duty,
Teach me to be your queen, and you my subjects:
O, serve me well, and teach yourselves that duty!
DORSET   Dispute not with her; she is lunatic.
Q. MARG.   Peace, master marquis, you are malapert:
Your fire-new stamp of honour is scarce current.
O, that your young nobility could judge
What 'twere to lose it, and be miserable!

	They that stand high have many blasts to shake them;	
	And if they fall, they dash themselves to pieces.	260
RICHARD	Good counsel, marry: learn it, learn it, marquis.	
DORSET	It touches you, my lord, as much as me.	
RICHARD	Ay, and much more: but I was born so high,	
	Our aery buildeth in the cedar's top,	
	And dallies with the wind, and scorns the sun.	
Q. MARG.	And turns the sun to shade; alas! alas!	
	Witness my son, now in the shade of death;	
	Whose bright out-shining beams thy cloudy wrath	
	Hath in eternal darkness folded up.	
	Your aery buildeth in our aery's nest.	270
	O God, that seest it, do not suffer it;	
	As it is won with blood, lost be it so!	
RICHARD	Peace, peace! For shame, if not for charity.	
Q. MARG.	Urge neither charity nor shame to me:	
	Uncharitably with me have you dealt,	
	And shamefully my hopes by you are butchered.	
	My charity is outrage, life my shame;	
	And in that shame still live my sorrow's rage!	
BUCK'HAM	Have done, have done.	
Q. MARG.	O princely Buckingham, I'll kiss thy hand,	280
	In sign of league and amity with thee:	
	Now fair befall thee and thy noble house!	
	Thy garments are not spotted with our blood,	
	Nor thou within the compass of my curse.	
BUCK'HAM	Nor no one here; for curses never pass	
	The lips of those that breathe them in the air.	
Q. MARG.	I will not think but they ascend the sky,	
	And there awake God's gentle-sleeping peace.	
	[aside] O Buckingham, take heed of yonder dog!	
	Look when he fawns, he bites; and when he bites,	290
	His venom tooth will rankle to the death:	
	Have not to do with him, beware of him;	
	Sin, death, and hell have set their marks on him,	
	And all their ministers attend on him.	
RICHARD	What doth she say, my Lord of Buckingham?	
BUCK'HAM	Nothing that I respect, my gracious lord.	
Q. MARG.	What, dost thou scorn me for my gentle counsel,	

	And soothe the devil that I warn thee from?	
	O, but remember this another day,	
	When he shall split thy very heart with sorrow,	300
	And say poor Margaret was a prophetess.	
	Live each of you the subjects to his hate,	
	And he to yours, and all of you to God's!	[*she goes*
HASTINGS	My hair doth stand on end to hear her curses.	
RIVERS	And so doth mine: I muse why she's at liberty.	
RICHARD	I cannot blame her: by God's holy mother,	
	She hath had too much wrong; and I repent	
	My part thereof that I have done to her.	
Q. ELIZAB.	I never did her any, to my knowledge.	
RICHARD	Yet you have all the vantage of her wrong.	310
	I was too hot to do somebody good,	
	That is too cold in thinking of it now.	
	Marry, for Clarence, he is well repaid;	
	He is franked up to fatting for his pains:	
	God pardon them that are the cause thereof!	
RIVERS	A virtuous and a Christian-like conclusion,	
	To pray for them that have done scathe to us!	
RICHARD	So do I ever – [*'speaks to himself'*] being well advised,	
	For had I cursed now, I had cursed myself.	

'Enter CATESBY*'*

CATESBY	Madam, his majesty doth call for you;	320
	And for your grace, and you, my gracious lords.	
Q. ELIZAB.	Catesby, I come. Lords, will you go with me?	
RIVERS	We wait upon your grace.	[*all but Gloucester go*
RICHARD	I do the wrong, and first begin to brawl.	
	The secret mischiefs that I set abroach	
	I lay unto the grievous charge of others.	
	Clarence, whom I indeed have cast in darkness,	
	I do beweep to many simple gulls,	
	Namely to Derby, Hastings, Buckingham;	
	And tell them 'tis the queen and her allies	330
	That stir the king against the duke my brother.	
	Now, they believe it; and withal whet me	
	To be revenged on Rivers, Dorset, Grey:	
	But then I sigh; and, with a piece of Scripture,	

Tell them that God bids us do good for evil:
And thus I clothe my naked villainy
With odd old ends stol'n forth of holy writ;
And seem a saint, when most I play the devil.

'Enter two Murderers'

But soft! Here come my executioners.
How now, my hardy stout resolvéd mates!   340
Are you now going to dispatch this thing?

I MURD.   We are, my lord, and come to have the warrant,
That we may be admitted where he is.

RICHARD   Well thought upon, I have it here about me.

[gives the warrant

When you have done, repair to Crosby Place.
But, sirs, be sudden in the execution,
Withal obdurate, do not hear him plead;
For Clarence is well-spoken, and perhaps
May move your hearts to pity, if you mark him.

I MURD.   Tut, tut, my lord, we will not stand to prate;   350
Talkers are no good doers: be assured
We go to use our hands and not our tongues.

RICHARD   Your eyes drop millstones, when fools' eyes fall tears.
I like you, lads: about your business straight.
Go, go, dispatch.

I MURD.   We will, my noble lord.

[they go

SCENE 4

London. The Tower

Enter CLARENCE *and* BRAKENBURY

BRAKEN.   Why looks your grace so heavily today?

CLARENCE   O, I have passed a miserable night,
So full of fearful dreams, of ugly sights,
That, as I am a Christian faithful man,
I would not spend another such a night,
Though 'twere to buy a world of happy days,
So full of dismal terror was the time!

BRAKEN. What was your dream, my lord? I pray you tell me.
CLARENCE Methoughts that I had broken from the Tower,
       And was embarked to cross to Burgundy,   10
       And in my company my brother Gloucester,
       Who from my cabin tempted me to walk
       Upon the hatches. Thence we looked toward England,
       And cited up a thousand heavy times,
       During the wars of York and Lancaster
       That had befall'n us. As we paced along
       Upon the giddy footing of the hatches,
       Methought that Gloucester stumbled, and in falling
       Struck me, that thought to stay him, overboard,
       Into the tumbling billows of the main.   20
       O Lord, methought what pain it was to drown!
       What dreadful noise of waters in mine ears!
       What sights of ugly death within mine eyes!
       Methoughts I saw a thousand fearful wracks;
       A thousand men that fishes gnawed upon;
       Wedges of gold, great ingots, heaps of pearl,
       Inestimable stones, unvalued jewels,
       All scatt'red in the bottom of the sea.
       Some lay in dead men's skulls; and in the holes
       Where eyes did once inhabit there were crept,   30
       As 'twere in scorn of eyes, reflecting gems,
       That wooed the slimy bottom of the deep,
       And mocked the dead bones that lay scatt'red by.
BRAKEN. Had you such leisure in the time of death
       To gaze upon these secrets of the deep?
CLARENCE Methought I had; and often did I strive
       To yield the ghost: but still the envious flood
       Stopped in my soul, and would not let it forth
       To find the empty, vast, and wand'ring air;
       But smothered it within my panting bulk,   40
       Who almost burst to belch it in the sea.
BRAKEN. Awaked you not in this sore agony?
CLARENCE No, no, my dream was lengthened after life.
       O, then began the tempest to my soul.
       I passed, methought, the melancholy flood,
       With that sour ferryman which poets write of,

Unto the kingdom of perpetual night.
The first that there did greet my stranger soul,
Was my great father-in-law, renownéd Warwick;
Who spake aloud, 'What scourge for perjury   50
Can this dark monarchy afford false Clarence?'
And so he vanished. Then came wand'ring by
A shadow like an angel, with bright hair
Dabbled in blood, and he shrieked out aloud,
'Clarence is come; false, fleeting, perjured Clarence,
That stabbed me in the field by Tewkesbury:
Seize on him, Furies, take him unto torment!'
With that, methought, a legion of foul fiends
Environed me, and howléd in mine ears
Such hideous cries that with the very noise   60
I trembling waked, and for a season after
Could not believe but that I was in hell,
Such terrible impression made my dream.

BRAKEN. No marvel, lord, though it affrighted you;
I am afraid, methinks, to hear you tell it.

CLARENCE Ah, Keeper, Keeper, I have done these things,
That now give evidence against my soul,
For Edward's sake, and see how he requites me!
O God! If my deep prayers cannot appease thee,
But thou wilt be avenged on my misdeeds,   70
Yet execute thy wrath in me alone;
O, spare my guiltless wife and my poor children!
Keeper, I prithee, sit by me awhile;
My soul is heavy, and I fain would sleep.

BRAKEN. I will, my lord: God give your grace good rest!

                                    [*Clarence sleeps*

Sorrow breaks seasons and reposing hours,
Makes the night morning and the noontide night.
Princes have but their titles for their glories,
An outward honour for an inward toil;
And for unfelt imaginations   80
They often feel a world of restless cares:
So that between their titles and low name
There's nothing differs but the outward fame.

                    Enter the two Murderers

1 MURD.	Ho! Who's here?
BRAKEN.	What wouldst thou, fellow? And how cam'st thou hither?
1 MURD.	I would speak with Clarence, and I came hither on my legs.
BRAKEN.	What, so brief?
2 MURD.	'Tis better, sir, than to be tedious. Let him see our 90 commission, and talk no more. *[Brakenbury reads it*
BRAKEN.	I am in this commanded to deliver
	The noble Duke of Clarence to your hands.
	I will not reason what is meant hereby,
	Because I will be guiltless from the meaning.
	There lies the duke asleep, and there the keys.
	I'll to the king, and signify to him
	That thus I have resigned to you my charge.
1 MURD.	You may, sir; 'tis a point of wisdom: fare you well.
	[Brakenbury goes
2 MURD.	What, shall I stab him as he sleeps? 100
1 MURD.	No; he'll say 'twas done cowardly, when he wakes.
2 MURD.	Why, he shall never wake until the great judgement-day.
1 MURD.	Why, then he'll say we stabbed him sleeping.
2 MURD.	The urging of that word 'judgement' hath bred a kind of remorse in me.
1 MURD.	What, art thou afraid?
2 MURD.	Not to kill him, having a warrant; but to be damned for killing him, from the which no warrant can defend me.
1 MURD.	I thought thou hadst been resolute. 110
2 MURD.	So I am, to let him live.
1 MURD.	I'll back to the Duke of Gloucester, and tell him so.
2 MURD.	Nay, I prithee, stay a little: I hope this passionate humour of mine will change; it was wont to hold me but while one tells twenty.
1 MURD.	How dost thou feel thyself now?
2 MURD.	Faith, some certain dregs of conscience are yet within me.
1 MURD.	Remember our reward when the deed's done.
2 MURD.	Zounds, he dies: I had forgot the reward. 120

1 MURD.	Where's thy conscience now?
2 MURD.	O, in the Duke of Gloucester's purse.
1 MURD.	When he opens his purse to give us our reward, thy conscience flies out.
2 MURD.	'Tis no matter, let it go; there's few or none will entertain it.
1 MURD.	What if it come to thee again?
2 MURD.	I'll not meddle with it: it makes a man a coward: a man cannot steal, but it accuseth him; a man cannot swear, but it checks him; a man cannot lie with his neighbour's wife, but it detects him: 'tis a blushing shamefaced spirit that mutinies in a man's bosom; it fills a man full of obstacles. It made me once restore a purse of gold, that (by chance) I found; it beggars any man that keeps it: it is turned out of towns and cities for a dangerous thing; and every man that means to live well endeavours to trust to himself and live without it.
1 MURD.	'Tis even now at my elbow, persuading me not to kill the duke.
2 MURD.	Take the devil in thy mind, and believe him not: he would insinuate with thee but to make thee sigh.
1 MURD.	I am strong-framed, he cannot prevail with me.
2 MURD.	Spoke like a tall man that respects thy reputation. Come, shall we fall to work?
1 MURD.	Take him on the costard with the hilts of thy sword, and then throw him into the malmsey-butt in the next room.
2 MURD.	O excellent device! And make a sop of him.
1 MURD.	Soft! He wakes.
2 MURD.	Strike!
1 MURD.	No, we'll reason with him.
CLARENCE	Where art thou, Keeper? Give me a cup of wine.
2 MURD.	You shall have wine enough, my lord, anon.
CLARENCE	In God's name, what art thou?
1 MURD.	A man, as you are.
CLARENCE	But not, as I am, royal.
2 MURD.	Nor you, as we are, loyal.
CLARENCE	Thy voice is thunder, but thy looks are humble.
1 MURD.	My voice is now the king's, my looks mine own.

130

140

150

CLARENCE	How darkly and how deadly dost thou speak!	160
	Your eyes do menace me: why look you pale?	
	Who sent you hither? Wherefore do you come?	
2 MURD.	To, to, to —	
CLARENCE	To murder me?	
BOTH	Ay, ay.	
CLARENCE	You scarcely have the hearts to tell me so,	
	And therefore cannot have the hearts to do it.	
	Wherein, my friends, have I offended you?	
1 MURD.	Offended us you have not, but the king.	
CLARENCE	I shall be reconciled to him again.	170
2 MURD.	Never, my lord; therefore prepare to die.	
CLARENCE	Are you drawn forth among a world of men	
	To slay the innocent? What is my offence?	
	Where is the evidence that doth accuse me?	
	What lawful quest have given their verdict up	
	Unto the frowning judge? Or who pronounced	
	The bitter sentence of poor Clarence' death?	
	Before I be convict by course of law,	
	To threaten me with death is most unlawful.	
	I charge you, as you hope to have redemption	180
	By Christ's dear blood shed for our grievous sins,	
	That you depart and lay no hands on me:	
	The deed you undertake is damnable.	
1 MURD.	What we will do, we do upon command.	
2 MURD.	And he that hath commanded is our king.	
CLARENCE	Erroneous vassals! The great King of kings	
	Hath in the tables of his law commanded	
	That thou shalt do no murder: will you then	
	Spurn at his edict, and fulfil a man's?	
	Take heed; for he holds vengeance in his hand,	190
	To hurl upon their heads that break his law.	
2 MURD.	And that same vengeance doth he hurl on thee,	
	For false forswearing, and for murder too:	
	Thou didst receive the sacrament to fight	
	In quarrel of the house of Lancaster.	
1 MURD.	And, like a traitor to the name of God,	
	Didst break that vow, and with thy treacherous blade	
	Unrip'st the bowels of thy sov'reign's son.	

2 MURD.   Whom thou wast sworn to cherish and defend.

1 MURD.   How canst thou urge God's dreadful law to us,   200
          When thou hast broke it in such dear degree?

CLARENCE   Alas! For whose sake did I that ill deed?
          For Edward, for my brother, for his sake.
          He sends you not to murder me for this;
          For in that sin he is as deep as I.
          If God will be avengéd for the deed,
          O, know you yet he doth it publicly.
          Take not the quarrel from his powerful arm;
          He needs no indirect or lawless course
          To cut off those that have offended him.   210

1 MURD.   Who made thee then a bloody minister,
          When gallant-springing brave Plantagenet,
          That princely novice, was struck dead by thee?

CLARENCE   My brother's love, the devil, and my rage.

1 MURD.   Thy brother's love, our duty, and thy faults,
          Provoke us hither now to slaughter thee.

CLARENCE   If you do love my brother, hate not me;
          I am his brother, and I love him well.
          If you are hired, for meed go back again,
          And I will send you to my brother Gloucester,   220
          Who shall reward you better for my life
          Than Edward will for tidings of my death.

2 MURD.   You are deceived, your brother Gloucester hates you.

CLARENCE   O, no, he loves me, and he holds me dear:
          Go you to him from me.

1 MURD.   Ay, so we will.

CLARENCE   Tell him, when that our princely father York
          Blessed his three sons with his victorious arm,
          And charged us from his soul to love each other,
          He little thought of this divided friendship:
          Bid Gloucester think of this, and he will weep.   230

1 MURD.   Ay, millstones, as he lessoned us to weep.

CLARENCE   O, do not slander him, for he is kind.

1 MURD.   As snow in harvest. Come, you deceive yourself:
          'Tis he that sends us to destroy you here.

CLARENCE   It cannot be; for he bewept my fortune,
          And hugged me in his arms, and swore with sobs,

           That he would labour my delivery.

1 MURD.   Why, so he doth, when he delivers you
           From this earth's thraldom to the joys of heaven.

2 MURD.   Make peace with God, for you must die, my lord.   240

CLARENCE   Have you that holy feeling in your souls,
           To counsel me to make my peace with God,
           And are you yet to your own souls so blind,
           That you will war with God by murd'ring me?
           O, sirs, consider, they that set you on
           To do this deed will hate you for the deed.

2 MURD.   What shall we do?

CLARENCE   Relent, and save your souls.
           Which of you, if you were a prince's son,
           Being pent from liberty, as I am now,
           If two such murderers as yourselves came to you,   250
           Would not entreat for life? Even so I beg
           As you would beg, were you in my distress.

1 MURD.   Relent! 'Tis cowardly and womanish.

CLARENCE   Not to relent is beastly, savage, devilish.
           My friend, I spy some pity in thy looks;
           O, if thine eye be not a flatterer,
           Come thou on my side, and entreat for me.
           A begging prince what beggar pities not?

2 MURD.   Look behind you, my lord.

1 MURD.   ['*stabs him*'] Take that, and that: if all this will not do,   260
           I'll drown you in the malmsey-butt within.
                           [*drags out the body*

2 MURD.   A bloody deed, and desperately dispatched!
           How fain, like Pilate, would I wash my hands
           Of this most grievous murder!

First Murderer returns

1 MURD.   How now! What mean'st thou, that thou help'st me not?
           By heavens, the duke shall know how slack you
                                have been!

2 MURD.   I would he knew that I had saved his brother!
           Take thou the fee, and tell him what I say,
           For I repent me that the duke is slain.   [*goes*

1 MURD.   So do not I: go, coward as thou art.   270

Well, I'll go hide the body in some hole,
Till that the duke give order for his burial:
And when I have my meed, I will away;
For this will out, and then I must not stay.

                                       [goes

ACT 2 SCENE I

London. The palace

Flourish. Enter KING EDWARD *sick, borne in a chair, with*
QUEEN ELIZABETH, DORSET, RIVERS, HASTINGS,
BUCKINGHAM, GREY, *and others*

K. EDWARD Why, so: now have I done a good day's work.
You peers, continue this united league:
I every day expect an embassage
From my Redeemer to redeem me hence;
And more at peace my soul shall part to heaven,
Since I have made my friends at peace on earth.
Hastings and Rivers, take each other's hand;
Dissemble not your hatred, swear your love.

RIVERS   By heaven, my soul is purged from grudging hate;
And with my hand I seal my true heart's love.   10

HASTINGS So thrive I, as I truly swear the like!

K. EDWARD Take heed you dally not before your king;
Lest he that is the supreme King of kings
Confound your hidden falsehood and award
Either of you to be the other's end.

HASTINGS So prosper I, as I swear perfect love!

RIVERS   And I, as I love Hastings with my heart!

K. EDWARD Madam, yourself is not exempt from this,
Nor you, son Dorset; Buckingham, nor you;
You have been factious one against the other.   20
Wife, love Lord Hastings, let him kiss your hand;
And what you do, do it unfeignedly.

Q. ELIZAB. There, Hastings; I will never more remember
Our former hatred, so thrive I and mine!

K. EDWARD Dorset, embrace him; Hastings, love lord marquis.

DORSET   This interchange of love, I here protest,
Upon my part shall be inviolable.

HASTINGS And so swear I.   [*they embrace*

K. EDWARD Now, princely Buckingham, seal thou this league
With thy embracements to my wife's allies,   30
And make me happy in your unity.

BUCK'HAM [*to the Queen*]
>Whenever Buckingham doth turn his hate
>Upon your grace, but with all duteous love
>Doth cherish you and yours, God punish me
>With hate in those where I expect most love!
>When I have most need to employ a friend,
>And most assuréd that he is a friend,
>Deep, hollow, treacherous, and full of guile,
>Be he unto me! This do I beg of God,
>When I am cold in love to you or yours. [*they 'embrace'*   40

K. EDWARD A pleasing cordial, princely Buckingham,
>Is this thy vow unto my sickly heart.
>There wanteth now our brother Gloucester here,
>To make the blessed period of this peace.

BUCK'HAM And in good time,
>Here comes Sir Richard Ratcliffe and the duke.

Enter RICHARD *and* RATCLIFFE

RICHARD   Good morrow to my sovereign king and queen;
>And, princely peers, a happy time of day!

K. EDWARD Happy indeed, as we have spent the day.
>Gloucester, we have done deeds of charity,   50
>Made peace of enmity, fair love of hate,
>Between these swelling wrong-incenséd peers.

RICHARD   A blesséd labour, my most sovereign lord.
>Among this princely heap, if any here,
>By false intelligence, or wrong surmise,
>Hold me a foe, if I unwittingly
>Have aught committed that is hardly borne
>By any in this presence, I desire
>To reconcile me to his friendly peace:
>'Tis death to me to be at enmity;   60
>I hate it, and desire all good men's love.
>First, madam, I entreat true peace of you,
>Which I will purchase with my duteous service;
>Of you, my noble cousin Buckingham,
>If ever any grudge were lodged between us;
>Of you, and you, Lord Rivers, and Lord Dorset,
>Of you, Lord Woodville, and Lord Scales of you,
>That all without desert have frowned on me;

Dukes, earls, lords, gentlemen; indeed, of all.
I do not know that Englishman alive   70
With whom my soul is any jot at odds
More than the infant that is born tonight:
I thank my God for my humility.

Q. ELIZAB. A holy day shall this be kept hereafter:
I would to God all strifes were well compounded.
My sovereign lord, I do beseech your highness
To take our brother Clarence to your grace.

RICHARD Why, madam, have I off'red love for this,
To be so flouted in this royal presence?
Who knows not that the gentle duke is dead?   80

                       [*'they all start'*

You do him injury to scorn his corse.

RIVERS Who knows not he is dead! Who knows he is?

Q. ELIZAB. All-seeing heaven, what a world is this!

BUCK'HAM Look I so pale, Lord Dorset, as the rest?

DORSET Ay, my good lord, and no man in the presence
But his red colour hath forsook his cheeks.

K. EDWARD Is Clarence dead? The order was reversed.

RICHARD But he, poor man, by your first order died,
And that a wingéd Mercury did bear;
Some tardy cripple bare the countermand   90
That came too lag to see him buriéd.
God grant that some, less noble and less loyal,
Nearer in bloody thoughts, but not in blood,
Deserve not worse than wretched Clarence did,
And yet go current from suspicion!

Enter LORD STANLEY

STANLEY A boon, my sovereign, for my service done!

K. EDWARD I prithee, peace: my soul is full of sorrow.

STANLEY I will not rise, unless your highness hear me.

K. EDWARD   Then say at once what is it thou requests.

STANLEY The forfeit, sovereign, of my servant's life;   100
Who slew today a riotous gentleman
Lately attendant on the Duke of Norfolk.

K. EDWARD Have I a tongue to doom my brother's death,
And shall that tongue give pardon to a slave?
My brother killed no man – his fault was thought,

And yet his punishment was bitter death.
Who sued to me for him? Who, in my wrath,
Kneeled at my feet and bid me be advised?
Who spoke of brotherhood? Who spoke of love?
Who told me how the poor soul did forsake   110
The mighty Warwick, and did fight for me?
Who told me, in the field at Tewkesbury
When Oxford had me down, he rescued me
And said 'Dear brother, live, and be a king'?
Who told me, when we both lay in the field
Frozen almost to death, how he did lap me
Even in his garments, and did give himself,
All thin and naked, to the numb cold night?
All this from my remembrance brutish wrath
Sinfully plucked, and not a man of you   120
Had so much grace to put it in my mind.
But when your carters or your waiting-vassals
Have done a drunken slaughter and defaced
The precious image of our dear Redeemer,
You straight are on your knees for pardon, pardon;
And I, unjustly too, must grant it you.   *[Stanley rises*
But for my brother not a man would speak,
Nor I, ungracious, speak unto myself
For him, poor soul. The proudest of you all
Have been beholding to him in his life;   130
Yet none of you would once beg for his life.
O God, I fear thy justice will take hold
On me, and you, and mine, and yours, for this!
Come, Hastings, help me to my closet. Ah,
                          poor Clarence!
                 [he is carried forth; Hastings, the Queen,
                         Rivers, and Dorset in attendance

RICHARD   This is the fruits of rashness. Marked you not
How that the guilty kindred of the queen
Looked pale when they did hear of Clarence' death?
O, they did urge it still unto the king!
God will revenge it. Come, lords, will you go
To comfort Edward with our company?   140
BUCK'HAM We wait upon your grace.   *[they follow*

SCENE 2

'Enter the old DUCHESS OF YORK, *with the two children of Clarence'*

BOY   Good grandam, tell us, is our father dead?
DUCHESS   No, boy.
GIRL   Why do you weep so oft, and beat your breast,
           And cry 'O Clarence, my unhappy son!'?
BOY   Why do you look on us, and shake your head,
           And call us orphans, wretches, castaways,
           If that our noble father were alive?
DUCHESS   My pretty cousins, you mistake me both.
           I do lament the sickness of the king,
           As loath to lose him, not your father's death;   10
           It were lost sorrow to wail one that's lost.
BOY   Then you conclude, my grandam, he is dead.
           The king mine uncle is to blame for it:
           God will revenge it, whom I will importune
           With earnest prayers, all to that effect.
GIRL   And so will I.
DUCHESS   Peace, children, peace! The king doth love you well.
           Incapable and shallow innocents,
           You cannot guess who caused your father's death.
BOY   Grandam, we can; for my good uncle Gloucester   20
           Told me the king, provoked to it by the queen,
           Devised impeachments to imprison him:
           And when my uncle told me so, he wept,
           And pitied me, and kindly kissed my cheek;
           Bade me rely on him as on my father,
           And he would love me dearly as a child.
DUCHESS   Ah, that deceit should steal such gentle shape,
           And with a virtuous vizor hide deep vice!
           He is my son, ay, and therein my shame;
           Yet from my dugs he drew not this deceit.   30
BOY   Think you my uncle did dissemble, grandam?
DUCHESS   Ay, boy.
BOY   I cannot think it. Hark! What noise is this?

'Enter the QUEEN *with her hair about her ears,*
RIVERS and DORSET *after her'*

Q. ELIZAB. Ah, who shall hinder me to wail and weep,
          To chide my fortune and torment myself?
          I'll join with black despair against my soul,
          And to myself become an enemy.
DUCHESS   What means this scene of rude impatience?
Q. ELIZAB. To mark an act of tragic violence.
          Edward, my lord, thy son, our king, is dead.   40
          Why grow the branches when the root is gone?
          Why wither not the leaves that want their sap?
          If you will live, lament; if die, be brief,
          That our swift-wingéd souls may catch the king's,
          Or, like obedient subjects, follow him
          To his new kingdom of ne'er-changing night.
DUCHESS   Ah, so much interest have I in thy sorrow
          As I had title in thy noble husband!
          I have bewept a worthy husband's death,
          And lived with looking on his images;   50
          But now two mirrors of his princely semblance
          Are cracked in pieces by malignant death,
          And I for comfort have but one false glass,
          That grieves me when I see my shame in him.
          Thou art a widow; yet thou art a mother,
          And hast the comfort of thy children left:
          But death hath snatched my husband from mine arms,
          And plucked two crutches from my feeble hands,
          Clarence and Edward. O, what cause have I,
          Thine being but a moiety of my moan,   60
          To overgo thy woes and drown thy cries!
BOY   Ah aunt! You wept not for our father's death,
          How can we aid you with our kindred tears?
GIRL   Our fatherless distress was left unmoaned;
          Your widow-dolour likewise be unwept!
Q. ELIZAB. Give me no help in lamentation;
          I am not barren to bring forth complaints:
          All springs reduce their currents to mine eyes,
          That I, being governed by the watery moon,
          May send forth plenteous tears to drown the world! 70
          Ah for my husband, for my dear lord Edward!
CHILDREN Ah for our father, for our dear Lord Clarence!

DUCHESS	Alas for both, both mine, Edward and Clarence!
Q. ELIZAB.	What stay had I but Edward? And he's gone.
CHILDREN	What stay had we but Clarence? And he's gone.
DUCHESS	What stays had I but they? And they are gone.
Q. ELIZAB.	Was never widow had so dear a loss.
CHILDREN	Were never orphans had so dear a loss.
DUCHESS	Was never mother had so dear a loss.

DUCHESS
　　　　　Alas, I am the mother of these griefs!　　　　　　80
　　　　　Their woes are parcelled, mine is general.
　　　　　She for an Edward weeps, and so do I;
　　　　　I for a Clarence weep, so doth not she:
　　　　　These babes for Clarence weep, and so do I;
　　　　　I for an Edward weep, so do not they:
　　　　　Alas, you three on me, threefold distressed,
　　　　　Pour all your tears! I am your sorrow's nurse,
　　　　　And I will pamper it with lamentation.

DORSET
　　　　　Comfort, dear mother: God is much displeased
　　　　　That you take with unthankfulness his doing.　　90
　　　　　In common worldly things 'tis called ungrateful
　　　　　With dull unwillingness to repay a debt
　　　　　Which with a bounteous hand was kindly lent;
　　　　　Much more to be thus opposite with heaven,
　　　　　For it requires the royal debt it lent you.

RIVERS
　　　　　Madam, bethink you, like a careful mother,
　　　　　Of the young prince your son: send straight for him;
　　　　　Let him be crowned; in him your comfort lives.
　　　　　Drown desperate sorrow in dead Edward's grave,
　　　　　And plant your joys in living Edward's throne.　100

> *Enter* RICHARD, BUCKINGHAM, DERBY,
> HASTINGS, *and* RATCLIFFE

RICHARD
　　　　　Sister, have comfort: all of us have cause
　　　　　To wail the dimming of our shining star;
　　　　　But none can help our harms by wailing them.
　　　　　Madam, my mother, I do cry you mercy;
　　　　　I did not see your grace. Humbly on my knee
　　　　　I crave your blessing.

DUCHESS
　　　　　God bless thee, and put meekness in thy breast,
　　　　　Love, charity, obedience, and true duty!

RICHARD
　　　　　Amen! [*aside*] And make me die a good old man!

| | That is the butt-end of a mother's blessing: | 110 |

That is the butt-end of a mother's blessing: 110
I marvel that her grace did leave it out.
BUCK'HAM You cloudy princes and heart-sorrowing peers,
That bear this heavy mutual load of moan,
Now cheer each other in each other's love:
Though we have spent our harvest of this king,
We are to reap the harvest of his son.
The broken rancour of your high-swoln hearts,
But lately splintered, knit, and joined together,
Must gently be preserved, cherished, and kept:
Me seemeth good that, with some little train, 120
Forthwith from Ludlow the young prince be fet
Hither to London, to be crowned our king.
RIVERS Why with some little train, my Lord of Buckingham?
BUCK'HAM Marry, my lord, lest by a multitude
The new-healed wound of malice should break out;
Which would be so much the more dangerous,
By how much the estate is green and yet ungoverned:
Where every horse bears his commanding rein,
And may direct his course as please himself,
As well the fear of harm as harm apparent, 130
In my opinion, ought to be prevented.
RICHARD I hope the king made peace with all of us;
And the compact is firm and true in me.
RIVERS And so in me; and so, I think, in all.
Yet, since it is but green, it should be put
To no apparent likelihood of breach,
Which haply by much company might be urged:
Therefore I say with noble Buckingham
That it is meet so few should fetch the prince.
HASTINGS And so say I. 140
RICHARD Then be it so; and go we to determine
Who they shall be that straight shall post to Ludlow.
Madam, and you, my sister, will you go
To give your censures in this business?
Q. ELIZAB. }
DUCHESS } With all our hearts.

                    [*all go in but Buckingham and Richard*
BUCK'HAM My lord, whoever journeys to the prince,

For God sake let not us two stay at home:
For by the way I'll sort occasion,
As index to the story we late talked of,
To part the queen's proud kindred from the prince.   150

RICHARD   My other self, my counsel's consistory,
My oracle, my prophet, my dear cousin!
I, as a child, will go by thy direction.
Toward Ludlow then, for we'll not stay behind.

                                  [they go

SCENE 3

London. A street

Enter two Citizens, meeting

1 CITIZEN   Good morrow, neighbour, whither away so fast?

2 CITIZEN   I promise you, I scarcely know myself:
Hear you the news abroad?

1 CITIZEN   Yes, that the king is dead.

2 CITIZEN   Ill news, by'r lady. Seldom comes the better.
I fear, I fear, 'twill prove a giddy world.

'Enter another Citizen'

3 CITIZEN   Neighbours, God speed!

1 CITIZEN   Give you good morrow, sir.

3 CITIZEN   Doth the news hold of good King Edward's death?

2 CITIZEN   Ay, sir, it is too true, God help the while!

3 CITIZEN   Then, masters, look to see a troublous world.

1 CITIZEN   No, no; by God's good grace his son shall reign.   10

3 CITIZEN   Woe to that land that's governed by a child!

2 CITIZEN   In him there is a hope of government,
Which, in his nonage, council under him,
And, in his full and ripened years, himself,
No doubt, shall then, and till then, govern well.

1 CITIZEN   So stood the state when Henry the Sixth
Was crowned in Paris but at nine months old.

3 CITIZEN   Stood the state so? No, no, good friends, God wot;
For then this land was famously enriched
With politic grave counsel; then the king   20

Had virtuous uncles to protect his grace.
1 CITIZEN Why, so hath this, both by his father and mother.
3 CITIZEN Better it were they all came by his father,
Or by his father there were none at all;
For emulation who shall now be nearest,
Will touch us all too near, if God prevent not.
O, full of danger is the Duke of Gloucester!
And the queen's sons and brothers haught and proud:
And were they to be ruled, and not to rule,
This sickly land might solace as before.   30
1 CITIZEN Come, come, we fear the worst; all will be well.
3 CITIZEN When clouds are seen, wise men put on their cloaks;
When great leaves fall, then winter is at hand;
When the sun sets, who doth not look for night?
Untimely storms makes men expect a dearth.
All may be well; but, if God sort it so,
'Tis more than we deserve, or I expect.
2 CITIZEN Truly, the hearts of men are full of fear:
You cannot reason almost with a man
That looks not heavily and full of dread.   40
3 CITIZEN Before the days of change, still is it so:
By a divine instinct men's minds mistrust
Ensuing danger; as by proof we see
The water swell before a boist'rous storm.
But leave it all to God. Whither away?
2 CITIZEN Marry, we were sent for to the justices.
3 CITIZEN And so was I: I'll bear you company.

[they pass on

SCENE 4

London. The palace

Enter the ARCHBISHOP OF YORK, *the young* DUKE OF YORK, QUEEN
ELIZABETH, *and the* DUCHESS OF YORK

ARCHB.   Last night, I hear, they lay at Stony Stratford;
And at Northampton they do rest tonight:
Tomorrow, or next day, they will be here,
DUCHESS I long with all my heart to see the prince:

            I hope he is much grown since last I saw him.

Q. ELIZAB. But I hear, no; they say my son of York
            Has almost overta'en him in his growth.

YORK   Ay, mother, but I would not have it so.

DUCHESS   Why, my good cousin, it is good to grow.

YORK   Grandam, one night, as we did sit at supper,   10
            My uncle Rivers talked how I did grow
            More than my brother: 'Ay,' quoth my uncle
                               Gloucester,
            'Small herbs have grace, ill weeds do grow apace'.
            And since, methinks, I would not grow so fast,
            Because sweet flowers are slow and weeds make haste.

DUCHESS   Good faith, good faith, the saying did not hold
            In him that did object the same to thee:
            He was the wretched'st thing when he was young,
            So long a-growing and so leisurely,
            That, if his rule were true, he should be gracious.   20

ARCHB.   And so, no doubt, he is, my gracious madam.

DUCHESS   I hope he is, but yet let mothers doubt.

YORK   Now, by my troth, if I had been rememb'red,
            I could have given my uncle's grace a flout,
            To touch his growth nearer than he touched mine.

DUCHESS   How, my young York? I prithee, let me hear it.

YORK   Marry, they say my uncle grew so fast
            That he could gnaw a crust at two hours old:
            'Twas full two years ere I could get a tooth.
            Grandam, this would have been a biting jest.   30

DUCHESS   I prithee, pretty York, who told thee this?

YORK   Grandam, his nurse.

DUCHESS   His nurse! Why, she was dead ere thou wast born.

YORK   If 'twere not she, I cannot tell who told me.

Q. ELIZAB. A parlous boy: go to, you are too shrewd.

ARCHB.   Good madam, be not angry with the child.

Q. ELIZAB. Pitchers have ears.

                  'Enter a Messenger'

ARCHB.   Here comes a messenger. What news?

MESSENGER Such news, my lord, as grieves me to report.

Q. ELIZAB. How doth the prince?

MESSENGER   Well, madam, and in health.   40

DUCHESS What is thy news?

MESSENGER   Lord Rivers and Lord Grey
Are sent to Pomfret, and with them
Sir Thomas Vaughan, prisoners.

DUCHESS Who hath committed them?

MESSENGER   The mighty dukes,
Gloucester and Buckingham.

ARCHB.   For what offence?

MESSENGER The sum of all I can, I have disclosed;
Why or for what the nobles were committed
Is all unknown to me, my gracious lord.

Q. ELIZAB. Ay me, I see the ruin of my house!
The tiger now hath seized the gentle hind;   50
Insulting tyranny begins to jet
Upon the innocent and aweless throne:
Welcome, destruction, blood, and massacre!
I see, as in a map, the end of all.

DUCHESS Accursèd and unquiet wrangling days,
How many of you have mine eyes beheld!
My husband lost his life to get the crown;
And often up and down my sons were tossed,
For me to joy and weep their gain and loss:
And being seated, and domestic broils   60
Clean overblown, themselves, the conquerors,
Make war upon themselves, brother to brother,
Blood to blood, self to self! Preposterous
And frantic outrage, end thy damnèd spleen;
Or let me die, to look on death no more!

Q. ELIZAB. Come, come, my boy; we will to sanctuary.
Madam, farewell.

DUCHESS   Stay, I will go with you.

Q. ELIZAB. You have no cause.

ARCHB.   My gracious lady, go;
And thither bear your treasure and your goods.
For my part, I'll resign unto your grace   70
The seal I keep: and so betide to me
As well I tender you and all of yours!
Go, I'll conduct you to the sanctuary.   [they go

ACT 3 SCENE I

London. A street

The trumpets sound. Enter the young PRINCE, RICHARD,
BUCKINGHAM, *the Lord* CARDINAL,
CATESBY, *and others*

BUCK'HAM Welcome, sweet prince, to London, to your chamber.

RICHARD Welcome, dear cousin, my thoughts' sovereign:
The weary way hath made you melancholy.

PRINCE No, uncle; but our crosses on the way
Have made it tedious, wearisome, and heavy:
I want more uncles here to welcome me.

RICHARD Sweet prince, the untainted virtue of your years
Hath not yet dived into the world's deceit:
Nor more can you distinguish of a man
Than of his outward show, which, God he knows,   10
Seldom or never jumpeth with the heart.
Those uncles which you want were dangerous;
Your grace attended to their sug'red words,
But looked not on the poison of their hearts:
God keep you from them, and from such false friends!

PRINCE God keep me from false friends! But they were none.

RICHARD My lord, the Mayor of London comes to greet you.

'Enter Lord Mayor'

MAYOR God bless your grace with health and happy days!

PRINCE I thank you, good my lord, and thank you all.
I thought my mother and my brother York   20
Would long ere this have met us on the way:
Fie, what a slug is Hastings, that he comes not
To tell us whether they will come or no!

'Enter LORD HASTINGS*'*

BUCK'HAM And, in good time, here comes the sweating lord.

PRINCE Welcome, my lord: what, will our mother come?

HASTINGS On what occasion God he knows, not I,
The queen your mother and your brother York

Have taken sanctuary: the tender prince
Would fain have come with me to meet your grace,
But by his mother was perforce withheld.   30

BUCK'HAM Fie, what an indirect and peevish course
Is this of hers! Lord Cardinal, will your grace
Persuade the queen to send the Duke of York
Unto his princely brother presently?
If she deny, Lord Hastings, go with him,
And from her jealous arms pluck him perforce.

CARDINAL My Lord of Buckingham, if my weak oratory
Can from his mother win the Duke of York,
Expect him here; but if she be obdurate
To mild entreaties, God in heaven forbid   40
We should infringe the holy privilege
Of blessed sanctuary! Not for all this land
Would I be guilty of so deep a sin.

BUCK'HAM You are too senseless-obstinate, my lord,
Too ceremonious and traditional.
Weigh it but with the grossness of this age,
You break not sanctuary in seizing him.
The benefit thereof is always granted
To those whose dealings have deserved the place
And those who have the wit to claim the place.   50
This prince hath neither claimed it nor deserved it;
Therefore, in mine opinion, cannot have it:
Then, taking him from thence that is not there,
You break no privilege nor charter there.
Oft have I heard of sanctuary men,
But sanctuary children ne'er till now.

CARDINAL My lord, you shall o'er-rule my mind for once.
Come on, Lord Hastings, will you go with me?

HASTINGS I go, my lord.

PRINCE Good lords, make all the speedy haste you may.   60
                    [Cardinal and Hastings depart
Say, uncle Gloucester, if our brother come,
Where shall we sojourn till our coronation?

RICHARD Where it seems best unto your royal self.
If I may counsel you, some day or two
Your highness shall repose you at the Tower:

Then where you please, and shall be thought most fit
For your best health and recreation.

PRINCE I do not like the Tower, of any place.
Did Julius Caesar build that place, my lord

BUCK'HAM He did, my gracious lord, begin that place;   70
Which, since, succeeding ages have re-edified.

PRINCE Is it upon record, or else reported
Successively from age to age, he built it?

BUCK'HAM Upon record, my gracious lord.

PRINCE But say, my lord, it were not regist'red,
Methinks the truth should live from age to age,
As 'twere retailed to all posterity,
Even to the general all-ending day.

RICHARD So wise so young, they say, do ne'er live long.

PRINCE What say you, uncle?   80

RICHARD I say, without characters, fame lives long.
[aside] Thus, like the formal vice, Iniquity,
I moralise two meanings in one word.

PRINCE That Julius Caesar was a famous man;
With what his valour did enrich his wit,
His wit set down to make his valour live:
Death makes no conquest of this conqueror,
For now he lives in fame, though not in life.
I'll tell you what, my cousin Buckingham –

BUCK'HAM What, my gracious lord?   90

PRINCE An if I live until I be a man,
I'll win our ancient right in France again,
Or die a soldier, as I lived a king.

RICHARD Short summers lightly have a forward spring.

HASTINGS and the CARDINAL return with young YORK

BUCK'HAM Now in good time, here comes the Duke of York.

PRINCE Richard of York! How fares our loving brother?

YORK Well, my dread lord; so must I call you now.

PRINCE Ay, brother, to our grief, as it is yours:
Too late he died that might have kept that title,
Which by his death hath lost much majesty.   100

RICHARD How fares our cousin, noble Lord of York?

YORK I thank you, gentle uncle. O, my lord,

	You said that idle weeds are fast in growth:
	The prince my brother hath outgrown me far.
RICHARD	He hath, my lord.
YORK	And therefore is he idle?
RICHARD	O, my fair cousin, I must not say so.
YORK	Then he is more beholding to you than I.
RICHARD	He may command me as my sovereign;
	But you have power in me as in a kinsman.
YORK	I pray you, uncle, give me this dagger. 110
RICHARD	My dagger, little cousin? With all my heart.
PRINCE	A beggar, brother?
YORK	Of my kind uncle, that I know will give't,
	Being but a toy, which is no grief to give.
RICHARD	A greater gift than that I'll give my cousin.
YORK	A greater gift! O, that's the sword to it.
RICHARD	Ay, gentle cousin, were it light enough.
YORK	O, then, I see you'll part but with light gifts;
	In weightier things you'll say a beggar nay.
RICHARD	It is too heavy for your grace to wear. 120
YORK	I'd weigh it lightly, were it heavier.
RICHARD	What, would you have my weapon, little lord?
YORK	I would, that I might thank you as you call me.
RICHARD	How?
YORK	Little.
PRINCE	My Lord of York will still be cross in talk:
	Uncle, your grace knows how to bear with him.
YORK	You mean, to bear me, not to bear with me:
	Uncle, my brother mocks both you and me;
	Because that I am little, like an ape, 130
	He thinks that you should bear me on your shoulders.
BUCK'HAM	With what a sharp-provided wit he reasons!
	To mitigate the scorn he gives his uncle,
	He prettily and aptly taunts himself:
	So cunning and so young is wonderful.
RICHARD	My lord, will't please you pass along?
	Myself and my good cousin Buckingham
	Will to your mother, to entreat of her
	To meet you at the Tower and welcome you.
YORK	What, will you go unto the Tower, my lord? 140

PRINCE	My Lord Protector needs will have it so.
YORK	I shall not sleep in quiet at the Tower.
RICHARD	Why, what should you fear?
YORK	Marry, my uncle Clarence' angry ghost:
	My grandam told me he was murdered there.
PRINCE	I fear no uncles dead.
RICHARD	Nor none that live, I hope.
PRINCE	An if they live, I hope I need not fear.
	But come, my lord; so with a heavy heart,
	Thinking on them, go I unto the Tower. 150

> ['A Sennet.' All go but Richard,
> Buckingham and Catesby]

BUCK'HAM	Think you, my lord, this little prating York
	Was not incensèd by his subtle mother
	To taunt and scorn you thus opprobriously?
RICHARD	No doubt, no doubt: O, 'tis a parlous boy;
	Bold, quick, ingenious, forward, capable:
	He is all the mother's, from the top to toe.
BUCK'HAM	Well, let them rest. Come, Catesby, thou art sworn
	As deeply to effect what we intend,
	As closely to conceal what we impart:
	Thou know'st our reasons urged upon the way. 160
	What think'st thou? Is it not an easy matter
	To make Lord William Hastings of our mind,
	For the instalment of this noble duke
	In the seat royal of this famous isle?
CATESBY	He for his father's sake so loves the prince
	That he will not be won to aught against him.
BUCK'HAM	What think'st thou then of Stanley? Will not he?
CATESBY	He will do all in all as Hastings doth.
BUCK'HAM	Well, then, no more but this: go, gentle Catesby,
	And, as it were far off, sound thou Lord Hastings 170
	How he doth stand affected to our purpose;
	And summon him tomorrow to the Tower,
	To sit about the coronation.
	If thou dost find him tractable to us,
	Encourage him, and tell him all our reasons:
	If he be leaden, icy-cold, unwilling,
	Be thou so too; and so break off the talk,

And give us notice of his inclination.
For we tomorrow hold divided councils,
Wherein thyself shalt highly be employed.   180

RICHARD   Commend me to Lord William: tell him, Catesby,
His ancient knot of dangerous adversaries
Tomorrow are let blood at Pomfret Castle;
And bid my lord, for joy of this good news,
Give Mistress Shore one gentle kiss the more.

BUCK'HAM Good Catesby, go, effect this business soundly.

CATESBY   My good lords both, with all the heed I can.

RICHARD   Shall we hear from you, Catesby, ere we sleep?

CATESBY   You shall, my lord.

RICHARD   At Crosby House, there shall you find us both.   190

[Catesby goes

BUCK'HAM My lord, what shall we do, if we perceive
Lord Hastings will not yield to our complots?

RICHARD   Chop off his head – something we will determine.
And look when I am king, claim thou of me
The earldom of Hereford, and all the movables
Whereof the king my brother was possessed.

BUCK'HAM I'll claim that promise at your grace's hand.

RICHARD   And look to have it yielded with all kindness.
Come, let us sup betimes, that afterwards
We may digest our complots in some form.   200

[they go

SCENE 2

Before Lord Hastings' house; night

'Enter a Messenger to the door of Hastings'

MESSENGER [knocks] My lord! My lord!

HASTINGS   [within] Who knocks?

MESSENGER One from the Lord Stanley.

HASTINGS   [within] What is't o'clock?

MESSENGER Upon the stroke of four.   [Hastings opens the door

HASTINGS Cannot my Lord Stanley sleep these tedious nights?

MESSENGER So it appears by that I have to say.
First, he commends him to your noble self.

HASTINGS What then?

MESSENGER Then certifies your lordship that this night   10
He dreamt the boar had razéd off his helm:
Besides, he says there are two councils kept;
And that may be determined at the one
Which may make you and him to rue at th'other.
Therefore he sends to know your lordship's pleasure –
If you will presently take horse with him,
And with all speed post with him toward the north,
To shun the danger that his soul divines.

HASTINGS Go, fellow, go, return unto thy lord;
Bid him not fear the separated councils: 20
His honour and myself are at the one,
And at the other is my good friend Catesby;
Where nothing can proceed that toucheth us
Whereof I shall not have intelligence.
Tell him his fears are shallow, without instance:
And for his dreams, I wonder he's so simple
To trust the mock'ry of unquiet slumbers.
To fly the boar before the boar pursues
Were to incense the boar to follow us
And make pursuit where he did mean no chase.   30
Go, bid thy master rise and come to me;
And we will both together to the Tower,
Where he shall see the boar will use us kindly.

MESSENGER I'll go, my lord, and tell him what you say.   *[goes*

'*Enter* CATESBY'

CATESBY Many good morrows to my noble lord!

HASTINGS Good morrow, Catesby, you are early stirring:
What news, what news, in this our tott'ring state?

CATESBY It is a reeling world indeed, my lord;
And I believe will never stand upright
Till Richard wear the garland of the realm.   40

HASTINGS How, wear the garland? Dost thou mean the crown?

CATESBY Ay, my good lord.

HASTINGS I'll have this crown of mine cut from my shoulders
          Before I'll see the crown so foul misplaced.
          But canst thou guess that he doth aim at it?
CATESBY   Ay, on my life, and hopes to find you forward
          Upon his party for the gain thereof:
          And thereupon he sends you this good news,
          That this same very day your enemies,
          The kindred of the queen, must die at Pomfret.   50
HASTINGS Indeed, I am no mourner for that news,
          Because they have been still my adversaries:
          But, that I'll give my voice on Richard's side,
          To bar my master's heirs in true descent,
          God knows I will not do it, to the death.
CATESBY   God keep your lordship in that gracious mind!
HASTINGS But I shall laugh at this a twelvemonth hence,
          That they which brought me in my master's hate,
          I live to look upon their tragedy.
          Well, Catesby, ere a fortnight make me older,   60
          I'll send some packing that yet think not on't.
CATESBY   'Tis a vile thing to die, my gracious lord,
          When men are unprepared and look not for it.
HASTINGS O monstrous, monstrous! And so falls it out
          With Rivers, Vaughan, Grey: and so 'twill do
          With some men else, that think themselves as safe
          As thou and I, who, as thou know'st, are dear
          To princely Richard and to Buckingham.
CATESBY   The princes both make high account of you —
          [aside] For they account his head upon the Bridge.   70
HASTINGS I know they do, and I have well deserved it.

                    'Enter LORD STANLEY'

          Come on, come on, where is your boar-spear, man?
          Bear you the boar, and go so unprovided?
STANLEY   My lord, good morrow; good morrow, Catesby:
          You may jest on, but, by the holy rood,
          I do not like these several councils, I.
HASTINGS I hold my life as dear as you do yours;
          And never in my days, I do protest,
          Was it so precious to me as 'tis now:

Think you, but that I know our state secure,   80
I would be so triumphant as I am?

STANLEY   The lords at Pomfret, when they rode from London,
Were jocund and supposed their states were sure,
And they indeed had no cause to mistrust;
But yet you see how soon the day o'ercast.
This sudden stab of rancour I misdoubt:
Pray God, I say, I prove a needless coward!
What, shall we toward the Tower? The day is spent.

HASTINGS   Come, come, have with you. Wot you what my lord?
Today the lords you talked of are beheaded.   90

STANLEY   They, for their truth, might better wear their heads
Than some that have accused them wear their hats.
But come, my lord, let's away.

                    'Enter a Pursuivant'

HASTINGS   Go on before; I'll talk with this good fellow.
                              [*Stanley and Catesby depart*
How now, sirrah? How goes the world with thee?

PURSUIV.   The better that your lordship please to ask.

HASTINGS   I tell thee, man, 'tis better with me now
Than when thou met'st me last where now we meet:
Then was I going prisoner to the Tower,
By the suggestion of the queen's allies;   100
But now, I tell thee (keep it to thyself)
This day those enemies are put to death,
And I in better state than e'er I was.

PURSUIV.   God hold it, to your honour's good content!

HASTINGS   Gramercy, fellow: there, drink that for me.
                              [*'throws him his purse'*

PURSUIV.   I thank your honour.   [*goes*

                    'Enter a Priest'

PRIEST   Well met, my lord; I am glad to see your honour.

HASTINGS   I thank thee, good Sir John, with all my heart.
I am in your debt for your last exercise;
Come the next Sabbath, and I will content you.   110
                              [*he whispers in his ear*

                    'Enter BUCKINGHAM*'*

BUCK'HAM What, talking with a priest, Lord Chamberlain?
            Your friends at Pomfret, they do need the priest:
            Your honour hath no shriving work in hand.
HASTINGS Good faith, and when I met this holy man,
            The men you talk of came into my mind.
            What, go you toward the Tower?
BUCK'HAM I do, my lord; but long I cannot stay there:
            I shall return before your lordship thence.
HASTINGS Nay, like enough, for I stay dinner there.
BUCK'HAM And supper too, although thou know'st it not.   120
            [*aloud*] Come, will you go?
HASTINGS   I'll wait upon your lordship.
                                                    [*they go*

                            SCENE 3

                        Pomfret Castle

        '*Enter* SIR RICHARD RATCLIFFE, *with halberds, carrying the*
        nobles' RIVERS, GREY, *and* VAUGHAN '*to death*'

RIVERS   Sir Richard Ratcliffe, let me tell thee this:
            Today shalt thou behold a subject die
            For truth, for duty, and for loyalty.
GREY   God bless the prince from all the pack of you!
            A knot you are of damnéd blood-suckers.
VAUGHAN   You live that shall cry woe for this hereafter.
RATCLIFFE Dispatch; the limit of your lives is out.
RIVERS   O Pomfret, Pomfret! O thou bloody prison,
            Fatal and ominous to noble peers!
            Within the guilty closure of thy walls   10
            Richard the Second here was hacked to death;
            And, for more slander to thy dismal seat,
            We give to thee our guiltless blood to drink.
GREY   Now Margaret's curse is fall'n upon our heads,
            When she exclaimed on Hastings, you, and I,
            For standing by when Richard stabbed her son.
RIVERS   Then cursed she Richard, then cursed she Buckingham,
            Then cursed she Hastings. O, remember, God,

To hear her prayer for them, as now for us!
And for my sister and her princely sons,   20
Be satisfied, dear God, with our true blood,
Which, as thou know'st, unjustly must be spilt.

RATCLIFFE Make haste; the hour of death is expiate.

RIVERS Come, Grey, come, Vaughan, let us here embrace:
Farewell, until we meet again in heaven.

[they are led away

SCENE 4

A room in the Tower of London

BUCKINGHAM, STANLEY, HASTINGS, *the* BISHOP OF ELY,
RATCLIFFE, LOVEL, *with others, at a table*

HASTINGS Now, noble peers, the cause why we are met
Is to determine of the coronation.
In God's name, speak! When is the royal day?

BUCK'HAM Is all things ready for the royal time?

STANLEY It is, and wants but nomination.

ELY Tomorrow then I judge a happy day.

BUCK'HAM Who knows the Lord Protector's mind herein?
Who is most inward with the noble duke?

ELY Your grace, we think, should soonest know his mind.

BUCK'HAM We know each other's faces: for our hearts,   10
He knows no more of mine than I of yours;
Or I of his, my lord, than you of mine.
Lord Hastings, you and he are near in love.

HASTINGS I thank his grace, I know he loves me well;
But, for his purpose in the coronation,
I have not sounded him, nor he delivered
His gracious pleasure any way therein:
But you, my honourable lords, may name the time;
And in the duke's behalf I'll give my voice,
Which, I presume, he'll take in gentle part.   20

Enter RICHARD

ELY In happy time, here comes the duke himself.

RICHARD My noble lords and cousins all, good morrow.

	I have been long a sleeper; but I trust	
	My absence doth neglect no great design,	
	Which by my presence might have been concluded.	
BUCK'HAM	Had you not come upon your cue, my lord,	
	William Lord Hastings had pronounced your part –	
	I mean, your voice for crowning of the king.	
RICHARD	Than my Lord Hastings no man might be bolder;	
	His lordship knows me well, and loves me well.	30
	My lord of Ely, when I was last in Holborn,	
	I saw good strawberries in your garden there:	
	I do beseech you send for some of them.	
ELY	Marry, and will, my lord, with all my heart. [he goes	
RICHARD	Cousin of Buckingham, a word with you.	
	[drawing him aside	
	Catesby hath sounded Hastings in our business,	
	And finds the testy gentleman so hot,	
	That he will lose his head ere give consent	
	His master's child, as worshipfully he terms it,	
	Shall lose the royalty of England's throne.	40
BUCK'HAM	Withdraw yourself a while, I'll go with you.	
	[they go out	
STANLEY	We have not yet set down this day of triumph.	
	Tomorrow, in my judgement, is too sudden;	
	For I myself am not so well provided	
	As else I would be, were the day prolonged.	

The BISHOP OF ELY *returns*

ELY	Where is my Lord the Duke of Gloucester?	
	I have sent for these strawberries.	
HASTINGS	His grace looks cheerfully and smooth this morning;	
	There's some conceit or other likes him well,	
	When that he bids good-morrow with such spirit.	50
	I think there's ne'er a man in Christendom	
	Can lesser hide his love or hate than he;	
	For by his face straight shall you know his heart.	
STANLEY	What of his heart perceive you in his face	
	By any likelihood he showed today?	
HASTINGS	Marry, that with no man here he is offended;	
	For, were he, he had shown it in his looks.	

RICHARD and BUCKINGHAM return

RICHARD　　I pray you all, tell me what they deserve
That do conspire my death with devilish plots
Of damnéd witchcraft, and that have prevailed　　60
Upon my body with their hellish charms?

HASTINGS　The tender love I bear your grace, my lord,
Makes me most forward in this princely presence
To doom th'offenders: whosoe'er they be,
I say, my lord, they have deservéd death.

RICHARD　　Then be your eyes the witness of their evil.
Look how I am bewitched; behold, mine arm
Is like a blasted sapling withered up:
And this is Edward's wife, that monstrous witch,
Consorted with that harlot, strumpet Shore,　　70
That by their witchcraft thus have markéd me.

HASTINGS　If they have done this deed, my noble lord –

RICHARD　　If! Thou protector of this damnéd strumpet,
Talk'st thou to me of 'ifs'? Thou art a traitor:
Off with his head! Now, by Saint Paul I swear,
I will not dine until I see the same.
Lovel and Ratcliffe, look that it be done:
The rest that love me, rise and follow me.
　　　　　　　　　　　[*all leave but Hastings, Ratcliffe and Lovel*

HASTINGS　Woe, woe for England! Not a whit for me;
For I, too fond, might have prevented this.　　80
Stanley did dream the boar did raze our helms,
And I did scorn it, and disdain to fly:
Three times today my foot-cloth horse did stumble,
And started when he looked upon the Tower,
As loath to bear me to the slaughter-house.
O, now I need the priest that spake to me:
I now repent I told the pursuivant,
As too triumphing, how mine enemies
Today at Pomfret bloodily were butchered,
And I myself secure in grace and favour.　　90
O Margaret, Margaret, now thy heavy curse
Is lighted on poor Hastings' wretched head!

RATCLIFFE Come, come, dispatch; the duke would be at dinner:
           Make a short shrift; he longs to see your head.
HASTINGS O momentary grace of mortal men,
           Which we more hunt for than the grace of God!
           Who builds his hope in air of your good looks
           Lives like a drunken sailor on a mast,
           Ready with every nod to tumble down
           Into the fatal bowels of the deep.   100
LOVEL Come, come, dispatch; 'tis bootless to exclaim.
HASTINGS O bloody Richard! Miserable England!
           I prophesy the fearfull'st time to thee
           That ever wretched age hath looked upon.
           Come, lead me to the block; bear him my head.
           They smile at me who shortly shall be dead.
                                     [he is led away

SCENE 5

The Tower-walls

Enter RICHARD *and* BUCKINGHAM, *'in rotten armour,*
marvellous ill-favoured'

RICHARD Come, cousin, canst thou quake, and change thy colour,
           Murder thy breath in middle of a word,
           And then again begin, and stop again,
           As if thou wert distraught and mad with terror?
BUCK'HAM Tut, I can counterfeit the deep tragedian,
           Speak and look back, and pry on every side,
           Tremble and start at wagging of a straw,
           Intending deep suspicion: ghastly looks
           Are at my service, like enforcéd smiles;
           And both are ready in their offices,   10
           At any time, to grace my stratagems.
           But what, is Catesby gone?
RICHARD He is; and, see, he brings the mayor along.

                'Enter the MAYOR *and* CATESBY'

BUCK'HAM Lord Mayor –   *[he starts*
RICHARD Look to the drawbridge there!

BUCK'HAM Hark! A drum.
RICHARD   Catesby, o'erlook the walls
BUCK'HAM Lord Mayor, the reason we have sent –
RICHARD   Look back, defend thee, here are enemies!
BUCK'HAM God and our innocence defend and guard us!   20
RICHARD   Be patient, they are friends, Ratcliffe and Lovel.

    'Enter LOVEL *and* RATCLIFFE, *with* HASTINGS' *head'*

LOVEL   Here is the head of that ignoble traitor,
          The dangerous and unsuspected Hastings.
RICHARD   So dear I loved the man, that I must weep.
          I took him for the plainest harmless creature
          That breathed upon the earth a Christian;
          Made him my book, wherein my soul recorded
          The history of all her secret thoughts.
          So smooth he daubed his vice with show of virtue
          That, his apparent open guilt omitted,   30
          I mean his conversation with Shore's wife,
          He lived from all attainder of suspects.
BUCK'HAM Well, well, he was the covert'st shelt'red traitor.
          Would you imagine, or almost believe,
          Were't not that, by great preservation,
          We live to tell it, that the subtle traitor
          This day had plotted, in the council-house
          To murder me and my good Lord of Gloucester?
MAYOR   Had he done so?
RICHARD   What! Think you we are Turks or infidels?   40
          Or that we would, against the form of law,
          Proceed thus rashly in the villain's death,
          But that the extreme peril of the case,
          The peace of England and our persons' safety,
          Enforced us to this execution?
MAYOR   Now, fair befall you! He deserved his death;
          And your good graces both have well proceeded,
          To warn false traitors from the like attempts.
BUCK'HAM I never looked for better at his hands,
          After he once fell in with Mistress Shore.   50
          Yet had we not determined he should die,
          Until your lordship came to see his end,
          Which now the loving haste of these our friends,

Something against our meanings, have prevented:
Because, my lord, I would have had you hear
The traitor speak and timorously confess
The manner and the purpose of his treasons;
That you might well have signified the same
Unto the citizens, who haply may
Misconster us in him and wail his death.   60

MAYOR   But, my good lord, your grace's words shall serve,
As well as I had seen and heard him speak:
And do not doubt, right noble princes both,
But I'll acquaint our duteous citizens
With all your just proceedings in this cause.

RICHARD   And to that end we wished your lordship here,
T'avoid the censures of the carping world.

BUCK'HAM Which since you come too late of our intent,
Yet witness what you hear we did intend:
And so, my good Lord Mayor, we bid farewell.   70
                              [*the Mayor takes leave*

RICHARD   Go, after, after, cousin Buckingham.
The mayor towards Guildhall hies him in all post:
There, at your meet'st advantage of the time,
Infer the bastardy of Edward's children:
Tell them how Edward put to death a citizen,
Only for saying he would make his son
Heir to the crown, meaning indeed his house,
Which, by the sign thereof, was terméd so.
Moreover, urge his hateful luxury
And bestial appetite in change of lust;   80
Which stretched unto their servants, daughters, wives,
Even where his raging eye or savage heart
Without control listed to make a prey.
Nay, for a need, thus far come near my person:
Tell them, when that my mother went with child
Of that insatiate Edward, noble York
My princely father then had wars in France;
And, by true computation of the time,
Found that the issue was not his begot;
Which well appearéd in his lineaments,   90
Being nothing like the noble duke my father:

         Yet touch this sparingly, as 'twere far off,
         Because, my lord, you know my mother lives.

BUCK'HAM Doubt not, my lord, I'll play the orator
         As if the golden fee for which I plead
         Were for myself: and so, my lord, adieu.

RICHARD   If you thrive well, bring them to Baynard's Castle,
         Where you shall find me well accompanied
         With reverend fathers and well-learnéd bishops.

BUCK'HAM I go, and towards three or four o'clock   100
         Look for the news that the Guildhall affords.   [goes

RICHARD   Go, Lovel, with all speed to Doctor Shaw;
         [To Catesby] Go thou to Friar Penker; bid them both
         Meet me within this hour at Baynard's Castle. [they go
         Now will I go to take some privy order
         To draw the brats of Clarence out of sight;
         And to give notice that no manner person
         Have any time recourse unto the princes.

                                         [he goes

SCENE 6

London. A street

'Enter a Scrivener', with a paper in his hand

SCRIVENER Here is the indictment of the good Lord Hastings,
         Which in a set hand fairly is engrossed,
         That it may be today read o'er in Paul's.
         And mark how well the sequel hangs together:
         Eleven hours I have spent to write it over,
         For yesternight by Catesby was it sent me;
         The precedent was full as long a-doing:
         And yet within these five hours Hastings lived,
         Untainted, unexamined, free, at liberty.
         Here's a good world the while! Who is so gross,   10
         That cannot see this palpable device?
         Yet who's so bold, but says he sees it not?
         Bad is the world; and all will come to nought,
         When such ill dealing must be seen in thought.

                                         [he goes

SCENE 7

A courtyard before Baynard's Castle

Enter RICHARD and BUCKINGHAM at different doors

RICHARD   How now, how now, what say the citizens?
BUCK'HAM Now, by the holy mother of our Lord,
        The citizens are mum, say not a word.
RICHARD   Touched you the bastardy of Edward's children?
BUCK'HAM I did; with his contract with Lady Lucy,
        And his contract by deputy in France;
        Th'insatiate greediness of his desire,
        And his enforcement of the city wives;
        His tyranny for trifles; his own bastardy,
        As being got, your father then in France,   10
        And his resemblance, being not like the duke:
        Withal I did infer your lineaments,
        Being the right idea of your father,
        Both in your form and nobleness of mind;
        Laid open all your victories in Scotland,
        Your discipline in war, wisdom in peace,
        Your bounty, virtue, fair humility;
        Indeed left nothing fitting for your purpose
        Untouched or slightly handled in discourse:
        And when mine oratory drew toward end,   20
        I bid them that did love their country's good
        Cry 'God save Richard, England's royal king!'
RICHARD   And did they so?
BUCK'HAM No, so God help me, they spake not a word;
        But, like dumb statues or breathing stones,
        Stared each on other, and looked deadly pale.
        Which when I saw, I reprehended them,
        And asked the Mayor what meant this wilful silence:
        His answer was, the people were not uséd
        To be spoke to but by the Recorder.   30
        Then he was urged to tell my tale again:
        'Thus saith the duke, thus hath the duke inferred';
        But nothing spoke in warrant from himself.
        When he had done, some followers of mine own

　　　　　At lower end of the hall hurled up their caps,
　　　　　And some ten voices cried 'God save King Richard!'
　　　　　And thus I took the vantage of those few:
　　　　　'Thanks, gentle citizens and friends,' quoth I,
　　　　　'This general applause and cheerful shout
　　　　　Argues your wisdoms and your love to Richard';　　40
　　　　　And even here brake off and came away.
RICHARD　What tongueless blocks were they! Would they
　　　　　　　　　　　　　　　　　　　　not speak?
BUCK'HAM　No, by my troth, my lord.
RICHARD　Will not the Mayor then and his brethren come?
BUCK'HAM　The Mayor is here at hand: intend some fear;
　　　　　Be not you spoke with, but by mighty suit:
　　　　　And look you get a prayer-book in your hand,
　　　　　And stand between two churchmen, good my lord;
　　　　　For on that ground I'll make a holy descant:
　　　　　And be not easily won to our requests;　　　　50
　　　　　Play the maid's part, still answer nay, and take it.
RICHARD　I go; and if you plead as well for them
　　　　　As I can say nay to thee for myself,
　　　　　No doubt we'll bring it to a happy issue.
BUCK'HAM　Go, go up to the leads; the Lord Mayor knocks.

　　　　　　　　　　　　　　　　　　[*Richard goes*

　　　　　The Mayor and Citizens enter the courtyard

　　　　　Welcome, my lord: I dance attendance here;
　　　　　I think the duke will not be spoke withal.

　　　　　　　　　　CATESBY *appears*

　　　　　Catesby, what says your lord to my request?
CATESBY　He doth entreat your grace, my noble lord,
　　　　　To visit him tomorrow or next day.　　　　　60
　　　　　He is within, with two right reverend fathers,
　　　　　Divinely bent to meditation;
　　　　　And in no worldly suits would he be moved,
　　　　　To draw him from his holy exercise.
BUCK'HAM　Return, good Catesby, to the gracious duke:
　　　　　Tell him, myself, the Mayor, and aldermen,
　　　　　In deep designs, in matter of great moment,
　　　　　No less importing than our general good,

Are come to have some conference with his grace.
CATESBY   I'll signify so much unto him straight.   [goes in 70
BUCK'HAM Ah, ha, my lord, this prince is not an Edward!
He is not lolling on a lewd love-bed,
But on his knees at meditation;
Not dallying with a brace of courtesans,
But meditating with two deep divines;
Not sleeping, to engross his idle body,
But praying, to enrich his watchful soul:
Happy were England, would this virtuous prince
Take on his grace the sovereignty thereof:
But, sure, I fear, we shall not win him to it.   80
MAYOR   Marry, God defend his grace should say us nay!
BUCK'HAM I fear he will. Here Catesby comes again.

CATESBY *returns*

Now, Catesby, what says his grace?
CATESBY   He wonders to what end you have assembled
Such troops of citizens to come to him,
His grace not being warned thereof before:
He fears, my lord, you mean no good to him.
BUCK'HAM Sorry I am my noble cousin should
Suspect me that I mean no good to him:
By heaven, we come to him in perfit love;   90
Ant so once more return and tell his grace.
                                    [*Catesby goes in again*
When holy and devout religious men
Are at their beads, 'tis much to draw them thence,
So sweet is zealous contemplation.

RICHARD *appears 'aloft, between two Bishops';* CATESBY *returns*

MAYOR   See, where his grace stands, 'tween two clergymen!
BUCK'HAM Two props of virtue for a Christian prince,
To stay him from the fall of vanity:
And, see, a book of prayer in his hand,
True ornaments to know a holy man.
Famous Plantagenet, most gracious prince,   100
Lend favourable ear to our requests;
And pardon us the interruption

Of thy devotion and right Christian zeal.

RICHARD My lord, there needs no such apology:
I do beseech your grace to pardon me,
Who, earnest in the service of my God,
Deferred the visitation of my friends.
But, leaving this, what is your grace's pleasure?

BUCK'HAM Even that, I hope, which pleaseth God above
And all good men of this ungoverned isle.   110

RICHARD I do suspect I have done some offence
That seems disgracious in the city's eye,
And that you come to reprehend my ignorance.

BUCK'HAM You have, my lord: would it might please your grace,
On our entreaties, to amend your fault!

RICHARD Else wherefore breathe I in a Christian land?

BUCK'HAM Know then, it is your fault that you resign
The supreme seat, the throne majestical,
The scept'red office of your ancestors,
Your state of fortune and your due of birth,   120
The lineal glory of your royal house,
To the corruption of a blemished stock:
Whiles, in the mildness of your sleepy thoughts,
Which here we waken to our country's good,
The noble isle doth want her proper limbs;
Her face defaced with scars of infamy,
Her royal stock graffed with ignoble plants,
And almost should'red in the swallowing gulf
Of dark forgetfulness and deep oblivion.
Which to recure, we heartily solicit   130
Your gracious self to take on you the charge
And kingly government of this your land;
Not as protector, steward, substitute,
Or lowly factor for another's gain;
But as successively, from blood to blood,
Your right of birth, your empery, your own.
For this, consorted with the citizens,
Your very worshipful and loving friends,
And by their vehement instigation,
In this just cause come I to move your grace.   140

RICHARD I cannot tell if to depart in silence

Or bitterly to speak in your reproof
Best fitteth my degree or your condition:
If not to answer, you might haply think
Tongue-tied ambition, not replying, yielded
To bear the golden yoke of sovereignty,
Which fondly you would here impose on me;
If to reprove you for this suit of yours,
So seasoned with your faithful love to me,
Then, on the other side, I checked my friends.   150
Therefore – to speak, and to avoid the first,
And then, in speaking, not to incur the last –
Definitively thus I answer you:
Your love deserves my thanks, but my desert
Unmeritable shuns your high request.
First, if all obstacles were cut away
And that my path were even to the crown,
As the ripe revenue and due of birth,
Yet so much is my poverty of spirit,
So mighty and so many my defects,   160
That I would rather hide me from my greatness,
Being a bark to brook no mighty sea,
Than in my greatness covet to be hid
And in the vapour of my glory smothered.
But, God be thanked, there is no need of me,
And much I need to help you, were there need:
The royal tree hath left us royal fruit,
Which, mellowed by the stealing hours of time,
Will well become the seat of majesty,
And make, no doubt, us happy by his reign.   170
On him I lay that you would lay on me,
The right and fortune of his happy stars,
Which God defend that I should wring from him!
BUCK'HAM My lord, this argues conscience in your grace;
But the respects thereof are nice and trivial,
All circumstances well consideréd.
You say that Edward is your brother's son:
So say we too, but not by Edward's wife;
For first was he contract to Lady Lucy –
Your mother lives a witness to his vow –   180

And afterward by substitute betrothed
To Bona, sister to the King of France.
These both put off, a poor petitioner,
A care-crazed mother to a many sons,
A beauty-waning and distresséd widow,
Even in the afternoon of her best days,
Made prize and purchase of his wanton eye,
Seduced the pitch and height of his degree
To base declension and loathed bigamy:
By her, in his unlawful bed, he got   190
This Edward, whom our manners call the prince.
More bitterly could I expostulate,
Save that, for reverence to some alive,
I give a sparing limit to my tongue.
Then, good my lord, take to your royal self
This proffered benefit of dignity;
If not to bless us and the land withal,
Yet to draw forth your noble ancestry
From the corruption of abusing times
Unto a lineal true-derivéd course.   200

MAYOR   Do, good my lord, your citizens entreat you.
BUCK'HAM Refuse not, mighty lord, this proffered love.
CATESBY   O, make them joyful, grant their lawful suit!
RICHARD   Alas, why would you heap this care on me?
I am unfit for state and majesty.
I do beseech you, take it not amiss;
I cannot nor I will not yield to you.
BUCK'HAM If you refuse it – as, in love and zeal,
Loath to depose the child, your brother's son;
As well we know your tenderness of heart   210
And gentle, kind, effeminate remorse,
Which we have noted in you to your kindred,
And egally indeed to all estates –
Yet know, whe'er you accept our suit or no,
Your brother's son shall never reign our king;
But we will plant some other in the throne,
To the disgrace and downfall of your house:
And in this resolution here we leave you.
Come, citizens. Zounds! I'll entreat no more.

RICHARD	O, do not swear, my lord of Buckingham. 220

                     [Buckingham, Mayor and citizens leave

CATESBY	Call him again, sweet prince, accept their suit:
	If you deny them, all the land will rue it.
RICHARD	Will you enforce me to a world of cares?
	Call them again: I am not made of stone,
	But penetrable to your kind entreaties,
	Albeit against my conscience and my soul.

          'BUCKINGHAM *and the rest'* return

          Cousin of Buckingham, and sage grave men,
          Since you will buckle fortune on my back,
          To bear her burthen, whe'er I will or no,
          I must have patience to endure the load.   230
          But if black scandal or foul-faced reproach
          Attend the sequel of your imposition,
          Your mere enforcement shall acquittance me
          From all the impure blots and stains thereof;
          For God doth know, and you may partly see,
          How far I am from the desire of this.

MAYOR	God bless your grace! We see it, and will say it.
RICHARD	In saying so, you shall but say the truth.
BUCK'HAM	Then I salute you with this royal title:
	Long live King Richard, England's worthy king! 240
ALL	Amen.
BUCK'HAM	Tomorrow may it please you to be crowned?
RICHARD	Even when you please, for you will have it so.
BUCK'HAM	Tomorrow then we will attend your grace:
	And so most joyfully we take our leave.
RICHARD	Come, let us to our holy work again.
	Farewell, my cousin; farewell, gentle friends.

                                   [they go

ACT 4 SCENE I

Before the Tower

Enter QUEEN ELIZABETH, DUCHESS OF YORK, *and* MARQUIS OF
DORSET; *meeting* ANNE, DUCHESS OF GLOUCESTER, *and* LADY
MARGARET PLANTAGENET, *Clarence's young daughter*

DUCHESS	Who meets us here? My niece Plantagenet,
	Led in the hand of her kind aunt of Gloucester?
	Now, for my life, she's wand'ring to the Tower,
	On pure heart's love to greet the tender princes.
	Daughter, well met.
ANNE	God give your graces both
	A happy and a joyful time of day!
Q. ELIZAB.	As much to you, good sister! Whither away?
ANNE	No farther than the Tower, and, as I guess,
	Upon the like devotion as yourselves,
	To gratulate the gentle princes there.
Q. ELIZAB.	Kind sister, thanks: we'll enter all together.

BRAKENBURY *comes from the Tower*

	And, in good time, here the lieutenant comes.
	Master Lieutenant, pray you, by your leave,
	How doth the prince, and my young son of York?
BRAKEN.	Right well, dear madam. By your patience,
	I may not suffer you to visit them;
	The king hath strictly charged the contrary.
Q. ELIZAB.	The king! Who's that?
BRAKEN.	I mean the Lord Protector.
Q. ELIZAB.	The Lord protect him from that kingly title!
	Hath he set bounds between their love and me?
	I am their mother; who shall bar me from them?
DUCHESS	I am their father's mother; I will see them.
ANNE	Their aunt I am in law, in love their mother:
	Then bring me to their sights; I'll bear thy blame,
	And take thy office from thee, on my peril.
BRAKEN.	No, madam, no; I may not leave it so:

10

20

I am bound by oath, and therefore pardon me.
                                    [*he goes within*

                LORD STANLEY *comes up*

STANLEY   Let me but meet you, ladies, one hour hence,
            And I'll salute your grace of York as mother,   30
            And reverend looker-on, of two fair queens.
            [*to Anne*] Come, madam, you must straight to
                                            Westminster,
            There to be crownéd Richard's royal queen.
Q. ELIZAB. Ah, cut my lace asunder,
            That my pent heart may have some scope to beat,
            Or else I swoon with this dead-killing news!
ANNE   Despiteful tidings! O unpleasing news!
DORSET   Be of good cheer: mother, how fares your grace?
Q. ELIZAB. O Dorset, speak not to me, get thee gone!
            Death and destruction dogs thee at thy heels;   40
            Thy mother's name is ominous to children.
            If thou wilt outstrip death, go cross the seas,
            And live with Richmond, from the reach of hell:
            Go, hie thee, hie thee from this slaughter-house,
            Lest thou increase the number of the dead;
            And make me die the thrall of Margaret's curse,
            Nor mother, wife, nor England's counted queen.
STANLEY   Full of wise care is this your counsel, madam.
            [*to Dorset*] Take all the swift advantage of the hours;
            You shall have letters from me to my son   50
            In your behalf, to meet you on the way:
            Be not ta'en tardy by unwise delay.
DUCHESS   O ill-dispersing wind of misery!
            O my acccurséd womb, the bed of death!
            A cockatrice hast thou hatched to the world,
            Whose unavoided eye is murderous.
STANLEY   Come, madam, come; I in all haste was sent.
ANNE   And I with all unwillingness will go.
            O, would to God that the inclusive verge
            Of golden metal that must round my brow   60
            Were red-hot steel, to sear me to the brains!
            Anointed let me be with deadly venom,

And die ere men can say, 'God save the queen!'

Q. ELIZAB. Go, go, poor soul, I envy not thy glory:
To feed my humour, wish thyself no harm.

ANNE No? Why, when he that is my husband now
Came to me, as I followed Henry's corse,
When scarce the blood was well washed from his hands
Which issued from my other angel husband,
And that dear saint which then I weeping followed –   70
O, when, I say, I looked on Richard's face,
This was my wish: 'Be thou', quoth I, 'accursed,
For making me, so young, so old a widow!
And, when thou wed'st, let sorrow haunt thy bed;
And be thy wife, if any be so, made
More miserable by the life of thee
Than thou hast made me by my dear lord's death!'
Lo, ere I can repeat this curse again,
Within so small a time, my woman's heart
Grossly grew captive to his honey words   80
And proved the subject of mine own soul's curse,
Which hitherto hath held mine eyes from rest;
For never yet one hour in his bed
Did I enjoy the golden dew of sleep,
But with his timorous dreams was still awaked.
Besides, he hates me for my father Warwick;
And will, no doubt, shortly be rid of me.

Q. ELIZAB. Poor heart, adieu! I pity thy complaining.

ANNE No more than with my soul I mourn for yours.

Q. ELIZAB. Farewell, thou woeful welcomer of glory!   90

ANNE Adieu, poor soul, that tak'st thy leave of it!

DUCHESS [to Dorset] Go thou to Richmond, and good fortune
                            guide thee!
[to Anne] Go thou to Richard, and good angels
                              tend thee!
[to Queen Elizabeth] Go thou to sanctuary, and
                        good thoughts possess thee!
I to my grave, where peace and rest lie with me!
Eighty odd years of sorrow have I seen,
And each hour's joy wracked with a week of teen.

Q. ELIZAB. Stay, yet look back with me unto the Tower.

Pity, you ancient stones, those tender babes
Whom envy hath immured within your walls!   100
Rough cradle for such little pretty ones!
Rude ragged nurse, old sullen playfellow
For tender princes, use my babies well!
So foolish sorrow bids your stones farewell.

                                        [*they depart*

SCENE 2

London. The palace

'*Sennet. Enter* RICHARD, *in pomp*', *crowned*;
BUCKINGHAM, CATESBY, *a Page, and others*

K.RICHARD Stand all apart. Cousin of Buckingham!
BUCK'HAM My gracious sovereign!
K.RICHARD Give me thy hand.   [*he ascends the throne*
                    Thus high, by thy advice,
And thy assistance, is King Richard seated:
But shall we wear these glories for a day?
Or shall they last, and we rejoice in them?
BUCK'HAM Still live they and for ever let them last!
K.RICHARD Ah Buckingham, now do I play the touch,
To try if thou be current gold indeed:
Young Edward lives; think now what I would speak.   10
BUCK'HAM Say on, my loving lord.
K.RICHARD Why, Buckingham, I say I would be king.
BUCK'HAM Why, so you are, my thrice renownéd lord.
K.RICHARD Ha? Am I king? 'Tis so – but Edward lives.
BUCK'HAM True, noble prince.
K.RICHARD   O bitter consequence!
That Edward still should live, 'true, noble prince'!
Cousin, thou wast not wont to be so dull.
Shall I be plain? I wish the bastards dead,
And I would have it suddenly performed.
What say'st thou now? Speak suddenly, be brief.   20
BUCK'HAM Your grace may do your pleasure.
K.RICHARD Tut, tut, thou art all ice, thy kindness freezes:

	Say, have I thy consent that they shall die?
BUCK'HAM	Give me some little breath, some pause, dear lord,
	Before I positively speak in this:
	I will resolve you herein presently. [*he goes*
CATESBY	The king is angry: see, he gnaws his lip.
K.RICHARD	I will converse with iron-witted fools
	And unrespective boys: none are for me
	[*descends from his throne*

That look into me with considerate eyes: 30
High-reaching Buckingham grows circumspect.
Boy!

PAGE   My lord?

K.RICHARD   Know'st thou not any whom corrupting gold
Will tempt unto a close exploit of death?

PAGE   I know a discontented gentleman
Whose humble means match not his haughty spirit:
Gold were as good as twenty orators,
And will, no doubt, tempt him to anything.

K.RICHARD   What is his name?

PAGE   His name, my lord, is Tyrrel.

K.RICHARD   I partly know the man: go, call him hither, boy.   40
                        [*Page goes*

The deep-revolving witty Buckingham
No more shall be the neighbour to my counsels.
Hath he so long held out with me untired,
And stops he now for breath? Well, be it so.

'Enter STANLEY'

How now, Lord Stanley!

STANLEY   Know, my loving lord,
The Marquis Dorset, as I hear, is fled
To Richmond in the parts where he abides.
                        [*stands apart*

K.RICHARD   Come hither, Catesby. Rumour it abroad
That Anne, my wife, is very grievous sick:
I will take order for her keeping close.   50
Inquire me out some mean poor gentleman,
Whom I will marry straight to Clarence' daughter:
The boy is foolish, and I fear not him.

Look, how thou dream'st! I say again, give out
That Anne, my queen, is sick and like to die.
About it! For it stands me much upon
To stop all hopes whose growth may damage me.
                              [*Catesby hurries forth*
I must be married to my brother's daughter,
Or else my kingdom stands on brittle glass.
Murder her brothers, and then marry her!   60
Uncertain way of gain! But I am in
So far in blood that sin will pluck on sin:
Tear-falling pity dwells not in this eye.

Re-enter Page with TYRREL

Is thy name Tyrrel?
TYRREL   James Tyrrel, and your most obedient subject.
K.RICHARD Art thou, indeed?
TYRREL   Prove me, my gracious lord.
K.RICHARD Dar'st thou resolve to kill a friend of mine?
TYRREL   Please you, I had rather kill two enemies.
K.RICHARD Why, there thou hast it: two deep enemies,
           Foes to my rest and my sweet sleep's disturbers,   70
           Are they that I would have thee deal upon:
           Tyrrel, I mean those bastards in the Tower.
TYRREL   Let me have open means to come to them,
           And soon I'll rid you from the fear of them.
K.RICHARD Thou sing'st sweet music. Hark, come hither, Tyrrel:
           Go, by this token; rise, and lend thine ear.   [*'whispers'*
           There is no more but so: say it is done,
           And I will love thee, and prefer thee for it.
TYRREL   I will dispatch it straight.   [*goes*

BUCKINGHAM *returns*

BUCK'HAM My lord, I have considered in my mind   80
           The late request that you did sound me in.
K.RICHARD Well, let that rest. Dorset is fled to Richmond.
BUCK'HAM I hear the news, my lord.
K.RICHARD Stanley, he is your wife's son: look unto it.
BUCK'HAM My lord, I claim the gift, my due by promise,
           For which your honour and your faith is pawned:
           Th'earldom of Hereford and the movables

            Which you have promiséd I shall possess.

K.RICHARD   Stanley, look to your wife: if she convey
            Letters to Richmond, you shall answer it.   90

BUCK'HAM   What says your highness to my just request?

K.RICHARD   I do remember me, Henry the Sixth
            Did prophesy that Richmond should be king,
            When Richmond was a little peevish boy.
            A king! Perhaps –

BUCK'HAM   My lord!

K.RICHARD   How chance the prophet could not at that time
            Have told me, I being by, that I should kill him?

BUCK'HAM   My lord, your promise for the earldom –

K.RICHARD   Richmond! When last I was at Exeter,   100
            The mayor in courtesy showed me the castle,
            And called it Rougemont: at which name I started,
            Because a bard of Ireland told me once
            I should not live long after I saw Richmond.

BUCK'HAM   My lord!

K.RICHARD   Ay, what's o'clock?

BUCK'HAM   I am thus bold to put your grace in mind
            Of what you promised me.

K.RICHARD   Well, but what's o'clock?

BUCK'HAM   Upon the stroke of ten.

K.RICHARD   Well, let it strike.

BUCK'HAM   Why let it strike?   110

K.RICHARD   Because that, like a Jack, thou keep'st the stroke
            Betwixt thy begging and my meditation.
            I am not in the giving vein today.

BUCK'HAM   May it please you to resolve me in my suit?

K.RICHARD   Thou troublest me, I am not in the vein.   [goes

BUCK'HAM   And is it thus? Repays he my deep service
            With such contempt? Made I him king for this?
            O, let me think on Hastings, and be gone
            To Brecknock, while my fearful head is on!

                                       [goes

SCENE 3

The same, later

'Enter TYRREL*'*

TYRREL   The tyrannous and bloody act is done,
         The most arch deed of piteous massacre
         That ever yet this land was guilty of.
         Dighton and Forrest, who I did suborn
         To do this piece of ruthless butchery,
         Albeit they were fleshed villains, bloody dogs,
         Melted with tenderness and mild compassion,
         Wept like two children in their death's sad story.
         'O, thus,' quoth Dighton, 'lay the gentle babes':
         'Thus, thus,' quoth Forrest, 'girdling one another   10
         Within their alabaster innocent arms:
         Their lips were four red roses on a stalk,
         Which in their summer beauty kissed each other.
         A book of prayers on their pillow lay;
         Which once,' quoth Forrest, 'almost changed my mind;
         But O! The devil' – there the villain stopped;
         Whilst Dighton thus told on: 'We smotheréd
         The most replenishéd sweet work of Nature
         That from the prime creation e'er she framed.'
         Hence all o'er gone with conscience and remorse,   20
         They could not speak; and so I left them both,
         To bear this tidings to the bloody king.
         And here he comes.

                 Enter KING RICHARD

                          All health, my sovereign lord!
K.RICHARD Kind Tyrrel, am I happy in thy news?
TYRREL   If to have done the thing you gave in charge
          Beget your happiness, be happy then,
          For it is done.
K.RICHARD   But didst thou see them dead?
TYRREL   I did, my lord.
K.RICHARD   And buried, gentle Tyrrel?
TYRREL   The chaplain of the Tower hath buried them;

           But where, to say the truth, I do not know.   30

K.RICHARD Come to me, Tyrrel, soon at after-supper,
           When thou shalt tell the process of their death.
           Meantime, but think how I may do thee good,
           And be inheritor of thy desire.
           Farewell till then.

TYRREL   I humbly take my leave.   [*he goes*

K.RICHARD The son of Clarence have I pent up close;
           His daughter meanly have I matched in marriage;
           The sons of Edward sleep in Abraham's bosom,
           And Anne my wife hath bid this world good night.
           Now, for I know the Breton Richmond aims   40
           At young Elizabeth, my brother's daughter,
           And, by that knot, looks proudly on the crown,
           To her go I, a jolly thriving wooer.

                '*Enter* RATCLIFFE'

RATCLIFFE My lord!

K.RICHARD Good or bad news, that thou com'st in so bluntly?

RATCLIFFE Bad news, my lord: Morton is fled to Richmond;
           And Buckingham, backed with the hardy Welshmen,
           Is in the field, and still his power increaseth.

K.RICHARD Ely with Richmond troubles me more near
           Than Buckingham and his rash-levied strength.   50
           Come, I have learned that fearful commenting
           Is leaden servitor to dull delay;
           Delay leads impotent and snail-paced beggary.
           Then fiery expedition be my wing,
           Jove's Mercury, and herald for a king!
           Go, muster men: my counsel is my shield;
           We must be brief when traitors brave the field.

                                  [*they go*

SCENE 4

Before the palace

'Enter old QUEEN MARGARET'

Q. MARG.   So now prosperity begins to mellow
           And drop into the rotten mouth of death.
           Here in these confines slily have I lurked,
           To watch the waning of mine enemies.
           A dire induction am I witness to,
           And will to France, hoping the consequence
           Will prove as bitter, black, and tragical.
           Withdraw thee, wretched Margaret: who comes here?
                                                              [*retires*

Enter QUEEN ELIZABETH *and the* DUCHESS OF YORK

Q. ELIZAB. Ah, my poor princes! Ah, my tender babes!   10
           My unblown flowers, new-appearing sweets!
           If yet your gentle souls fly in the air
           And be not fixed in doom perpetual,
           Hover about me with your airy wings
           And hear your mother's lamentation!
Q. MARG.   Hover about her; say, that right for right
           Hath dimmed your infant morn to agéd night.
DUCHESS   So many miseries have crazed my voice,
           That my woe-wearied tongue is still and mute.
           Edward Plantagenet, why art thou dead?   20
Q. MARG.   Plantagenet doth quit Plantagenet,
           Edward for Edward pays a dying debt.
Q. ELIZAB. Wilt thou, O God, fly from such gentle lambs,
           And throw them in the entrails of the wolf?
           When didst thou sleep when such a deed was done?
Q. MARG.   When holy Harry died, and my sweet son.
DUCHESS   Dead life, blind sight, poor mortal living ghost,
           Woe's scene, world's shame, grave's due by life usurped,
           Brief abstract and record of tedious days,
           Rest thy unrest on England's lawful earth,
           Unlawfully made drunk with innocent blood!   [*sits* 30
Q. ELIZAB. Ah, that thou wouldst as soon afford a grave

As thou canst yield a melancholy seat!
Then would I hide my bones, not rest them here.
Ah, who hath any cause to mourn but we?

                                       [sits down by her

Q. MARG.   *[advancing]* If ancient sorrow be most reverend,
Give mine the benefit of seniory,
And let my griefs frown on the upper hand.
If sorrow can admit society,   *[sits down with them*
Tell o'er your woes again by viewing mine:
I had an Edward, till a Richard killed him;   40
I had a Harry, till a Richard killed him:
Thou hadst an Edward, till a Richard killed him;
Thou hadst a Richard, till a Richard killed him.

DUCHESS I had a Richard too, and thou didst kill him;
I had a Rutland too, thou holp'st to kill him.

Q. MARG. Thou hadst a Clarence too, and Richard killed him.
From forth the kennel of thy womb hath crept
A hell-hound that doth hunt us all to death:
That dog, that had his teeth before his eyes,
To worry lambs and lap their gentle blood;   50
That foul defacer of God's handiwork;
That excellent grand tyrant of the earth,
That reigns in galléd eyes of weeping souls –
Thy womb let loose, to chase us to our graves.
O upright, just, and true-disposing God,
How do I thank thee, that this carnal cur
Preys on the issue of his mother's body,
And makes her pew-fellow with others' moan!

DUCHESS O Harry's wife, triumph not in my woes!
God witness with me, I have wept for thine.   60

Q. MARG. Bear with me; I am hungry for revenge,
And now I cloy me with beholding it.
Thy Edward he is dead, that killed my Edward;
Thy other Edward dead, to quit my Edward;
Young York he is but boot, because both they
Matched not the high perfection of my loss:
Thy Clarence he is dead that stabbed my Edward;
And the beholders of this frantic play,
Th'adulterate Hastings, Rivers, Vaughan, Grey,

Untimely smothered in their dusky graves. 70
Richard yet lives, hell's black intelligencer,
Only reserved their factor, to buy souls
And send them thither: but at hand, at hand,
Ensues his piteous and unpitied end:
Earth gapes, hell burns, fiends roar, saints pray,
To have him suddenly conveyed from hence;
Cancel his bond of life, dear God, I plead,
That I may live and say 'The dog is dead!'

Q. ELIZAB. O, thou didst prophesy the time would come
That I should wish for thee to help me curse 80
That bottled spider, that foul bunch-backed toad!

Q. MARG. I called thee then vain flourish of my fortune;
I called thee then poor shadow, painted queen,
The presentation of but what I was;
The flattering index of a direful pageant;
One heaved a-high, to be hurled down below;
A mother only mocked with two fair babes;
A dream of what thou wast, a garish flag,
To be the aim of every dangerous shot;
A sign of dignity, a breath, a bubble; 90
A queen in jest, only to fill the scene.
Where is thy husband now? Where be thy brothers?
Where be thy two sons? Wherein dost thou joy?
Who sues, and kneels and says, 'God save the queen'?
Where be the bending peers that flattered thee?
Where be the thronging troops that followed thee?
Decline all this, and see what now thou art:
For happy wife, a most distressed widow;
For joyful mother, one that wails the name;
For queen, a very caitiff crowned with care; 100
For one being sued to, one that humbly sues;
For she that scorned at me, now scorned of me;
For she being feared of all, now fearing one;
For she commanding all, obeyed of none.
Thus hath the course of Justice whirled about,
And left thee but a very prey to time;
Having no more but thought of what thou wast,
To torture thee the more, being what thou art.

Thou didst usurp my place, and dost thou not
Usurp the just proportion of my sorrow?   110
Now thy proud neck bears half my burthened yoke;
From which even here I slip my weary head,
And leave the burthen of it all – on thee.
Farewell, York's wife, and queen of sad mischance:
These English woes shall make me smile in France.

Q. ELIZAB. O thou well skilled in curses, stay awhile,
And teach me how to curse mine enemies!

Q. MARG. Forbear to sleep the nights, and fast the days;
Compare dead happiness with living woe;
Think that thy babes were sweeter than they were,   120
And he that slew them fouler than he is.
Bett'ring thy loss makes the bad causer worse:
Revolving this will teach thee how to curse.

Q. ELIZAB. My words are dull; O, quicken them with thine!

Q. MARG. Thy woes will make them sharp and pierce like mine.
                                  [*she goes*

DUCHESS Why should calamity be full of words?

Q. ELIZAB. Windy attorneys to their client woes,
Airy succeeders of intestate joys,
Poor breathing orators of miseries!
Let them have scope: though what they will impart   130
Help nothing else, yet do they ease the heart.

DUCHESS If so, then be not tongue-tied: go with me,
And in the breath of bitter words let's smother
My damnèd son, that thy two sweet sons smothered.
The trumpet sounds: be copious in exclaims.

'Enter KING RICHARD *and his train', marching with
drums and trumpets*

K.RICHARD Who intercepts me in my expedition?

DUCHESS O, she that might have intercepted thee,
By strangling thee in her accursèd womb,
From all the slaughters, wretch, that thou hast done!

Q. ELIZAB. Hid'st thou that forehead with a golden crown,   140
Where should be branded, if that right were right,
The slaughter of the prince that owed that crown,
And the dire death of my poor sons and brothers?
Tell me, thou villain slave, where are my children?

DUCHESS   Thou toad, thou toad, where is thy brother Clarence?
          And little Ned Plantagenet, his son?
Q. ELIZAB. Where is the gentle Rivers, Vaughan, Grey?
DUCHESS   Where is kind Hastings?
K.RICHARD A flourish, trumpets! Strike alarum, drums!
          Let not the heavens hear these tell-tale women   150
          Rail on the Lord's anointed: strike, I say!
                              ['Flourish. Alarums'
          Either be patient, and entreat me fair,
          Or with the clamorous report of war
          Thus will I drown your exclamations.
DUCHESS   Art thou my son?
K.RICHARD Ay, I thank God, my father, and yourself.
DUCHESS   Then patiently hear my impatience.
K.RICHARD Madam, I have a touch of your condition,
          That cannot brook the accent of reproof.
DUCHESS   O, let me speak!
K.RICHARD   Do then; but I'll not hear.   160
DUCHESS   I will be mild and gentle in my words.
K.RICHARD And brief, good mother, for I am in haste.
DUCHESS   Art thou so hasty? I have stayed for thee,
          God knows, in torment and in agony.
K.RICHARD And came I not at last to comfort you?
DUCHESS   No, by the holy rood, thou know'st it well,
          Thou cam'st on earth to make the earth my hell.
          A grievous burthen was thy birth to me;
          Tetchy and wayward was thy infancy;
          Thy school-days frightful, desp'rate, wild, and furious; 170
          Thy prime of manhood daring, bold, and venturous;
          Thy age confirmed, proud, subtle, sly and bloody,
          More mild but yet more harmful-kind in hatred.
          What comfortable hour canst thou name
          That ever graced me with thy company?
K.RICHARD Faith, none, but Humphrey Hour, that called your grace
          To breakfast once forth of my company.
          If I be so disgracious in your eye,
          Let me march on, and not offend you, madam.
          Strike up the drum.
DUCHESS   I prithee, hear me speak.   180

K.RICHARD You speak too bitterly.
DUCHESS   Hear me a word;
          For I shall never speak to thee again.
K.RICHARD So.
DUCHESS   Either thou wilt die, by God's just ordinance,
          Ere from this war thou turn a conqueror,
          Or I with grief and extreme age shall perish
          And never more behold thy face again.
          Therefore take with thee my most grievous curse,
          Which, in the day of battle, tire thee more
          Than all the complete armour that thou wear'st!   190
          My prayers on the adverse party fight;
          And there the little souls of Edward's children
          Whisper the spirits of thine enemies
          And promise them success and victory.
          Bloody thou art, bloody will be thy end;
          Shame serves thy life and doth thy death attend.
                                                    [*she goes*
Q. ELIZAB. Though far more cause, yet much less spirit to curse
          Abides in me; I say amen to her.
K.RICHARD Stay, madam; I must talk a word with you.
Q. ELIZAB. I have no moe sons of the royal blood   200
          For thee to slaughter: for my daughters, Richard,
          They shall be praying nuns, not weeping queens;
          And therefore level not to hit their lives.
K.RICHARD You have a daughter called Elizabeth,
          Virtuous and fair, royal and gracious.
Q. ELIZAB. And must she die for this? O, let her live,
          And I'll corrupt her manners, stain her beauty,
          Slander myself as false to Edward's bed,
          Throw over her the veil of infamy:
          So she may live unscarred of bleeding slaughter,   210
          I will confess she was not Edward's daughter.
K.RICHARD Wrong not her birth, she is a royal princess.
Q. ELIZAB. To save her life, I'll say she is not so.
K.RICHARD Her life is safest only in her birth.
Q. ELIZAB. And only in that safety died her brothers.
K.RICHARD No, at their births good stars were opposite.

Q. ELIZAB. No, to their lives ill friends were contrary.

K.RICHARD All unavoided is the doom of destiny.

Q. ELIZAB. True, when avoided grace makes destiny:
    My babes were destined to a fairer death,   220
    If grace had blessed thee with a fairer life.

K.RICHARD You speak as if that I had slain my cousins!

Q. ELIZAB. Cousins indeed, and by their uncle cozened
    Of comfort, kingdom, kindred, freedom, life.
    Whose hand soever lanced their tender hearts,
    Thy head, all indirectly, gave direction:
    No doubt the murd'rous knife was dull and blunt
    Till it was whetted on thy stone-hard heart
    To revel in the entrails of my lambs.
    But that still use of grief makes wild grief tame,   230
    My tongue should to thy ears not name my boys
    Till that my nails were anchored in thine eyes;
    And I, in such a desp'rate bay of death,
    Like a poor bark, of sails and tackling reft,
    Rush all to pieces on thy rocky bosom.

K.RICHARD Madam, so thrive I in my enterprise
    And dangerous success of bloody wars,
    As I intend more good to you and yours
    Than ever you or yours by me were harmed!

Q. ELIZAB. What good is covered with the face of heaven,   240
    To be discovered, that can do me good?

K.RICHARD Th'advancement of your children, gentle lady.

Q. ELIZAB. Up to some scaffold, there to lose their heads?

K.RICHARD Unto the dignity and height of fortune,
    The high imperial type of this earth's glory.

Q. ELIZAB. Flatter my sorrow with report of it;
    Tell me what state, what dignity, what honour,
    Canst thou demise to any child of mine?

K.RICHARD Even all I have; ay, and myself and all,
    Will I withal endow a child of thine;   250
    So in the Lethe of thy angry soul
    Thou drown the sad remembrance of those wrongs
    Which thou supposest I have done to thee.

Q. ELIZAB. Be brief; lest that the process of thy kindness
    Last longer telling than thy kindness' date.

K.RICHARD Then know, that from my soul I love thy daughter.

Q. ELIZAB. My daughter's mother thinks it with her soul.

K.RICHARD What do you think?

Q. ELIZAB. That thou dost love my daughter from thy soul:
            So from thy soul's love didst thou love her brothers;   260
            And from my heart's love I do thank thee for it.

K.RICHARD Be not so hasty to confound my meaning:
            I mean that with my soul I love thy daughter,
            And do intend to make her Queen of England.

Q. ELIZAB. Well then, who dost thou mean shall be her king?

K.RICHARD Even he that makes her queen: who else should be?

Q. ELIZAB. What, thou?

K.RICHARD Even so: how think you of it?

Q. ELIZAB. How canst thou woo her?

K.RICHARD   That would I learn of you,
            As one being best acquainted with her humour.   270

Q. ELIZAB. And wilt thou learn of me?

K.RICHARD   With all my heart.

Q. ELIZAB. Send to her, by the man that slew her brothers,
            A pair of bleeding hearts; thereon engrave
            'Edward' and 'York'; then haply will she weep:
            Therefore present to her – as sometimes Margaret
            Did to thy father, steeped in Rutland's blood –
            A handkerchief; which, say to her, did drain
            The purple sap from her sweet brother's body,
            And bid her wipe her weeping eyes withal.
            If this inducement move her not to love,   280
            Send her a letter of thy noble deeds;
            Tell her thou mad'st away her uncle Clarence,
            Her uncle Rivers; ay, and for her sake
            Mad'st quick conveyance with her good aunt Anne.

K.RICHARD You mock me, madam; this is not the way
            To win your daughter.

Q. ELIZAB.   There is no other way;
            Unless thou couldst put on some other shape,
            And not be Richard that hath done all this.

K.RICHARD Say that I did all this for love of her.

Q. ELIZAB. Nay, then indeed she cannot choose but hate thee,   290
            Having bought love with such a bloody spoil.

K.RICHARD Look what is done cannot be now amended:
          Men shall deal unadvisedly sometimes,
          Which after-hours gives leisure to repent.
          If I did take the kingdom from your sons,
          To make amends I'll give it to your daughter.
          If I have killed the issue of your womb,
          To quicken your increase I will beget
          Mine issue of your blood upon your daughter.
          A grandam's name is little less in love   300
          Than is the doting title of a mother;
          They are as children but one step below,
          Even of your mettle, of your very blood;
          Of all one pain, save for a night of groans
          Endured of her, for whom you bid like sorrow.
          Your children were vexation to your youth,
          But mine shall be a comfort to your age.
          The loss you have is but a son being king,
          And by that loss your daughter is made queen.
          I cannot make you what amends I would,   310
          Therefore accept such kindness as I can.
          Dorset your son, that with a fearful soul
          Leads discontented steps in foreign soil,
          This fair alliance quickly shall call home
          To high promotions and great dignity:
          The king, that calls your beauteous daughter wife,
          Familiarly shall call thy Dorset brother;
          Again shall you be mother to a king,
          And all the ruins of distressful times
          Repaired with double riches of content.   320
          What! We have many goodly days to see:
          The liquid drops of tears that you have shed
          Shall come again, transformed to orient pearl,
          Advantaging their loan with interest
          Of ten times double gain of happiness.
          Go, then, my mother, to thy daughter go;
          Make bold her bashful years with your experience;
          Prepare her ears to hear a wooer's tale;
          Put in her tender heart th'aspiring flame

Of golden sovereignty; acquaint the princess   330
With the sweet silent hours of marriage joys:
And when this arm of mine hath chastiséd
The petty rebel, dull-brained Buckingham,
Bound with triumphant garlands will I come
And lead thy daughter to a conqueror's bed;
To whom I will retail my conquest won,
And she shall be sole victoress, Caesar's Caesar.

Q. ELIZAB. What were I best to say? Her father's brother
Would be her lord? Or shall I say her uncle?
Or he that slew her brothers and her uncles?   340
Under what title shall I woo for thee,
That God, the law, my honour, and her love,
Can make seem pleasing to her tender years?

K. RICHARD Infer fair England's peace by this alliance.

Q. ELIZAB. Which she shall purchase with still-lasting war.

K. RICHARD Tell her the king, that may command, entreats.

Q. ELIZAB. That at her hands which the king's King forbids.

K. RICHARD Say she shall be a high and mighty queen.

Q. ELIZAB. To vail the title, as her mother doth.

K. RICHARD Say I will love her everlastingly.   350

Q. ELIZAB. But how long shall that title 'ever' last?

K. RICHARD Sweetly in force unto her fair life's end.

Q. ELIZAB. But how long fairly shall her sweet life last?

K. RICHARD As long as heaven and nature lengthens it.

Q. ELIZAB. As long as hell and Richard likes of it.

K. RICHARD Say, I, her sovereign, am her subject love.

Q. ELIZAB. But she, your subject, loathes such sovereignty.

K. RICHARD Be eloquent in my behalf to her.

Q. ELIZAB. An honest tale speeds best being plainly told.

K. RICHARD Then plainly to her tell my loving tale.   360

Q. ELIZAB. Plain and not honest is too harsh a style.

K. RICHARD Your reasons are too shallow and too quick.

Q. ELIZAB. O no, my reasons are too deep and dead;
Too deep and dead, poor infants, in their graves.

K. RICHARD Harp not on that string, madam; that is past.

ELIZABETH. Harp on it still shall I till heartstrings break.

K. RICHARD Now, by my George, my garter, and my crown –

Q. ELIZAB. Profaned, dishonoured, and the third usurped.

K.RICHARD I swear —
Q. ELIZAB.   By nothing; for this is no oath:
          Thy George, profaned, hath lost his lordly honour;   370
          Thy garter, blemished, pawned his knightly virtue;
          Thy crown, usurped, disgraced his kingly glory.
          If something thou wouldst swear to be believed,
          Swear then by something that thou hast not wronged.
K.RICHARD Then, by my self —
Q. ELIZAB.   Thy self is self-misused.
K.RICHARD Now, by the world —
Q. ELIZAB.   'Tis full of thy foul wrongs.
RICHARD My father's death —
Q. ELIZAB.   Thy life hath it dishonoured.
K.RICHARD Why then, by God —
Q. ELIZAB.   God's wrong is most of all.
          If thou didst fear to break an oath with Him,
          The unity the king my husband made   380
          Thou hadst not broken, nor my brothers died:
          If thou hadst feared to break an oath by Him,
          Th'imperial metal, circling now thy head,
          Had graced the tender temples of my child,
          And both the princes had been breathing here,
          Which now, two tender bedfellows for dust,
          Thy broken faith hath made the prey for worms.
          What canst thou swear by now?
K.RICHARD   The time to come.
Q. ELIZAB. That thou hast wrongéd in the time o'erpast;
          For I myself have many tears to wash   390
          Hereafter time, for time past wronged by thee.
          The children live whose fathers thou hast slaughtered,
          Ungoverned youth, to wail it in their age;
          The parents live whose children thou hast butchered,
          Old barren plants, to wail it with their age.
          Swear not by time to come; for that thou hast
          Misused ere used, by times ill-used o'erpast.
K.RICHARD As I intend to prosper and repent,
          So thrive I in my dangerous affairs
          Of hostile arms! Myself myself confound!   400
          Heaven and fortune bar me happy hours!

Day, yield me not thy light; nor, night, thy rest!
Be opposite, all planets of good luck,
To my proceeding! – if, with dear heart's love,
Immaculate devotion, holy thoughts,
I tender not thy beauteous princely daughter!
In her consists my happiness and thine;
Without her, follows to myself and thee,
Herself, the land, and many a Christian soul,
Death, desolation, ruin, and decay.   410
It cannot be avoided but by this;
It will not be avoided but by this.
Therefore, dear mother – I must call you so –
Be the attorney of my love to her;
Plead what I will be, not what I have been,
Not my deserts, but what I will deserve;
Urge the necessity and state of times,
And be not peevish-fond in great designs.

Q. ELIZAB. Shall I be tempted of the devil thus?

K.RICHARD Ay, if the devil tempt you to do good.   420

Q. ELIZAB. Shall I forget myself to be myself?

K.RICHARD Ay, if yourself's remembrance wrong yourself.

Q. ELIZAB. Yet thou didst kill my children.

K.RICHARD But in your daughter's womb I bury them:
       Where in that nest of spicery they will breed
       Selves of themselves, to your recomforture.

Q. ELIZAB. Shall I go win my daughter to thy will?

K.RICHARD And be a happy mother by the deed.

Q. ELIZAB. I go. Write to me very shortly,
       And you shall understand from me her mind.   430

K.RICHARD Bear her my true love's kiss; and so, farewell. [*she goes*
       Relenting fool, and shallow-changing woman!

         '*Enter* RATCLIFFE', CATESBY *following*

       How now! What news?

RATCLIFFE Most mighty sovereign, on the western coast
       Rideth a puissant navy; to our shores
       Throng many doubtful hollow-hearted friends,
       Unarmed, and unresolved to beat them back:
       'Tis thought that Richmond is their admiral;

   And there they hull, expecting but the aid
   Of Buckingham to welcome them ashore.   440
K.RICHARD Some light-foot friend post to the Duke of Norfolk:
   Ratcliffe, thyself – or Catesby; where is he?
CATESBY Here, my good lord.
K.RICHARD   Catesby, fly to the duke.
CATESBY I will, my lord, with all convenient haste.
K.RICHARD Ratcliffe, come hither! Post to Salisbury:
   When thou comest thither – [*to Catesby*]
          Dull unmindful villain,
   Why stay'st thou here, and go'st not to the duke?
CATESBY First, mighty liege, tell me your highness' pleasure,
   What from your grace I shall deliver to him.
K.RICHARD O, true, good Catesby: bid him levy straight   450
   The greatest strength and power that he can make,
   And meet me suddenly at Salisbury.
CATESBY I go.   [*he goes*
RATCLIFFE What, may it please you, shall I do at Salisbury?
K.RICHARD Why, what wouldst thou do there before I go?
RATCLIFFE Your highness told me I should post before.
K.RICHARD My mind is changed.

      '*Enter* LORD STANLEY'

       Stanley, what news with you?
STANLEY None good, my liege, to please you with the hearing;
   Nor none so bad, but well may be reported.
K.RICHARD Hoyday, a riddle! Neither good nor bad!   460
   What need'st thou run so many miles about,
   When thou mayest tell thy tale the nearest way?
   Once more, what news?
STANLEY   Richmond is on the seas.
K.RICHARD There let him sink, and be the seas on him!
   White-livered runagate, what doth he there?
STANLEY I know not, mighty sovereign, but by guess.
K.RICHARD Well, as you guess?
STANLEY Stirred up by Dorset, Buckingham, and Morton,
   He makes for England, here to claim the crown.
K.RICHARD Is the chair empty? Is the sword unswayed?   470
   Is the king dead? The empire unpossessed?
   What heir of York is there alive but we?

And who is England's king but great York's heir?
Then, tell me, what makes he upon the seas?

STANLEY Unless for that, my liege, I cannot guess.

K.RICHARD Unless for that he comes to be your liege,
You cannot guess wherefore the Welshman comes.
Thou wilt revolt and fly to him, I fear.

STANLEY No, my good lord; therefore mistrust me not.

K.RICHARD Where is thy power then to beat him back? 480
Where be thy tenants and thy followers?
Are they not now upon the western shore,
Safe-conducting the rebels from their ships?

STANLEY No, my good lord, my friends are in the north.

K.RICHARD Cold friends to me: what do they in the north,
When they should serve their sovereign in the west?

STANLEY They have not been commanded, mighty king:
Pleaseth your majest to give me leave,
I'll muster up my friends, and meet your grace
Where and what time your majesty shall please. 490

K.RICHARD Ay, ay, thou wouldst be gone to join with Richmond:
But I'll not trust thee.

STANLEY Most mighty sovereign,
You have no cause to hold my friendship doubtful:
I never was nor never will be false.

K.RICHARD Go then, and muster men; but leave behind
Your son, George Stanley: look your heart be firm,
Or else his head's assurance is but frail.

STANLEY So deal with him as I prove true to you. [goes

'Enter a Messenger'

MESSENGER My gracious sovereign, now in Devonshire,
As I by friends am well advértiséd, 500
Sir Edward Courtney, and the haughty prelate,
Bishop of Exeter, his elder brother,
With many moe confederates, are in arms.

'Enter another Messenger'

2 MESSENG. In Kent, my liege, the Guildfords are in arms;
And every hour more competitors
Flock to the rebels and their power grows strong.

'Enter another Messenger'

3 MESSENG. My lord, the army of great Buckingham –
K.RICHARD Out on you, owls! Nothing but songs of death?
                                                        [*he strikes him*
                There, take thou that, till thou bring better news.
4 MESSENG. The news I have to tell your majesty   510
                Is that, by sudden floods and fall of waters,
                Buckingham's army is dispersed and scattered;
                And he himself wand'red away alone,
                No man knows whither.
K.RICHARD   I cry thee mercy:
                There is my purse to cure that blow of thine.
                Hath any well-adviséd friend proclaimed
                Reward to him that brings the traitor in?
3 MESSENG. Such proclamation hath been made, my lord.

                        'Enter another Messenger'

4 MESSENG. Sir Thomas Lovel and Lord Marquis Dorset,
                'Tis said, my liege, in Yorkshire are in arms.   520
                But this good comfort bring I to your highness,
                The Breton navy is dispersed by tempest:
                Richmond, in Dorsetshire, sent out a boat
                Unto the shore, to ask those on the banks
                If they were his assistants, yea or no;
                Who answered him, they came from Buckingham
                Upon his party: he, mistrusting them,
                Hoised sail and made his course again for Brittany.
K.RICHARD March on, march on, since we are up in arms;
                If not to fight with foreign enemies,   530
                Yet to beat down these rebels here at home.

                        CATESBY *returns*

CATESBY   My liege, the Duke of Buckingham is taken;
                That is the best news: that the Earl of Richmond
                Is with a mighty power landed at Milford
                Is colder tidings, yet they must be told.
K.RICHARD Away towards Salisbury! While we reason here,
                A royal battle might be won and lost:
                Some one take order Buckingham be brought
                To Salisbury; the rest march on with me.
                                                      [*a flourish as they go*

SCENE 5

Lord Stanley's house

LORD STANLEY *and* SIR CHRISTOPHER URSWICK, *a priest*

STANLEY   Sir Christopher, tell Richmond this from me:
That in the sty of the most deadly boar
My son George Stanley is franked up in hold:
If I revolt, off goes young George's head;
The fear of that holds off my present aid.
So, get thee gone; commend me to thy lord.
Withal say that the queen hath heartily consented
He should espouse Elizabeth her daughter.
But, tell me, where is princely Richmond now?

CHRIS'PHER   At Pembroke, or at Ha'rford-west, in Wales.   10

STANLEY   What men of name resort to him?

CHRIS'PHER   Sir Walter Herbert, a renownéd soldier;
Sir Gilbert Talbot, Sir William Stanley,
Oxford, redoubted Pembroke, Sir James Blunt,
And Rice ap Thomas, with a valiant crew,
And many other of great name and worth:
And towards London do they bend their power,
If by the way they be not fought withal.

STANLEY   Well, hie thee to thy lord; I kiss his hand:
My letter will resolve him of my mind.   20
Farewell.

                                         [they go

ACT 5 SCENE I

Salisbury. An open place

Enter a Sheriff 'with halberds', leading BUCKINGHAM *'to execution'*

BUCK'HAM Will not King Richard let me speak with him?
SHERIFF   No, my good lord; therefore be patient.
BUCK'HAM Hastings, and Edward's children, Grey and Rivers,
         Holy King Henry, and thy fair son Edward,
         Vaughan, and all that have miscarriéd
         By underhand corrupted foul injustice,
         If that your moody discontented souls
         Do through the clouds behold this present hour,
         Even for revenge mock my destruction!
         This is All-Souls' day, fellow, is it not?   10
SHERIFF   It is, my lord.
BUCK'HAM Why, then All-Souls' day is my body's doomsday.
         This is the day which in King Edward's time
         I wished might fall on me when I was found
         False to his children and his wife's allies;
         This is the day wherein I wished to fall
         By the false faith of him whom most I trusted;
         This, this All-Souls' day to my fearful soul
         Is the determined respite of my wrongs:
         That high All-Seer which I dallied with   20
         Hath turned my feignéd prayer on my head,
         And given in earnest what I begged in jest.
         Thus doth He force the swords of wicked men
         To turn their own points in their masters' bosoms:
         Thus Margaret's curse falls heavy on my neck;
         'When he', quoth she, 'shall split thy heart with sorrow,
         Remember Margaret was a prophetess.'
         Come, lead me, officers, to the block of shame;
         Wrong hath but wrong, and blame the due of blame.
                                              [*they pass on*

SCENE 2

The camp near Tamworth

'Enter RICHMOND, OXFORD, BLUNT, HERBERT,
and others, with drum and colours'

RICHMOND   Fellows in arms, and my most loving friends,
           Bruised underneath the yoke of tyranny,
           Thus far into the bowels of the land
           Have we marched on without impediment;
           And here receive we from our father Stanley
           Lines of fair comfort and encouragement.
           The wretched, bloody, and usurping boar,
           That spoils your summer fields and fruitful vines,
           Swills your warm blood like wash, and makes his trough
           In your embowelled bosoms – this foul swine   10
           Is now even in the centre of this isle,
           Near to the town of Leicester, as we learn.
           From Tamworth thither is but one day's march.
           In God's name, cheerly on, courageous friends,
           To reap the harvest of perpetual peace
           By this one bloody trial of sharp war.

OXFORD   Every man's conscience is a thousand men,
           To fight against this guilty homicide.

HERBERT   I doubt not but his friends will turn to us.

BLUNT   He hath no friends but what are friends for fear,   20
           Which in his dearest need will fly from him.

RICHMOND   All for our vantage. Then, in God's name, march:
           True hope is swift, and flies with swallow's wings;
           Kings it makes gods, and meaner creatures kings.

                                                    [*they go*

SCENE 3

Bosworth Field

'*Enter* KING RICHARD *in arms with* NORFOLK',
the EARL OF SURREY, *and others*

K.RICHARD Here pitch our tent, even here in Bosworth field.
           My Lord of Surrey, why look you so sad?
SURREY   My heart is ten times lighter than my looks.
K.RICHARD My Lord of Norfolk —
NORFOLK   Here, most gracious liege.
K.RICHARD Norfolk, we must have knocks, ha? Must we not?
NORFOLK We must both give and take, my loving lord.
K.RICHARD Up with my tent! Here will I lie tonight;
           But where tomorrow? Well, all's one for that.
           Who hath descried the number of the traitors?
NORFOLK Six or seven thousand is their utmost power.   10
K.RICHARD Why, our battalia trebles that account:
           Besides, the king's name is a tower of strength,
           Which they upon the adverse faction want.
           Up with the tent! Come, noble gentlemen,
           Let us survey the vantage of the ground.
           Call for some men of sound direction:
           Let's lack no discipline, make no delay;
           For, lords, tomorrow is a busy day.

                                         [*they go*

Enter, on the other side of the field, RICHMOND, SIR WILLIAM
BRANDON, OXFORD, *and others. Soldiers pitch Richmond's tent*

RICHMOND The weary sun hath made a golden set,
           And by the bright tract of his fiery car   20
           Gives token of a goodly day tomorrow.
           Sir William Brandon, you shall bear my standard.
           Give me some ink and paper in my tent:
           I'll draw the form and model of our battle,
           Limit each leader to his several charge,
           And part in just proportion our small power.
           My Lord of Oxford, you, Sir William Brandon,

And you, Sir Walter Herbert, stay with me.
The Earl of Pembroke keeps his regiment:
Good Captain Blunt, bear my good-night to him,   30
And by the second hour in the morning
Desire the earl to see me in my tent:
Yet one thing more, good captain, do for me –
Where is Lord Stanley quartered, do you know?

BLUNT   Unless I have mista'en his colours much,
Which well I am assured I have not done,
His regiment lies half a mile at least
South from the mighty power of the king.

RICHMOND   If without peril it be possible,
Sweet Blunt, make some good means to speak
                               with him,   40
And give him from me this most needful note.

BLUNT   Upon my life, my lord, I'll undertake it;
And so, God give you quiet rest tonight!

RICHMOND   Good night, good Captain Blunt. Come, gentlemen,
Let us consult upon tomorrow's business:
In to my tent! The dew is raw and cold.
                    [*'they withdraw into the tent'*

      Enter, to his tent, KING RICHARD, NORFOLK,
         RATCLIFFE, CATESBY, *and others*

K.RICHARD   What is't o'clock?

CATESBY   It's supper-time, my lord;
It's nine o'clock.

K.RICHARD   I will not sup tonight.
Give me some ink and paper.
What, is my beaver easier than it was?   50
And all my armour laid into my tent?

CATESBY   It is, my liege; and all things are in readiness.

K.RICHARD   Good Norfolk, hie thee to thy charge;
Use careful watch, choose trusty sentinels.

NORFOLK   I go, my lord.

K.RICHARD   Stir with the lark tomorrow, gentle Norfolk.

NORFOLK   I warrant you, my lord.   [*he goes*

K.RICHARD   Catesby!

CATESBY   My lord?
K.RICHARD   Send out a pursuivant-at-arms
           To Stanley's regiment; bid him bring his power   60
           Before sunrising, lest his son George fall
           Into the blind cave of eternal night.   [*Catesby goes*
           Fill me a bowl of wine. Give me a watch.
           Saddle white Surrey for the field tomorrow.
           Look that my staves be sound, and not too heavy.
           Ratcliffe!
RATCLIFFE My lord?
K.RICHARD Saw'st thou the melancholy Lord Northumberland?
RATCLIFFE Thomas the Earl of Surrey and himself,
           Much about cock-shut time, from troop to troop   70
           Went through the army, cheering up the soldiers.
K.RICHARD So, I am satisfied. A bowl of wine:
           I have not that alacrity of spirit
           Nor cheer of mind that I was wont to have.
           Set it down. Is ink and paper ready?
RATCLIFFE It is, my lord.
K.RICHARD   Bid my guard watch. Leave me.
           Ratcliffe, about the mid of night come to my tent
           And help to arm me. Leave me, I say.
                    [*Ratcliffe goes; Richard withdraws into his tent*

               Enter STANLEY *'to* RICHMOND *in his tent',*
                    Lords and others attending

STANLEY   Fortune and victory sit on thy helm!
RICHMOND   All comfort that the dark night can afford   80
           Be to thy person, noble father-in-law!
           Tell me, how fares our loving mother?
STANLEY   I, by attorney, bless thee from thy mother,
           Who prays continually for Richmond's good:
           So much for that. The silent hours steal on,
           And flaky darkness breaks within the east.
           In brief, for so the season bids us be,
           Prepare thy battle early in the morning,
           And put thy fortune to th'arbitrement
           Of bloody strokes and mortal-staring war.   90
           I, as I may – that which I would I cannot –

With best advantage will deceive the time,
And aid thee in this doubtful shock of arms:
But on thy side I may not be too forward,
Lest, being seen, thy brother, tender George,
Be executed in his father's sight.
Farewell: the leisure and the fearful time
Cuts off the ceremonious vows of love
And ample interchange of sweet discourse
Which so long sund'red friends should dwell upon.   100
God give us leisure for these rites of love!
Once more, adieu: be valiant, and speed well!

RICHMOND   Good lords, conduct him to his regiment:
I'll strive with troubled thoughts to take a nap,
Lest leaden slumber peise me down tomorrow,
When I should mount with wings of victory.
Once more, good night, kind lords and gentlemen.

                        [*they leave: Richmond kneels*

O Thou, whose captain I account myself,
Look on my forces with a gracious eye;
Put in their hands thy bruising irons of wrath,   110
That they may crush down with a heavy fall
Th'usurping helmets of our adversaries!
Make us thy ministers of chastisement,
That we may praise thee in the victory!
To thee I do commend my watchful soul
Ere I let fall the windows of mine eyes:
Sleeping and waking, O, defend me still!

                               [*'sleeps'*

'The Ghost of PRINCE EDWARD, *son to Henry the Sixth*',
            appears between the tents

GHOST   [*'to Richard'*] Let me sit heavy on thy soul tomorrow!
Think how thou stab'st me in my prime of youth
At Tewkesbury: despair therefore, and die!   120
[*'to Richmond'*] Be cheerful, Richmond; for the
                           wrongéd souls
Of butchered princes fight in thy behalf:
King Henry's issue, Richmond, comforts thee.

    'The Ghost of HENRY THE SIXTH' *appears*

GHOST   [*to Richard*] When I was mortal, my anointed body
        By thee was punchéd full of deadly holes:
        Think on the Tower and me: despair, and die!
        Harry the Sixth bids thee despair and die!
        [*'to Richmond'*] Virtuous and holy, be thou conqueror!
        Harry, that prophesied thou shouldst be king,
        Doth comfort thee in thy sleep: live and flourish.   130
                                          [*vanishes*

        'The Ghost of CLARENCE' *appears*

GHOST   [*to Richard*] Let me sit heavy on thy soul tomorrow!
        I that was washed to death with fulsome wine,
        Poor Clarence, by thy guile betrayed to death.
        Tomorrow in the battle think on me,
        And fall thy edgeless sword: despair, and die!
        [*'to Richmond'*] Thou offspring of the house of
                                  Lancaster,
        The wrongéd heirs of York do pray for thee:
        Good angels guard thy battle! Live, and flourish!
                                          [*vanishes*

      'The Ghosts of RIVERS, GREY, and VAUGHAN' *appear*

RIVERS   Let me sit heavy on thy soul tomorrow,
        Rivers, that died at Pomfret! Despair, and die!   140
GREY   Think upon Grey, and let thy soul despair!
VAUGHAN Think upon Vaughan, and, with guilty fear,
        Let fall thy lance: despair, and die!
ALL   [*'to Richmond'*] Awake, and think our wrongs in
                              Richard's bosom
        Will conquer him! Awake, and win the day!
                                      [*they vanish*

       'The Ghost of LORD HASTINGS' *appears*

GHOST   [*to Richard*] Bloody and guilty, guiltily awake,
        And in a bloody battle end thy days!
        Think on Lord Hastings: despair, and die!
        [*'to Richmond'*] Quiet untroubled soul, awake, awake!
        Arm, fight, and conquer, for fair England's sake!   150
                                          [*vanishes*

      'The Ghosts of the two young Princes' *appear*

GHOSTS   [*to Richard*] Dream on thy cousins smotheréd in
                                      the Tower:
           Let us be lead within thy bosom, Richard,
           And weigh thee down to ruin, shame, and death!
           Thy nephews' souls bid thee despair and die!
           [*'to Richmond'*] Sleep, Richmond, sleep in peace,
                                  and wake in joy;
           Good angels guard thee from the boar's annoy!
           Live, and beget a happy race of kings!
           Edward's unhappy sons do bid thee flourish.
                                           [*they vanish*

               '*The Ghost of* ANNE *his wife*' appears

GHOST   [*'to Richard'*] Richard, thy wife, that wretched
                                   Anne thy wife,
           That never slept a quiet hour with thee,   160
           Now fills thy sleep with perturbations:
           Tomorrow in the battle think on me,
           And fall thy edgeless sword: despair, and die!
           [*'to Richmond'*] Thou quiet soul, sleep thou a
                                    quiet sleep:
           Dream of success and happy victory!
           Thy adversary's wife doth pray for thee.   [*vanishes*

             '*The Ghost of* BUCKINGHAM' appears

GHOST   [*'to Richard'*] The first was I that helped thee to
                                      the crown;
           The last was I that felt thy tyranny:
           O, in the battle think on Buckingham,
           And die in terror of thy guiltiness!   170
           Dream on, dream on, of bloody deeds and death:
           Fainting, despair; despairing, yield thy breath!
           [*'to Richmond'*] I died for hope ere I could lend thee aid:
           But cheer thy heart, and be thou not dismayed:
           God and good angels fight on Richmond's side;
           And Richard falls in height of all his pride.   [*vanishes*

              '*RICHARD starts out of his dream*'

K.RICHARD Give me another horse! Bind up my wounds!
           Have mercy, Jesu! – Soft, I did but dream.

O coward conscience, how dost thou afflict me!
The lights burn blue. It is now dead midnight.   180
Cold fearful drops stand on my trembling flesh.
What do I fear? Myself? There's none else by.
Richard loves Richard; that is, I am I.
Is there a murderer here? No – yes, I am:
Then fly. What, from myself? Great reason why –
Lest I revenge. Myself upon myself?
Alack, I love myself. For any good
That I myself have done unto myself?
O, no! Alas, I rather hate myself
For hateful deeds committed by myself!   190
I am a villain: yet I lie, I am not.
Fool, of thyself speak well: fool, do not flatter.
My conscience hath a thousand several tongues,
And every tongue brings in a several tale,   10
And every tale condemns me for a villain.
Perjury, perjury, in the high'st degree;
Murder, stern murder, in the dir'st degree;
All several sins, all used in each degree,
Throng to the bar, crying all 'Guilty! Guilty!'
I shall despair. There is no creature loves me;   200
And if I die, no soul will pity me:
Nay, wherefore should they, since that I myself
Find in myself no pity to myself?
Methought the souls of all that I had murdered
Came to my tent, and every one did threat
Tomorrow's vengeance on the head of Richard.

RATCLIFFE *comes to the tent*

RATCLIFFE My lord!
K.RICHARD Zounds! Who is there?
RATCLIFFE My lord; 'tis I. The early village cock
Hath twice done salutation to the morn;   210
Your friends are up, and buckle on their armour.
K.RICHARD O Ratcliffe, I have dreamed a fearful dream!
What thinkest thou, will all our friends prove true?
RATCLIFFE No doubt, my lord.
K.RICHARD   Ratcliffe, I fear, I fear –

RATCLIFFE Nay, good my lord, be not afraid of shadows.
K.RICHARD By the apostle Paul, shadows tonight
         Have struck more terror to the soul of Richard
         Than can the substance of ten thousand soldiers
         Arméd in proof, and led by shallow Richmond.
         'Tis not yet near day. Come, go with me;   220
         Under our tents I'll play the eavesdropper,
         To hear if any mean to shrink from me.   [*they go*

     '*Enter the Lords to* RICHMOND, *sitting in his tent*'

LORDS   Good morrow, Richmond!
RICHMOND Cry mercy, lords and watchful gentlemen,
         That you have ta'en a tardy sluggard here!
LORDS   How have you slept, my lord?
RICHMOND The sweetest sleep and fairest boding dreams
         That ever ent'red in a drowsy head
         Have I since your departure had, my lords.
         Methought their souls whose bodies Richard murdered   230
         Came to my tent and cried on victory:
         I promise you my soul is very jocund
         In the remembrance of so fair a dream.
         How far into the morning is it, lords?
LORDS   Upon the stroke of four.
RICHMOND Why, then 'tis time to arm and give direction.

     '*His oration to his soldiers*', *who gather about the tent*

         More than I have said, loving countrymen,
         The leisure and enforcement of the time
         Forbids to dwell upon: yet remember this,
         God and our good cause fight upon our side;   240
         The prayers of holy saints and wrongéd souls,
         Like high-reared bulwarks, stand before our faces.
         Richard except, those whom we fight against
         Had rather have us win than him they follow:
         For what is he they follow? Truly, gentlemen,
         A bloody tyrant and a homicide;
         One raised in blood, and one in blood established;
         One that made means to come by what he hath,
         And slaughtered those that were the means to help him;
         A base foul stone, made precious by the foil   250

Of England's chair, where he is falsely set;
One that hath ever been God's enemy.
Then, if you fight against God's enemy,
God will in justice ward you as his soldiers;
If you do sweat to put a tyrant down,
You sleep in peace, the tyrant being slain;
If you do fight against your country's foes,
Your country's fat shall pay your pains the hire;
If you do fight in safeguard of your wives,
Your wives shall welcome home the conquerors;   260
If you do free your children from the sword,
Your children's children quits it in your age.
Then, in the name of God and all these rights,
Advance your standards, draw your willing swords.
For me, the ransom of my bold attempt
Shall be this cold corpse on the earth's cold face;
But if I thrive, the gain of my attempt
The least of you shall share his part thereof.
Sound drums and trumpets bold and cheerfully;
God and Saint George! Richmond and victory!   270
                                        [they march away

KING RICHARD *returns with* RATCLIFFE

K.RICHARD What said Northumberland as touching Richmond?
RATCLIFFE That he was never trainéd up in arms.
K.RICHARD He said the truth: and what said Surrey then?
RATCLIFFE He smiled and said, 'The better for our purpose.'
K.RICHARD He was in the right; and so indeed it is.   [*'clock strikes'*
          Tell the clock there. Give me a calendar.
          Who saw the sun today?
RATCLIFFE   Not I, my lord.
K.RICHARD Then he disdains to shine; for by the book
          He should have braved the east an hour ago:
          A black day will it be to somebody.   280
          Ratcliffe!
RATCLIFFE My lord?
K.RICHARD   The sun will not be seen today;
          The sky doth frown and lour upon our army.
          I would these dewy tears were from the ground.

Not shine today! Why, what is that to me
More than to Richmond? For the selfsame heaven
That frowns on me looks sadly upon him.

NORFOLK enters in haste

NORFOLK   Arm, arm, my lord; the foe vaunts in the field.
K.RICHARD   Come, bustle, bustle. Caparison my horse;
Call up Lord Stanley, bid him bring his power.   290
I will lead forth my soldiers to the plain,
And thus my battle shall be orderéd:
My foreward shall be drawn out all in length,
Consisting equally of horse and foot;
Our archers shall be placéd in the midst:
John Duke of Norfolk, Thomas Earl of Surrey,
Shall have the leading of this foot and horse.
They thus directed, we will follow
In the main battle, whose puissance on either side
Shall be well wingéd with our chiefest horse.   300
This, and Saint George to boot! What think'st
                     thou, Norfolk?
NORFOLK   A good direction, warlike sovereign.
This found I on my tent this morning.

[he shows him a paper

K.RICHARD *[reads]* 'Jockey of Norfolk, be not too bold,
        For Dickon thy master is bought and sold.'
A thing deviséd by the enemy.
Go, gentlemen, every man unto his charge:
Let not our babbling dreams affright our souls:
Conscience is but a word that cowards use,
Devised at first to keep the strong in awe.   310
Our strong arms be our conscience, swords our law.
March on, join bravely, let us to it pell-mell;
If not to heaven, then hand in hand to hell.

'His oration to his army'

What shall I say more than I have inferred?
Remember whom you are to cope withal –
A sort of vagabonds, rascals, and runaways,
A scum of Bretons, and base lackey peasants,
Whom their o'er-cloyéd country vomits forth

To desperate ventures and assured destruction.
You sleeping safe, they bring to you unrest;   320
You having lands, and blest with beauteous wives,
They would distrain the one, distain the other.
And who doth lead them but a paltry fellow,
Long kept in Bretagne at our mother's cost?
A milksop, one that never in his life
Felt so much cold as over shoes in snow?
Let's whip these stragglers o'er the seas again,
Lash hence these overweening rags of France,
These famished beggars, weary of their lives,
Who, but for dreaming on this fond exploit,   330
For want of means, poor rats, had hanged themselves.
If we be conquered, let men conquer us,
And not these bastard Bretons, whom our fathers
Have in their own land beaten, bobbed, and
                                        thumped,
And in record left them the heirs of shame.
Shall these enjoy our lands, lie with our wives,
Ravish our daughters? [*'drum afar off'*] Hark! I hear
                                        their drum.
Fight, gentlemen of England! Fight, bold yeomen!
Draw, archers, draw your arrows to the head!
Spur your proud horses hard, and ride in blood!   340
Amaze the welkin with your broken staves!

                    'Enter a Messenger'

What says Lord Stanley? Will he bring his power?
MESSENGER My lord, he doth deny to come.
K.RICHARD Off with his son George's head!
NORFOLK My lord, the enemy is past the marsh:
                    After the battle let George Stanley die.
K.RICHARD A thousand hearts are great within my bosom:
                    Advance our standards, set upon our foes;
                    Our ancient word of courage, fair Saint George,
                    Inspire us with the spleen of fiery dragons!   350
                    Upon them! Victory sits on our helms.
                                        [*they charge*

SCENE 4

'Alarum: excursions'. Re-enter NORFOLK, *and
forces fighting; to him* CATESBY

CATESBY   Rescue, my Lord of Norfolk, rescue, rescue!
           The king enacts more wonders than a man,
           Daring and opposite to every danger:
           His horse is slain, and all on foot he fights,
           Seeking for Richmond in the throat of death.
           Rescue, fair lord, or else the day is lost!

'Alarums. Enter RICHARD*'*

K.RICHARD   A horse! A horse! My kingdom for a horse!
CATESBY   Withdraw, my lord; I'll help you to a horse.
K.RICHARD   Slave, I have set my life upon a cast,
           And I will stand the hazard of the die.   10
           I think there be six Richmonds in the field;
           Five have I slain today instead of him.
           A horse! A horse! My kingdom for a horse!

                                  [they pass on

SCENE 5

'Alarum. Enter RICHARD *with* RICHMOND; *they fight;
RICHARD *is slain'*

A retreat is sounded; then with a flourish re-enter RICHMOND, *and*
STANLEY *'bearing the crown, with divers other lords'*

RICHMOND   God and your arms be praised, victorious friends!
           The day is ours; the bloody dog is dead.
STANLEY   Courageous Richmond, well hast thou acquit thee.
           Lo, here, this long usurpéd royalty
           From the dead temples of this bloody wretch
           Have I plucked off, to grace thy brows withal:
           Wear it, enjoy it, and make much of it.
RICHMOND   Great God of heaven, say Amen to all!
           But, tell me, is thy young George Stanley living?
STANLEY   He is, my lord, and safe in Leicester town;   10

Whither, if it please you, we may now withdraw us.
RICHMOND What men of name are slain on either side?
STANLEY John Duke of Norfolk, Walter Lord Ferrers,
Sir Robert Brakenbury, and Sir William Brandon.
RICHMOND Inter their bodies as becomes their births.
Proclaim a pardon to the soldiers fled
That in submission will return to us:
And then, as we have ta'en the sacrament,
We will unite the white rose and the red.
Smile heaven upon this fair conjunction,   20
That long have frowned upon their enmity!
What traitor hears me, and says not Amen?
England hath long been mad, and scarred herself;
The brother blindly shed the brother's blood,
The father rashly slaughtered his own son,
The son, compelled, been butcher to the sire:
All that divided York and Lancaster,
Divided in their dire division,
O, now let Richmond and Elizabeth,
The true succeeders of each royal house,   30
By God's fair ordinance conjoin together!
And let their heirs, God if his will be so,
Enrich the time to come with smooth-faced peace,
With smiling plenty and fair prosperous days!
Abate the edge of traitors, gracious Lord,
That would reduce these bloody days again,
And make poor England weep in streams of blood!
Let them not live to taste this land's increase
That would with treason wound this fair land's peace!
Now civil wounds are stopped, Peace lives again: 40
That she may long live here, God say Amen!

                                    [they go

RICHARD II

Mahood ; Play on words :

breath   title   name   honour

tongue   sentence   word

breath = respiration, life, time for breathing
         utterance, will expressed in words

title = legal right, appellation of honour,
       label

name = label, inherent reputation,

honour = ?

tongue = organ of speech, complex
       organisation of a language

sentence = unit of speech, judgment,
       apophthegm, significance

word = unit of speech, convention,
       command, promise, apophthegm,
       divine utterance.

INTRODUCTION

Shakespeare's account of the reign of Richard II shows him returning to the start of the story of which *Richard III* had formed the end: the usurpation of Richard II's throne by Henry Bolingbroke set in train the long years of civil war – the Wars of the Roses – which were finally absolved in uniting of the houses of York and Lancaster in the person of Henry VII crowned at the conclusion of *Richard III:* 'Now civil wounds are stopped: peace lives again.' Shakespeare wrote his play in about 1595, and it was first published in 1597, although early printed editions did not include the episode in Act 4 in which Richard gives up the crown to Bolingbroke. This textual suppression registers the particular topicality of *Richard II* to contemporary audiences. Elizabeth I is said to have identified herself with Richard: both monarchs could be said to have encouraged court favourites, and both had no obvious heir. Such parallels ensured that the play was politically sensitive. When the Earl of Essex mounted his ill-fated rebellion against Elizabeth, his followers paid for a special performance of a play about Richard II, probably Shakespeare's, to drum up support for their actions. If a king could be got rid of in 1400, perhaps this dramatic example could prompt a repetition two centuries later.

For all this, however, Shakespeare's presentation of Richard is not a hatchet job like his image of Richard III. Richard II is an altogether more ambiguous character who has moments of considerable sympathy and pathos. On the one hand, he is weak and selfish and his decision to seize John of Gaunt's estate is a manifest abuse of sovereign power. His sense of his authority is repeatedly bolstered by aggrandising imagery: he is the sun, Christ, God's elected deputy. His instincts are to rhetoric and self-pity rather

than action. 'Let us sit upon the ground', he bemoans at Scroop's
news of military setbacks, 'And tell sad stories of the death of kings'
(3.2.155–56). He cannot resist a good scene, or an opportunity to
take centre stage. When Bolingbroke is urging him to resign the
crown in 4.1, Richard's procrastinating poetic loquacity is in
marked contrast to the urgent political agenda of his rival. On the
other hand, Richard's introspection is often sympathetic, as he
struggles to understand his changing situation. In Act 5 he has his
only soliloquy – a moment of emotional truth before his brutal
murder – in which he recognises 'I wasted time, and now time
doth waste me' (5.5.49). His language, always highly poetic, here
conveys real self-knowledge rather than self-dramatisation. His last
action contrasts with his lassitude earlier in the play, as he defends
himself with vigour and courage against Exton's assassins.

   The first editions of the play described it as a tragedy, and this
suggests that the play is primarily about the downfall of a significant, noble, flawed individual. Its later incorporation into the
genre of history may, by contrast, give more of a stress to historical
process and continuity – unlike a tragedy such as King Lear, in
which descent of the tragic protagonist maps the trajectory of the
play and there is no one in corresponding ascendance. King Lear is,
in fact, an illuminating companion-play for Richard II: both are
concerned with whether and how a king can become a man (and,
to some extent in Richard II, vice versa), and what a king is without
his trappings of authority. However, where the end of King Lear is
the death of the tragic hero and the shattered remnants of government, Richard II ends with a new king and a new political order,
albeit one overshadowed by the crimes of the past. Richard himself
uses an image of correspondence to refer to the transfer of authority: his decline and Bolingbroke's ascent are inseparable, 'like a
deep well That owes two buckets, filling one another, The emptier
ever dancing in the air, The other down, unseen, and full of water'
(4.1.183–86). Tragedy ends. The action is complete – the idea of a
sequel to King Lear is unthinkable. History continues – so that the
consequences of Richard's unkinging reverberate through subsequent generations and subsequent plays.

   Richard's image of the balancing well-buckets could be extended
to the play as a whole. Rather than approving or condemning
Bolingbroke's actions, rather than declaring itself a partisan for

either faction, the play seems concerned to display the ways in which, as the Gardener reasons, 'their fortunes both are weighed' (3.4.85). Equivalencies of similarity or contrast can be discerned between the two kings: Richard's love of metaphor and imagery is countered by Bolingbroke's laconic stage presence, although it is striking that when Bolingbroke rejects the comforts of metaphor he uses highly metaphorical language to do so: 'who can hold a fire in his hand By thinking on the frosty Caucasus?' (1.3.294–95). Richard speaks, Bolingbroke acts. Some commentators have seen a contrast between a medieval feudal Richard and a modern individualistic Bolingbroke, or between a divinely ordained monarch and a politically pragmatic one. When John Barton directed the play for the Royal Shakespeare Company in the 1970s, he had the actors playing Richard and Bolingbroke swap roles on alternate nights, emphasising their similarities rather than their absolute opposition. It is, however, impossible to judge where Shakespeare's own sympathies lay, or how early audiences might have responded. Balance is the keynote of Shakespeare's presentation of the transfer of dramatic and sovereign authority. Against Richard's flaws are set his claims to divinely ordained kingship; Bolingbroke's quiet determination is set against his actions as a rebel. Taken as a complete and finished play, *Richard II* does not punish Bolingbroke's action in taking the crown, although of course subsequent (and previous) plays dramatise its consequences. There is no response to the Bishop of Carlisle's fierce denunciation of Bolingbroke's actions in naming himself king, and his defence of the divine right of kings is not countered: 'And shall the figure of God's majesty, His captain, steward, deputy-elect, Anointed, crownéd, planted many years, Be judged by subject and inferior breath . . . ' (4.1.125–28). The evidence of history supports his prophecy that 'The blood of English shall manure the ground, And future ages groan for this foul act' (4.1.137–38). Richard is not a just king, but against the question-able morality of his sovereignty must be set the questionable legality of Bolingbroke's. A homily appointed by the Elizabethan authorities to be read in churches preached the terrible conse-quences of rebellion against a ruler, arguing that 'a rebel is worse than the worst prince, and rebellion worse than the worst govern-ment of the worst prince that hitherto hath been.' Yet

Bolingbroke's demeanour is not that of an ambitious rebel, and his final words, expressing deep regret for what has happened, are far from triumphalist: 'my soul is full of woe . . . I'll make a voyage to the Holy Land, To wash this blood off from my guilty hand.' (5.6.45, 48–49). Balance is the play's predominant ethical position.

The violence and fighting which accompany the usurpation are all reported, not staged. This places an added emphasis on the play's language. Unusually, *Richard II* is all in verse – even the Gardener, who might be expected to speak less formally, delivers his lugubrious pronouncements on the garden of England in blank verse – and it makes frequent use of end-rhyme. Language often explicitly replaces action: in the opening scene the quarrel between Bolingbroke and Mowbray is verbal, and conducted through the highly ritualised formal language of oaths sworn, and challenges and accusations delivered. Both men vow to consolidate this spoken argument through physical action – 'What my tongue speaks my right drawn sword may prove' (1.1.46) – but Richard intervenes to postpone this. Even when the two parties reappear at the Coventry lists, a formal sequence of declarations and proclamations precedes and then is a substitute for armed combat. The real subject of the argument, the truth about Gloucester's death, implicates Richard and cannot therefore be settled. Instead the king uses his verbal powers, sentencing the combatants to exile. As Bolingbroke wryly remarks, when his term of banishment is reduced, 'How long a time lies in one little word! Four lagging winters and four wanton springs End in a word – such is the breath of kings' (1.3.213–15). In fact the play is unusually static, with relatively little movement on stage and instead a series of set-piece and formal speeches, such as Gaunt's famous, nostalgic evocation of England's past in 2.1. Only one scene offers any significant physical action: in Act 4 Richard and Bolingbroke each handle the crown as the visible stage property comes to symbolise the whole sacred and political freight of kingship, and then Richard calls for a mirror in which to regard his unkinged self. Reserving most of the stage business for this climactic scene reinforces its dramatic and historical significance, as Richard, and the dramatist, invent the almost unprecedented ceremony for un-coronation: 'With mine own hands I give away my crown, With mine own tongue deny my sacred state' (4.1.208–09). The coining of a new negative, 'unkinged', to express Richard's new position, demonstrates its extraordinariness: a situation beyond what existing language can register. Language and its uses, the gap between words and their referents, the obfuscations and deception of ceremonial rhetoric, all play an important role in *Richard II*, as they reveal the narrative of a poet-king who could almost be seen to talk himself into deposition and death: 'such is the breath of kings.'

Sh's adaptations of history

1. Queen = 12
2. Hotspur = 35 (older than R II + Bol)
3. Hal = 12
4. Duchess of York not Aumerle's mother
5. Gaunt unscrupulous, self-seeking politician, unsuccessful general, unpopular administrator (taxes)
6. Duchess of Gloucester died later
7. Telescoping of events, eg no 2 haw gap for conference; Bol sets off for England in scene in which Gaunt dies
8. Aumerle changed to Bol's side before Voendreny.

The scene: England and Wales

CHARACTERS IN THE PLAY

KING RICHARD THE SECOND
JOHN OF GAUNT, *Duke of Lancaster* ⎱ *uncles to the king*
EDMUND, *Duke of York* ⎰
HENRY BOLINGBROKE, *Duke of Hereford,*
     son to John of Gaunt; afterwards King Henry IV
DUKE OF AUMERLE, *son to the Duke of York*
THOMAS MOWBRAY, *Duke of Norfolk*
DUKE OF SURREY
EARL OF SALISBURY
LORD BERKELEY
BUSHY ⎱
BAGOT ⎰ *servants to King Richard*
GREEN
EARL OF NORTHUMBERLAND
HENRY PERCY, *his son*
LORD ROSS
LORD WILLOUGHBY
LORD FITZWATER
BISHOP OF CARLISLE
ABBOT OF WESTMINSTER
SIR STEPHEN SCROOP
SIR PIERCE OF EXTON
Lord Marshal
Captain of a band of Welshmen

QUEEN *to King Richard*
DUCHESS OF YORK
DUCHESS OF GLOUCESTER
Lady attending on the Queen

Lords, Heralds, Officers, Soldiers, two Gardeners, Keeper,
Messenger, Groom, and other Attendants

RICHARD II

ACT I SCENE I *1398*

A great scaffold within the castle at Windsor, with seats thereon, and a space of ground before it

'*Enter* KING RICHARD, JOHN OF GAUNT, *with the* DUKE OF SURREY, *other nobles and attendants.*' *They ascend the scaffold and sit in their places, the King in a chair of justice in the midst*

K.RICHARD   Old John of Gaunt, time-honoured Lancaster,   *= 58*
               Hast thou according to thy oath and band   *(York 57)*
               Brought hither Henry Hereford thy bold son,
               Here to make good the boist'rous late appeal,
               Which then our leisure would not let us hear,
               Against the Duke of Norfolk, Thomas Mowbray?

GAUNT   I have, my liege.

K.RICHARD   Tell me, moreover, hast thou sounded him,   *R II as just*
               If he appeal the duke on ancient malice,
               Or worthily as a good subject should   10
               On some known ground of treachery in him?

GAUNT   As near as I could sift him on that argument,
               On some apparent danger seen in him
               Aimed at your highness, no inveterate malice.

K.RICHARD   Then call them to our presence – face to face,
               And frowning brow to brow, ourselves will hear
               The accuser and the accusèd freely speak:
               High-stomached are they both and full of ire,
               In rage, deaf as the sea, hasty as fire.

           '*Enter* BOLINGBROKE *and* MOWBRAY'   *= Gaunt's castle in Lincs.*

B'BROKE   Many years of happy days befall   20
               My gracious sovereign, my most loving liege!

MOWBRAY   Each day still better other's happiness,
               Until the heavens, envying earth's good hap,
               Add an immortal title to your crown!

K.RICHARD   We thank you both, yet one but flatters us,
               As well appeareth by the cause you come,
               Namely, to appeal each other of high treason:

Cousin of Hereford, what dost thou object
Against the Duke of Norfolk, Thomas Mowbray?

B'BROKE First, heaven be the record to my speech,   30
In the devotion of a subject's love,
Tend'ring the precious safety of my prince,
And free from other misbegotten hate,
Come I appellant to this princely presence.
Now, Thomas Mowbray, do I turn to thee,
And mark my greeting well: for what I speak
My body shall make good upon this earth,
Or my divine soul answer it in heaven:
Thou art a traitor and a miscreant,
Too good to be so, and too bad to live,   40
Since the more fair and crystal is the sky,
The uglier seem the clouds that in it fly:
Once more, the more to aggravate the note,
With a foul traitor's name stuff I thy throat,
And wish (so please my sovereign) ere I move,
What my tongue speaks my right drawn sword may
                              prove.

MOWBRAY Let not my cold words here accuse my zeal.
'Tis not the trial of a woman's war,
The bitter clamour of two eager tongues,
Can arbitrate this cause betwixt us twain.   50
The blood is hot that must be cooled for this.
Yet can I not of such tame patience boast
As to be hushed and nought at all to say.
First, the fair reverence of your highness curbs me
From giving reins and spurs to my free speech,
Which else would post until it had returned
These terms of treason doubled down his throat:
Setting aside his high blood's royalty,
And let him be no kinsman to my liege,
I do defy him, and I spit at him,   60
Call him a slanderous coward, and a villain,
Which to maintain I would allow him odds,
And meet him were I tied to run afoot,
Even to the frozen ridges of the Alps,
Or any other ground inhabitable,

         Where ever Englishman durst set his foot.

         Mean time, let this defend my loyalty –

         By all my hopes most falsely doth he lie.

B'BROKE   Pale trembling coward, there I throw my gage,

                        [he casts it at Mowbray's feet

         Disclaiming here the kindred of the king,   70

         And lay aside my high blood's royalty,

         Which fear, not reverence, makes thee to except.

         If guilty dread have left thee so much strength,

         As to take up mine honour's pawn, then stoop.

         By that, and all the rites of knighthood else,

         Will I make good against thee, arm to arm,

         What I have spoke, or thou canst worse devise.

MOWBRAY I take it up, and by that sword I swear,

         Which gently laid my knighthood on my shoulder,

         I'll answer thee in any fair degree,   80

         Or chivalrous design of knightly trial:

         And when I mount, alive may I not light,

         If I be traitor or unjustly fight!

K.RICHARD What doth our cousin lay to Mowbray's charge?

         It must be great that can inherit us

         So much as of a thought of ill in him.

B'BROKE   Look what I speak, my life shall prove it true,

         That Mowbray hath received eight thousand nobles

         In name of lendings for your highness' soldiers,

         The which he hath detained for lewd employments,   90

         Like a false traitor, and injurious villain:

         Besides I say, and will in battle prove,

         Or here, or elsewhere to the furthest verge

         That ever was surveyed by English eye,

         That all the treasons for these eighteen years

         Complotted and contrivéd in this land.

         Fetch from false Mowbray their first head and spring!

         Further I say, and further will maintain

         Upon his bad life to make all this good,

         That he did plot the Duke of Gloucester's death,   100

         Suggest his soon-believing adversaries,

         And consequently, like a traitor coward,

         Sluiced out his innocent soul through streams of blood,

(Handwritten note at top: ① How should the actor interpret this?)

    Which blood, like sacrificing Abel's, cries,
    Even from the tongueless caverns of the earth, *(imagery)*
    To me for justice and rough chastisement:
    And by the glorious worth of my descent, *(rhyme)*
    This arm shall do it, or this life be spent.

K.RICHARD How high a pitch his resolution soars! *(imagery (falcon))*
    Thomas of Norfolk, what say'st thou to this?   110

MOWBRAY O, let my sovereign turn away his face,
    And bid his ears a little while be deaf,
    Till I have told this slander of his blood, *(slander = disgrace)*
    How God and good men hate so foul a liar.

K.RICHARD Mowbray, impartial are our eyes and ears;
    Were he my brother, nay, my kingdom's heir, *(irony?)*
    As he is but my father's brother's son,
    Now by my sceptre's awe I make a vow, *(R II as just.)*
    Such neighbour nearness to our sacred blood
    Should nothing privilege him nor partialise   120
    The unstooping firmness of my upright soul.
    He is our subject, Mowbray, so art thou; *(rhyme)*
    Free speech and fearless I to thee allow.

MOWBRAY Then, Bolingbroke, as low as to thy heart
    Through the false passage of thy throat, thou liest!
    Three parts of that receipt I had for Calais *(Repudiates 1st charge)*
    Disbursed I duly to his highness' soldiers,
    The other part reserved I by consent,
    For that my sovereign liege was in my debt,
    Upon remainder of a dear account,   130
    Since last I went to France to fetch his queen: ②
    Now swallow down that lie. For Gloucester's death,
    I slew him not, but to my own disgrace *(slipped)* **NB**
    Neglected my sworn duty in that case: *(Ambiguous: rebuttal of 3rd charge)*
    For you, my noble lord of Lancaster,
    The honourable father to my foe, *(relationship explained!)*
    Once did I lay an ambush for your life,
    A trespass that doth vex my grievéd soul:
    But ere I last received the sacrament,
    I did confess it, and exactly begged   140
    Your grace's pardon, and I hope I had it.

(Handwritten note at bottom: ② Mowbray to France 1395 to negotiate 2nd marriage to Isabel, Charles VI's daughter. But R II went to Calais 1396 for wedding.)

This is my fault – as for the rest appealed,
It issues from the rancour of a villain,
A recreant and most degenerate traitor,
Which in myself I boldly will defend,
And interchangeably hurl down my gage
Upon this overweening traitor's foot,
To prove myself a loyal gentleman,
Even in the best blood chambered in his bosom,   150
In haste whereof most heartily I pray
Your highness to assign our trial day.

K.RICHARD Wrath-kindled gentlemen, be ruled by me;
Let's purge this choler without letting blood.
This we prescribe, though no physician –
Deep malice makes too deep incision:
Forget, forgive, conclude and be agreed.
Our doctors say this is no month to bleed.
Good uncle, let this end where it begun,
We'll calm the Duke of Norfolk, you your son.   160

GAUNT To be a make-peace shall become my age.
Throw down, my son, the Duke of Norfolk's gage.

K.RICHARD And, Norfolk, throw down his.

GAUNT   When, Harry? When?
Obedience bids I should not bid again.

K.RICHARD Norfolk, throw down we bid, there is no boot.

MOWBRAY Myself I throw, dread sovereign, at thy foot.
My life thou shalt command, but not my shame;
The one my duty owes, but my fair name,
Despite of death that lives upon my grave,
To dark dishonour's use thou shalt not have: 170
I am disgraced, impeached, and baffled here,
Pierced to the soul with slander's venomed spear,
The which no balm can cure but his heart-blood
Which breathed this poison.

K.RICHARD   Rage must be withstood.
Give me his gage; lions make leopards tame.

MOWBRAY Yea, but not change his spots: take but my shame,
And I resign my gage. My dear dear lord,
The purest treasure mortal times afford
Is spotless reputation; that away,

Men are but gilded loam, or painted clay.   180
A jewel in a ten times barred-up chest
Is a bold spirit in a loyal breast:
Mine honour is my life, both grow in one,
Take honour from me, and my life is done: Falstaff:
Then, dear my liege, mine honour let me try;   What is honour?
In that I live, and for that will I die.

K. RICHARD Cousin, throw up your gage, do you begin.

B'BROKE O God defend my soul from such deep sin!
Shall I seem crest-fallen in my father's sight?
Or with pale beggar-fear impeach my height   190
Before this out-dared dastard? Ere my tongue
Shall wound my honour with such feeble wrong,
Or sound so base a parle, my teeth shall tear   image
The slavish motive of recanting fear,   image
And spit it bleeding in his high disgrace,
Where shame doth harbour, even in Mowbray's face.

K. RICHARD We were not born to sue, but to command,   1st sign
Which since we cannot do, to make you friends,   of weakness
Be ready, as your lives shall answer it,
At Coventry upon Saint Lambert's day. = 17 Sept.   200
There shall your swords and lances arbitrate
The swelling difference of your settled hate.
Since we can not atone you, we shall see
Justice design the victor's chivalry.
Lord marshal, command our officers at arms
Be ready to direct these home alarms.   [they go

NB
No rhyme

Duke of Lancaster?

                    SCENE 2 (largely Sh's invention
Convenient break between 2 similar scenes (also time
        A room in the Duke of Lancaster's house gap), presenting
                                                to emotional
'Enter JOHN OF GAUNT with the DUCHESS OF GLOUCESTER' reality.

GAUNT Alas, the part I had in Woodstock's blood
Doth more solicit me than your exclaims
To stir against the butchers of his life;
But since correction lieth in those hands,   = R II's
Which made the fault that we cannot correct,
Put we our quarrel to the will of heaven,

Who, when they see the hours ripe on earth,
Will rain hot vengeance on offenders' heads.

DUCHESS Finds brotherhood in thee no sharper spur?
Hath love in thy old blood no living fire? 10
Edward's seven sons, whereof thyself art one,
Were as seven vials of his sacred blood,
Or seven fair branches springing from one root:
Some of those seven are dried by nature's course,
Some of those branches by the Destinies cut:
But Thomas, my dear lord, my life, my Gloucester,
One vial full of Edward's sacred blood,
One flourishing branch of his most royal root,
Is cracked, and all the precious liquor spilt,
Is hacked down, and his summer leaves all faded, 20
By envy's hand, and murder's bloody axe. [she weeps
Ah, Gaunt, his blood was thine! That bed, that womb,
That mettle, that self mould, that fashioned thee
Made him a man; and though thou livest and
breathest,
Yet art thou slain in him. Thou dost consent
In some large measure to thy father's death,
In that thou seest thy wretched brother die,
Who was the model of thy father's life,
Call it not patience, Gaunt, it is despair.
In suff'ring thus thy brother to be slaught'red, 30
Thou showest the naked pathway to thy life,
Teaching stern murder how to butcher thee:
That which in mean men we entitle patience,
Is pale cold cowardice in noble breasts.
What shall I say? To safeguard thine own life,
The best way is to venge my Gloucester's death.

GAUNT God's is the quarrel; for God's substitute,
His deputy anointed in His sight,
Hath caused his death, the which if wrongfully,
Let heaven revenge, for I may never lift 40
An angry arm against His minister.

DUCHESS Where then, alas, may I complain myself?

GAUNT   To God, the widow's champion and defence.
DUCHESS   Why then, I will. Farewell, old Gaunt.
           Thou goest to Coventry, there to behold
           Our cousin Hereford and fell Mowbray fight.
           O, sit my husband's wrongs on Hereford's spear,
           That it may enter butcher Mowbray's breast!
           Or if misfortune miss the first career,
           Be Mowbray's sins so heavy in his bosom,   50
           That they may break his foaming courser's back,
           And throw the rider headlong in the lists,
           A caitiff recreant to my cousin Hereford!
           Farewell old Gaunt, thy sometimes brother's wife
           With her companion Grief must end her life.
GAUNT   Sister, farewell, I must to Coventry.
           As much good stay with thee, as go with me!
DUCHESS   Yet one word more – grief boundeth where it falls,
           Not with the empty hollowness, but weight:
           I take my leave before I have begun,   60
           For sorrow ends not when it seemeth done:
           Commend me to thy brother, Edmund York.
           Lo, this is all – nay, yet depart not so;
           Though this be all, do not so quickly go;
           I shall remember more. Bid him – ah, what? –
           With all good speed at Plashy visit me.
           Alack, and what shall good old York there see
           But empty lodgings and unfurnished walls,
           Unpeopled offices, untrodden stones?
           And what hear there for welcome but my groans?   70
           Therefore commend me, let him not come there,
           To seek out sorrow that dwells every where.
           Desolate, desolate, will I hence and die:
           The last leave of thee takes my weeping eye.

                                              [they go

SCENE 3

The lists at Coventry; to the side a platform, with a throne (richly hanged and adorned) for the king, and seats for his court; at either end of the lists chairs for the combatants; a great throng of spectators.
Heralds, etc. attending

'*Enter the Lord Marshal and the* DUKE AUMERLE'

MARSHAL	My Lord Aumerle, is Harry Hereford armed?
AUMERLE	Yea, at all points, and longs to enter in.
MARSHAL	The Duke of Norfolk, sprightfully and bold,
	Stays but the summons of the appellant's trumpet.
AUMERLE	Why then, the champions are prepared, and stay
	For nothing but his majesty's approach.

The trumpets sound and the KING, *bearing a truncheon, enters with his nobles (*GAUNT *among them): when they are set, enter the* DUKE OF NORFOLK *in arms defendant*

K.RICHARD Marshal, demand of yonder champion
           The cause of his arrival here in arms.
           Ask him his name, and orderly proceed
           To swear him in the justice of his cause.   10
MARSHAL   In God's name and the king's, say who thou art,
           And why thou comest thus knightly clad in arms,
           Against what man thou com'st, and what thy quarrel.
           Speak truly, on thy knighthood, and thy oath,
           And so defend thee heaven and thy valour!
MOWBRAY   My name is Thomas Mowbray, Duke of Norfolk,
           Who hither come engagéd by my oath
           (Which God defend a knight should violate!)
           Both to defend my loyalty and truth,
           To God, my king, and my succeeding issue,   20
           Against the Duke of Hereford that appeals me,
           And by the grace of God, and this mine arm,
           To prove him, in defending of myself,
           A traitor to my God, my king, and me.
           And as I truly fight, defend me heaven!
                                              [*he takes his seat*

The trumpets sound. Enter the DUKE OF HEREFORD
                appellant in armour

K. RICHARD Marshal, ask yonder knight in arms,
            Both who he is, and why he cometh hither,
            Thus plated in habiliments of war,
            And formally, according to our law,
            Depose him in the justice of his cause.   30
MARSHAL   What is thy name? And wherefore com'st thou hither,
            Before King Richard in his royal lists?
            Against whom comest thou? And what's thy quarrel?
            Speak like a true knight, so defend thee heaven!
B'BROKE   Harry of Hereford, Lancaster and Derby
            Am I, who ready here do stand in arms
            To prove by God's grace, and my body's valour
            In lists, on Thomas Mowbray, Duke of Norfolk,
            That he is a traitor foul and dangerous,
            To God of heaven, King Richard and to me.   40
            And as I truly fight, defend me heaven!
MARSHAL   On pain of death, no person be so bold,
            Or daring-hardy, as to touch the lists,
            Except the marshal and such officers
            Appointed to direct these fair designs.
B'BROKE   Lord marshal, let me kiss my sovereign's hand,
            And bow my knee before his majesty,
            For Mowbray and myself are like two men
            That vow a long and weary pilgrimage.
            Then let us take a ceremonious leave,   50
            And loving farewell of our several friends.
MARSHAL   The appellant in all duty greets your highness;
            And craves to kiss your hand, and take his leave.
K. RICHARD [*rises*] We will descend and fold him in our arms.
            Cousin of Hereford, as thy cause is right,
            So be thy fortune in this royal fight.
                            [*he descends with* GAUNT *and other nobles
                            into the lists and embraces Bolingbroke*
            Farewell, my blood, which if today thou shed,
            Lament we may, but not revenge thee dead.
B'BROKE   O, let no noble eye profane a tear
            For me, if I be gored with Mowbray's spear.   60

As confident as is the falcon's flight
Against a bird, do I with Mowbray fight.
My loving lord, [*to the Marshal*] I take my leave of you:
Of you, my noble cousin, Lord Aumerle –
Not sick, although I have to do with death,
But lusty, young, and cheerly drawing breath.
Lo, as at English feasts, so I regreet
The daintiest last, to make the end most sweet.

[*to Gaunt*

O thou, the earthly author of my blood,
Whose youthful spirit in me regenerate   *more feelingly* 70
Doth with a twofold vigour lift me up
To reach at victory above my head,
Add proof unto mine armour with thy prayers,
And with thy blessings steel my lance's point,
That it may enter Mowbray's waxen coat,
And furbish new the name of John a Gaunt,
Even in the lusty haviour of his son.

GAUNT   God in thy good cause make thee prosperous!
Be swift like lightning in the execution,
And let thy blows, doubly redoubled,   80
Fall like amazing thunder on the casque
Of thy adverse pernicious enemy!
Rouse up thy youthful blood, be valiant and live.

B'BROKE   Mine innocency and Saint George to thrive!

[*he takes his seat*

MOWBRAY [*rising*] However God or fortune cast my lot, *superundane power*
There lives or dies true to King Richard's throne,
A loyal, just, and upright gentleman:
Never did captive with a freer heart
Cast off his chains of bondage, and embrace   *Language*
His golden uncontrolled enfranchisement,
More than my dancing soul doth celebrate   *(not just* 90
This feast of battle with mine adversary.   *RII – the poet)*
Most mighty liege, and my companion peers,
Take from my mouth the wish of happy years:
As gentle and as jocund as to jest
Go I to fight: truth hath a quiet breast.

K.RICHARD   Farewell, my lord, securely I espy

Virtue with valour couchéd in thine eye.
Order the trial, marshal, and begin.

[the King and his lords return to their seats;
Bolingbroke and Mowbray don their helmets
and lower the visors

MARSHAL Harry of Hereford, Lancaster, and Derby,   100
Receive thy lance, and God defend the right!

B'BROKE Strong as a tower in hope, I cry 'amen'.

MARSHAL *[to a knight]* Go bear this lance to Thomas, Duke of
Norfolk.

1 HERALD Harry of Hereford, Lancaster, and Derby,
Stands here, for God, his sovereign, and himself,
On pain to be found false and recreant,
To prove the Duke of Norfolk, Thomas Mowbray,
A traitor to his God, his king, and him,
And dares him to set forward to the fight.

2 HERALD Here standeth Thomas Mowbray, Duke of Norfolk,   110
On pain to be found false and recreant,
Both to defend himself, and to approve
Henry of Hereford, Lancaster, and Derby,
To God, his sovereign, and to him disloyal,
Courageously and with a free desire
Attending but the signal to begin.

MARSHAL Sound, trumpets, and set forward, combatants.

'A charge sounded.' The champions are about to join battle, when
the KING rises and casts his truncheon into the lists

Stay, the king hath thrown his warder down.

K.RICHARD Let them lay by their helmets and their spears,
And both return back to their chairs again.   120
Withdraw with us, and let the trumpets sound,
While we return these dukes what we decree.

After some moments, the KING returns and summons
the combatants to him

Draw near,
And list what with our council we have done.
For that our kingdom's earth should not be soiled
With that dear blood which it hath fosteréd;
And for our eyes do hate the dire aspect

Of civil wounds ploughed up with neighbours' swords,
And for we think the eagle-wingéd pride
Of sky-aspiring and ambitious thoughts,   130
With rival-hating envy, set on you
To wake our peace, which in our country's cradle
Draws the sweet infant breath of gentle sleep;
Which so roused up with boist'rous untuned drums,
With harsh-resounding trumpets' dreadful bray,
And grating shock of wrathful iron arms,
Might from our quiet confines fright fair peace,
And make us wade even in our kindred's blood;
Therefore we banish you our territories:
You, cousin Hereford, upon pain of life,   140
Till twice five summers have enriched our fields,
Shall not regreet our fair dominions,
But tread the stranger paths of banishment.

B'BROKE   Your will be done; this must my comfort be,
That sun that warms you here, shall shine on me,
And those his golden beams to you here lent,
Shall point on me, and gild my banishment.

K.RICHARD   Norfolk, for thee remains a heavier doom,
Which I with some unwillingness pronounce.
The sly slow hours shall not determinate   150
The dateless limit of thy dear exile.
The hopeless word of 'never to return'
Breathe I against thee, upon pain of life.

MOWBRAY   A heavy sentence, my most sovereign liege,
And all unlooked for from your highness' mouth.
A dearer merit, not so deep a maim
As to be cast forth in the common air,
Have I deservéd at your highness' hands.
The language I have learnt these forty years,
My native English, now I must forgo,   160
And now my tongue's use is to me no more
Than an unstringéd viol or a harp,
Or like a cunning instrument cased up,
Or being open, put into his hands
That knows no touch to tune the harmony:
Within my mouth you have engaoled my tongue,

  Doubly portcullised with my teeth and lips,
  And dull unfeeling barren ignorance
  Is made my gaoler to attend on me:
  I am too old to fawn upon a nurse,   170
  Too far in years to be a pupil now;
  What is thy sentence then but speechless death,
  Which robs my tongue from breathing native breath?

K. RICHARD It boots thee not to be compassionate;
  After our sentence plaining comes too late.

MOWBRAY Then thus I turn me from my country's light,
  To dwell in solemn shades of endless night.

         [he moves away

K. RICHARD Return again, and take an oath with thee.
  Lay on our royal sword your banished hands:
  Swear by the duty that you owe to God   180
  (Our part therein we banish with yourselves),
  To keep the oath that we administer:
  You never shall, so help you truth and God,
  Embrace each other's love in banishment,
  Nor never look upon each other's face,
  Nor never write, regreet, nor reconcile
  This louring tempest of your home-bred hate,
  Nor never by advisèd purpose meet,
  To plot, contrive, or complot any ill,
  'Gainst us, our state, our subjects, or our land. 190

B'BROKE I swear.

MOWBRAY And I, to keep all this.

B'BROKE Norfolk, so fare as to mine enemy:
  By this time, had the king permitted us,
  One of our souls had wand'red in the air,
  Banished this frail sepulchre of our flesh,
  As now our flesh is banished from this land.
  Confess thy treasons ere thou fly the realm –
  Since thou hast far to go, bear not along
  The clogging burthen of a guilty soul.   200

MOWBRAY No, Bolingbroke, if ever I were traitor,
  My name be blotted from the book of life,
  And I from heaven banished as from hence:
  But what thou art, God, thou, and I do know,

And all too soon, I fear, the king shall rue:
Farewell, my liege. Now no way can I stray:
Save back to England all the world's my way. [*he goes*

K.RICHARD   Uncle, even in the glasses of thine eyes
I see thy grievéd heart: thy sad aspect
Hath from the number of his banished years   210
Plucked four away. [*to Bolingbroke*] Six frozen
                                                winters spent,
Return with welcome home from banishment.

B'BROKE   How long a time lies in one little word!
Four lagging winters and four wanton springs
End in a word – such is the breath of kings.

GAUNT   I thank my liege that, in regard of me,
He shortens four years of my son's exile,
But little vantage shall I reap thereby:
For, ere the six years that he hath to spend
Can change their moons, and bring their times about,   220
My oil-dried lamp and time-bewasted light
Shall be extinct with age and endless night,
My inch of taper will be burnt and done,
And blindfold Death not let me see my son.

K.RICHARD   Why, uncle, thou hast many years to live.

GAUNT   But not a minute, king, that thou canst give;
Shorten my days thou canst with sullen sorrow,
And pluck nights from me, but not lend a morrow:
Thou canst help time to furrow me with age,
But stop no wrinkle in his pilgrimage: 230
Thy word is current with him for my death,
But dead, thy kingdom cannot buy my breath.

K.RICHARD   Thy son is banished upon good advice,
Whereto thy tongue a party-verdict gave;
Why at our justice seem'st thou then to lour?

GAUNT   Things sweet to taste, prove in digestion sour.
You urged me as a judge, but I had rather,
You would have bid me argue like a father:
O, had it been a stranger, not my child,
To smooth his fault I should have been more mild.   240
A partial slander sought I to avoid,
And in the sentence my own life destroyed.

    Alas, I looked when some of you should say,
    I was too strict to make mine own away:
    But you gave leave to my unwilling tongue,
    Against my will to do myself this wrong.

K. RICHARD Cousin, farewell – and uncle, bid him so,
    Six years we banish him and he shall go.

     [*'Flourish'. The King departs with his train*

AUMERLE Cousin, farewell, what presence must not know,
    From where you do remain let paper show.   250

MARSHAL My lord, no leave take I, for I will ride
    As far as land will let me by your side.

GAUNT O, to what purpose dost thou hoard thy words,
    That thou returnest no greeting to thy friends?

B'BROKE I have too few to take my leave of you,
    When the tongue's office should be prodigal
    To breathe the abundant dolour of the heart.

GAUNT Thy grief is but thy absence for a time.

B'BROKE Joy absent, grief is present for that time.

GAUNT What is six winters? They are quickly gone –   260

B'BROKE To men in joy; but grief makes one hour ten.

GAUNT Call it a travel that thou tak'st for pleasure.

B'BROKE My heart will sigh when I miscall it so,
    Which finds it an enforcéd pilgrimage.

GAUNT The sullen passage of thy weary steps
    Esteem as <u>foil</u> wherein thou art to set
    The precious jewel of thy home return.

B'BROKE Nay, rather, every tedious stride I make
    Will but remember me what a deal of world
    I wander from the jewels that I love.   270
    Must I not serve a long apprenticehood
    To foreign passages, and in the end,
    Having my freedom, boast of nothing else,
    But that I was a journeyman to grief?

GAUNT All places that the eye of heaven visits
    Are to a wise man ports and happy havens:
    Teach thy necessity to reason thus –
    There is no virtue like necessity.
    Think not the king did banish thee,
    But thou the king. Woe doth the heavier sit,   280

Where it perceives it is but faintly borne:
Go, say I sent thee forth to purchase honour,
And not the king exiled thee; or suppose
Devouring pestilence hangs in our air,
And thou art flying to a fresher clime:
Look, what thy soul holds dear, imagine it
To lie that way thou goest, not whence thou com'st:
Suppose the singing birds musicians,
The grass whereon thou tread'st the presence strewed,
The flowers fair ladies, and thy steps no more   290
Than a delightful measure or a dance,
For gnarling sorrow hath less power to bite
The man that mocks at it and sets it light.

B'BROKE O, who can hold a fire in his hand
By thinking on the frosty Caucasus?
Or cloy the hungry edge of appetite
By bare imagination of a feast?
Or wallow naked in December snow
By thinking on fantastic summer's heat?
O no, the apprehension of the good   300
Gives but the greater feeling to the worse:
Fell sorrow's tooth doth never rankle more
Than when he bites, but lanceth not the sore.

GAUNT   Come, come, my son, I'll bring thee on thy way;
Had I thy youth and cause, I would not stay.

B'BROKE Then England's ground, farewell, sweet soil adieu,
My mother and my nurse that bears me yet!
Where'er I wander, boast of this I can,
Though banished, yet a trueborn Englishman.

[*they go*

Johnson ended Act I here.

SCENE 4

The court   ~~favoriles~~

'Enter the KING' with BAGOT and GREEN' 'at one door, and the
                    LORD AUMERLE at another'

in medias res

K.RICHARD We did observe. Cousin Aumerle,
          How far brought you high Hereford on his way?

AUMERLE   I brought high Hereford, if you call him so,
          But to the next highway, and there I left him.

K.RICHARD And say, what store of parting tears were shed?

AUMERLE   Faith, none for me, except the north-east wind   *A's scorn*
          Which then blew bitterly against our faces,   *for Bol.*
          Awaked the sleeping rheum, and so by chance
          Did grace our hollow parting with a tear.

K.RICHARD What said our cousin when you parted with him?   10

AUMERLE   'Farewell' –
          And for my heart disdainéd that my tongue
          Should so profane the word, that taught me craft
          To counterfeit oppression of such grief
          That words seemed buried in my sorrow's grave:
          Marry, would the word 'farewell' have
                                        length'ned hours,
          And added years to his short banishment,
          He should have had a volume of farewells:
          But since it would not, he had none of me.   *R II Bol +*
                                                         Aum. all ears
K.RICHARD He is our cousin's cousin, but 'tis doubt,   *of 2 Ed III's*
          When time shall call him home from banishment, *sons.*
    ?   Whether our kinsman come to see his friends.
          Ourself and Bushy
          Observed his courtship to the common people,   *Below popular*
          How he did seem to dive into their hearts,
          With humble and familiar courtesy,
          What reverence he did throw away on slaves,
          Wooing poor craftsmen with the craft of smiles
          And patient underbearing of his fortune,   *= endurance*
          As 'twere to banish their affects with him.   *= affection* 30
          Off goes his bonnet to an oyster-wench,
          A brace of draymen bid God speed him well,

And had the tribute of his supple knee,
With 'Thanks, my countrymen, my loving friends' –
As were our England in reversion his,　　　　*NB*
And he our subjects' next degree in hope.

GREEN　Well, he is gone; and with him go these thoughts.
Now for the rebels which stand out in Ireland,
Expedient manage must be made, my liege,
Ere further leisure yield them further means　　40
For their advantage and your highness' loss.

K.RICHARD　We will ourself in person to this war,
And for our coffers with too great a court
And liberal largess are grown somewhat light,
We are enforced to farm our royal realm,
The revenue whereof shall furnish us
For our affairs in hand – if that come short,
Our substitutes at home shall have blank charters,
Whereto, when they shall know what men are rich,
They shall subscribe them for large sums of gold,　　50
And send them after to supply our wants;
For we will make for Ireland presently.

BUSHY *enters*

What news?
BUSHY　Old John of Gaunt is grievous sick, my lord,
Suddenly taken, and hath sent post haste
To entreat your majesty to visit him.
K.RICHARD　Where lies he?
BUSHY　At Ely House.
K.RICHARD　Now put it, God, in the physician's mind,
To help him to his grave immediately!　　*NB*　60
The lining of his coffers shall make coats
To deck our soldiers for these Irish wars.
Come, gentlemen, let's all go visit him;
Pray God we may make haste and come too late!
ALL　Amen.　　　　　　　　　　　　　*[they go out*

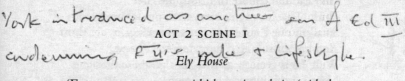

York introduced as another son of Ed III
condemning R II's rule & lifestyle.

ACT 2 SCENE 1

Ely House

'Enter JOHN OF GAUNT *sick*' borne in a chair, '*with the*
DUKE OF YORK, *etc.*'

GAUNT   Will the king come that I may breathe my last
         In wholesome counsel to his unstaid youth?

YORK   Vex not yourself, nor strive not with your breath,
         For all in vain comes counsel to his ear.

GAUNT   O, but they say the tongues of dying men
         Enforce attention like deep harmony:
         Where words are scarce they are seldom spent in vain,
         For they breathe truth that breathe their words in pain:
         He that no more must say is listened more
         Than they whom youth and ease have taught to glose;   10
         More are men's ends marked than their lives before:
         The setting sun, and music at the close,
         As the last taste of sweets, is sweetest last,
         Writ in remembrance more than things long past.
         Though Richard my life's counsel would not hear,
         My death's sad tale may yet undeaf his ear.

chiasmus
in an
patterned play

YORK   No, it is stopped with other flattering sounds,
         As praises, of whose taste the wise are fond,
         Lascivious metres, to whose venom sound
         The open ear of youth doth always listen,
         Report of fashions in proud Italy,   20
         Whose manners still our tardy apish nation
         Limps after in base imitation:
         Where doth the world thrust forth a vanity –
         So it be new, there's no respect how vile –
         That is not quickly buzzed into his ears?
         Then all too late comes counsel to be heard,
         Where will doth mutiny with wit's regard:
         Direct not him whose way himself will choose,
         'Tis breath thou lack'st, and that breath wilt thou lose.   30

GAUNT   Methinks I am a prophet new inspired,
         And thus expiring do foretell of him:

I Various
fashion

nothing
changes

image

His rash fierce blaze of riot cannot last;
For violent fires soon burn out themselves,
Small showers last long, but sudden storms are short:
He tires betimes that spurs too fast betimes:
With eager feeding food doth choke the feeder:
Light vanity, insatiate cormorant,
Consuming means, soon preys upon itself.
This royal throne of kings, this sceptered isle,   40
This earth of majesty, this seat of Mars,
This other Eden, demi-paradise,
This fortress built by nature for herself
Against infection and the hand of war,
This happy breed of men, this little world,
This precious stone set in the silver sea,
Which serves it in the office of a wall,
Or as a moat defensive to a house,
Against the envy of less happier lands;
This blessed plot, this earth, this realm, this England,   50
This nurse, this teeming womb of royal kings,
Feared by their breed, and famous by their birth,
Renownéd for their deeds as far from home,
For Christian service and true chivalry,
As is the sepulchre in stubborn Jewry
Of the world's ransom, blessed Mary's Son:
This land of such dear souls, this dear dear land,
Dear for her reputation through the world,
Is now leased out – I die pronouncing it –
Like to a tenement or pelting farm.   60
England, bound in with the triumphant sea,
Whose rocky shore beats back the envious siege
Of wat'ry Neptune, is now bound in with shame,
With inky blots, and rotten parchment bonds:
That England, that was wont to conquer others,
Hath made a shameful conquest of itself.
Ah, would the scandal vanish with my life,
How happy then were my ensuing death!

'Enter KING, QUEEN, AUMERLE, BUSHY, GREEN, BAGOT, ROSS,
and WILLOUGHBY'

YORK	The king is come; deal mildly with his youth,
	For young hot colts, being ragged, do rage the more. 70
QUEEN	How fares our noble uncle, Lancaster?
K. RICHARD	What comfort, man? How is't with aged Gaunt?
GAUNT	O, how that name befits my composition!
	Old Gaunt indeed, and gaunt in being old:
	Within me grief hath kept a tedious fast,
	And who abstains from meat that is not gaunt?
	For sleeping England long time have I watched;
	Watching breeds leanness, leanness is all gaunt:
	The pleasure that some fathers feed upon
	Is my strict fast; I mean my children's looks, 80
	And therein fasting hast thou made me gaunt:
	Gaunt am I for the grave, gaunt as a grave,
	Whose hollow womb inherits nought but bones.
K. RICHARD	Can sick men play so nicely with their names?
GAUNT	No, misery makes sport to mock itself:
	Since thou dost seek to kill my name in me,
	I mock my name, great king, to flatter thee.
K. RICHARD	Should dying men flatter with those that live?
GAUNT	No, no, men living flatter those that die.
K. RICHARD	Thou now a–dying sayest thou flatterest me. 90
GAUNT	Oh no, thou diest, though I the sicker be.
K. RICHARD	I am in health, I breathe, and see thee ill.
GAUNT	Now He that made me knows I see thee ill,
	Ill in myself to see, and in thee, seeing ill.
	Thy death–bed is no lesser than thy land,
	Wherein thou liest in reputation sick,
	And thou too careless patient as thou art
	Commit'st thy anointed body to the cure
	Of those physicians that first wounded thee.
	A thousand flatterers sit within thy crown, 100
	Whose compass is no bigger than thy head,
	And yet incagéd in so small a verge,
	The waste is no whit lesser than thy land.
	O, had thy grandsire with a prophet's eye
	Seen how his son's son should destroy his sons,
	From forth thy reach he would have laid thy shame,
	Deposing thee before thou wert possessed,

Which art possessed now to depose thyself. *2nd pun*

Why, cousin, wert thou regent of the world,

It were a shame to let this land by lease;   110

But for thy world enjoying but this land,

Is it not more than shame to shame it so?

Landlord of England art thou now, not king,   *NB*

Thy state of law is bondslave to the law,

And thou –   *interruption*

K.RICHARD   A lunatic lean-witted fool,

Presuming on an ague's privilege,

Darest with thy frozen admonition

Make pale our cheek, chasing the royal blood

With fury from his native residence.

Now by my seat's right royal majesty,   120

Wert thou not brother to great Edward's son,   *= Bl. Prince*

This tongue that runs so roundly in thy head

Should run thy head from thy unreverent shoulders.

GAUNT   O, spare me not, my brother Edward's son,

For that I was his father Edward's son;

That blood already, like the pelican,

Hast thou tapped out and drunkenly caroused.

My brother Gloucester, plain well-meaning soul,

Direct   Whom fair befall in heaven 'mongst happy souls,

accusation May be a precedent and witness good.

That thou respect'st not spilling Edward's blood!   *NB* 130

Join with the present sickness that I have,

And thy unkindness be like crooked age,

To crop at once a too long withered flower.

Live in thy shame, but die not shame with thee!

These words hereafter thy tormentors be!

Convey me to my bed, then to my grave:

Love they to live that love and honour have.

                 [*he is borne out by attendants*

K.RICHARD And let them die that age and sullens have,   *= sulks*

For both hast thou, and both become the grave.   140

YORK   I do beseech your majesty, impute his words

To wayward sickliness and age in him.   *York as*

He loves you, on my life, and holds you dear   *conciliator*

red rag   As Harry Duke of Hereford, were he here.

to a bull

Gaunt dies off stage in 8 lines!

K.RICHARD Right, you say true – as Hereford's love, so his;
           As theirs, so mine, and all be as it is.

           NORTHUMBERLAND *enters*

NORTH.   My liege, old Gaunt commends him to your majesty.
K.RICHARD What says he?
NORTH.   Nay, nothing, all is said:
           His tongue is now a stringless instrument;
           Words, life, and all, old Lancaster hath spent.   150
YORK   Be York the next that must be bankrupt so!
           Though death be poor, it ends a mortal woe.
K.RICHARD The ripest fruit first falls, and so doth he,
           His time is spent, our pilgrimage must be;
           So much for that. Now for our Irish wars –
           We must supplant those rough rug-headed kerns,
           Which live like venom, where no venom else
           But only they have privilege to live.
           And for these great affairs do ask some charge,
           Towards our assistance we do seize to us   160
           The plate, coin, revenues, and moveables,
           Whereof our uncle Gaunt did stand possessed.
YORK   How long shall I be patient? Ah, how long
           Shall tender duty make me suffer wrong?
           Not Gloucester's death, nor Hereford's banishment,
           Not Gaunt's rebukes, nor England's private wrongs,
           Nor the prevention of poor Bolingbroke
           About his marriage, nor my own disgrace,
           Have ever made me sour my patient cheek,
           Or bend one wrinkle on my sovereign's face.   170
           I am the last of noble Edward's sons,
           Of whom thy father, Prince of Wales, was first.
           In war was never lion raged more fierce,
           In peace was never gentle lamb more mild,
           Than was that young and princely gentleman:
           His face thou hast, for even so looked he,
           Accomplished with the number of thy hours;
           But when he frowned it was against the French,
           And not against his friends; his noble hand
           Did win what he did spend, and spent not that   180

[Handwritten marginalia: NB; in age; man of action; ditto; see pp 114, etc; Ed III; = Bl. Pr.; York accuses R II; NB; R II prevented Bol from marrying French king's cousin by denouncing him as committer of treasons offences]

Which his triumphant father's hand had won:
His hands were guilty of no kindred blood,
But bloody with the enemies of his kin:
O, Richard! York is too far gone with grief,
Or else he never would compare between –

K.RICHARD Why, uncle, what's the matter?

YORK   O, my liege,
Pardon me, if you please – if not, I pleased
Not to be pardoned, am content withal.
Seek you to seize and gripe into your hands
The royalties and rights of banished Hereford?   190
Is not Gaunt dead? And doth not Hereford live?
Was not Gaunt just? And is not Harry true?
Did not the one deserve to have an heir?
Is not his heir a well-deserving son?
Take Hereford's rights away, and take from Time
His charters and his customary rights;
Let not tomorrow then ensue today;
Be not thyself – for how art thou a king
But by fair sequence and succession?
Now, afore God – God forbid I say true! –   200
If you do wrongfully seize Hereford's rights,
Call in the letters-patents that he hath
By his attorneys-general to sue
His livery, and deny his off'red homage,
You pluck a thousand dangers on your head,
You lose a thousand well-disposéd hearts,
And prick my tender patience to those thoughts
Which honour and allegiance cannot think.

K.RICHARD Think what you will, we seize into our hands
His plate, his goods, his money and his lands.   210

YORK I'll not be by the while – my liege, farewell.
What will ensue hereof there's none can tell:
But by bad courses may be understood,
That their events can never fall out good.   [he goes

K.RICHARD Go, Bushy, to the Earl of Wiltshire straight,
Bid him repair to us to Ely House,
To see this business: tomorrow next

We will for Ireland, and 'tis time, I trow.
And we create, in absence of ourself,
Our uncle York lord governor of England;   220
For he is just, and always loved us well.
Come on, our queen, tomorrow must we part;
Be merry, for our time of stay is short.

> [*he leads out the Queen, followed by*
> *Bushy, Aumerle, Green, and Bagot*

NORTH.   Well, lords, the Duke of Lancaster is dead.
ROSS   And living too, for now his son is duke.
WILLO'BY Barely in title, not in revenues.
NORTH.   Richly in both, if justice had her right.
ROSS   My heart is great, but it must break with silence,
          Ere't be disburdened with a liberal tongue.
NORTH.   Nay, speak thy mind, and let him ne'er speak more   230
          That speaks thy words again to do thee harm.
WILLO'BY Tends that thou wouldst speak to the Duke of
                                                  Hereford?
          If it be so, out with it boldly, man.
          Quick is mine ear to hear of good towards him.
ROSS   No good at all that I can do for him,
          Unless you call it good to pity him,
          Bereft, and gelded of his patrimony.
NORTH.   Now afore God 'tis shame such wrongs are borne
          In him, a royal prince, and many moe
          Of noble blood in this declining land.   240
          The king is not himself, but basely led
          By flatterers, and what they will inform,
          Merely in hate, 'gainst any of us all,
          That will the king severely prosecute
          'Gainst us, our lives, our children, and our heirs.
ROSS   The commons hath he pilled with grievous taxes,
          And quite lost their hearts. The nobles hath he fined
          For ancient quarrels, and quite lost their hearts.
WILLO'BY And daily new exactions are devised,
          As blanks, benevolences, and I wot not what: 250
          But what, a God's name, doth become of this?
NORTH.   Wars hath not wasted it, for warred he hath not,

But basely yielded upon compromise
That which his noble ancestors achieved with blows.
More hath he spent in peace than they in wars.

ROSS   The Earl of Wiltshire hath the realm in farm.   *yet again*

WILLO'BY   The king's grown bankrupt like a broken man.

NORTH.   Reproach and dissolution hangeth over him.

ROSS   He hath not money for these Irish wars,
           His burthenous taxations notwithstanding,   260
           But by the robbing of the banished duke.

NORTH.   His noble kinsman — most degenerate king!
           But, lords, we hear this fearful tempest sing,
           Yet seek no shelter to avoid the storm:
           We see the wind sit sore upon our sails,
           And yet we strike not, but securely perish.

ROSS   We see the very wrack that we must suffer,
           And unavoided is the danger now,
           For suffering so the causes of our wrack.

NORTH.   Not so, even through the hollow eyes of death   270
           I spy life peering, but I dare not say   *usage*
           How near the tidings of our comfort is.   *= Bol.*

WILLO'BY   Nay, let us share thy thoughts as thou dost ours.

ROSS   Be confident to speak, Northumberland;
           We three are but thyself, and speaking so
           Thy words are but as thoughts, therefore be bold.

NORTH.   Then thus — I have from le Port Blanc, a bay
           In Brittany, received intelligence
           That Harry Duke of Hereford, Rainold Lord Cobham,
           [The son of Richard Earl of Arundel,]   280
           That late broke from the Duke of Exeter,
           His brother, Archbishop late of Canterbury,
           Sir Thomas Erpingham, Sir John Ramston,
           Sir John Norbery, Sir Robert Waterton, and
                                                    Francis Coint —
           All these, well furnished by the Duke of Britain,
           With eight tall ships, three thousand men of war,
           Are making hither with all due expedience,
           And shortly mean to touch our northern shore:
           Perhaps they had ere this, but that they stay

① Compression of time.

The first departing of the king for Ireland.   290
If then we shall shake off our slavish yoke,
Imp out our drooping country's broken wing,
Redeem from broking pawn the blemished crown,
Wipe off the dust that hides our sceptre's gilt,
And make high majesty look like itself,
Away with me in post to Ravenspurgh:
But if you faint, as fearing to do so,
Stay, and be secret, and myself will go.

ROSS   To horse, to horse! Urge doubts to them that fear.
WILLO'BY   Hold out my horse, and I will first be there.   300

[they hurry out

SCENE 2

Windsor Castle

'Enter the QUEEN, BUSHY, and BAGOT'

BUSHY   Madam, your majesty is too much sad.
            You promised, when you parted with the king,
            To lay aside life-harming heaviness,
            And entertain a cheerful disposition.

QUEEN   To please the king I did – to please myself
            I cannot do it; yet I know no cause
            Why I should welcome such a guest as grief,
            Save bidding farewell to so sweet a guest
            As my sweet Richard: yet again methinks
            Some unborn sorrow ripe in Fortune's womb   10
            Is coming towards me, and my inward soul
            With nothing trembles, yet at something grieves,
            More than with parting from my lord the king.

BUSHY   Each substance of a grief hath twenty shadows,
            Which shows like grief itself, but is not so:
            For Sorrow's eye, glazéd with blinding tears,
            Divides one thing entire to many objects,
            Like perspectives, which rightly gazed upon
            Show nothing but confusion; eyed awry,
            Distinguish form: so your sweet majesty,   20
            Looking awry upon your lord's departure,

Find shapes of grief more than himself to wail,
Which looked on as it is, is nought but shadows
Of what it is not; then, thrice-gracious queen,
More than your lord's departure weep not – more
                                   is not seen,
Or if it be, 'tis with false Sorrow's eye,
Which, for things true, weeps things imaginary.

QUEEN   It may be so; but yet my inward soul
Persuades me it is otherwise: howe'er it be,
I cannot but be sad; so heavy sad,   30
As, though on thinking on no thought I think,
Makes me with heavy nothing faint and shrink.

BUSHY   'Tis nothing but conceit, my gracious lady.

QUEEN   'Tis nothing less: conceit is still derived
From some forefather grief. Mine is not so,
For nothing hath begot my something grief,
Or something hath the nothing that I grieve;
'Tis in reversion that I do possess –
But what it is that is not yet known, what
I cannot name, 'tis nameless woe, I wot.   40

                GREEN *enters*

GREEN   God save your majesty! And well met, gentlemen.
I hope the king is not yet shipped for Ireland.

QUEEN   Why hopest thou so? 'Tis better hope he is,
For his designs crave haste, his haste good hope:
Then wherefore dost thou hope he is not shipped?

GREEN   That he, our hope, might have retired his power,
And driven into despair an enemy's hope,
Who strongly hath set footing in this land.
The banished Bolingbroke repeals himself,
And with uplifted arms is safe arrived   50
At Ravenspurgh.

QUEEN   Now God in heaven forbid!

GREEN   Ah, madam, 'tis too true, and that is worse,
The Lord Northumberland, his son young
                         Henry Percy,
The Lords of Ross, Beaumond, and Willoughby,
With all their powerful friends, are fled to him.

BUSHY   Why have you not proclaimed Northumberland
         And all the rest revolted faction traitors?

GREEN   We have, whereupon the Earl of Worcester
         Hath broken his staff, resigned his stewardship,
         And all the household servants fled with him   60
         To Bolingbroke.

QUEEN   So, Green, thou art the midwife to my woe,
         And Bolingbroke my sorrow's dismal heir.
         Now hath my soul brought forth her prodigy,
         And I, a gasping new-delivered mother,
         Have woe to woe, sorrow to sorrow joined.

BUSHY   Despair not, madam.

QUEEN   Who shall hinder me?
         I will despair, and be at enmity
         With cozening Hope: he is a flatterer,
         A parasite, a keeper back of Death,   70
         Who gently would dissolve the bands of life,
         Which false Hope lingers in extremity.

              YORK *enters with his gorget on*

GREEN   Here comes the Duke of York.

QUEEN   With signs of war about his aged neck.
         O, full of careful business are his looks!
         Uncle, for God's sake, speak comfortable words.

YORK   Should I do so, I should belie my thoughts.
         Comfort's in heaven, and we are on the earth,
         Where nothing lives but crosses, cares, and grief:
         Your husband he is gone to save far off,   80
         Whilst others come to make him lose at home:
         Here am I left to underprop his land,
         Who weak with age cannot support myself.
         Now comes the sick hour that his surfeit made,
         Now shall he try his friends that flattered him.

              A servingman enters

SERVING. My lord, your son was gone before I came.

YORK   He was? Why, so! Go all which way it will!
         The nobles they are fled, the commons cold,
         And will, I fear, revolt on Hereford's side.
         Sirrah,   90

    Get thee to Plashy, to my sister Gloucester,
    Bid her send me presently a thousand pound.
    Hold, take my ring.
SERVING. My lord, I had forgot to tell your lordship:
    Today, as I came by, I calléd there –
    But I shall grieve you to report the rest.
YORK What is't, knave?
SERVING. An hour before I came the duchess died.
YORK God for his mercy, what a tide of woes
    Comes rushing on this woeful land at once!   100
    I know not what to do: I would to God,
    So my untruth had not provoked him to it,
    The king had cut off my head with my brother's.
    What, are there no posts dispatched for Ireland?
    How shall we do for money for these wars?
    Come, sister – cousin, I would say – pray pardon me:
    Go, fellow, get thee home, provide some carts,
    And bring away the armour that is there.
             [the servingman goes
    Gentlemen, will you go muster men?
    If I know   110
    How or which way to order these affairs,
    Thus thrust disorderly into my hands,
    Never believe me. Both are my kinsmen:
    Th'one is my sovereign, whom both my oath
    And duty bids defend; th'other again
    Is my kinsman, whom the king hath wronged,
    Whom conscience and my kindred bids to right.
    Well, somewhat we must do. Come, cousin, I'll
    Dispose of you:
    Gentlemen, go, muster up your men,
    And meet me presently at Berkeley: 120
    I should to Plashy too,
    But time will not permit: all is uneven,
    And everything is left at six and seven.
            [he leads the Queen out
BUSHY The wind sits fair for news to go to Ireland,
    But none returns. For us to levy power
    Proportionable to the enemy

Is all unpossible.

GREEN   Besides, our nearness to the king in love
         Is near the hate of those love not the king.   130

BAGOT   And that is the wavering commons, for their love
         Lies in their purses; and whoso empties them,
         By so much fills their hearts with deadly hate.

BUSHY   Wherein the king stands generally condemned.

BAGOT   If judgement lie in them, then so do we,
         Because we ever have been near the king.

GREEN   Well, I will for refuge straight to Bristol Castle –
         The Earl of Wiltshire is already there.

BUSHY   Thither will I with you, for little office
         The hateful commons will perform for us,   140
         Except like curs to tear us all to pieces:
         Will you go along with us?

BAGOT   No, I will to Ireland to his majesty.
         Farewell: if heart's presages be not vain,
         We three here part that ne'er shall meet again.

BUSHY   That's as York thrives to beat back Bolingbroke.

GREEN   Alas, poor duke! The task he undertakes
         Is numb'ring sands, and drinking oceans dry.
         Where one on his side fights, thousands will fly:
         Farewell at once, for once, for all, and ever.   150

BUSHY   Well, we may meet again.

BAGOT   I fear me, never.

                                                    [they go

SCENE 3

Near Berkeley Castle

BOLINGBROKE and NORTHUMBERLAND, marching with forces up a hill

B'BROKE How far is it, my lord, to Berkeley now?

NORTH.   Believe me, noble lord,
         I am a stranger here in Gloucestershire.
         These high wild hills and rough uneven ways
         Draws out our miles and makes them wearisome;
         And yet your fair discourse hath been as sugar,
         Making the hard way sweet and delectable.

> But I bethink me what a weary way
> From Ravenspurgh to Cotswold will be found
> In Ross and Willoughby, wanting your company,   10
> Which I protest hath very much beguiled
> The tediousness and process of my travel:
> But theirs is sweet'ned with the hope to have
> The present benefit which I possess,
> And hope to joy is little less in joy
> Than hope enjoyed; by this the weary lords
> Shall make their way seem short, as mine hath done
> By sight of what I have, your noble company.

B'BROKE   Of much less value is my company
> Than your good words. But who comes here?   20

HARRY PERCY *enters*

NORTH.   It is my son, young Harry Percy,
> Sent from my brother Worcester, whencesoever.
> Harry, how fares your uncle?

PERCY   I had thought, my lord, to have learned his
>   health of you.

NORTH.   Why, is he not with the queen?

PERCY   No, my good lord, he hath forsook the court,
> Broken his staff of office, and dispersed
> The household of the king.

NORTH.   What was his reason.?
> He was not so resolved, when last we spake together.

PERCY   Because your lordship was proclaiméd traitor.   30
> But he, my lord, is gone to Ravenspurgh,
> To offer service to the Duke of Hereford,
> And sent me over by Berkeley to discover
> What power the Duke of York had levied there,
> Then with directions to repair to Ravenspurgh.

NORTH.   Have you forgot the Duke of Hereford, boy?

PERCY   No, my good lord, for that is not forgot
> Which ne'er I did remember: to my knowledge,
> I never in my life did look on him.

NORTH.   Then learn to know him now. This is the duke.   40

PERCY   My gracious lord, I tender you my service,
> Such as it is, being tender, raw, and young,

Which elder days shall ripen and confirm
To more appróvéd service and desert.

B'BROKE   I thank thee, gentle Percy, and be sure
I count myself in nothing else so happy
As in a soul rememb'ring my good friends;
And as my fortune ripens with thy love,
It shall be still thy true love's recompense.
My heart this covenant makes, my hand thus seals it.   50

NORTH.   How far is it to Berkeley? And what stir
Keeps good old York there with his men of war?

PERCY   There stands the castle, by yon tuft of trees,
Manned with three hundred men, as I have heard,
And in it are the Lords of York, Berkeley, and
                                 Seymour –
None else of name and noble estimate.

             ROSS *and* WILLOUGHBY *come up*

NORTH.   Here come the Lords of Ross and Willoughby,
Bloody with spurring, fiery-red with haste.

B'BROKE   Welcome, my lords. I wot your love pursues
A banished traitor: all my treasury   60
Is yet but unfelt thanks, which more enriched
Shall be your love and labour's recompense.

ROSS   Your presence makes us rich, most noble lord.

WILLO'BY   And far surmounts our labour to attain it.

B'BROKE   Evermore thank's the exchequer of the poor,
Which till my infant fortune comes to years,
Stands for my bounty: but who comes here?

             BERKELEY *approaches*

NORTH.   It is my Lord of Berkeley, as I guess.

BERKELEY   My Lord of Hereford, my message is to you.

B'BROKE   My lord, my answer is to 'Lancaster',   70
And I am come to seek that name in England;
And I must find that title in your tongue,
Before I make reply to aught you say.

BERKELEY   Mistake me not, my lord, 'tis not my meaning
To raze one title of your honour out:
To you, my lord, I come, what lord you will,
From the most gracious regent of this land,

	The Duke of York; to know what pricks you on	
	To take advantage of the absent time,	
	And fright our native peace with self-borne arms.	80

YORK *with a retinue draws near*

B'BROKE	I shall not need transport my words by you;	
	Here comes his grace in person.	
	My noble uncle! [*he kneels*	N B
YORK	Show me thy humble heart, and not thy knee,	
	Whose duty is deceivable and false.	
B'BROKE	My gracious uncle!	
YORK	Tut, tut!	
	Grace me no grace, nor uncle me no uncle,	
	I am no traitor's uncle, and that word 'grace'	
	In an ungracious mouth is but profane:	
	Why have those banished and forbidden legs	90
	Dared once to touch a dust of England's ground?	
	But then more 'why?' Why have they dared to march	
	So many miles upon her peaceful bosom,	
	Frighting her pale-faced villages with war,	
	And ostentation of despised arms?	
	Com'st thou because the anointed king is hence?	
	Why, foolish boy, the king is left behind,	
	And in my loyal bosom lies his power.	
	Were I but now the lord of such hot youth,	
	As when brave Gaunt, thy father, and myself,	100
	Rescued the Black Prince, that young Mars of men,	
	From forth the ranks of many thousand French,	
	O, then how quickly should this arm of mine,	
	Now prisoner to the palsy, chastise thee,	
	And minister correction to thy fault!	
B'BROKE	My gracious uncle, let me know my fault,	
	On what condition stands it and wherein?	
YORK	Even in condition of the worst degree –	
	In gross rebellion and detested treason.	
	Thou art a banished man, and here art come,	110
	Before the expiration of thy time,	
	In braving arms against thy sovereign.	
B'BROKE	As I was banished, I was banished Hereford,	

But as I come, I come for Lancaster.
And, noble uncle, I beseech your grace
Look on my wrongs with an indifferent eye:
You are my father, for methinks in you
I see old Gaunt alive. O then my father,
Will you permit that I shall stand condemned
A wandering vagabond, my rights and royalties   120
Plucked from my arms perforce, and given away
To upstart unthrifts? Wherefore was I born?
If that my cousin king be king in England,
It must be granted I am Duke of Lancaster.
You have a son, Aumerle, my noble cousin;
Had you first died, and he been thus trod down,
He should have found his uncle Gaunt a father,
To rouse his wrongs and chase them to the bay.
I am denied to sue my livery here,
And yet my letters-patents give me leave.   130
My father's goods are all distrained and sold,
And these and all are all amiss employed.
What would you have me do? I am a subject;
And I challenge law. Attorneys are denied me,
And therefore personally I lay my claim
To my inheritance of free descent.

NORTH.   The noble duke hath been too much abused.
ROSS   It stands your grace upon to do him right.
WILLO'BY Base men by his endowments are made great.
YORK   My lords of England, let me tell you this: 140
          I have had feeling of my cousin's wrongs,
          And laboured all I could to do him right:
          But in this kind to come, in braving arms,
          Be his own carver and cut out his way,
          To find out right with wrong, it may not be;
          And you that do abet him in this kind
          Cherish rebellion, and are rebels all.
NORTH.   The noble duke hath sworn his coming is
          But for his own; and for the right of that
          We all have strongly sworn to give him aid: 150
          And let him never see joy that breaks that oath.
YORK   Well, well, I see the issue of these arms.

I cannot mend it, I must needs confess,
Because my power is weak and all ill left:
But if I could, by Him that gave me life,
I would attach you all, and make you stoop
Unto the sovereign mercy of the king;
But, since I cannot, be it known unto you,
I do remain as neuter. So, fare you well,
Unless you please to enter in the castle,
And there repose you for this night.   160

B'BROKE   An offer, uncle, that we will accept.
But we must win your grace to go with us
To Bristow castle, which they say is held
By Bushy, Bagot, and their complices,
The caterpillars of the commonwealth,
Which I have sworn to weed and pluck away.

YORK   It may be I will go with you – but yet I'll pause,
For I am loath to break our country's laws.
Nor friends nor foes, to me welcome you are: 170
Things past redress are now with me past care.

                             [they go forward

SCENE 4

A camp in Wales

SALISBURY, *and a Welsh Captain*

CAPTAIN   My Lord of Salisbury, we have stayed ten days,
And hardly kept our countrymen together,
And yet we hear no tidings from the king;
Therefore we will disperse ourselves. Farewell.

SALISBURY Stay yet another day, thou trusty Welshman;
The king reposeth all his confidence in thee.

CAPTAIN   'Tis thought the king is dead; we will not stay.
The bay-trees in our country are all withered,
And meteors fright the fixéd stars of heaven;
The pale-faced moon looks bloody on the earth,   10
And lean-looked prophets whisper fearful change,
Rich men look sad, and ruffians dance and leap –
The one in fear to lose what they enjoy,

The other to enjoy by rage and war:
These signs forerun the death or fall of kings.
Farewell. Our countrymen are gone and fled,
As well assured Richard their king is dead.   *[he goes*

SALISBURY Ah, Richard! With the eyes of heavy mind
I see thy glory like a shooting star
Fall to the base earth from the firmament.   20
Thy sun sets weeping in the lowly west,
Witnessing storms to come, woe, and unrest.
Thy friends are fled to wait upon thy foes,
And crossly to thy good all fortune goes.

                                                                   [he goes

ACT 3 SCENE I

Bristol. Before the castle

Enter BOLINGBROKE, YORK, NORTHUMBERLAND, *with* BUSHY
and GREEN, *prisoners*

B'BROKE   Bring forth these men.
            Bushy and Green, I will not vex your souls,
            Since presently your souls must part your bodies,
            With too much urging your pernicious lives,
            For 'twere no charity; yet to wash your blood
            From off my hands, here in the view of men,
            I will unfold some causes of your deaths:
            You have misled a prince, a royal king,
            A happy gentleman in blood and lineaments,
            By you unhappied and disfigured clean.   10
            You have in manner with your sinful hours
            Made a divorce betwixt his queen and him,
            Broke the possession of a royal bed,
            And stained the beauty of a fair queen's cheeks
            With tears, drawn from her eyes by your foul wrongs.
            Myself, a prince by fortune of my birth,
            Near to the king in blood, and near in love,
            Till you did make him misinterpret me,
            Have stooped my neck under your injuries,
            And sighed my English breath in foreign clouds,   20
            Eating the bitter bread of banishment,
            Whilst you have fed upon my signories,
            Disparked my parks, and felled my forest woods;
            From my own windows torn my household coat,
            Razed out my imprese, leaving me no sign,
            Save men's opinions and my living blood,
            To show the world I am a gentleman.
            This and much more, much more than twice all this,
            Condemns you to the death. See them
                                 delivered over
            To execution and the hand of death.   30
BUSHY   More welcome is the stroke of death to me

Than Bolingbroke to England. Lords, farewell.

GREEN   My comfort is, that heaven will take our souls,
And plague injustice with the pains of hell.

B'BROKE   My Lord Northumberland, see them dispatched.

[*Northumberland and others depart with the prisoners*

Uncle, you say, the queen is at your house;
For God's sake fairly let her be entreated.
Tell her I send to her my kind commends;
Take special care my greetings be delivered.

YORK   A gentleman of mine I have dispatched   40
With letters of your love to her at large.

B'BROKE   Thanks, gentle uncle. Come, lords, away,
To fight with Glendower and his complices.
Awhile to work, and after holiday.   [*they go*

SCENE 2

Near the coast of Wales

KING RICHARD, *the* BISHOP OF CARLISLE, AUMERLE,
and Soldiers, newly disembarked

K.RICHARD   Barkloughly Castle call they this at hand?   = Harlech

AUMERLE   Yea, my lord. How brooks your grace the air,
After your late tossing on the breaking seas?

K.RICHARD   Needs must I like it well. I weep for joy
To stand upon my kingdom once again:
Dear earth, I do salute thee with my hand,
Though rebels wound thee with their horses' hoofs:
As a long-parted mother with her child
Plays fondly with her tears and smiles in meeting;
So, weeping, smiling, greet I thee, my earth,
And do thee favours with my royal hands;
Feed not thy sovereign's foe, my gentle earth,   10
Nor with thy sweets comfort his ravenous sense,
But let thy spiders that suck up thy venom,
And heavy-gaited toads, lie in their way,
Doing annoyance to the treacherous feet,
Which with usurping steps do trample thee.

           Yield stinging nettles to mine enemies:
           And when they from thy bosom pluck a flower,
           Guard it, I pray thee, with a lurking adder,   20
           Whose double tongue may with a mortal touch
           Throw death upon thy sovereign's enemies.
           Mock not my senseless conjuration, lords;
           This earth shall have a feeling, and these stones
           Prove arméd soldiers, ere her native king
           Shall falter under foul rebellion's arms.   [he rises

CARLISLE   Fear not, my lord. That Power that made you king,
           Hath power to keep you king in spite of all.
           The means that heaven yields must be embraced,
           And not neglected; else, if heaven would,   30
           And we will not, heaven's offer we refuse,
           The proffered means of succour and redress.

AUMERLE   He means, my lord, that we are too remiss,
           Whilst Bolingbroke, through our security,
           Grows strong and great in substance and in power.

K.RICHARD Discomfortable cousin! Know'st thou not
           That when the searching eye of heaven is hid,
           Behind the globe, that lights the lower world,
           Then thieves and robbers range abroad unseen,
           In murders and in outrage, boldly here;
           But when from under this terrestrial ball   40
           He fires the proud tops of the eastern pines,
           And darts his light through every guilty hole,
           Then murders, treasons, and detested sins,
           The cloak of night being plucked from off their backs,
           Stand bare and naked, trembling at themselves?
           So when this thief, this traitor, Bolingbroke,
           Who all this while hath revelled in the night,
           Whilst we were wand'ring with the antipodes,
           Shall see us rising in our throne the east,   50
           His treasons will sit blushing in his face,
           Not able to endure the sight of day,
           But self-affrighted tremble at his sin.
           Not all the water in the rough rude sea
           Can wash the balm off from an anointed king.
           The breath of worldly men cannot depose

The deputy elected by the Lord.
For every man that Bolingbroke hath pressed
To lift shrewd steel against our golden crown,
God for his Richard hath in heavenly pay   60
A glorious angel; then, if angels fight,
Weak men must fall, for heaven still guards the right.

SALISBURY *comes up*

Welcome, my lord: how far off lies your power?
SALISBURY Nor near nor farther off, my gracious lord,
Than this weak arm; discomfort guides my tongue,
And bids me speak of nothing but despair.
One day too late, I fear me, noble lord,
Hath clouded all thy happy days on earth:
O, call back yesterday, bid time return,
And thou shalt have twelve thousand fighting men!   70
Today, today, unhappy day too late,
O'erthrows thy joys, friends, fortune and thy state;
For all the Welshmen, hearing thou wert dead,
Are gone to Bolingbroke, dispersed and fled.
AUMERLE Comfort, my liege, why looks your grace so pale?
K.RICHARD But now the blood of twenty thousand men
Did triumph in my face, and they are fled:
And till so much blood thither come again,
Have I not reason to look pale and dead?
All souls that will be safe, fly from my side,   80
For time hath set a blot upon my pride.
AUMERLE Comfort, my liege, remember who you are.
K.RICHARD I had forgot myself, am I not king?
Awake, thou coward majesty! Thou sleepest.
Is not the king's name twenty thousand names?
Arm, arm, my name! A puny subject strikes
At thy great glory. Look not to the ground,
Ye favourites of a king, are we not high?
High be our thoughts. I know my uncle York
Hath power enough to serve our turn: but who
                                        comes here? 90

SCROOP *is seen approaching*

SCROOP   More health and happiness betide my liege
             Than can my care-tuned tongue deliver him.

K.RICHARD Mine ear is open, and my heart prepared;
             The worst is worldly loss thou canst unfold.
             Say, is my kingdom lost? Why, 'twas my care,
             And what loss is it to be rid of care?
             Strives Bolingbroke to be as great as we?
             Greater he shall not be. If he serve God,
             We'll serve him too, and be his fellow so:
             Revolt our subjects? That we cannot mend,   100
             They break their faith to God as well as us:
             Cry woe, destruction, ruin, and decay,
             The worst is death, and death will have his day.

SCROOP   Glad am I, that your highness is so armed
             To bear the tidings of calamity.
             Like an unseasonable stormy day,
             Which makes the silver rivers drown their shores,
             As if the world were all dissolved to tears;
             So high above his limits swells the rage
             Of Bolingbroke, covering your fearful land   110
             With hard bright steel, and hearts harder than steel.
             White-beards have armed their thin and hairless scalps
             Against thy majesty: boys, with women's voices,
             Strive to speak big and clap their female joints
             In stiff unwieldy arms against thy crown;
             Thy very beadsmen learn to bend their bows
             Of double-fatal yew against thy state,
             Yea, distaff-women manage rusty bills
             Against thy seat. Both young and old rebel,
             And all goes worse than I have power to tell.   120

K.RICHARD Too well, too well thou tell'st a tale so ill.
             Where is the Earl of Wiltshire? Where is Bagot?
             What is become of Bushy? Where is Green?
             That they have let the dangerous enemy
             Measure our confines with such peaceful steps?
             If we prevail, their heads shall pay for it:
             I warrant they have made peace with Bolingbroke.

SCROOP   Peace have they made with him, indeed, my lord.

K.RICHARD O villains, vipers, damned without redemption!

Dogs, easily won to fawn on any man!   130
Snakes, in my heart-blood warmed, that sting my heart!
Three Judases, each one thrice worse than Judas!
Would they make peace? Terrible hell
Make war upon their spotted souls for this!

SCROOP   Sweet love, I see, changing his property,
Turns to the sourest and most deadly hate.
Again uncurse their souls, their peace is made
With heads and not with hands; those whom you curse
Have felt the worst of death's destroying wound,
And lie full low graved in the hollow ground.   140

AUMERLE   Is Bushy, Green, and the Earl of Wiltshire dead?

SCROOP   Ay, all of them at Bristow lost their heads.

AUMERLE   Where is the duke my father with his power?

K.RICHARD   No matter where, of comfort no man speak:
Let's talk of graves, of worms, and epitaphs,
Make dust our paper, and with rainy eyes
Write sorrow on the bosom of the earth.
Let's choose executors and talk of wills:
And yet not so, for what can we bequeath,
Save our deposéd bodies to the ground?   150
Our lands, our lives, and all are Bolingbroke's,
And nothing can we call our own, but death,
And that small model of the barren earth,
Which serves as paste and cover to our bones.
For God's sake let us sit upon the ground,
And tell sad stories of the death of kings:
How some have been deposed, some slain in war,
Some haunted by the ghosts they have deposed,
Some poisoned by their wives, some sleeping killed;
All murdered – for within the hollow crown   160
That rounds the mortal temples of a king,
Keeps Death his court, and there the antic sits,
Scoffing his state and grinning at his pomp;
Allowing him a breath, a little scene,
To monarchise, be feared, and kill with looks,
Infusing him with self and vain conceit,
As if this flesh which walls about our life,
Were brass impregnable; and humoured thus,

Comes at the last, and with a little pin
Bores through his castle wall, and farewell king!   170
Cover your heads, and mock not flesh and blood
With solemn reverence, throw away respect,
Tradition, form, and ceremonious duty,
For you have but mistook me all this while:
I live with bread like you, feel want,
Taste grief, need friends – subjected thus,
How can you say to me, I am a king?

CARLISLE   My lord, wise men ne'er sit and wail their woes,   ①
But presently prevent the ways to wail.
To fear the foe, since fear oppresseth strength,   180
Gives in your weakness strength unto your foe,
And so your follies fight against yourself.   alliteration
Fear and be slain, no worse can come to fight,
And fight and die is death destroying death,
Where fearing dying pays death servile breath.

AUMERLE   My father hath a power; inquire of him,
And learn to make a body of a limb.

K.RICHARD Thou chid'st me well. Proud Bolingbroke, I come   Swings again
To change blows with thee for our day of doom.
This ague fit of fear is over-blown;   ''   190
An easy task it is to win our own.
Say, Scroop, where lies our uncle with his power?
Speak sweetly, man, although thy looks be sour.

SCROOP   Men judge by the complexion of the sky
The state and inclination of the day;
So may you by my dull and heavy eye,
My tongue hath but a heavier tale to say.
I play the torturer by small and small
To lengthen out the worst that must be spoken:
Blow 4   Your uncle York is joined with Bolingbroke,   200
And all your northern castles yielded up,
And all your southern gentlemen in arms
Upon his party.

K.RICHARD   Thou hast said enough.   [to Aumerle
Beshrew thee, cousin, which didst lead me forth
Of that sweet way I was in to despair!
What say you now? What comfort have we now?

> By heaven, I'll hate him everlastingly
> That bids me be of comfort any more.
> Go to Flint castle, there I'll pine away:
> A king, woe's slave, shall kingly woe obey.   210
> That power I have, discharge, and let them go
> To ear the land that hath some hope to grow,
> For I have none. Let no man speak again
> To alter this, for counsel is but vain.

AUMERLE My liege, one word.

K.RICHARD   He does me double wrong
> That wounds me with the flatteries of his tongue.
> Discharge my followers, let them hence away,
> From Richard's night, to Bolingbroke's fair day.

[they go

SCENE 3

Wales. Before Flint Castle

Enter marching with drum and colours, BOLINGBROKE, YORK,
NORTHUMBERLAND, *and their forces*

B'BROKE So that by this intelligence we learn
> The Welshmen are dispersed, and Salisbury
> Is gone to meet the king, who lately landed
> With some few private friends upon this coast.

NORTH. The news is very fair and good, my lord.
> Richard not far from hence hath hid his head.

YORK It would beseem the Lord Northumberland
> To say 'King Richard': alack the heavy day,
> When such a sacred king should hide his head.

NORTH. Your grace mistakes; only to be brief   10
> Left I his title out.

YORK   The time hath been,
> Would you have been so brief with him, he would
> Have been so brief with you, to shorten you,
> For taking so the head, your whole head's length.

B'BROKE Mistake not, uncle, further than you should.

YORK Take not, good cousin, further than you should,
> Lest you mistake: the heavens are o'er our heads.

B'BROKE   I know it, uncle, and oppose not myself
           Against their will. But who comes here?
                        Enter PERCY *(= 37 yrs old in fact)*

           Welcome, Harry; what, will not this castle yield?   20
PERCY   The castle royally is manned, my lord,
           Against thy entrance.
B'BROKE   Royally!
           Why, it contains no king?
PERCY   Yes, my good lord,
           It doth contain a king. King Richard lies
           Within the limits of yon lime and stone,
           And with him are the Lord Aumerle, Lord Salisbury,
           Sir Stephen Scroop, besides a clergyman
           Of holy reverence; who, I cannot learn.
NORTH.   O, belike it is the Bishop of Carlisle.   30
B'BROKE   Noble lord,   [*to Northumberland*
           Go to the rude ribs of that ancient castle;
           Through brazen trumpet send the breath of parley
           Into his ruined ears, and thus deliver:
           Henry Bolingbroke
           On both his knees doth kiss King Richard's hand,
           And sends allegiance and true faith of heart
           To his most royal person: hither come
           Even at his feet to lay my arms and power,
           Provided that my banishment repealed   40
           And lands restored again be freely granted;
           If not, I'll use the advantage of my power,
           And lay the summer's dust with showers of blood,
           Rained from the wounds of slaughtered Englishmen,
           The which, how far off from the mind of Bolingbroke
           It is such crimson tempest should bedrench
           The fresh green lap of fair King Richard's land,
           My stooping duty tenderly shall show.
           Go, signify as much, while here we march
           Upon the grassy carpet of this plain.   50
                              [*Northumberland advances to the
                                      castle, with a trumpeter*

Poetry from Bol.

What do we make of Bol here?

Wonderful
language
throughout

Let's march without the noise of threat'ning drum,
That from this castle's tattered battlements
Our fair appointments may be well perused.
Methinks, King Richard and myself should meet
With no less terror than the elements
Of fire and water, when their thund'ring shock
At meeting tears the cloudy cheeks of heaven.
Be he the fire, I'll be the yielding water;
The rage be his, whilst on the earth I rain
My waters – on the earth, and not on him.   60
March on, and mark King Richard how he looks.

NORTHUMBERLAND *sounds a parle without, and is*
answered within: then a flourish. Enter on the walls
KING RICHARD, *the* BISHOP OF CARLISLE, AUMERLE,
SCROOP, *and* SALISBURY

See, see, King Richard doth himself appear,
As doth the blushing discontented sun
From out the fiery portal of the east,
When he perceives the envious clouds are bent
To dim his glory, and to stain the track
Of his bright passage to the occident.
YORK   Yet looks he like a king. Behold his eye,
As bright as is the eagle's, lightens forth
Controlling majesty; alack, alack, for woe,   70
That any harm should stain so fair a show!
K.RICHARD [*to Northumberland*]
We are amazed, and thus long have we stood
To watch the fearful bending of thy knee,
Because we thought ourself thy lawful king:
And if we be, how dare thy joints forget
To pay their awful duty to our presence?
If we be not, show us the hand of God
That hath dismissed us from our stewardship;
For well we know no hand of blood and bone
Can gripe the sacred handle of our sceptre,
Unless he do profane, steal, or usurp.   80
And though you think that all, as you have done,
Have torn their souls, by turning them from us,

NB

And we are barren and bereft of friends,
Yet know my master, God omnipotent,
Is mustering in his clouds, on our behalf,
Armies of pestilence, and they shall strike
Your children yet unborn, and unbegot,
That lift your vassal hands against my head,
And threat the glory of my precious crown.   90
Tell Bolingbroke – for yon methinks he stands –
That every stride he makes upon my land
Is dangerous treason: he is come to open
The purple testament of bleeding war.
But ere the crown he looks for live in peace,
Ten thousand bloody crowns of mothers' sons
Shall ill become the flower of England's face,
Change the complexion of her maid-pale peace
To scarlet indignation, and bedew
Her pasture's grass with faithful English blood.   100

NORTH.   The king of heaven forbid our lord the king
Should so with civil and uncivil arms
Be rushed upon! Thy thrice noble cousin,
Harry Bolingbroke, doth humbly kiss thy hand,
And by the honourable tomb he swears,
That stands upon your royal grandsire's bones,
And by the royalties of both your bloods,
Currents that spring from one most gracious head,
And by the buried hand of warlike Gaunt,
And by the worth and honour of himself,   110
Comprising all that may be sworn or said:
His coming hither hath no further scope
Than for his lineal royalties, and to beg
Enfranchisement immediate on his knees,
Which on thy royal party granted once,
His glittering arms he will commend to rust,
His barbéd steeds to stables, and his heart
To faithful service of your majesty.
This swears he, as he is a prince, is just;
And, as I am a gentleman, I credit him.   120

K.RICHARD Northumberland, say thus the king returns:
His noble cousin is right welcome hither,

And all the number of his fair demands

Shall be accomplished without contradiction.
With all the gracious utterance thou hast,
Speak to his gentle hearing kind commends.

                    [*Richard turns to Aumerle*

We do debase ourselves, cousin, do we not,
To look so poorly, and to speak so fair?
Shall we call back Northumberland and send
Defiance to the traitor, and so die?   130

AUMERLE   No, good my lord; let's fight with gentle words,
          Till time lend friends, and friends their helpful swords.
K.RICHARD O God, O God! That e'er this tongue of mine,
          That laid the sentence of dread banishment
          On yon proud man, should take it off again
          With words of sooth! O, that I were as great
          As is my grief, or lesser than my name!
          Or that I could forget what I have been!
          Or not remember what I must be now!
          Swell'st thou, proud heart? I'll give thee scope to beat,   140
          Since foes have scope to beat both thee and me.
AUMERLE   Northumberland comes back from Bolingbroke.
K.RICHARD What must the king do now? Must he submit?

          The king shall do it. Must he be deposed?
          The king shall be contented. Must he lose
          The name of king? A God's name let it go:
          I'll give my jewels for a set of beads,
          My gorgeous palace for a hermitage,
          My gay apparel for an almsman's gown,
          My figured goblets for a dish of wood,   150
          My sceptre for a palmer's walking-staff,
          My subjects for a pair of carvéd saints,
          And my large kingdom for a little grave,
          A little, little grave, an obscure grave;
          Or I'll be buried in the king's highway,
          Some way of common trade, where subjects' feet
          May hourly trample on their sovereign's head;
          For on my heart they tread now whilst I live:
          And buried once, why not upon my head?
          Aumerle, thou weep'st, my tender-hearted cousin.   160

We'll make foul weather with despiséd tears;

Our sighs and they shall lodge the summer corn, = beat down.

And make a dearth in this revolting land:

Or shall we play the wantons with our woes,

And make some pretty match with shedding tears? = game

As thus to drop them still upon one place,

Till they have fretted us a pair of graves

Within the earth, and therein laid: there lies

Two kinsmen digged their graves with weeping eyes.

puns   Would not this ill do well? Well, well, I see   170

✓✓   I talk but idly, and you laugh at me.

Most mighty prince, my Lord Northumberland,

What says King Bolingbroke? Will his majesty

Give Richard leave to live till Richard die?

You make a leg, and Bolingbroke says 'ay'.

NORTH.   My lord, in the base court he doth attend,

To speak with you; may it please you to come down?

K.RICHARD Down, down I come, like glist'ring Phaethon:

Wanting the manage of unruly jades.

emphasis   In the base court? Base court, where kings grow base, 180

on word   To come at traitors' calls, and do them grace.

In the base court? Come down? Down court!

Down king!

For night-owls shriek where mounting larks should sing.

[*he goes down from the battlements*

B'BROKE   [*coming forward*] What says his majesty?

NORTH.   Sorrow and grief of heart

Makes him speak fondly like a frantic man,

Yet he is come.

KING RICHARD, *the* DUKE OF YORK *and attendants come forth*

B'BROKE   Stand all apart,

And show fair duty to his majesty.

My gracious lord –   [*'he kneels down'*

K.RICHARD Fair cousin, you debase your princely knee,   190

To make the base earth proud with kissing it:

Me rather had my heart might feel your love,

Than my unpleased eye see your courtesy.

Up, cousin, up – your heart is up, I know,

Thus high at least, [*touching his own head*]
                    although your knee below.

B'BROKE   My gracious lord, I come but for mine own.   NB

K.RICHARD Your own is yours, and I am yours, and all.

B'BROKE   So far be mine, my most redoubted lord,
           As my true service shall deserve your love.

K.RICHARD Well you deserve: they well deserve to have,   200
           That know the strong'st and surest way to get.
           Uncle, give me your hands, nay, dry your eyes;
           Tears show their love, but want their remedies.
           Cousin, I am too young to be your father,
           Though you are old enough to be my heir.
           What you will have, I'll give, and willing too,
           For do we must, what force will have us do.
           Set on towards London, cousin, is it so?

B'BROKE   Yea, my good lord.

K.RICHARD   Then I must not say no.

                                                   [*they go*

                              SCENE 4

                     The Duke of York's garden

                     Enter the QUEEN *and two ladies*

Stylised conversation

QUEEN   What sport shall we devise here in this garden,
           To drive away the heavy thought of care?

LADY   Madam, we'll play at bowls.

QUEEN   'Twill make me think the world is full of rubs,
           And that my fortune runs against the bias.

LADY   Madam, we'll dance.

QUEEN   My legs can keep no measure in delight,
           When my poor heart no measure keeps in grief.
           Therefore, no dancing, girl: some other sport.

LADY   Madam, we'll tell tales.   10

QUEEN   Of sorrow or of joy?

LADY   Of either, madam.

QUEEN   Of neither, girl:
           For if of joy, being altogether wanting,

It doth remember me the more of sorrow;
Or if of grief, being altogether had,
It adds more sorrow to my want of joy:
For what I have I need not to repeat,
And what I want it boots not to complain.

LADY   Madam, I'll sing.

QUEEN   'Tis well that thou hast cause;
But thou shouldst please me better, wouldst thou weep. 20

LADY   I could weep, madam, would it do you good.

QUEEN   And I could sing, would weeping do me good,
And never borrow any tear of thee.

                'Enter Gardeners'

But stay, here come the gardeners.
Let's step into the shadow of these trees.
My wretchedness unto a row of pins,
They will talk of state, for every one doth so
Against a change: woe is forerun with woe.

                  [*The Queen and her ladies retire*

GARDENER [*to one of his men*]
      Go, bind thou up yon dangling apricocks,
Which like unruly children make their sire   30
Stoop with oppression of their prodigal weight;
Give some supportance to the bending twigs.
[*to the other*] Go thou, and like an executioner
Cut off the heads of too fast growing sprays,
That look too lofty in our commonwealth:
All must be even in our government.
You thus employed, I will go root away
The noisome weeds which without profit suck
The soil's fertility from wholesome flowers.

MAN   Why should we, in the compass of a pale,   40
Keep law and form and due proportion,
Showing as in a model our firm estate,
When our sea-walléd garden, the whole land,
Is full of weeds, her fairest flowers choked up,
Her fruit trees all unpruned, her hedges ruined,
Her knots disordered, and her wholesome herbs
Swarming with caterpillars?

GARDENER   Hold thy peace.

He that hath suffered this disordered spring
Hath now himself met with the fall of leaf.
The weeds which his broad-spreading leaves did shelter,   50
That seemed in eating him to hold him up,
Are plucked up root and all by Bolingbroke –
I mean the Earl of Wiltshire, Bushy, Green.

MAN   What, are they dead?

GARDENER   They are, and Bolingbroke
Hath seized the wasteful king. O, what pity is it
That he had not so trimmed and dressed his land,
As we this garden! We at time of year
Do wound the bark, the skin of our fruit trees,
Lest being over-proud in sap and blood,
With too much riches it confound itself.   60
Had he done so to great and growing men,
They might have lived to bear, and he to taste,
Their fruits of duty. Superfluous branches
We lop away, that bearing boughs may live:
Had he done so, himself had borne the crown,
Which waste of idle hours hath quite thrown down.

MAN   What, think you then the king shall be deposed?

GARDENER Depressed he is already, and deposed
'Tis doubt he will be. Letters came last night
To a dear friend of the good Duke of York's,   70
That tell black tidings.

QUEEN   O, I am pressed to death through want of speaking!
                                              [comes forth
Thou, old Adam's likeness, set to dress this garden,
How dares thy harsh rude tongue sound this
                                              unpleasing news?
What Eve, what serpent, hath suggested thee
To make a second fall of cursèd man?
Why dost thou say King Richard is deposed?
Dar'st thou, thou little better thing than earth,
Divine his downfal? Say, where, when, and how,
Cam'st thou by these ill tidings? Speak, thou wretch!   80

GARDENER Pardon me, madam. Little joy have I
To breathe this news, yet what I say is true.
King Richard, he is in the mighty hold

Of Bolingbroke: their fortunes both are weighed.
In your lord's scale is nothing but himself,
And some few vanities that make him light;
But in the balance of great Bolingbroke,
Besides himself, are all the English peers,
And with that odds he weighs King Richard down.
Post you to London, and you will find it so;   90
I speak no more than every one doth know.

QUEEN   Nimble mischance, that art so light of foot,
Doth not thy embassage belong to me,
And am I last that knows it? O, thou thinkest
To serve me last, that I may longest keep
Thy sorrow in my breast. Come, ladies, go,
To meet at London London's king in woe.
What, was I born to this, that my sad look
Should grace the triumph of great Bolingbroke?
Gardener, for telling me these news of woe,   100
Pray God the plants thou graft'st may never grow.
                 [*she leaves the garden with her ladies*

GARDENER   Poor queen, so that thy state might be no worse,
I would my skill were subject to thy curse.
Here did she fall a tear, here in this place
I'll set a bank of rue, sour herb of grace.
Rue, even for ruth, here shortly shall be seen,
In the remembrance of a weeping queen.
                             [*they go*

ACT 4 SCENE I

Westminster Hall, with the king's throne

Enter as to the Parliament BOLINGBROKE, AUMERLE, SURREY,
NORTHUMBERLAND, PERCY, FITZWATER, *and other lords,*
the BISHOP OF CARLISLE, *and the* ABBOT OF WESTMINSTER;
Herald and Officers with BAGOT

B'BROKE	Call forth Bagot. [*he is brought forward*
	Now, Bagot, freely speak thy mind,
	What thou dost know of noble Gloucester's death,
	Who wrought it with the king, and who performed
	The bloody office of his timeless end.
BAGOT	Then set before my face the Lord Aumerle.
B'BROKE	Cousin, stand forth, and look upon that man.
BAGOT	My Lord Aumerle, I know your daring tongue
	Scorns to unsay what once it hath delivered.
	In that dead time when Gloucester's death was plotted, 10
	I heard you say, 'Is not my arm of length,
	That reacheth from the restful English court
	As far as Calais, to my uncle's head?'
	Amongst much other talk that very time
	I heard you say that you had rather refuse
	The offer of an hundred thousand crowns
	Than Bolingbroke's return to England;
	Adding withal, how blest this land would be,
	In this your cousin's death.
AUMERLE	Princes and noble lords,
	What answer shall I make to this base man? 20
	Shall I so much dishonour my fair stars,
	On equal terms to give him chastisement?
	Either I must, or have mine honour soiled
	With the attainder of his slanderous lips.
	There is my gage, the manual seal of death,
	That marks thee out for hell! I say thou liest,
	And will maintain what thou hast said is false
	In thy heart-blood, though being all too base

(handwritten marginalia:)

① Confusion of chronology

① Trying to discover facts abt G's death
But TURMOIL of accusation + counter-
                                        accusation

	To stain the temper of my knightly sword.	
B'BROKE	Bagot, forbear, thou shalt not take it up.	30
AUMERLE	Excepting one, I would he were the best	
	In all this presence that hath moved me so.	
FITZWATER	If that thy valour stand on sympathy,	
	There is my gage, Aumerle, in gage to thine:	
	By that fair sun which shows me where thou stand'st,	
	I heard thee say, and vauntingly thou spak'st it,	
	That thou wert cause of noble Gloucester's death.	
	If thou deniest it twenty times, thou liest,	
	And I will turn thy falsehood to thy heart,	
	Where it was forgéd, with my rapier's point.	40
AUMERLE	Thou dar'st not, coward, live to see that day.	
FITZWATER	Now, by my soul, I would it were this hour.	
AUMERLE	Fitzwater, thou art damned to hell for this.	
PERCY	Aumerle, thou liest, his honour is as true	
	In this appeal as thou art all unjust;	
	And that thou art so, there I throw my gage,	
	To prove it on thee to the extremest point	
	Of mortal breathing. Seize it if thou dar'st.	
AUMERLE	An if I do not, may my hands rot off,	
	And never brandish more revengeful steel	50
	Over the glittering helmet of my foe!	
A LORD	I task the earth to the like, forsworn Aumerle,	
	And spur thee on with full as many lies	
	As may be holloa'd in thy treacherous ear	
	From sun to sun. There is my honour's pawn;	
	Engage it to the trial if thou darest.	
AUMERLE	Who sets me else? By heaven, I'll throw at all!	
	I have a thousand spirits in one breast,	
	To answer twenty thousand such as you.	
SURREY	My Lord Fitzwater, I do remember well	60
	The very time Aumerle and you did talk.	
FITZWATER	'Tis very true, you were in presence then,	
	And you can witness with me this is true.	
SURREY	As false, by heaven, as heaven itself is true.	
FITZWATER	Surrey, thou liest.	
SURREY	Dishonourable boy!	

[handwritten marginal note: Dramatic moment.]

This scene takes us back to Act 1 with accusations of treason over his death.

That lie shall lie so heavy on my sword,
That it shall render vengeance and revenge,
Till thou the lie-giver, and that lie, do lie
In earth as quiet as thy father's skull.
In proof whereof, there is my honour's pawn: 70
Engage it to the trial if thou dar'st.

FITZWATER How fondly dost thou spur a forward horse!
If I dare eat, or drink, or breathe, or live,
I dare meet Surrey in a wilderness,
And spit upon him, whilst I say he lies,
And lies, and lies: there is my bond of faith,
To tie thee to my strong correction.
As I intend to thrive in this new world,
Aumerle is guilty of my true appeal.
Besides, I heard the banished Norfolk say   80
That thou, Aumerle, didst send two of thy men
To execute the noble duke at Calais.

AUMERLE Some honest Christian trust me with a gage,
That Norfolk lies; here do I throw down this,
If he may be repealed to try his honour.

B'BROKE These differences shall all rest under gage,
Till Norfolk be repealed. Repealed he shall be,

just note.

And, though mine enemy, restored again
To all his lands and signories: when he's returned,
Against Aumerle we will enforce his trial.   90

CARLISLE That honourable day shall ne'er be seen.
Many a time hath banished Norfolk fought
For Jesu Christ in glorious Christian field,
Streaming the ensign of the Christian cross
Against black pagans, Turks, and Saracens,
And, toiled with works of war, retired himself
To Italy, and there at Venice gave
His body to that pleasant country's earth,
And his pure soul unto his captain Christ
Under whose colours he had fought so long.   100

B'BROKE Why, bishop, is Norfolk dead?

CARLISLE As surely as I live, my lord.

B'BROKE Sweet peace conduct his sweet soul to the bosom
Of good old Abraham! Lords appellants,

Bol acting as king.

A much lengthier process in Holinshed

> Your differences shall all rest under gage,
> Till we assign you to your days of trial.

YORK enters

YORK   Great Duke of Lancaster, I come to thee
            From plume-plucked Richard, who with willing soul
            Adopts thee heir, and his high sceptre yields
            To the possession of thy royal hand.   110
            Ascend his throne, descending now from him,
            And long live Henry, of that name the fourth!

B'BROKE   In God's name, I'll ascend the regal throne.   (1)

CARLISLE   Marry, God forbid!
            Worst in this royal presence may I speak,   ?
            Yet best beseeming me to speak the truth.
            Would God that any in this noble presence
            Were enough noble to be upright judge
            Of noble Richard. Then true noblesse would
            Learn him forbearance from so foul a wrong.   120
            What subject can give sentence on his king?
            And who sits here that is not Richard's subject?
            Thieves are not judged but they are by to hear,
            Although apparent guilt be seen in them;
            And shall the figure of God's majesty,   *Divine R*
            His captain, steward, deputy-elect,   *of K.*
            Anointed, crownéd, planted many years,
            Be judged by subject and inferior breath,
            And he himself not present? O, forfend it, God,
            That in a Christian climate souls refined   130
            Should show so heinous, black, obscene a deed!
            I speak to subjects, and a subject speaks,
            Stirred up by God thus boldly for his king.
            My Lord of Hereford here, whom you call king,
            Is a foul traitor to proud Hereford's king,
            And if you crown him, let me prophesy,
            The blood of English shall manure the ground,
            And future ages groan for this foul act;
            Peace shall go sleep with Turks and infidels,
            And, in this seat of peace, tumultuous wars   140
            Shall kin with kin, and kind with kind confound;

civil war

Upset of order

Disorder, horror, fear, and mutiny
Shall here inhabit, and this land be called
The field of Golgotha and dead men's skulls.
O, if you raise this house against this house,
It will the woefullest division prove
That ever fell upon this curséd earth.
Prevent it, resist it, let it not be so,
Lest child, child's children, cry against you woe.

NORTH·   Well have you argued, sir, and, for your pains,   150

Dramatic moment

Of capital treason we arrest you here:
My Lord of Westminster, be it your charge
To keep him safely till his day of trial.
May it please you, lords, to grant the commons' suit?

B'BROKE   Fetch hither Richard, that in common view
He may surrender; so we shall proceed   *must be*
Without suspicion.   *done openly*

YORK   I will be his conduct.   *[he goes*

B'BROKE   Lords, you that here are under our arrest,   *cf p 161*
Procure your sureties for your days of answer:
Little are we beholding to your love,   160
And little looked for at your helping hands.

YORK *returns with* KING RICHARD, *guarded and stripped of his royal
robes; Officers follow bearing the Crown, etc.*

K. RICHARD Alack, why am I sent for to a king,
Before I have shook off the regal thoughts
Wherewith I reigned? I hardly yet have learned
To insinuate, flatter, bow, and bend my knee:
Give sorrow leave awhile to tutor me
To this submission. Yet I well remember
The favours of these men: were they not mine?
Did they not sometime cry 'all hail!' to me?

cf p 166 So Judas did to Christ: but he, in twelve,   170
Found truth in all but one; I, in twelve
                                      thousand, none.
God save the king! Will no man say amen?
Am I both priest and clerk? Well then, amen.
God save the king! Although I be not he;
And yet, amen, if heaven do think him me.

To do what service am I sent for hither?

YORK   To do that office of thine own good will,
Which tired majesty did make thee offer:
The resignation of thy state and crown
To Henry Bolingbroke.   180

K.RICHARD Give me the crown. Here, cousin, seize the crown:
Here, cousin,
On this side, my hand, and on that side, thine.
Now is this golden crown like a deep well
That owes two buckets, filling one another,
The emptier ever dancing in the air,
The other down, unseen, and full of water:
That bucket down, and full of tears, am I,
Drinking my griefs, whilst you mount up on high.

B'BROKE   I thought you had been willing to resign.   190

K.RICHARD My crown I am, but still my griefs are mine:
You may my glories and my state depose,
But not my griefs; still am I king of those.

B'BROKE   Part of your cares you give me with your crown.

K.RICHARD Your cares set up do not pluck my cares down.
My care is loss of care, by old care done,
Your care is gain of care, by new care won:
The cares I give, I have, though given away;
They tend the crown, yet still with me they stay.

B'BROKE   Are you contented to resign the crown?   200

K.RICHARD Ay, no; no, ay; for I must nothing be:
Therefore no 'no', for I resign to thee.
Now mark me how I will undo myself:
I give this heavy weight from off my head,
And this unwieldy sceptre from my hand,
The pride of kingly sway from out my heart;
With mine own tears I wash away my balm,
With mine own hands I give away my crown,
With mine own tongue deny my sacred state,
With mine own breath release all duteous oaths.   210
All pomp and majesty I do forswear;
My manors, rents, revenues, I forgo;
My acts, decrees, and statutes, I deny:
God pardon all oaths that are broke to me!

God keep all vows unbroke are made to thee!
Make me, that nothing have, with nothing grieved,
And thou with all pleased, that hast all achieved!
Long mayst thou live in Richard's seat to sit,
And soon lie Richard in an earthy pit.
God save King Henry, unkinged Richard says,   220
And send him many years of sunshine days.
What more remains?

NORTH.   No more, but that you read
These accusations and these grievous crimes,
Committed by your person and your followers
Against the state and profit of this land;
That, by confessing them, the souls of men
May deem that you are worthily deposed.

K. RICHARD Must I do so? And must I ravel out
My weaved-up follies? Gentle Northumberland,
If thy offences were upon record,   230
Would it not shame thee, in so fair a troop,
To read a lecture of them? If thou wouldst,
There shouldst thou find one heinous article,
Containing the deposing of a king,
And cracking the strong warrant of an oath,
Marked with a blot, damned in the book of heaven.
Nay, all of you, that stand and look upon me,
Whilst that my wretchedness doth bait myself,
Though some of you, with Pilate, wash your hands,
Showing an outward pity; yet you Pilates   240
Have here delivered me to my sour cross,
And water cannot wash away your sin.

NORTH. My lord, dispatch, read o'er these articles.

K. RICHARD Mine eyes are full of tears, I cannot see:
And yet salt water blinds them not so much,
But they can see a sort of traitors here.
Nay, if I turn mine eyes upon myself,
I find myself a traitor with the rest:
For I have given here my soul's consent
T' undeck the pompous body of a king;   250
Made glory base, and sovereignty a slave,
Proud majesty a subject, state a peasant.

NORTH.   My lord —

K.RICHARD No lord of thine, thou haught, insulting man,
           Nor no man's lord; I have no name, no title,
           No, not that name was given me at the font,
           But 'tis usurped: alack the heavy day,
           That I have worn so many winters out,
           And know not now what name to call myself!
           O, that I were a mockery king of snow,   260
           Standing before the sun of Bolingbroke,
           To melt myself away in water drops!
           Good king, great king, and yet not greatly good,
           An if my word be sterling yet in England,
           Let it command a mirror hither straight,
           That it may show me what a face I have,
           Since it is bankrupt of his majesty.

B'BROKE   Go some of you, and fetch a looking-glass.

                               [an attendant goes out

NORTH.   Read o'er this paper, while the glass doth come.

K.RICHARD Fiend, thou torments me ere I come to hell.   270

B'BROKE   Urge it no more, my Lord Northumberland.

NORTH.   The commons will not then be satisfied.

K.RICHARD They shall be satisfied; I'll read enough,
           When I do see the very book indeed
           Where all my sins are writ, and that's myself.

          The attendant returns with a glass

           Give me that glass, and therein will I read.
           No deeper wrinkles yet? Hath sorrow struck
           So many blows upon this face of mine,
           And made no deeper wounds? O, flatt'ring glass,
           Like to my followers in prosperity,   280
           Thou dost beguile me! Was this face the face
           That every day under his household roof
           Did keep ten thousand men? Was this the face
           That like the sun did make beholders wink?
           Was this the face that faced so many follies,
           And was at last out-faced by Bolingbroke?
           A brittle glory shineth in this face;
           As brittle as the glory is the face.

                        [he dashes the glass to the ground

For there it is, cracked in a hundred shivers.
Mark, silent king, the moral of this sport,   290
How soon my sorrow hath destroyed my face.

B'BROKE   The shadow of your sorrow hath destroyed
The shadow of your face.

K.RICHARD   Say that again.
The shadow of my sorrow – ha! Let's see:
'Tis very true, my grief lies all within,
And these external manners of lament
Are merely shadows to the unseen grief,
That swells with silence in the tortured soul.
There lies the substance; and I thank thee, king,
For thy great bounty, that not only giv'st   300
Me cause to wail, but teachest me the way
How to lament the cause. I'll beg one boon,
And then be gone, and trouble you no more.
Shall I obtain it?

B'BROKE   Name it, fair cousin.

K.RICHARD Fair cousin! I am greater than a king.
For when I was a king, my flatterers
Were then but subjects; being now a subject,
I have a king here to my flatterer.
Being so great, I have no need to beg.

B'BROKE   Yet ask.   310

K.RICHARD And shall I have?

B'BROKE   You shall.

K.RICHARD Then give me leave to go.

B'BROKE   Whither?

K.RICHARD Whither you will, so I were from your sights.

B'BROKE   Go, some of you, convey him to the Tower.

K.RICHARD O, good! Convey! Conveyers are you all,
That rise thus nimbly by a true king's fall.

                          [certain lords conduct Richard
                              guarded from the hall

B'BROKE   On Wednesday next we solemnly set down
Our coronation: lords, prepare yourselves.   320

BOLINGBROKE *and the Lords depart in procession:* the ABBOT OF
WESTMINSTER, *the* BISHOP OF CARLISLE *and* AUMERLE *linger behind*

ABBOT	A woeful pageant have we here beheld.
CARLISLE	The woe's to come – the children yet unborn
	Shall feel this day as sharp to them as thorn.
AUMERLE	You holy clergymen, is there no plot
	To rid the realm of this pernicious blot?
ABBOT	My lord,
	Before I freely speak my mind herein,
(X)	You shall not only take the sacrament
	To bury mine intents, but also to effect
	Whatever I shall happen to devise.
	I see your brows are full of discontent,
	Your hearts of sorrow, and your eyes of tears.
	Come home with me to supper; I will lay
	A plot shall show us all a merry day.

The problems of valuing the sacrament by force.

330

[they go

ACT 5 SCENE I

London. A street leading to the Tower

'Enter the QUEEN *with her attendants'*

QUEEN   This way the king will come, this is the way
     To Julius Caesar's ill-erected tower,
     To whose flint bosom my condemnèd lord
     Is doomed a prisoner by proud Bolingbroke.
     Here let us rest, if this rebellious earth
     Have any resting for her true king's queen.

     RICHARD *with guards comes into the street*

     But soft, but see, or rather do not see,
     My fair rose wither. Yet look up, behold,
     That you in pity may dissolve to dew,
     And wash him fresh again with true-love tears.   10
     Ah, thou, the model where old Troy did stand!
     Thou map of honour, thou King Richard's tomb,
     And not King Richard; thou most beauteous inn,
     Why should hard-favoured grief be lodged in thee,
     When triumph is become an alehouse guest?

K. RICHARD Join not with grief, fair woman, do not so,
     To make my end too sudden. Learn, good soul,
     To think our former state a happy dream,
     From which awaked, the truth of what we are
     Shows us but this: I am sworn brother, sweet,   20
     To grim Necessity, and he and I
     Will keep a league till death. Hie thee to France,
     And cloister thee in some religious house.
     Our holy lives must win a new world's crown,
     Which our profane hours here have throwen down.

QUEEN   What, is my Richard both in shape and mind
     Transformed and weak'ned? Hath Bolingbroke
                              deposed
     Thine intellect? Hath he been in thy heart?
     The lion dying thrusteth forth his paw,
     And wounds the earth, if nothing else, with rage   30

Handwritten: ① How do we regard R o R?

    To be o'erpowered; and wilt thou pupil-like
    Take the correction, mildly kiss the rod,
    And fawn on rage with base humility,
    Which art a lion and the king of beasts?   *NB*

K.RICHARD   A king of beasts, indeed! If aught but beasts,
    I had been still a happy king of men.
    Good sometimes queen, prepare thee hence for France.
    Think I am dead, and that even here thou takest
    As from my death-bed thy last living leave;
    In winter's tedious nights sit by the fire   40
    With good old folks, and let them tell thee tales *pathos*
    Of woeful ages long ago betid;
    And ere thou bid good night, to quit their griefs,
    Tell thou the lamentable fall of me,   *= tragedy*
    And send the hearers weeping to their beds:
    For why, the senseless brands will sympathise
    The heavy accent of thy moving tongue,
    And in compassion weep the fire out,
    And some will mourn in ashes, some coal-black,
    For the deposing of a rightful king.   50

         NORTHUMBERLAND *comes up*

NORTH.   My lord, the mind of Bolingbroke is changed;
    You must to Pomfret, not unto the Tower.
    And, madam, there is order ta'en for you,
    With all swift speed you must away to France.

K.RICHARD   Northumberland, thou ladder wherewithal
    The mounting Bolingbroke ascends my throne,
    The time shall not be many hours of age
    More than it is, ere foul sin gathering head
    Shall break into corruption. Thou shalt think,
    Though he divide the realm and give thee half,   60
    It is too little, helping him to all.
    And he shall think that thou, which knowest the way
    To plant unrightful kings, wilt know again,
    Being ne'er so little urged another way,
    To pluck him headlong from the usurped throne.
    The love of wicked men converts to fear,
    That fear to hate, and hate turns one or both

Handwritten: ② Prophecy of rebellion. H IV 1.

To worthy danger and deservéd death.

NORTH.   My guilt be on my head, and there an end:
         Take leave and part, for you must part forthwith.   *Blunt*   70

K.RICHARD Doubly divorced! Bad men, you violate
         A twofold marriage – 'twixt my crown and me,
         And then betwixt me and my married wife.
         Let me unkiss the oath 'twixt thee and me;
         And yet not so, for with a kiss 'twas made.
         Part us, Northumberland: I towards the north,
         Where shivering cold and sickness pines the clime;
         My wife to France, from whence set forth in pomp
         She came adornéd hither like sweet May,
         Sent back like Hallowmas or short'st of day.   80

QUEEN   And must we be divided? Must we part?

K.RICHARD Ay, hand from hand, my love, and heart from heart.

QUEEN   Banish us both, and send the king with me.

NORTH.   That were some love, but little policy.

QUEEN   Then whither he goes, thither let me go.

K.RICHARD So two, together weeping, make one woe.
         Weep thou for me in France, I for thee here;
         Better far off than near, be ne'er the near.
         Go, count thy way with sighs, I mine with groans.

QUEEN   So longest way shall have the longest moans.   90

K.RICHARD Twice for one step I'll groan, the way being short,
         And piece the way out with a heavy heart.
         Come, come, in wooing sorrow let's be brief,
         Since, wedding it, there is such length in grief.
         One kiss shall stop our mouths, and dumbly part;
         Thus give I mine, and thus take I thy heart.   [*they kiss*

QUEEN   Give me mine own again; 'twere no good part
         To take on me to keep and kill thy heart.
                                               [*they kiss again*
         So, now I have mine own again, be gone,
         That I may strive to kill it with a groan.   100

K.RICHARD We make woe wanton with this fond delay.
         Once more, adieu; the rest let sorrow say.
                                                    [*they go*

SCENE 2

The Duke of York's palace

The DUKE OF YORK *and the* DUCHESS

DUCHESS My lord, you told me you would tell the rest,
When weeping made you break the story off,
Of our two cousins coming into London.

YORK Where did I leave?

DUCHESS   At that sad stop, my lord,
Where rude misgoverned hands, from windows' tops,
Threw dust and rubbish on King Richard's head.

YORK Then, as I said, the duke, great Bolingbroke,
Mounted upon a hot and fiery steed,
Which his aspiring rider seemed to know,
With slow but stately pace kept on his course,   10
Whilst all tongues cried 'God save thee, Bolingbroke!'
You would have thought the very windows spake,
So many greedy looks of young and old
Through casements darted their desiring eyes
Upon his visage, and that all the walls
With painted imagery had said at once
'Jesu preserve thee! Welcome, Bolingbroke!'
Whilst he from one side to the other turning,
Bareheaded, lower than his proud steed's neck,
Bespake them thus: 'I thank you, countrymen':   20
And thus still doing, thus he passed along.

DUCHESS Alack, poor Richard! Where rode he the whilst?

YORK As in a theatre the eyes of men,
After a well-graced actor leaves the stage,
Are idly bent on him that enters next,
Thinking his prattle to be tedious;
Even so, or with much more contempt, men's eyes
Did scowl on Richard; no man cried, 'God save him!'
No joyful tongue gave him his welcome home,
But dust was thrown upon his sacred head;   30
Which with such gentle sorrow he shook off,
His face still combating with tears and smiles,
The badges of his grief and patience,

That had not God for some strong purpose steeled
The hearts of men, they must perforce have melted,
And barbarism itself have pitied him.
But heaven hath a hand in these events,
To whose high will we bound our calm contents.
To Bolingbroke are we sworn subjects now,
Whose state and honour I for aye allow.   40

AUMERLE *comes to the door*

DUCHESS Here comes my son Aumerle.
YORK   Aumerle that was,
But that is lost for being Richard's friend.
And, madam, you must call him Rutland now:
I am in parliament pledge for his truth
And lasting fealty to the new-made king.
DUCHESS Welcome, my son. Who are the violets now,
That strew the green lap of the new come spring?
AUMERLE Madam, I know not, nor I greatly care not.
God knows I had as lief be none as one.
YORK Well, bear you well in this new spring of time,   50
Lest you be cropped before you come to prime.
What news from Oxford? Do these justs and
                                        triumphs hold?
AUMERLE For aught I know, my lord, they do.
YORK You will be there, I know.
AUMERLE If God prevent not, I purpose so.
YORK What seal is that, that hangs without thy bosom?
Yea, look'st thou pale? Let me see the writing.
AUMERLE My lord, 'tis nothing.
YORK   No matter then who see it.
I will be satisfied; let me see the writing.
AUMERLE I do beseech your grace to pardon me;   60
It is a matter of small consequence,
Which for some reasons I would not have seen.
YORK Which for some reasons, sir, I mean to see.
I fear, I fear –
DUCHESS   What should you fear?
'Tis nothing but some bond that he is ent'red into
For gay apparel 'gainst the triumph day.

YORK	Bound to himself! What doth he with a bond,
	That he is bound to? Wife, thou art a fool.
	Boy, let me see the writing.
AUMERLE	I do beseech you, pardon me, I may not show it. 70
YORK	I will be satisfied; let me see it, I say.

               [*'he plucks it out of his bosom and reads it'*

✓ H IV

	<u>Treason</u>! Foul treason! Villain! Traitor! Slave!
DUCHESS	What is the matter, my lord? (1)
YORK	Ho! Who is within there? Saddle my horse.

                           [*he reads again*

	God for his mercy! What treachery is here!
DUCHESS	Why, what is it, my lord? (1 b)
YORK	Give me my boots, I say; saddle my horse.

                           [*he reads again*

	Now by mine honour, by my life, by my troth,
	I will appeach the villain.
DUCHESS	What is the matter? (1c)
YORK	Peace, foolish woman. 80
DUCHESS	I will not peace. What is the matter, Aumerle? (1 d)
AUMERLE	Good mother, be content – it is no more
	Than my poor life must answer.
DUCHESS	Thy life answer!
YORK	Bring me my boots, I will unto the king.

              '*His man enters with his boots*'

DUCHESS	Strike him, Aumerle. Poor boy, thou art amazed.
	Hence, villain! Never more come in my sight.
YORK	Give me my boots, I say. [*the man helps him into them*
DUCHESS	Why, York, what wilt thou do?
	Wilt thou not hide the trespass of thine own?
	<u>Have</u> we <u>more sons</u>? Or are we like to have?
	Is not my teeming date drunk up with time? 90
	And wilt thou pluck my fair son from mine age,
	And rob me of a happy mother's name?
	Is he not like thee? Is he not thine own?
YORK	Thou fond mad woman,
	Wilt thou conceal this dark conspiracy?
	A dozen of them here have <u>ta'en the sacrament</u>, (X) f p 187
	And interchangeably set down their hands,

To kill the king at Oxford.

DUCHESS   He shall be none.
We'll keep him here, then what is that to him?   100

YORK   Away, fond woman! Were he twenty times my son,
I would appeach him.

DUCHESS   Hadst thou groaned for him
As I have done, thou wouldst be more pitiful.
But now I know thy mind: thou dost suspect
That I have been disloyal to thy bed,
And that he is a bastard, not thy son:
Sweet York, sweet husband, be not of that mind,
He is as like thee as a man may be,
Not like to me, or any of my kin,
And yet I love him.

YORK   Make way, unruly woman.   110

[he goes

DUCHESS   After, Aumerle; mount thee upon his horse,
Spur post, and get before him to the king,
And beg thy pardon ere he do accuse thee.
I'll not be long behind; though I be old,
I doubt not but to ride as fast as York,
And never will I rise up from the ground,
Till Bolingbroke have pardoned thee: away, be gone!

[they hurry out

SCENE 3

Windsor Castle

Enter BOLINGBROKE, PERCY *and other nobles*

B'BROKE   Can no man tell me of my unthrifty son?
'Tis full three months since I did see him last.
If any plague hang over us, 'tis he:
I would to God, my lords, he might be found.
Inquire at London, 'mongst the taverns there,
For there, they say, he daily doth frequent,
With unrestrainèd loose companions,
Even such, they say, as stand in narrow lanes,

	And beat our watch, and rob our passengers,	
	While he, young wanton and effeminate boy,	10
	Takes on the point of honour to support	
	So dissolute a crew.	
PERCY	My lord, some two days since I saw the prince,	
	And told him of those triumphs held at Oxford.	
B'BROKE	And what said the gallant?	
PERCY	His answer was, he would unto the stews,	
	And from the common'st creature pluck a glove,	
	And wear it as a favour, and with that	
	He would unhorse the lustiest challenger.	
B'BROKE	As dissolute as desperate; yet through both	20
	I see some sparks of better hope, which elder years *i.e. H V*	
	May happily bring forth. But who comes here?	

'Enter AUMERLE amazed'

AUMERLE	Where is the king?	
B'BROKE	What means our cousin, that he stares and looks	
	So wildly?	
AUMERLE	God save your grace, I do beseech your majesty,	
	To have some conference with your grace alone.	
B'BROKE	Withdraw yourselves, and leave us here alone.	
	[*Percy and the rest withdraw*	
	What is the matter with our cousin now?	
AUMERLE	[*kneels*] For ever may my knees grow to the earth,	30
	My tongue cleave to my roof within my mouth,	
	Unless a pardon ere I rise or speak.	
B'BROKE	Intended, or committed, was this fault?	
	If on the first, how heinous e'er it be,	
	To win thy after-love, I pardon thee.	
AUMERLE	Then give me leave that I may turn the key,	
	That no man enter till my tale be done.	
B'BROKE	Have thy desire. [*the key is turned*	

'The DUKE OF YORK knocks at the door and crieth'

YORK	My liege, beware, look to thyself;	
	Thou hast a traitor in thy presence there.	40
B'BROKE	Villain, I'll make thee safe. = *harmless* [*he draws* ?	
AUMERLE	[*kneels again*] Stay thy revengeful hand; thou hast	
	no cause to fear.	

YORK   Open the door, secure, foolhardy king.
            Shall I for love speak treason to thy face?
            Open the door, or I will break it open.

        BOLINGBROKE *opens, admits* YORK *and locks the door again*

B'BROKE   What is the matter, uncle? Speak, recover breath,
            Tell us how near is danger,
            That we may arm us to encounter it.
YORK   Peruse this writing here, and thou shalt know
            The treason that my haste forbids me show.   50

                            [*he delivers the indenture*

AUMERLE   Remember, as thou read'st, thy promise passed.
            I do repent me, read not my name there;
            My heart is not confederate with my hand.
YORK   It was, villain, ere thy hand did set it down.
            I tore it from the traitor's bosom, king.
            Fear, and not love, begets his penitence:
            Forget to pity him, lest thy pity prove
            A serpent that will sting thee to the heart.
B'BROKE   O heinous, strong, and bold conspiracy!
            O loyal father of a treacherous son!   60
            Thou sheer, immaculate and silver fountain,
            From whence this stream, through muddy passages,
            Hath held his current, and defiled himself!
            Thy overflow of good converts to bad;
            And thy abundant goodness shall excuse
            This deadly blot in thy digressing son.
YORK   So shall my virtue be his vice's bawd,
            And he shall spend mine honour with his shame,
            As thriftless sons their scraping fathers' gold:
            Mine honour lives when his dishonour dies,   70
            Or my shamed life in his dishonour lies.
            Thou kill'st me in his life: giving him breath,
            The traitor lives, the true man's put to death.
DUCHESS   [*without*] What ho, my liege! For God's sake, let
                                              me in.
B'BROKE   What shrill-voiced suppliant makes this eager cry?
DUCHESS   A woman, and thy aunt, great king, 'tis I.
            Speak with me, pity me, open the door;
            A beggar begs that never begged before.

(handwritten: ① light-hearted Bd?)

B'BROKE	Our scene is altered from a serious thing,
	And now changed to 'The Beggar and the King'. ? *80* ①
	My dangerous cousin, let your mother in;
	I know she is come to pray for your foul sin.
YORK	If thou do pardon whosoever pray,
	More sins for this forgiveness prosper may.
	This fest'red joint cut off, the rest rest sound:
	This let alone will all the rest confound.

AUMERLE *admits the* DUCHESS

DUCHESS	O king, believe not this hard-hearted man!
	Love loving not itself, none other can.
YORK	Thou frantic woman, what dost thou make here?
	Shall thy old dugs once more a traitor rear? *90*
DUCHESS	Sweet York, be patient. Hear me, gentle liege.

[*she kneels*

B'BROKE	Rise up, good aunt.
DUCHESS	Not yet, I thee beseech.
	For ever will I walk upon my knees,
	And never see day that the happy sees,
	Till thou give joy – until thou bid me joy,
	By pardoning Rutland, my transgressing boy.
AUMERLE	Unto my mother's prayers I bend my knee. [*kneels*
YORK	Against them both my true joints bended be. [*kneels*
	Ill mayst thou thrive, if thou grant any grace!
DUCHESS	Pleads he in earnest? Look upon his face; *100*
	His eyes do drop no tears, his prayers are in jest.
	His words come from his mouth, ours from our breast.
	He prays but faintly, and would be denied,
	We pray with heart and soul, and all beside.
	His weary joints would gladly rise, I know,
	Our knees shall kneel till to the ground they grow.
	His prayers are full of false hypocrisy,
	Ours of true zeal and deep integrity.
	Our prayers do out-pray his; then let them have
	That mercy which true prayer ought to have. *110*
B'BROKE	Good aunt, stand up.
DUCHESS	Nay, do not say 'stand up';
	Say 'pardon' first, and afterwards 'stand up'.

(handwritten margin note: Difficult to bring ff?)

(handwritten margin note: Balanced clauses)

An if I were thy nurse, thy tongue to teach,
'Pardon' should be the first word of thy speech.
I never longed to hear a word till now;
Say 'pardon', king, let pity teach thee how.
The word is short, but not so short as sweet,
No word like 'pardon' for kings' mouths so meet.

YORK   Speak it in French, king, say 'pardonne moy'. = polite refusal

DUCHESS   Dost thou teach pardon pardon to destroy?   120
Ah, my sour husband, my hard-hearted lord,
That sets the word itself against the word!
Speak 'pardon' as 'tis current in our land;
The chopping French we do not understand.
Thine eye begins to speak, set thy tongue there;
Or in thy piteous heart plant thou thine ear,
That hearing how our plaints and prayers do pierce,
Pity may move thee 'pardon' to rehearse.

B'BROKE   Good aunt, stand up.

DUCHESS   I do not sue to stand. ✓
Pardon is all the suit I have in hand.   130

ⓙ B'BROKE   I pardon him, as God shall pardon me. ✓

DUCHESS   O happy vantage of a kneeling knee!
Yet am I sick for fear, speak it again.
Twice saying 'pardon' doth not pardon twain,
But makes one pardon strong.

B'BROKE   With all my heart
I pardon him.

DUCHESS   A god on earth thou art.

B'BROKE   But for our trusty brother-in-law, and the abbot,
With all the rest of that consorted crew,
Destruction straight shall dog them at the heels.
Good uncle, help to order several powers   140
To Oxford, or where'er these traitors are.
They shall not live within this world, I swear,
But I will have them, if I once know where.
Uncle, farewell, and cousin too, adieu: died at Agincourt
Your mother well hath prayed, and prove you true!

DUCHESS   Come, my old son; I pray God make thee new.

                                              [they go

SCENE 4

Plot scene

SIR PIERCE OF EXTON *enters with his manservant*

EXTON   Didst thou not mark the king, what words he spake?
'Have I no friend will rid me of this living fear?'
Was it not so?

SERVANT   These were his very words.

EXTON   'Have I no friend?' quoth he. He spake it twice,
And urged it twice together, did he not?

SERVANT   He did.

EXTON   And, speaking it, he wishtly looked on me,   = *steadfastly,*
As who should say, 'I would thou wert the man   *earnestly*
That would divorce this terror from my heart',
Meaning the king at Pomfret. Come, let's go,   10
I am the king's friend, and will rid his foe.   *The problem!*

                                       [they go

SCENE 5

Pomfret Castle

'RICHARD *alone*'

Soliloquy: early in the play

K.RICHARD   I have been studying how I may compare   *The meditative*
This prison where I live unto the world: *R, contemplative,*
And for because the world is populous,   *in 'epithet' of note*
And here is not a creature but myself,   *solitude*
I cannot do it; yet I'll hammer it out.
My brain I'll prove the female to my soul,
My soul the father, and these two beget
A generation of still-breeding thoughts:
And these same thoughts people this little world,
In humours like the people of this world.   10
For no thought is contented: the better sort,
As thoughts of things divine, are intermixed
With scruples, and do set the word itself
Against the word,
As thus: 'Come, little ones', and then again,   *N, T.*
'It is as hard to come, as for a camel

To thread the postern of a small needle's eye.'
Thoughts tending to ambition, they do plot
Unlikely wonders: how these vain weak nails
May tear a passage through the flinty ribs   20
Of this hard world, my ragged prison walls;
And, for they cannot, die in their own pride.
Thoughts tending to content flatter themselves
That they are not the first of fortune's slaves,
Nor shall not be the last; like silly beggars
Who sitting in the stocks refuge their shame,
That many have and others must sit there:
And in this thought they find a kind of ease,
Bearing their own misfortunes on the back
Of such as have before endured the like.   30
Thus play I in one person many people,
And none contented. Sometimes am I king,
Then treasons make me wish myself a beggar,
And so I am: then crushing penury
Persuades me I was better when a king;
Then am I kinged again, and by and by
Think that I am unkinged by Bolingbroke,
And straight am nothing. But whate'er I be,
Nor I, nor any man that but man is,
With nothing shall be pleased, till he be eased   40
With being nothing.   ['music plays'
                    Music do I hear?
Ha, ha! Keep time! How sour sweet music is,
When time is broke and no proportion kept!
So is it in the music of men's lives:
And here have I the daintiness of ear
To check time broke in a disordered string,
But for the concord of my state and time
Had not an ear to hear my true time broke.
I wasted time, and now doth time waste me:
For now hath time made me his numb'ring clock;   50
My thoughts are minutes, and with sighs they jar
Their watches on unto mine eyes, the outward watch,
Whereto my finger, like a dial's point,
Is pointing still, in cleansing them from tears.

Now, sir, the sound that tells what hour it is
Are clamorous groans which strike upon my heart,
Which is the bell. So sighs, and tears, and groans,
Show minutes, times, and hours; but my time
Runs posting on in Bolingbroke's proud joy,
While I stand fooling here, his Jack of the clock.   60
This music mads me; let it sound no more,
For though it have holp madmen to their wits,
In me it seems it will make wise men mad.
Yet blessing on his heart that gives it me!
For 'tis a sign of love; and love to Richard
Is a strange brooch in this all-hating world.

        'Enter a Groom of the stable'

GROOM   Hail, royal prince!
K.RICHARD   Thanks, noble peer;
The cheapest of us is ten groats too dear.
What art thou? And how comest thou hither,
Where no man never comes, but that sad dog   70
That brings me food to make misfortune live?
GROOM   I was a poor groom of thy stable, king,
When thou wert king; who, travelling towards York,
With much ado at length have gotten leave
To look upon my sometimes royal master's face:
O, how it erned my heart, when I beheld
In London streets that coronation day,
When Bolingbroke rode on roan Barbary!
That horse that thou so often hast bestrid,
That horse that I so carefully have dressed.   80
K.RICHARD Rode he on Barbary? Tell me, gentle friend,
How went he under him?
GROOM   So proudly as if he disdained the ground.
K.RICHARD So proud that Bolingbroke was on his back.
That jade hath eat bread from my royal hand,
This hand hath made him proud with clapping him.
Would he not stumble? Would he not fall down,
Since pride must have a fall, and break the neck
Of that proud man that did usurp his back?
Forgiveness, horse! Why do I rail on thee,   90
Since thou, created to be awed by man,

Wast born to bear? I was not made a horse,
And yet I bear a burthen like an ass,
Spurred, galled, and tired by jauncing Bolingbroke.

'Enter one to Richard with meat'

KEEPER　　　[*to the Groom*] Fellow, give place, here is no
　　　　　　　　　　　　　　　　　　　　　　　longer stay.
K. RICHARD　If thou love me, 'tis time thou wert away.
GROOM　　　What my tongue dares not, that my heart shall say.
　　　　　　　　　　　　　　　　　　　　　　　[*he goes*

KEEPER　　　[*placing the dish upon the table*]
　　　　　　My lord, will't please you to fall to?
K. RICHARD　Taste of it first, as thou art wont to do.
KEEPER　　　My lord, I dare not. Sir Pierce of Exton, who lately
　　　　　　came from the king, commands the contrary.
K. RICHARD　The devil take Henry of Lancaster and thee!
　　　　　　Patience is stale, and I am weary of it.
　　　　　　　　　　　　　　　　　　　　　　　[*he beats the Keeper*

KEEPER　　　Help, help, help!

　　　　　　　EXTON *and the other murderers rush in*

K. RICHARD　How now! What means death in this rude assault?
　　　　　　Villain, thy own hand yields thy death's instrument.
　　　　　　　　　　　　　[*he snatches an axe from one and kills him*
　　　　　　Go thou, and fill another room in hell.
　　　　　　　　　　　[*he kills another, but 'here Exton strikes him down'*
　　　　　　That hand shall burn in never-quenching fire
　　　　　　That staggers thus my person: Exton, thy fierce hand
　　　　　　Hath with the king's blood stained the king's
　　　　　　　　　　　　　　　　　　　own land.　　110
　　　　　　Mount, mount, my soul! Thy seat is up on high,
　　　　　　Whilst my gross flesh sinks downward, here to die.
　　　　　　　　　　　　　　　　　　　　　　　[*he dies*

EXTON　　　As full of valour as of royal blood:
　　　　　　Both have I spilled. O, would the deed were good!
　　　　　　For now the devil that told me I did well
　　　　　　Says that this deed is chronicled in hell.
　　　　　　This dead king to the living king I'll bear:
　　　　　　Take hence the rest, and give them burial here.
　　　　　　　　　　　　　　　　　　　　　　　[*they carry out the bodies*

Bol's allies ensure his kingship.

SCENE 6

Windsor Castle

BOLINGBROKE *and the* **DUKE OF YORK**

B'BROKE   Kind uncle York, the latest news we hear,
Is that the rebels have consumed with fire
Our town of Cicester in Gloucestershire;   *NB. pronunce*
But whether they be ta'en or slain we hear not.

NORTHUMBERLAND *enters*

Welcome, my lord, what is the news?
NORTH.   First, to thy sacred state wish I all happiness.   *NB*
The next news is, I have to London sent
The heads of Salisbury, Spencer, Blunt and Kent.
The manner of their taking may appear
At large discoursèd in this paper here.   [*he presents it* 10
B'BROKE   We thank thee, gentle Percy, for thy pains,
And to thy worth will add right worthy gains.

FITZWATER *enters*

FITZWATER   My lord, I have from Oxford sent to London
The heads of Brocas and Sir Bennet Seely,
Two of the dangerous consorted traitors,
That sought at Oxford thy dire overthrow.
B'BROKE   Thy pains, Fitzwater, shall not be forgot;
Right noble is thy merit, well I wot.

PERCY *enters, with the* **BISHOP OF CARLISLE** *guarded*

PERCY   The grand conspirator, Abbot of Westminster,
With clog of conscience and sour melancholy   20
Hath yielded up his body to the grave.
But here is Carlisle living, to abide
Thy kingly doom and sentence of his pride.
B'BROKE   Carlisle, this is your doom:
Choose out some secret place, some reverend room,
More than thou hast, and with it joy thy life;
So as thou liv'st in peace, die free from strife:
For though mine enemy thou hast ever been,
High sparks of honour in thee have I seen.

Bol the clement,
the magnanimous

Enter EXTON, *with persons bearing a coffin*

EXTON   Great king, within this coffin I present   30
           Thy buried fear: herein all breathless lies
           The mightiest of thy greatest enemies,
           Richard of Bordeaux, by me hither brought.
B'BROKE   Exton, I thank thee not, for thou hast wrought
           A deed of slander with thy fatal hand
           Upon my head and all this famous land.
EXTON   From your own mouth, my lord, did I this deed.
B'BROKE   They love not poison that do poison need,
           Nor do I thee; though I did wish him dead,
           I hate the murderer, love him murderéd.   40
           The guilt of conscience take thou for thy labour,
           But neither my good word, nor princely favour.
           With Cain go wander through the shades of night,
           And never show thy head by day nor light.
           Lords, I protest, my soul is full of woe,
           That blood should sprinkle me to make me grow:
           Come, mourn with me for what I do lament,
           And put on sullen black incontinent.
           I'll make a voyage to the Holy Land,
           To wash this blood off from my guilty hand.   50
           March sadly after, grace my mournings here,
           In weeping after this untimely bier.
                         [*The coffin is borne slowly out, Bolingbroke
                                      and the rest following*

HENRY IV Part 1

INTRODUCTION

The end of *Richard II* sees Bolingbroke, now Henry IV, troubled by his position of power and concerned about his wayward son Prince Harry, 'As dissolute as desperate – yet through both I see Some sparks of better hope, which elder years May happily bring forth' (5.3.20–22). In *1 Henry IV* these hints form the main dramatic dynamic: the cares of and threats to his office, and the development both of Hal's dissolution and 'sparks of better hope' are the prominent themes of the play. Written around 1596–97, *1 Henry IV* was first published in 1598 and ran to seven editions before the publication of the Folio edition of 1623. The earliest text bears the title 'The History of Henrie the Fourth, With the battell at Shrewsburie, between the King and Lord Henry Percy, surnamed Henrie Hotspur of the North. With the humorous conceits of Sir John Falstaffe'. This extended title is revelatory: there is no mention of the play as a first part, perhaps suggesting that the second part was conceived later as a response to the popularity of this play. Indeed, no other play of Shakespeare enjoyed comparable contemporary popularity, and one reason above all, as the title page suggests, can account for this: the character of Falstaff.

The huge presence of Sir John Falstaff threatens to overwhelm the play and its reception. Although the play's structure carefully juxtaposes the scenes in Eastcheap with those at Westminster, its heart seems to be in the warm, beery tavern-world of Hal, Falstaff, Quickly and their crew, rather than in the austere and careworn corridors of government. Like Hal, the audience longs to slip away from the anxious machinations of the uncertain Henry IV, whose throne, so decisively taken in *Richard II*, is now continually troubled by rebellion. Westminster is preoccupied with strategy and disquiet; Eastcheap is full of bawdy jokes and practical tricks. Falstaff is the undisputed king of the urban underworld of Eastcheap, and his function as a foil to Henry IV is made clear in the scene where he and Hal act out an interview with the king (2.4). His enormous girth symbolises his gourmandising and hedonism, and this larger-than-life character seems a huge metaphor rather than a man. Even his mock resurrection after his cowardice – avoiding injury at Shrewsbury by feigning death – serves to enforce the impression that he is immune to the normal cycles of life and death. Other characters will be consumed by history and its relentless movement, but Falstaff is rescued, supposedly at the instigation of Elizabeth I, for a role in contemporary Windsor in *The Merry Wives of Windsor*. In *I Henry IV*, he is cynical and amoral, full of bombast as well as sack. His representation draws on popular feast-day and carnival traditions of anarchic gratification presided over by the Lord of Misrule, and also on earlier, morality-type drama, as Hal points out: 'that reverend vice, that grey iniquity' (2.4.436). Falstaff's character also has an historical source: in the earliest texts of the play, and possibly in original performance, Falstaff was given the name Oldcastle. Oldcastle was a friend of Prince Hal and was eventually martyred as a Lollard, or Protestant dissident, in the reign of Henry V. His martyrdom was celebrated by writers such as John Foxe and John Bale, and his descendants, the influential Cobham family, may have put pressure on Shakespeare's company to expunge references to their ancestor in the irreverent portrait of the character who became known as Falstaff. Traces of the original name can be traced in the banter on 'my old lad of the castle' (1.2.41), in some irregular verse lines, and in the pointed disclaimer delivered by the Epilogue to *2 Henry IV*: 'Oldcastle died a martyr, and this is not the man' (p. 400). Shakespeare's traducing of the historical Oldcastle was countered by the rival theatre company, the Admiral's Men, who produced the suitably hagiographic play *Sir John Oldcastle* on the celebrated martyr. It does not seem to have been as popular as Shakespeare's version.

Falstaff's disquisition on honour: 'What is honour? A word. What is in that word honour? What is that honour? Air.' (5.1.133–35) articulates a self-serving philosophy entirely at odds with the code of chivalry motivating Hotspur and, less clearly, Hal himself. It is a subversive moment in a play which is struggling to contain and bring to heel all kinds of rebellion: personal (Hal), social (Eastcheap), and political (Hotspur). The play does not end on victory, although it may have effected a kind of resolution. Instead the king is predicting, as he disposes his forces to meet the insurgents, 'Rebellion in this land shall lose his sway' (5.5.41). It is a bright pronouncement, but in its echo of Henry IV's opening speech 'The edge of war, like an ill-sheathed knife, No more shall cut his master' (1.1.17–18), and with the benefit of historical hindsight, it sounds but a false dawn.

I Henry IV is haunted by the memory of Richard's death. Henry IV repeats his promise to make a pilgrimage to the Holy Land to atone for his sin, but domestic unrest keeps him at home. Even the tavern scenes allude to recent history. Falstaff's mock-serious 'Depose me?' (2.4.412), when Hal takes over the role of king in their parody of the court, reverberates with the deposition of Richard. As Marx observed, history repeats itself, 'first time as tragedy, the second as farce'. Henry himself is a relatively minor character in the play which bears his name: like Holinshed's *Chronicles* which takes the name of the sovereign as a running-title for the account of events which happen under his reign, the title *Henry IV* registers a period of time rather than an individual. The play's interest is with the next generation. In his private conference with his son in Act 3 Scene 2, Henry speaks at length about his route to the throne. He advises Hal of the importance of public image, recounting the success of his own strategy of withholding himself from view, so that 'By being seldom seen, I could not stir But like a comet I was wond'red at' (3.2.46–47). Hal, he fears, is too like the deposed king: 'For all the world As thou art to this hour was Richard then' (93–94), one who has 'lost thy princely privilege With vile participation' (85–86). This is a king acutely aware of his own political past, who fears that his son will not inherit his acuity. He need not worry, however, for Hal has already revealed his own awareness of the role of appearance for the successful monarch. At the end of his first scene, he articulates a degree of calculation about his sojourn in Eastcheap which may seem chilling to modern readers and audiences. He tells the audience in a soliloquy that he is only acting the part of a dissolute so as to add lustre to his eventual reformation, and he uses the consciously regal imagery of the sun to illustrate this: 'herein will I imitate the sun Who doth permit the base contagious clouds To smother up his beauty from the world That, when he please again to be himself Being wanted he may be more wonder'd at' (1.2.185–89).

From the beginning of the play, therefore, we are made aware that Hal is merely biding his time, allowing us to enjoy the Eastcheap scenes without worrying about the future king's involvement with such disreputable companions. It is the first hint that there will come a time when the heir to the throne cuts loose from Falstaff and the others, a suggestion echoed in Hal's ominous assertion in response to Falstaff's pleading 'banish not him thy Harry's company, banish plump Jack, and banish all the world': 'I do, I will' (2.4.454–56). Perhaps Hal is spending time in Eastcheap in order better to know his subjects and therefore become a better king; perhaps, as more cynical commentators have suggested, he is doing this in order better to subjugate them. Hal's own analysis, 'when I am king of England, I shall command all the good lads in Eastcheap' (2.4.13–14) is, like much of his self-consciously profligate behaviour, ambiguous on this point.

Hal's behaviour throughout is, of course, contrasted with that of Hotspur. One of the major changes Shakespeare made to his historical source material from Holinshed's *Chronicles* was in the age of Hotspur. The historical Henry Percy was closer in age to Henry IV than to his son; Shakespeare's alteration serves to emphasise the importance of the parallel with Hal in the ongoing personal and moral rivalry between them. These two young Henrys swap roles during the action. At the opening it is Hotspur who has distinguished himself in battle and whom the king wishes to own as his son, and by the conclusion, Hotspur is dead and Hal has come into his moral and filial inheritance as 'son Harry' (5.5.39). The play is concerned with multiple facets of father–son relationships, both public and private, and including the role of Falstaff as a surrogate father-figure. One of the play's overarching analogues is the parable of the prodigal son, as the Prince of Wales sows his wild oats in the knowledge of the welcome he will receive on his eventual reformation. The play proceeds through the use of parallels and foils: Hal's recognition that his own correction will be more effective than 'that which hath no foil to set it off' (1.2.203) could stand as a structural principle for the play as a whole. Court is juxtaposed with tavern, formal verse with informal prose, the high-flown rhetoric of monarchy with the earthy demotic of the populace. Hal and Hotspur are parallels, as are Falstaff and Henry. The rebellious Mortimer recalls Henry's own act of rebellion in taking the crown. Bravery and cowardice, honour and cynicism, candour and deceit – all are heightened through contrast.

The scene: England

CHARACTERS IN THE PLAY

KING HENRY THE FOURTH
HENRY, *Prince of Wales* } *sons to the king*
LORD JOHH OF LANCASTER
EARL OF WESTMORELAND
SIR WALTER BLUNT
THOMAS PERCY, *Earl of Worcester*
HENRY PERCY, *Earl of Northumberland*
HENRY PERCY, *surnamed* HOTSPUR, *his son*
EDMUND MORTIMER, *Earl of March*
RICHARD SCROOP, *Archbishop of York*
ARCHIBALD, *Earl of Douglas*
OWEN GLENDOWER
SIR RICHARD VERNON
SIR MICHAEL, *of the household of the Archbishop of York*
EDWARD POINS, *gentleman-in-waiting to Prince Henry*
SIR JOHN FALSTAFF
GADSHILL
PETO
BARDOLPH

LADY PERCY, *wife to Hotspur, and sister to Mortimer*
LADY MORTIMER, *daughter to Glendower, and wife to Mortimer*
MISTRESS QUICKLY, *hostess of the Boar's Head tavern, Eastcheap*

Lords, Officers, Sheriff, Vintner, Chamberlain, Drawers, two Carriers, Travellers, and Attendants

ACT I SCENE I

London. The Palace

KING HENRY *with* SIR WALTER BLUNT, *meeting* WESTMORELAND
and others

KING   So shaken as we are, so wan with care,
Find we a time for frighted peace to pant,
And breathe short-winded accents of new broils
To be commenced in strands afar remote.
No more the thirsty entrance of this soil
Shall daub her lips with her own children's blood,
No more shall trenching war channel her fields,
Nor bruise her flowerets with the arméd hoofs
Of hostile paces: those opposéd eyes,
Which, like the meteors of a troubled heaven,   10
All of one nature, of one substance bred,
Did lately meet in the intestine shock
And furious close of civil butchery,
Shall now, in mutual well-beseeming ranks,
March all one way, and be no more opposed
Against acquaintance, kindred, and allies.
The edge of war, like an ill-sheathéd knife,
No more shall cut his master. Therefore, friends,
As far as to the sepulchre of Christ,
Whose soldier now, under whose blesséd cross   20
We are impresséd and engaged to fight,
Forthwith a power of English shall we levy,
Whose arms were moulded in their mothers' womb
To chase these pagans in those holy fields
Over whose acres walked those blesséd feet
Which fourteen hundred years ago were nailed
For our advantage on the bitter cross.
But this our purpose now is twelve month old,
And bootless 'tis to tell you we will go:
Therefore we meet not now. Then let me hear   30
Of you, my gentle cousin Westmoreland,

What yesternight our council did decree
In forwarding this dear expedience.
WEST'LAND My liege, this haste was hot in question,
And many limits of the charge set down
But yesternight, when all athwart there came
A post from Wales, loaden with heavy news,
Whose worst was that the noble Mortimer,
Leading the men of Herefordshire to fight
Against the irregular and wild Glendower,   40
Was by the rude hands of that Welshman taken,
A thousand of his people butcheréd;
Upon whose dead corpse there was such misuse,
Such beastly shameless transformation,
By those Welshwomen done, as may not be
Without much shame retold or spoken of.
KING   It seems then that the tidings of this broil
Brake off our business for the Holy Land.
WEST'LAND This matched with other did, my gracious lord,
For more uneven and unwelcome news   50
Came from the north, and thus it did import:
On Holy-rood day the gallant Hotspur there,
Young Harry Percy, and brave Archibald,
That ever-valiant and approvéd Scot,
At Holmedon met,
Where they did spend a sad and bloody hour;
As by discharge of their artillery,
And shape of likelihood, the news was told;
For he that brought them, in the very heat
And pride of their contention did take horse,   60
Uncertain of the issue any way.
KING   Here is a dear, a true industrious friend,
Sir Walter Blunt, new lighted from his horse,
Stained with the variation of each soil
Betwixt that Holmedon and this seat of ours;
And he hath brought us smooth and welcome news.
The Earl of Douglas is discomfited,
Ten thousand bold Scots, two and twenty knights,
Balked in their own blood did Sir Walter see
On Holemedon's plains. Of prisoners, Hotspur took   70

   Mordake the Earl of Fife, and eldest son
   To beaten Douglas, and the Earl of Athol,
   Of Murray, Angus, and Menteith.
   And is not this an honourable spoil?
   A gallant prize? Ha, cousin, is it not?
WEST'LAND In faith,
   It is a conquest for a prince to boast of.
KING Yea, there thou mak'st me sad, and mak'st me sin
   In envy, that my Lord Northumberland
   Should be the father to so blest a son,   80
   A son who is the theme of honour's tongue,
   Amongst a grove the very straightest plant,
   Who is sweet Fortune's minion and her pride;
   Whilst I by looking on the praise of him
   See riot and dishonour stain the brow
   Of my young Harry. O that it could be proved
   That some night-tripping fairy had exchanged
   In cradle-clothes our children where they lay,
   And called mine Percy, his Plantagenet,
   Then would I have his Harry, and he mine. 90
   But let him from my thoughts. What think you, coz,
   Of this young Percy's pride? The prisoners,
   Which he in this adventure hath surprised,
   To his own use he keeps, and sends me word,
   I shall have none but Mordake Earl of Fife.
WEST'LAND This is his uncle's teaching, this is Worcester,
   Malevolent to you in all aspects,
   Which makes him prune himself, and bristle up
   The crest of youth against your dignity.
KING But I have sent for him to answer this;
   And for this cause awhile we must neglect 100
   Our holy purpose to Jerusalem.
   Cousin, on Wednesday next our council we
   Will hold at Windsor; so inform the lords.
   But come yourself with speed to us again,
   For more is to be said and to be done
   Than out of anger can be utteréd.
WEST'LAND I will, my liege.

               [they go

SCENE 2

London. A room in the house of the Prince of Wales

SIR JOHN FALSTAFF *lies upon a bench. The* PRINCE OF WALES *enters and rouses him*

FALSTAFF Now, Hal, what time of day is it, lad?

PRINCE Thou art so fat-witted with drinking of old sack, and
unbuttoning thee after supper, and sleeping upon
benches after noon, that thou hast forgotten to demand that truly which thou wouldest truly know.
What a devil hast thou to do with the time of the day?
Unless hours were cups of sack, and minutes capons,
and clocks the tongues of bawds, and dials the signs of
leaping-houses, and the blessed sun himself a fair hot
wench in flame-coloured taffeta, I see no reason why 10
thou shouldst be so superfluous to demand the time of
the day.

FALSTAFF Indeed, you come near me now, Hal, for we that take
purses go by the moon and the seven stars, and not by
Phoebus, he 'that wandering knight so fair'. And, I
prithee, sweet wag, when thou art king, as God save
thy grace – majesty, I should say, for grace thou wilt
have none.

PRINCE What, none?

FALSTAFF No, by my troth, not so much as will serve to be 20
prologue to an egg and butter.

PRINCE Well, how then? Come, roundly, roundly.

FALSTAFF Marry then, sweet wag, when thou art king let not us
that are squires of the night's body be called thieves of
the day's beauty; let us be Diana's foresters, gentlemen
of the shade, minions of the moon, and let men say we
be men of good government, being governed as the
sea is by our noble and chaste mistress the moon,
under whose countenance we steal.

PRINCE Thou sayest well, and it holds well too, for the fortune 30
of us that are the moon's men doth ebb and flow like
the sea, being governed as the sea is by the moon – as

for proof now, a purse of gold most resolutely snatched on Monday night and most dissolutely spent on Tuesday morning, got with swearing 'lay by' and spent with crying 'bring in' — now in as low an ebb as the foot of the ladder, and by and by in as high a flow as the ridge of the gallows.

FALSTAFF By the Lord, thou sayst true, lad, and is not my hostess of the tavern a most sweet wench? 40

PRINCE As the honey of Hybla, my old lad of the castle, and is not a buff jerkin a most sweet robe of durance?

FALSTAFF How now, how now, mad wag? What, in thy quips and thy quiddities? What a plague have I to do with a buff jerkin?

PRINCE Why, what a pox have I to do with my hostess of the tavern?

FALSTAFF Well, thou hast called her to a reckoning many a time and oft.

PRINCE Did I ever call for thee to pay thy part? 50

FALSTAFF No, I'll give thee thy due, thou hast paid all there.

PRINCE Yea, and elsewhere, so far as my coin would stretch; and where it would not, I have used my credit.

FALSTAFF Yea, and so used it that, were it not here apparent that thou art heir apparent — but, I prithee, sweet wag, shall there be gallows standing in England when thou art king? And resolution thus fubbed as it is with the rusty curb of old father Antic the law? Do not thou, when thou art king, hang a thief.

PRINCE No, thou shalt. 60

FALSTAFF Shall I? O rare! By the Lord, I'll be a brave judge!

PRINCE Thou judgest false already. I mean, thou shalt have the hanging of the thieves and so become a rare hangman.

FALSTAFF Well, Hal, well; and in some sort it jumps with my humour, as well as waiting in the court, I can tell you.

PRINCE For obtaining of suits?

FALSTAFF Yea, for obtaining of suits, whereof the hangman hath no lean wardrobe. 'Sblood, I am as melancholy as a gib cat or a lugged bear.

PRINCE Or an old lion, or a lover's lute. 70

FALSTAFF Yea, or the drone of a Lincolnshire bagpipe.

PRINCE   What sayest thou to a hare, or the melancholy of
Moor Ditch?

FALSTAFF   Thou hast the most unsavoury similes and art indeed the
most comparative, rascalliest, sweet young prince. But,
Hal, I prithee, trouble me no more with vanity. I would
to God thou and I knew where a commodity of good
names were to be bought: an old lord of the council
rated me the other day in the street about you, sir, but I
marked him not; and yet he talked very wisely, but I 80
regarded him not; and yet he talked wisely and in the
street too.

PRINCE   Thou didst well, for wisdom cries out in the streets,
and no man regards it.

FALSTAFF   O, thou hast damnable iteration, and art indeed able to
corrupt a saint: thou hast done much harm upon me,
Hal – God forgive thee for it. Before I knew thee, Hal,
I knew nothing, and now am I, if a man should speak
truly, little better than one of the wicked. I must give
over this life, and I will give it over: by the Lord, an I 90
do not, I am a villain. I'll be damned for never a king's
son in Christendom.

PRINCE   Where shall we take a purse to-morrow, Jack?

FALSTAFF   'Zounds, where thou wilt, lad, I'll make one; an I do
not, call me villain and baffle me.

PRINCE   I see a good amendment of life in thee, from praying
to purse-taking.

FALSTAFF   Why, Hal, 'tis my vocation, Hal, 'tis no sin for a man
to labour in his vocation.

POINS *enters*

Poins! Now shall we know if Gadshill have set a 100
match. O, if men were to be saved by merit, what hole
in hell were hot enough for him? This is the most
omnipotent villain that ever cried 'Stand' to a true
man.

PRINCE   Good morrow, Ned.

POINS   Good morrow, sweet Hal. What says Monsieur Remorse? What says Sir John Sack and Sugar? Jack, how
agrees the devil and thee about thy soul, that thou
soldest him on Good Friday last, for a cup of Madeira

	and a cold capon's leg? 110
PRINCE	Sir John stands to his word, the devil shall have his bargain; for he was never yet a breaker of proverbs: he will give the devil his due.
POINS	Then art thou damned for keeping thy word with the devil.
PRINCE	Else he had been damned for cozening the devil.
POINS	But, my lads, my lads, tomorrow morning, by four o'clock, early at Gad's Hill, there are pilgrims going to Canterbury with rich offerings, and traders riding to London with fat purses. I have vizards for you all, you have horses for yourselves. Gadshill lies tonight in Rochester, I have bespoke supper tomorrow night in Eastcheap: we may do it as secure as sleep. If you will go, I will stuff your purses full of crowns; if you will not, tarry at home and be hanged.
FALSTAFF	Hear ye, Yedward, if I tarry at home and go not, I'll hang you for going.
POINS	You will, chops?
FALSTAFF	Hal, wilt thou make one?
PRINCE	Who, I? Rob? I a thief? Not I, by my faith. 130
FALSTAFF	There's neither honesty, manhood, nor good fellowship in thee, nor thou cam'st not of the blood royal, if thou darest not stand for ten shillings.

[Poins makes signals behind Falstaff's back

PRINCE	Well then, once in my days I'll be a madcap.
FALSTAFF	Why, that's well said.
PRINCE	Well, come what will, I'll tarry at home.
FALSTAFF	By the Lord, I'll be a traitor then, when thou art king.
PRINCE	I care not.
POINS	Sir John, I prithee, leave the prince and me alone, I will lay him down such reasons for this adventure that 140 he shall go.
FALSTAFF	Well, God give thee the spirit of persuasion, and him the ears of profiting, that what thou speakest may move, and what he hears may be believed, that the true prince may, for recreation sake, prove a false thief; for the poor abuses of the time want countenance. Farewell, you shall find me in Eastcheap.

PRINCE   Farewell, the latter spring! Farewell, All-hallown
          summer!   [*Falstaff goes*

POINS   Now, my good sweet honey lord, ride with us to- 150
          morrow. I have a jest to execute that I cannot manage
          alone. Falstaff, Bardolph, Peto and Gadshill shall rob
          those men that we have already waylaid. Yourself and
          I will not be there: and when they have the booty, if
          you and I do not rob them, cut this head off from my
          shoulders.

PRINCE   How shall we part with them in setting forth?

POINS   Why, we will set forth before or after them, and
          appoint them a place of meeting, wherein it is at our
          pleasure to fail; and then will they adventure upon the 160
          exploit themselves, which they shall have no sooner
          achieved but we'll set upon them.

PRINCE   Yea, but 'tis like that they will know us by our horses,
          by our habits, and by every other appointment, to be
          ourselves.

POINS   Tut! Our horses they shall not see, I'll tie them in the
          wood; our vizards we will change after we leave them;
          and, sirrah, I have cases of buckram for the nonce, to
          immask our noted outward garments.

PRINCE   Yea, but I doubt they will be too hard for us.   170

POINS   Well, for two of them, I know them to be as true-bred
          cowards as ever turned back; and for the third, if he
          fight longer than he sees reason, I'll forswear arms.
          The virtue of this jest will be the incomprehensible lies
          that this same fat rogue will tell us when we meet at
          supper, how thirty at least he fought with, what wards,
          what blows, what extremities he endured; and in the
          reproof of this lives the jest.

PRINCE   Well, I'll go with thee. Provide us all things necessary,
          and meet me tomorrow night in Eastcheap; there I'll 180
          sup. Farewell.

POINS   Farewell, my lord.   [*Poins goes*

PRINCE   I know you all, and will awhile uphold
          The unyoked humour of your idleness.
          Yet herein will I imitate the sun,
          Who doth permit the base contagious clouds

To smother up his beauty from the world,
That when he please again to be himself,
Being wanted he may be more wond'red at,
By breaking through the foul and ugly mists   190
Of vapours that did seem to strangle him.
If all the year were playing holidays,
To sport would be as tedious as to work;
But when they seldom come, they wished for come,
And nothing pleaseth but rare accidents:
So, when this loose behaviour I throw off,
And pay the debt I never promiséd,
By how much better than my word I am,
By so much shall I falsify men's hopes,
And like bright metal on a sullen ground,   200
My reformation, glitt'ring o'er my fault,
Shall show more goodly, and attract more eyes,
Than that which hath no foil to set it off.
I'll so offend, to make offence a skill,
Redeeming time when men think least I will.

[*he goes*

SCENE 3

Windsor. The Council Chamber

Enter the KING, NORTHUMBERLAND, WORCESTER, HOTSPUR,
SIR WALTER BLUNT, *with others*

KING   My blood hath been too cold and temperate,
Unapt to stir at these indignities,
And you have found me; for accordingly
You tread upon my patience. But be sure
I will from henceforth rather be myself,
Mighty and to be feared, than my condition,
Which hath been smooth as oil, soft as young down,
And therefore lost that title of respect
Which the proud soul ne'er pays but to the proud.

WORCESTER Our house, my sovereign liege, little deserves   10
The scourge of greatness to be used on it,
And that same greatness too which our own hands
Have holp to make so portly.

NORTH.   My lord —
KING   Worcester, get thee gone, for I do see
            Danger and disobedience in thine eye:
            O, sir, your presence is too bold and peremptory,
            And majesty might never yet endure
            The moody frontier of a servant brow.
            You have good leave to leave us. When we need   20
            Your use and counsel, we shall send for you.
                                          [*Worcester goes out*
            You were about to speak.
NORTH.   Yea, my good lord.
            Those prisoners in your highness' name demanded,
            Which Harry Percy here at Holmedon took,
            Were, as he says, not with such strength denied
            As is delivered to your majesty.
            Either envy, therefore, or misprision
            Is guilty of this fault, and not my son.
HOTSPUR   My liege, I did deny no prisoners;
            But I remember, when the fight was done,   30
            When I was dry with rage and extreme toil,
            Breathless and faint, leaning upon my sword,
            Came there a certain lord, neat and trimly dressed,
            Fresh as a bridegroom, and his chin new reaped
            Showed like a stubble-land at harvest-home.
            He was perfuméd like a milliner,
            And 'twixt his finger and his thumb he held
            A pouncet-box, which ever and anon
            He gave his nose and took't away again;
            Who therewith angry, when it next came there,   40
            Took it in snuff — and still he smiled and talked:
            And as the soldiers bore dead bodies by,
            He called them untaught knaves, unmannerly,
            To bring a slovenly unhandsome corse
            Betwixt the wind and his nobility.
            With many holiday and lady terms
            He questioned me, amongst the rest demanded
            My prisoners in your majesty's behalf.
            I then, all smarting with my wounds being cold,
            To be so pestered with a popinjay,   50

Out of my grief and my impatience,
Answered neglectingly I know not what –
He should, or he should not; for he made me mad
To see him shine so brisk, and smell so sweet,
And talk so like a waiting-gentlewoman
Of guns, and drums, and wounds, God save the mark!
And telling me the sovereignest thing on earth
Was parmaceti for an inward bruise,
And that it was great pity, so it was,
This villainous salt-petre should be digged   60
Out of the bowels of the harmless earth,
Which many a good tall fellow had destroyed
So cowardly; and but for these vile guns
He would himself have been a soldier.
This bald unjointed chat of his, my lord,
I answered indirectly, as I said,
And I beseech you, let not his report
Come current for an accusation
Betwixt my love and your high majesty.

BLUNT   The circumstance considered, good my lord,   70
Whate'er Lord Harry Percy then had said
To such a person, and in such a place,
At such a time, with all the rest retold,
May reasonably die, and never rise
To do him wrong, or any way impeach
What then he said, so he unsay it now.

KING   Why, yet he doth deny his prisoners,
But with proviso and exception –
That we at our own charge shall ransom straight
His brother-in-law, the foolish Mortimer,   80
Who, on my soul, hath wilfully betrayed
The lives of those that he did lead to fight
Against the great magician, damned Glendower,
Whose daughter, as we hear, that Earl of March
Hath lately married. Shall our coffers then
Be emptied to redeem a traitor home?
Shall we buy treason, and indent with fears,
When they have lost and forfeited themselves?
No, on the barren mountains let him starve;

For I shall never hold that man my friend,   90
Whose tongue shall ask me for one penny cost
To ransom home revolted Mortimer.

HOTSPUR   Revolted Mortimer!
He never did fall off, my sovereign liege,
But by the chance of war. To prove that true
Needs no more but one tongue for all those wounds,
Those mouthéd wounds, which valiantly he took,
When on the gentle Severn's sedgy bank,
In single opposition, hand to hand,
He did confound the best part of an hour   100
In changing hardiment with great Glendower.
Three times they breathed and three times did
                                        they drink,
Upon agreement, of swift Severn's flood,
Who then affrighted with their bloody looks,
Ran fearfully among the trembling reeds,
And hid his crisp head in the hollow bank
Bloodstainéd with these valiant combatants.
Never did bare and rotten policy
Colour her working with such deadly wounds,
Nor never could the noble Mortimer   110
Receive so many, and all willingly.
Then let him not be slandered with revolt.

KING   Thou dost belie him, Percy, thou dost belie him.
He never did encounter with Glendower:
I tell thee,
He durst as well have met the devil alone,
As Owen Glendower for an enemy.
Art thou not ashamed? But, sirrah, henceforth
Let me not hear you speak of Mortimer:
Send me your prisoners with the speediest means,   120
Or you shall hear in such a kind from me
As will displease you. My Lord Northumberland,
We license your departure with your son.
Send us your prisoners, or you'll hear of it.

                    [*King Henry, Blunt and other nobles*
                                        leave the chamber

HOTSPUR   And if the devil come and roar for them,

I will not send them: I will after straight
And tell him so, for I will ease my heart,
Albeit I make a hazard of my head.

NORTH.　What, drunk with choler? Stay and pause awhile,
Here comes your uncle.

WORCESTER *returns*

HOTSPUR　　　　　　　　Speak of Mortimer!　　　130
'Zounds, I will speak of him, and let my soul
Want mercy if I do not join with him:
Yea, on his part, I'll empty all these veins,
And shed my dear blood drop by drop in the dust,
But I will lift the down-trod Mortimer
As high in the air as this unthankful king,
As this ingrate and cank'red Bolingbroke.

NORTH.　Brother, the king hath made your nephew mad.

WORCESTER Who struck this heat up after I was gone?

HOTSPUR　He will forsooth have all my prisoners,　　　140
And when I urged the ransom once again
Of my wife's brother, then his cheek looked pale,
And on my face he turned an eye of death,
Trembling even at the name of Mortimer.

WORCESTER I cannot blame him: was not he proclaimed,
By Richard that dead is, the next of blood?

NORTH.　He was, I heard the proclamation:
And then it was when the unhappy king
(Whose wrongs in us God pardon!) did set forth
Upon his Irish expedition;　　　150
From whence he intercepted did return
To be deposed and shortly murderéd.

WORCESTER And for whose death we in the world's wide mouth
Live scandalised and foully spoken of.

HOTSPUR　But soft, I pray you, did King Richard then
Proclaim my brother Edmund Mortimer
Heir to the crown?

NORTH.　　　　　　He did, myself did hear it.

HOTSPUR　Nay, then I cannot blame his cousin king,
That wished him on the barren mountains starve.
But shall it be that you, that set the crown　　　160

Upon the head of this forgetful man,
And for his sake wear the detested blot
Of murderous subornation, shall it be
That you a world of curses undergo,
Being the agents, or base second means,
The cords, the ladder, or the hangman rather?
O, pardon me that I descend so low,
To show the line, and the predicament,
Wherein you range under this subtle king!
Shall it for shame be spoken in these days,   170
Or fill up chronicles in time to come,
That men of your nobility and power
Did gage them both in an unjust behalf –
As both of you, God pardon it, have done –
To put down Richard, that sweet lovely rose,
And plant this thorn, this canker, Bolingbroke?
And shall it in more shame be further spoken,
That you are fooled, discarded, and shook off
By him for whom these shames ye underwent?
No, yet time serves wherein you may redeem   180
Your banished honours, and restore yourselves
Into the good thoughts of the world again:
Revenge the jeering and disdained contempt
Of this proud king, who studies day and night
To answer all the debt he owes to you,
Even with the bloody payment of your deaths:
Therefore, I say –

WORCESTER   Peace, cousin, say no more.
And now I will unclasp a secret book,
And to your quick-conceiving discontents
I'll read you matter deep and dangerous,   190
As full of peril and adventurous spirit
As to o'er-walk a current roaring loud
On the unsteadfast looting of a spear.

HOTSPUR   If he fall in, good night! Or sink or swim.
Send danger from the east unto the west,
So honour cross it from the north to south,
And let them grapple: O, the blood more stirs
To rouse a lion than to start a hare!

NORTH. Imagination of some great exploit
    Drives him beyond the bounds of patience. 200
HOTSPUR By heaven, methinks it were an easy leap,
    To pluck bright honour from the pale-faced moon,
    Or dive into the bottom of the deep,
    Where fathom-line could never touch the ground,
    And pluck up drownéd honour by the locks,
    So he that doth redeem her thence might wear
    Without corrival all her dignities:
    But out upon this half-faced fellowship!
WORCESTER He apprehends a world of figures here,
    But not the form of what he should attend. 210
    Good cousin, give me audience for a while.
HOTSPUR I cry you mercy.
WORCESTER   Those same noble Scots
    That are your prisoners –
HOTSPUR   I'll keep them all;
    By God, he shall not have a Scot of them.
    No, if a Scot would save his soul, he shall not.
    I'll keep them, by this hand.
WORCESTER   You start away,
    And lend no ear unto my purposes.
    Those prisoners you shall keep.
HOTSPUR   Nay, I will: that's flat.
    He said he would not ransom Mortimer,
    Forbad my tongue to speak of Mortimer, 220
    But I will find him when he lies asleep,
    And in his ear I'll holla 'Mortimer!'
    Nay,
    I'll have a starling shall be taught to speak
    Nothing but 'Mortimer', and give it him
    To keep his anger still in motion.
WORCESTER Hear you, cousin, a word.
HOTSPUR All studies here I solemnly defy,
    Save how to gall and pinch this Bolingbroke.
    And that same sword-and-buckler Prince of Wales, 230
    But that I think his father loves him not
    And would be glad he met with some mischance,
    I would have him poisoned with a pot of ale.

WORCESTER Farewell, kinsman! I'll talk to you
           When you are better tempered to attend.
NORTH.   Why, what a wasp-stung and impatient fool
           Art thou, to break into this woman's mood,
           Tying thine ear to no tongue but thine own!
HOTSPUR   Why, look you, I am whipped and scourged with rods,
           Nettled, and stung with pismires, when I hear   240
           Of this vile politician, Bolingbroke.
           In Richard's time – what d'ye call the place?
           A plague upon't, it is in Gloucestershire;
           'Twas where the madcap duke his uncle kept,
           His uncle York – where I first bowed my knee
           Unto this king of smiles, this Bolingbroke –
           'Sblood! When you and he came back from
                                           Ravenspurgh –
NORTH.   At Berkeley castle.
HOTSPUR   You say true.
           Why, what a candy deal of courtesy   250
           This fawning greyhound then did proffer me!
           'Look when his infant fortune came to age',
           And, 'gentle Harry Percy', and 'kind cousin':
           O, the devil take such cozeners! God forgive me!
           Good uncle, tell your tale – I have done.
WORCESTER Nay, if you have not, to it again,
           We will stay your leisure.
HOTSPUR   I have done, i'faith.
WORCESTER Then once more to your Scottish prisoners.
           Deliver them up without their ransom straight,
           And make the Douglas' son your only mean   260
           For powers in Scotland, which, for divers reasons
           Which I shall send you written, be assured
           Will easily be granted. You, my lord, [to Northumberland
           Your son in Scotland being thus employed,
           Shall secretly into the bosom creep
           Of that same noble prelate, well beloved,
           The archbishop.
HOTSPUR   Of York, is't not?
WORCESTER   True; who bears hard
           His brother's death at Bristow, the Lord Scroop.

       I speak not this in estimation,
       As what I think might be, but what I know
       Is ruminated, plotted, and set down,   270
       And only stays but to behold the face
       Of that occasion that shall bring it on.

HOTSPUR   I smell it. Upon my life, it will do well.

NORTH.   Before the game's afoot thou still let'st slip.

HOTSPUR   Why, it cannot choose but be a noble plot.
       And then the power of Scotland and of York
       To join with Mortimer, ha?

WORCESTER   And so they shall.

HOTSPUR   In faith, it is exceedingly well aimed.

WORCESTER And 'tis no little reason bids us speed,
       To save our heads by raising of a head,   280
       For, bear ourselves as even as we can,
       The king will always think him in our debt,
       And think we think ourselves unsatisfied,
       Till he hath found a time to pay us home.
       And see already how he doth begin
       To make us strangers to his looks of love.

HOTSPUR   He does, he does; we'll be revenged on him.

WORCESTER Cousin, farewell. No further go in this
       Than I by letters shall direct your course.
       When time is ripe, which will be suddenly,   290
       I'll steal to Glendower and Lord Mortimer,
       Where you and Douglas and our powers at once,
       As I will fashion it, shall happily meet,
       To bear our fortunes in our own strong arms,
       Which now we hold at much uncertainty.

NORTH.   Farewell, good brother: we shall thrive, I trust.

HOTSPUR   Uncle, adieu: O, let the hours be short,
       Till fields, and blows, and groans applaud our sport!

                                        [they go

ACT 2 SCENE I

An inn yard at Rochester

'Enter a Carrier with a lantern in his hand'

1 CARRIER Heigh-ho! An't be not four by the day, I'll be hanged.
Charles' wain is over the new chimney, and yet our
horse not packed. What, ostler!

OSTLER [*within*] Anon, anon.

1 CARRIER I prithee, Tom, beat Cut's saddle, put a few flocks in
the point; poor jade is wrung in the withers, out of all
cess.

'Enter another Carrier'

2 CARRIER Peas and beans are as dank here as a dog, and that is the
next way to give poor jades the bots: this house is
turned upside down since Robin Ostler died.   10

1 CARRIER Poor fellow never joyed since the price of oats rose, it
was the death of him.

2 CARRIER I think this be the most villainous house in all London
road for fleas, I am stung like a tench.

1 CARRIER Like a tench! By the mass, there is ne'er a king christen
could be better bit than I have been since the first
cock.

2 CARRIER Why, they will allow us ne'er a jordan, and then we
leak in your chimney, and your chamber-lye breeds
fleas like a loach.   20

1 CARRIER What, ostler! Come away, and be hanged, come away.

2 CARRIER I have a gammon of bacon, and two razes of ginger, to
be delivered as far as Charing Cross.

1 CARRIER God's body! The turkeys in my pannier are quite starved.
What, ostler! A plague on thee! Hast thou never an eye
in thy head? Canst not hear? An 'twere not as good deed
as drink, to break the pate on thee, I am a very villain.
Come, and be hanged! Hast no faith in thee?

Enter GADSHILL

GADSHILL Good morrow, carriers, what's o'clock?

1 CARRIER I think it be two o'clock.   30

GADSHILL I prithee, lend me thy lantern to see my gelding in the
          stable.

1 CARRIER Nay by God, soft, I know a trick worth two of that,
          ay, faith!

GADSHILL I pray thee, lend me thine.

2 CARRIER Ay when? Canst tell? Lend me thy lantern, quoth 'a?
          Marry, I'll see thee hanged first.

GADSHILL Sirrah carrier, what time do you mean to come to
          London?

2 CARRIER Time enough to go to bed with a candle, I warrant 40
          thee. Come, neighbour Mugs, we'll call up the gentle-
          men. They will along with company, for they have
          great charge.   [*the carriers go inside*

GADSHILL What, ho! Chamberlain!

CHAMB.   At hand, quoth pick-purse.

GADSHILL That's even as fair as — at hand, quoth the chamberlain:
          for thou variest no more from picking of purses than
          giving direction doth from labouring; thou layest the
          plot how.

                 A Chamberlain comes from the inn

CHAMB.   Good morrow, Master Gadshill. It holds current that I 50
          told you yesternight. There's a franklin in the wild of
          Kent, hath brought three hundred marks with him in
          gold. I heard him tell it to one of his company last night
          at supper, a kind of auditor, one that hath abundance of
          charge too, God knows what. They are up already, and
          call for eggs and butter. They will away presently.

GADSHILL Sirrah, if they meet not with Saint Nicholas' clerks, I'll
          give thee this neck.

CHAMB.   No, I'll none of it. I pray thee, keep that for the
          hangman, for I know thou worshippest Saint Nicholas, 60
          as truly as a man of falsehood may.

GADSHILL What talkest thou to me of the hangman? If I hang, I'll
          make a fat pair of gallows: for, if I hang, old Sir John
          hangs with me, and thou knowest he's no starveling.
          Tut! There are other Trojans that thou dream'st not of,
          the which for sport sake are content to do the profession
          some grace, that would, if matters should be looked into,

for their own credit sake make all whole. I am joined
with no foot-landrakers, no long-staff sixpenny strikers,
none of these mad mustachio purple-hued malt-worms, 70
but with nobility and tranquillity, burgomasters and great
oneyers, such as can hold in, such as will strike sooner
than speak, and speak sooner than drink, and drink
sooner than pray. And yet, zounds, I lie, for they pray
continually to their saint, the commonwealth, or rather
not pray to her, but prey on her, for they ride up and
down on her, and make her their boots.

CHAMB.   What, the commonwealth their boots? Will she hold
out water in foul way?

GADSHILL   She will, she will – Justice hath liquored her: we steal 80
as in a castle, cock-sure: we have the receipt of fern-
seed, we walk invisible.

CHAMB.   Nay, by my faith, I think you are more beholding to
the night than to fern-seed for your walking invisible.

GADSHILL   Give me thy hand; thou shalt have a share in our
purchase, as I am a true man.

CHAMB.   Nay, rather let me have it, as you are a false thief.

GADSHILL   Go to, 'homo' is a common name to all men: bid the
ostler bring my gelding out of the stable. Fare well,
you muddy knave.   90

                                                    [*they go*

SCENE 2

*A narrow lane, near the top of Gad's Hill, some two miles
from Rochester; bushes and trees. A dark night*

The PRINCE, PETO *and* BARDOLPH *come up the hill;*
                POINS hurrying after

POINS   Come, shelter, shelter! I have removed Falstaff's horse,
and he frets like a gummed velvet.

PRINCE   Stand close.   [*Poins hides behind a bush*

            FALSTAFF *comes up, breathless*

FALSTAFF   Poins! Poins, and be hanged! Poins!

PRINCE   Peace, ye fat-kidneyed rascal! What a brawling dost
thou keep!

FALSTAFF   Where's Poins, Hal?
PRINCE   He is walked up to the top of the hill; I'll go seek him.
                                                          [*he joins Poins*

FALSTAFF   I am accursed to rob in that thief's company. The
           rascal hath removed my horse, and tied him I know   10
           not where. If I travel but four foot by the squier further
           afoot, I shall break my wind. Well, I doubt not but to
           die a fair death for all this, if I 'scape hanging for killing
           that rogue. I have forsworn his company hourly any
           time this two and twenty years, and yet I am bewitched
           with the rogue's company. If the rascal have not given
           me medicines to make me love him, I'll be hanged. It
           could not be else: I have drunk medicines. Poins! Hal!
           a plague upon you both! Bardolph! Peto! I'll starve ere
           I'll rob a foot further. An 'twere not as good a deed as 20
           drink, to turn true man and to leave these rogues, I am
           the veriest varlet that ever chewed with a tooth. Eight
           yards of uneven ground is threescore and ten miles
           afoot with me, and the stony-hearted villains know it
           well enough. A plague upon't, when thieves cannot be
           true one to another! [*'they whistle'*] Whew! A plague
           upon you all! Give me my horse, you rogues, give me
           my horse and be hanged.
PRINCE   [*coming forward*] Peace, ye fat-guts! Lie down, lay thine
           ear close to the ground and list if thou canst hear the   30
           tread of travellers.
FALSTAFF   Have you any levers to lift me up again, being down?
           'Sblood, I'll not bear mine own flesh so far afoot again
           for all the coin in thy father's exchequer. What a
           plague mean ye to colt me thus?
PRINCE   Thou liest, thou art not colted, thou art uncolted.
FALSTAFF   I prithee, good Prince Hal, help me to my horse, good
           king's son.
PRINCE   Out, ye rogue! Shall I be your ostler?
FALSTAFF   Go hang thyself in thine own heir-apparent garters! If I   40
           be ta'en, I'll peach for this. An I have not ballads made
           on you all and sung to filthy tunes, let a cup of sack be
           my poison; when a jest is so forward, and afoot too! I
           hate it.

GADSHILL *approaches, coming down the hill*

GADSHILL Stand!

FALSTAFF So I do, against my will.

POINS, BARDOLPH, *and* PETO *come forward*

POINS O, 'tis our setter. I know his voice.

BARDOLPH What news?

GADSHILL Case ye, case ye, on with your vizards, there's money
of the king's coming down the hill, 'tis going to the 50
king's exchequer.

FALSTAFF You lie, ye rogue, 'tis going to the king's tavern.

GADSHILL There's enough to make us all.

FALSTAFF To be hanged.

PRINCE Sirs, you four shall front them in the narrow lane: Ned
Poins and I will walk lower. If they 'scape from your
encounter, then they light on us.

PETO How many be there of them?

GADSHILL Some eight, or ten.

FALSTAFF Zounds, will they not rob us?   60

PRINCE What, a coward, Sir John Paunch?

FALSTAFF Indeed, I am not John of Gaunt, your grandfather, but
yet no coward, Hal.

PRINCE Well, we leave that to the proof.

POINS Sirrah Jack, thy horse stands behind the hedge. When
thou need'st him, there thou shalt find him. Farewell,
and stand fast.

FALSTAFF Now cannot I strike him, if I should be hanged.

PRINCE Ned, where are our disguises?

POINS Here, hard by; stand close.   70

[*The Prince and Poins slip away*

FALSTAFF Now, my masters, happy man be his dole, say I; every
man to his business.

The Travellers are heard coming down the hill

I TRAV. Come, neighbour, the boy shall lead our horses down
the hill. We'll walk afoot awhile and ease our legs.

THIEVES Stand!

TRAV'ERS Jesus bless us!

FALSTAFF Strike, down with them, cut the villains' throats! Ah,

whoreson caterpillars! Bacon-fed knaves! They hate us
youth. Down with them, fleece them.

1 TRAV.   O, we are undone, both we and ours for ever.   80

FALSTAFF   Hang ye, gorbellied knaves, are ye undone? No, ye fat
chuffs. I would your store were here! On, bacons, on!
What, ye knaves? Young men must live. You are
grand-jurors, are ye? We'll jure ye, faith.

> ['Here they rob them and bind them' and
> then drive them down the hill

The PRINCE *and* POINS *steal from the bushes, disguised*

PRINCE   The thieves have bound the true men. Now, could
thou and I rob the thieves, and go merrily to London,
it would be argument for a week, laughter for a
month, and a good jest for ever.

POINS   Stand close, I hear them coming.

The Thieves return

FALSTAFF   Come, my masters, let us share, and then to horse   90
before day. An the Prince and Poins be not two arrant
cowards, there's no equity stirring. There's no more
valour in that Poins than in a wild-duck.

> ['As they are sharing, the Prince and
> Poins set upon them'

PRINCE   Your money!

POINS   Villains!

> ['They all run away, leaving the booty behind them,
> and Falstaff, after a blow or two, runs away too'

PRINCE   Got with much ease. Now merrily to horse: the thieves
are all scattered, and possessed with fear so strongly that
they dare not meet each other. Each takes his fellow for
an officer. Away, good Ned. Falstaff sweats to death,
and lards the lean earth as he walks along. Were't not   100
for laughing, I should pity him.

POINS   How the fat rogue roared!

> [*they go*

SCENE 3

A room in Warkworth Castle

'Enter HOTSPUR, *solus, reading a letter' and striding to and fro*

HOTSPUR 'But, for mine own part, my lord, I could be well
contented to be there, in respect of the love I bear
your house.'

He could be contented: why is he not then? In
respect of the love he bears our house: he shows in
this, he loves his own barn better than he loves our
house. Let me see some more.

'The purpose you undertake is dangerous.'

Why, that's certain. 'Tis dangerous to take a cold, to
sleep, to drink, but I tell you, my lord fool, out of this   10
nettle, danger, we pluck this flower, safety.

'The purpose you undertake is dangerous, the friends
you have named uncertain, the time itself unsorted, and
your whole plot too light for the counterpoise of so
great an opposition.'

Say you so, say you so? I say unto you again, you are
a shallow cowardly hind, and you lie. What a lack-
brain is this! By the Lord, our plot is a good plot as ever
was laid, our friends true and constant: a good plot,
good friends, and full of expectation: an excellent plot,   20
very good friends. What a frosty-spirited rogue is this!
Why, my lord of York commends the plot and the
general course of the action. 'Zounds, an I were now
by this rascal, I could brain him with his lady's fan. Is
there not my father, my uncle, and myself? Lord
Edmund Mortimer, my lord of York, and Owen
Glendower? Is there not besides the Douglas? Have I
not all their letters to meet me in arms by the ninth of
the next month? And are they not some of them set
forward already? What a pagan rascal is this! An infidel!   30
Ha! You shall see now, in very sincerity of fear and
cold heart, will he to the king, and lay open all our
proceedings! O, I could divide myself and go to buffets,
for moving such a dish of skim milk with so honourable

an action! Hang him! Let him tell the king, we are
prepared: I will set forward tonight.

             'Enter his Lady'

How now, Kate? I must leave you within these two
hours.

LADY PERCY O my good lord, why are you thus alone?
             For what offence have I this fortnight been   40
             A banished woman from my Harry's bed?
             Tell me, sweet lord, what is't that takes from thee
             Thy stomach, pleasure, and thy golden sleep?
             Why dost thou bend thine eyes upon the earth,
             And start so often when thou sit'st alone?
             Why hast thou lost the fresh blood in thy cheeks,
             And given my treasures and my rights of thee
             To thick-eyed musing and curst melancholy?
             In thy faint slumbers I by thee have watched,
             And heard thee murmur tales of iron wars,   50
             Speak terms of manage to thy bounding steed,
             Cry 'Courage! To the field!' And thou hast talked
             Of sallies and retires, of trenches, tents,
             Of palisadoes, frontiers, parapets,
             Of basilisks, of cannon, culverin,
             Of prisoners' ransom, and of soldiers slain,
             And all the currents of a heady fight.
             Thy spirit within thee hath been so at war,
             And thus hath so bestirred thee in thy sleep,
             That beads of sweat have stood upon thy brow,   60
             Like bubbles in a late-disturbéd stream,
             And in thy face strange motions have appeared,
             Such as we see when men restrain their breath
             On some great sudden hest. O, what portents are these?
             Some heavy business hath my lord in hand,
             And I must know it, else he loves me not.

HOTSPUR What, ho!

             A servant enters

             Is Gilliams with the packet gone?

SERVANT He is, my lord, an hour ago.

HOTSPUR Hath Butler brought those horses from the sheriff?

SERVANT	One horse, my lord, he brought even now.	70
HOTSPUR	What horse? A roan, a crop-ear, is it not?	
SERVANT	It is, my lord.	
HOTSPUR	That roan shall be my throne.	

HOTSPUR   That roan shall be my throne.
    Well, I will back him straight: O esperance!
    Bid Butler lead him forth into the park. [*the servant goes*

LADY PERCY But hear you, my lord.

HOTSPUR What say'st thou, my lady?

LADY PERCY What is it carries you away?

HOTSPUR Why, my horse, my love, my horse.

LADY PERCY Out, you mad-headed ape!
    A weasel hath not such a deal of spleen   80
    As you are tossed with. In faith,
    I'll know your business, Harry, that I will.
    I fear my brother Mortimer doth stir
    About his title, and hath sent for you
    To line his enterprise. But if you go –

HOTSPUR So far afoot, I shall be weary, love.

LADY PERCY Come, come, you paraquito, answer me
    Directly unto this question that I ask.
    In faith, I'll break thy little finger, Harry,
    An if thou wilt not tell me all things true.   90

HOTSPUR Away,
    Away, you trifler! Love! I love thee not,
    I care not for thee, Kate. This is no world
    To play with mammets and to tilt with lips.
    We must have bloody noses and cracked crowns,
    And pass them current too. God's me, my horse!
    What say'st thou, Kate? What wouldst thou have
              with me?

LADY PERCY Do you not love me? Do you not, indeed?
    Well, do not then, for since you love me not
    I will not love myself. Do you not love me?   100
    Nay, tell me if you speak in jest or no.

HOTSPUR Come, wilt thou see me ride?
    And when I am a-horseback, I will swear
    I love thee infinitely. But hark you, Kate,
    I must not have you henceforth question me

Whither I go, nor reason whereabout.
Whither I must, I must. And, to conclude,
This evening must I leave you, gentle Kate.
I know you wise, but yet no farther wise
Than Harry Percy's wife; constant you are,   110
But yet a woman: and for secrecy,
No lady closer, for I well believe
Thou wilt not utter what thou dost not know.
And so far will I trust thee, gentle Kate!

LADY PERCY   How! So far?

HOTSPUR   Not an inch further. But hark you, Kate,
Whither I go, thither shall you go too:
Today will I set forth, tomorrow you.
Will this content you, Kate?

LADY PERCY   It must, of force.

                              [they go

SCENE 4

A room at the Boar's Head Tavern in Eastcheap

The PRINCE *enters at one door, crosses the room,*
opens a door opposite and calls

PRINCE   Ned, prithee, come out of that fat room, and lend me
thy hand to laugh a little.

POINS   Where hast been, Hal?   *[comes forth*

PRINCE   With three or four loggerheads, amongst three or four
score hogsheads. I have sounded the very base-string
of humility. Sirrah, I am sworn brother to a leash of
drawers, and can call them all by their christen names,
as Tom, Dick, and Francis. They take it already upon
their salvation, that though I be but Prince of Wales,
yet I am the king of courtesy, and tell me flatly I am   10
no proud Jack like Falstaff, but a Corinthian, a lad of
mettle, a good boy (by the Lord, so they call me!) and
when I am king of England, I shall command all the
good lads in Eastcheap. They call drinking deep 'dyeing
scarlet', and when you breathe in your watering, they

cry 'hem!' and bid you 'play it off'. To conclude, I am
so good a proficient in one quarter of an hour, that I
can drink with any tinker in his own language during
my life. I tell thee, Ned, thou hast lost much honour,
that thou wert not with me in this action. But, sweet 20
Ned – to sweeten which name of Ned, I give thee this
pennyworth of sugar, clapped even now into my hand
by an underskinker, one that never spake other English
in his life than 'Eight shillings and sixpence', and 'You
are welcome', with this shrill addition, 'Anon, anon, sir!
Score a pint of bastard in the Half-moon', or so. But,
Ned, to drive away the time till Falstaff come, I prithee,
do thou stand in some by-room, while I question my
puny drawer to what end he gave me the sugar; and do
thou never leave calling 'Francis', that his tale to me 30
may be nothing but 'Anon'. Step aside, and I'll show
thee a precedent.

> POINS *returns to the room whence he came,*
> *leaving the door open behind him*

POINS	[*calls*] Francis!
PRINCE	Thou art perfect.
POINS	Francis!

> FRANCIS *bustles in through the other door*

FRANCIS	Anon, anon, sir.	[*turns back*
	Look down into the Pomgarnet, Ralph.	
PRINCE	Come hither, Francis.	
FRANCIS	My lord?	
PRINCE	How long hast thou to serve, Francis?	40
FRANCIS	Forsooth, five years, and as much as to –	
POINS	[*within*] Francis!	
FRANCIS	Anon, anon, sir.	
PRINCE	Five year! By'r lady, a long lease for the clinking of pewter; But, Francis, darest thou be so valiant as to play the coward with thy indenture and show it a fair pair of heels and run from it?	
FRANCIS	O Lord, sir! I'll be sworn upon all the books in England, I could find in my heart –	
POINS	[*within*] Francis!	50

FRANCIS	Anon, sir.
PRINCE	How old art thou, Francis?
FRANCIS	Let me see – about Michaelmas next I shall be –
POINS	[*within*] Francis!
FRANCIS	Anon, sir. Pray stay a little, my lord.

                                    [*he makes towards the by-room*

PRINCE	[*checks him*] Nay, but hark you, Francis. For the sugar thou gavest me – 'twas a pennyworth, was't not?
FRANCIS	O Lord, I would it had been two!
PRINCE	I will give thee for it a thousand pound. Ask me when thou wilt, and thou shalt have it –

    60

POINS	[*within*] Francis!
FRANCIS	Anon, anon.
PRINCE	Anon, Francis? No, Francis, but tomorrow, Francis; or, Francis, a-Thursday; or, indeed, Francis, when thou wilt. But, Francis!
FRANCIS	My lord?
PRINCE	Wilt thou rob this leathern jerkin, crystal-button, knot-pated, agate-ring, puke-stocking, caddis-garter, smooth-tongue, Spanish-pouch –
FRANCIS	O Lord, sir, who do you mean?

    70

PRINCE	Why then, your brown bastard is your only drink! For, look you, Francis, your white canvas doublet will sully. In Barbary, sir, it cannot come to so much.
FRANCIS	What, sir?
POINS	[*within*] Francis!
PRINCE	Away, you rogue, dost thou not hear them call?

                     [*'Here they both call him; the drawer stands*
                            amazed, not knowing which way to go'

The VINTNER *comes in*

VINTNER	What! Stand'st thou still, and hear'st such a calling? Look to the guests within. [*Francis goes.*] My lord, old Sir John, with half-a-dozen more, are at the door. Shall I let them in?

    80

PRINCE	Let them alone awhile, and then open the door. [*Vintner goes.*] Poins!
POINS	[*returning*] Anon, anon, sir.
PRINCE	Sirrah, Falstaff and the rest of the thieves are at the

door. Shall we be merry?

POINS   As merry as crickets, my lad. But hark ye, what cunning match have you made with this jest of the
drawer? Come, what's the issue?

PRINCE   I am now of all humours that have showed themselves
humours since the old days of goodman Adam to the   90
pupil age of this present twelve o'clock at midnight.
[*Francis hurries past.*] What's o'clock, Francis?

FRANCIS   Anon, anon, sir.   [*he goes out*

PRINCE   That ever this fellow should have fewer words than a
parrot, and yet the son of a woman! His industry is up-
stairs and down-stairs, his eloquence the parcel of a
reckoning. I am not yet of Percy's mind, the Hotspur
of the north, he that kills me some six or seven dozen
of Scots at a breakfast, washes his hands, and says to his
wife, 'Fie upon this quiet life! I want work.' 'O my   100
sweet Harry,' says she, 'how many hast thou killed
today?' 'Give my roan horse a drench', says he, and
answers, 'Some fourteen', an hour after; 'a trifle, a
trifle.' I prithee, call in Falstaff. I'll play Percy, and that
damned brawn shall play Dame Mortimer his wife.
'Rivo!' says the drunkard: call in Ribs, call in Tallow.

FALSTAFF *enters with* GADSHILL, BARDOLPH *and* PETO;
FRANCIS *follows with cups of sack*

POINS   Welcome, Jack. Where hast thou been?

FALSTAFF   [*to himself*] A plague of all cowards, I say, and a vengeance too! Marry, and amen! Give me a cup of sack, boy.
Ere I lead this life long, I'll sew nether-stocks, and   110
mend them, and foot them too. A plague of all cowards!
Give me a cup of sack, rogue. Is there no virtue extant?
[*'he drinketh'*

PRINCE   Didst thou never see Titan kiss a dish of butter (pitiful-
hearted Titan!) that melted at the sweet tale of the
sun's? If thou didst, then behold that compound.

FALSTAFF   [*giving Francis the empty cup*] You rogue, here's lime in
this sack too. There is nothing but roguery to be found
in villainous man, yet a coward is worse than a cup of
sack with lime in it. A villainous coward! Go thy ways,

old Jack, die when thou wilt. If manhood, good man-   120
hood, be not forgot upon the face of the earth, then am
I a shotten herring. There lives not three good men
unhanged in England, and one of them is fat, and grows
old. God help the while! A bad world, I say. I would I
were a weaver – I could sing psalms or any thing. A
plague of all cowards, I say still.

PRINCE   How now, wool-sack! What mutter you?

FALSTAFF   A king's son! If I do not beat thee out of thy kingdom
with a dagger of lath, and drive all thy subjects afore
thee like a flock of wild geese, I'll never wear hair on   130
my face more. You, Prince of Wales!

PRINCE   Why you whoreson round man! What's the matter?

FALSTAFF   Are not you a coward? Answer me to that – and Poins
there?

POINS   'Zounds, ye fat paunch, an ye call me coward, by the
Lord I'll stab thee.   [he draws his dagger

FALSTAFF   I call thee coward! I'll see thee damned ere I call thee
coward – but I would give a thousand pound I could
run as fast as thou canst. You are straight enough in the
shoulders, you care not who sees your back: call you   140
that backing of your friends? A plague upon such
backing! Give me them that will face me. [to Francis]
Give me a cup of sack – I am a rogue if I drunk today.

PRINCE   O villain! Thy lips are scarce wiped since thou
drunk'st last.

FALSTAFF   All's one for that. ['he drinketh'] A plague of all cowards,
still say I.

PRINCE   What's the matter?

FALSTAFF   What's the matter? There be four of us here have ta'en
a thousand pound this day morning.   150

PRINCE   Where is it, Jack? Where is it?

FALSTAFF   Where is it? Taken from us it is: a hundred upon poor
four of us.

PRINCE   What, a hundred, man?

FALSTAFF   I am a rogue, if I were not at half-sword with a dozen
of them two hours together. I have 'scaped by miracle.
I am eight times thrust through the doublet, four
through the hose, my buckler cut through and through,

my sword hacked like a handsaw, ecce signum! [*he*
draws it] I never dealt better since I was a man: all would   160
not do. A plague of all cowards! Let them speak. If they
speak more or less than truth, they are villains and the
sons of darkness.

PRINCE   Speak, sirs, how was it?

GADSHILL We four set upon some dozen –

FALSTAFF Sixteen at least, my lord.

GADSHILL And bound them.

PETO   No, no, they were not bound.

FALSTAFF You rogue, they were bound, every man of them, or I
am a Jew else, an Ebrew Jew.   170

GADSHILL As we were sharing, some six or seven fresh men set
upon us –

FALSTAFF And unbound the rest, and then come in the other.

PRINCE   What, fought you with them all?

FALSTAFF All! I know not what you call all, but if I fought not
with fifty of them I am a bunch of radish: if there were
not two or three and fifty upon poor old Jack, then am
I no two-legged creature.

PRINCE   Pray God you have not murdered some of them.

FALSTAFF Nay, that's past praying for. I have peppered two of   180
them. Two I am sure I have paid, two rogues in
buckram suits. I tell thee what, Hal, if I tell thee a lie,
spit in my face, call me horse. Thou knowest my old
ward: here I lay, and thus I bore my point. Four
rogues in buckram let drive at me –

PRINCE   What, four? Thou said'st but two even now.

FALSTAFF Four, Hal, I told thee four.

POINS   Ay, ay, he said four.

FALSTAFF These four came all afront, and mainly thrust at me. I
made me no more ado, but took all their seven points   190
in my target, thus.

PRINCE   Seven? Why, there were but four even now.

FALSTAFF In buckram?

POINS   Ay, four, in buckram suits.

FALSTAFF Seven, by these hilts, or I am a villain else.

PRINCE   [*aside*] Prithee, let him alone, we shall have more anon.

FALSTAFF Dost thou hear me, Hal?

PRINCE	Ay, and mark thee too, Jack.
FALSTAFF	Do so, for it is worth the listening to. These nine in buckram that I told thee of –
PRINCE	So, two more already.
FALSTAFF	Their points being broken –
POINS	Down fell their hose.
FALSTAFF	Began to give me ground: but I followed me close, came in foot and hand, and with a thought, seven of the eleven I paid.
PRINCE	O monstrous! Eleven buckram men grown out of two!
FALSTAFF	But, as the devil would have it, three misbegotten knaves in Kendal green came at my back, and let drive at me, for it was so dark, Hal, that thou couldest not see thy hand.
PRINCE	These lies are like their father that begets them, gross as a mountain, open, palpable. Why, thou clay-brained guts, thou knotty-pated fool, thou whoreson, obscene, greasy tallow-catch –
FALSTAFF	What, art thou mad? Art thou mad? Is not the truth the truth?
PRINCE	Why, how couldst thou know these men in Kendal green, when it was so dark thou couldst not see thy hand? Come tell us your reason. What sayest thou to this?
POINS	Come, your reason, Jack, your reason.
FALSTAFF	What, upon compulsion? Zounds, an I were at the strappado, or all the racks in the world, I would not tell you on compulsion. Give you a reason on compulsion! If reasons were as plentiful as blackberries, I would give no man a reason upon compulsion, I.
PRINCE	I'll be no longer guilty of this sin. This sanguine coward, this bed-presser, this horseback-breaker, this huge hill of flesh –
FALSTAFF	'Sblood, you starveling, you eel-skin, you dried neat's-tongue, you bull's-pizzle, you stock-fish! O, for breath to utter what is like thee! You tailor's-yard, you sheath, you bow-case, you vile standing tuck –
PRINCE	Well, breathe awhile, and then to it again, and when thou hast tired thyself in base comparisons, hear me speak but this.

200

210

220

230

POINS   Mark, Jack.

PRINCE   We two saw you four set on four, and bound them
            and were masters of their wealth. Mark now, how a
            plain tale shall put you down. Then did we two set on   240
            you four, and with a word, out-faced you from your
            prize, and have it, yea, and can show it you here in the
            house: and, Falstaff, you carried your guts away as
            nimbly, with as quick dexterity, and roared for mercy,
            and still run and roared, as ever I heard bull-calf. What
            a slave art thou, to hack thy sword as thou hast done,
            and then say it was in fight! What trick, what device,
            what starting-hole, canst thou now find out, to hide
            thee from this open and apparent shame?

POINS   Come, let's hear, Jack — what trick hast thou now?   250

FALSTAFF   By the Lord, I knew ye as well as he that made ye.
            Why, hear you, my masters — was it for me to kill the
            heir-apparent? Should I turn upon the true prince?
            Why, thou knowest I am as valiant as Hercules: but
            beware instinct — the lion will not touch the true
            prince. Instinct is a great matter — I was now a coward
            on instinct. I shall think the better of myself and thee
            during my life; I for a valiant lion, and thou for a true
            prince. But, by the Lord, lads, I am glad you have the
            money. Hostess, clap to the doors. Watch tonight, pray 260
            tomorrow. Gallants, lads, boys, hearts of gold, all the
            titles of good fellowship come to you! What, shall we
            be merry? Shall we have a play extempore?

PRINCE   Content — and the argument shall be thy running
            away.

FALSTAFF   Ah! No more of that, Hal, an thou lovest me.

                          HOSTESS *enters*

HOSTESS   O Jesu, my lord the prince —

PRINCE   How now, my lady the hostess! What say'st thou to me?

HOSTESS   Marry, my lord, there is a nobleman of the court at
            door would speak with you: he says he comes from   270
            your father.

PRINCE   Give him as much as will make him a royal man, and
            send him back again to my mother.

FALSTAFF   What manner of man is he?

HOSTESS   An old man.

FALSTAFF   What doth gravity out of his bed at midnight? Shall I give him his answer?

PRINCE   Prithee, do, Jack.

FALSTAFF   Faith, and I'll send him packing.   [*he goes out*

PRINCE   Now, sirs! By'r lady, you fought fair, so did you, Peto, so 280 did you, Bardolph. You are lions too, you ran away upon instinct, you will not touch the true prince, no, fie!

BARDOLPH   Faith, I ran when I saw others run.

PRINCE   Faith, tell me now in earnest, how came Falstaff's sword so hacked?

PETO   Why, he hacked it with his dagger, and said he would swear truth out of England but he would make you believe it was done in fight, and persuaded us to do the like.

BARDOLPH   Yea, and to tickle our noses with spear-grass to make 290 them bleed, and then to beslubber our garments with it, and swear it was the blood of true men. I did that I did not this seven year before; I blushed to hear his monstrous devices.

PRINCE   O villain, thou stolest a cup of sack eighteen years ago, and wert taken with the manner, and ever since thou hast blushed extempore. Thou hadst fire and sword on thy side, and yet thou ran'st away. What instinct hadst thou for it?

BARDOLPH   [*thrusts forward his face*] My lord, do you see these 300 meteors? Do you behold these exhalations?

PRINCE   I do.

BARDOLPH   What think you they portend?

PRINCE   Hot livers, and cold purses.

BARDOLPH   Choler, my lord, if rightly taken.

PRINCE   No, if rightly taken, halter.

FALSTAFF *returns*

Here comes lean Jack, here comes bare-bone. How now, my sweet creature of bombast? How long is't ago, Jack, since thou sawest thine own knee?

FALSTAFF   My own knee! When I was about thy years, Hal, I was 310

not an eagle's talon in the waist, I could have crept
into any alderman's thumb-ring: a plague of sighing
and grief! It blows a man up like a bladder. There's
villainous news abroad. Here was Sir John Bracy from
your father: you must to the court in the morning.
That same mad fellow of the north, Percy, and he of
Wales, that gave Amaimon the bastinado, and made
Lucifer cuckold, and swore the devil his true liegeman
upon the cross of a Welsh hook. What a plague call
you him?   320

POINS   Owen Glendower.

FALSTAFF   Owen, Owen, the same — and his son-in-law,
Mortimer, and old Northumberland, and that sprightly
Scot of Scots, Douglas, that runs a-horseback up a hill
perpendicular —

PRINCE   He that rides at high speed, and with his pistol kills a
sparrow flying.

FALSTAFF   You have hit it.

PRINCE   So did he never the sparrow.

FALSTAFF   Well, that rascal hath good mettle in him, he will not   330
run.

PRINCE   Why, what a rascal art thou then, to praise him so for
running.

FALSTAFF   A-horseback, ye cuckoo, but afoot he will not budge a
foot.

PRINCE   Yes, Jack, upon instinct.

FALSTAFF   I grant ye, upon instinct. Well, he is there too, and
one Mordake, and a thousand blue-caps more.
Worcester is stolen away tonight, thy father's beard is
turned white with the news. You may buy land now   340
as cheap as stinking mackerel.

PRINCE   Why then, it is like, if there come a hot June, and this
civil buffeting hold, we shall buy maidenheads as they
buy hob-nails, by the hundreds.

FALSTAFF   By the mass, lad, thou sayest true, it is like we shall
have good trading that way. But, tell me, Hal, art not
thou horrible afeard? Thou being heir-apparent, could
the world pick thee out three such enemies again, as
that fiend Douglas, that spirit Percy, and that devil

Glendower? Art thou not horribly afraid? Doth not 350
thy blood thrill at it?

PRINCE   Not a whit, i'faith, I lack some of thy instinct.

FALSTAFF   Well, thou wilt be horribly chid tomorrow when thou
comest to thy father. If thou love me, practise an answer.

PRINCE   Do thou stand for my father, and examine me upon
the particulars of my life.

FALSTAFF   Shall I? Content. This chair shall be my state, this
dagger my sceptre, and this cushion my crown.

PRINCE   Thy state is taken for a joined-stool, thy golden sceptre
for a leaden dagger, and thy precious rich crown for a 360
pitiful bald crown!

FALSTAFF   Well, an the fire of grace be not quite out of thee, now
shalt thou be moved. Give me a cup of sack to make
my eyes look red, that it may be thought I have wept –
for I must speak in passion, and I will do it in King
Cambyses' vein.

PRINCE   [bows] Well, here is my leg.

FALSTAFF   And here is my speech. Stand aside, nobility.

HOSTESS   O Jesu, this is excellent sport, i'faith.

FALSTAFF   Weep not, sweet queen, for trickling tears are vain.   370

HOSTESS   O, the father, how he holds his countenance!

FALSTAFF   For God's sake, lords, convey my tristful queen,
For tears do stop the flood-gates of her eyes.

HOSTESS   O Jesu, he doth it as like one of these harlotry players
as ever I see!

FALSTAFF   Peace, good pint-pot, peace, good tickle-brain.
Harry, I do not only marvel where thou spendest thy
time, but also how thou art accompanied: for though
the camomile, the more it is trodden on the faster it
grows, yet youth, the more it is wasted the sooner it 380
wears. That thou art my son, I have partly thy mother's
word, partly my own opinion, but chiefly a villainous
trick of thine eye, and a foolish hanging of thy nether
lip, that doth warrant me. If then thou be son to me,
here lies the point – why, being son to me, art thou so
pointed at? Shall the blessed sun of heaven prove a
micher and eat blackberries? A question not to be
asked. Shall the son of England prove a thief and take

purses? A question to be asked. There is a thing, Harry,
which thou hast often heard of, and it is known to   390
many in our land by the name of pitch. This pitch (as
ancient writers do report) doth defile; so doth the company thou keepest: for, Harry, now I do not speak to
thee in drink, but in tears; not in pleasure, but in
passion; not in words only, but in woes also: and yet
there is a virtuous man whom I have often noted in thy
company, but I know not his name.

PRINCE   What manner of man, an it like your majesty?

FALSTAFF   A goodly portly man, i'faith, and a corpulent, of a
cheerful look, a pleasing eye, and a most noble carriage,   400
and as I think his age some fifty, or by'r lady inclining
to threescore. And now I remember me, his name is
Falstaff. If that man should be lewdly given, he
deceiveth me; for, Harry, I see virtue in his looks. If
then the tree may be known by the fruit, as the fruit by
the tree, then, peremptorily I speak it, there is virtue in
that Falstaff – him keep with, the rest banish. And tell
me now, thou naughty varlet, tell me, where hast thou
been this month?

PRINCE   Dost thou speak like a king? Do thou stand for me,   410
and I'll play my father.

FALSTAFF   Depose me? If thou dost it half so gravely, so majestically,
both in word and matter, hang me up by the heels for a
rabbit-sucker, or a poulter's hare.   [they change places

PRINCE   Well, here I am set.

FALSTAFF   And here I stand – judge, my masters.

PRINCE   Now, Harry, whence come you?

FALSTAFF   My noble lord, from Eastcheap.

PRINCE   The complaints I hear of thee are grievous.

FALSTAFF   'Sblood, my lord, they are false: [aside] nay, I'll tickle   420
ye for a young prince, i'faith.

PRINCE   Swearest thou, ungracious boy? Henceforth ne'er look
on me. Thou art violently carried away from grace:
there is a devil haunts thee in the likeness of an old fat
man; a tun of man is thy companion: why dost thou
converse with that trunk of humours, that bolting-
hutch of beastliness, that swollen parcel of dropsies, that

huge bombard of sack, that stuffed cloak-bag of guts,
that roasted Manningtree ox with the pudding in his
belly, that reverend vice, that grey iniquity, that father 430
ruffian, that vanity in years? Wherein is he good, but to
taste sack and drink it? Wherein neat and cleanly, but to
carve a capon and eat it? Wherein cunning, but in craft?
Wherein crafty, but in villainy? Wherein villainous, but
in all things? Wherein worthy, but in nothing?

FALSTAFF   I would your grace would take me with you. Whom
means your grace?

PRINCE   That villainous abominable misleader of youth,
Falstaff, that old white-bearded Satan.

FALSTAFF   My lord, the man I know.   440

PRINCE   I know thou dost.

FALSTAFF   But to say I know more harm in him than in myself,
were to say more than I know: that he is old, the more
the pity, his white hairs do witness it; but that he is,
saving your reverence, a whoremaster, that I utterly
deny. If sack and sugar be a fault, God help the
wicked! If to be old and merry be a sin, then many an
old host that I know is damned. If to be fat be to be
hated, then Pharaoh's lean kine are to be loved. No,
my good lord – banish Peto, banish Bardolph, banish 450
Poins, but for sweet Jack Falstaff, kind Jack Falstaff,
true Jack Falstaff, valiant Jack Falstaff, and therefore
more valiant being as he is old Jack Falstaff, banish not
him thy Harry's company, banish not him thy Harry's
company. Banish plump Jack, and banish all the world.

PRINCE   I do, I will.

'Enter BARDOLPH, *running'*

BARDOLPH   O, my lord, my lord, the sheriff with a most monstrous
watch is at the door!

FALSTAFF   Out, ye rogue! Play out the play. I have much to say in
the behalf of that Falstaff.

'Enter the HOSTESS*'*

                                                                        460

HOSTESS   O Jesu, my lord, my lord!

PRINCE   Heigh, heigh! The devil rides upon a fiddle-stick.
What's the matter?

HOSTESS   The sheriff and all the watch are at the door, they are
           come to search the house. Shall I let them in?
FALSTAFF   Dost thou hear, Hal? Never call a true piece of gold a
           counterfeit. Thou art essentially made, without seeming
           so.
PRINCE   And thou a natural coward, without instinct.
FALSTAFF   I deny your major, if you will deny the sheriff; so, if   470
           not, let him enter. If I become not a cart as well as
           another man, a plague on my bringing up! I hope I
           shall as soon be strangled with a halter as another.
PRINCE   Go, hide thee behind the arras, the rest walk up above.
           Now, my masters, for a true face and good conscience.
FALSTAFF   Both which I have had, but their date is out, and
           therefore I'll hide me.
                    [he does so; all but the Prince and Poins go out
PRINCE   Call in the sheriff.

              'Enter Sheriff and the Carrier'

           Now, master sheriff, what is your will with me?
SHERIFF   First, pardon me, my lord. A hue and cry   480
           Hath followed certain men unto this house.
PRINCE   What men?
SHERIFF   One of them is well known, my gracious lord,
           A gross fat man.
CARRIER   As fat as butter.
PRINCE   The man, I do assure you, is not here,
           For I myself at this time have employed him:
           And, sheriff, I will engage my word to thee
           That I will by tomorrow dinner-time
           Send him to answer thee, or any man,   490
           For any thing he shall be charged withal,
           And so let me entreat you leave the house.
SHERIFF   I will, my lord. There are two gentlemen
           Have in this robbery lost three hundred marks.
PRINCE   It may be so: if he have robbed these men,
           He shall be answerable – and so, farewell.
SHERIFF   Good night, my noble lord.
PRINCE   I think it is good morrow, is it not?
SHERIFF   Indeed, my lord, I think it be two o'clock.
                             [Sheriff and Carrier depart

PRINCE	This oily rascal is known as well as Paul's. Go, call him	500
	forth.	
POINS	[*lifts the arras*] Falstaff! Fast asleep behind the arras, and	
	snorting like a horse.	
PRINCE	Hark, how hard he fetches breath. Search his pockets.	
	[*'He searcheth his pocket, and findeth certain papers'*] What	
	hast thou found?	
POINS	Nothing but papers, my lord.	
PRINCE	Let's see what they be: read them.	

POINS	Item, A capon	2s. 2d.	
	Item, Sauce	4d.	
	Item, Sack, two gallons	5s. 8d.	510
	Item, Anchovies and sack after supper	2s. 6d.	
	Item, Bread	ob.	

PRINCE	O monstrous! But one half-pennyworth of bread to
	this intolerable deal of sack! What there is else keep
	close, we'll read it at more advantage; there let him
	sleep till day. I'll to the court in the morning. We must
	all to the wars, and thy place shall be honourable. I'll
	procure this fat rogue a charge of foot, and I know his
	death will be a march of twelve-score. The money shall
	be paid back again with advantage. Be with me betimes 520
	in the morning, and so good morrow, Poins.
POINS	Good morrow, good my lord.

[*they go*

ACT 3 SCENE 1

Wales. A room in Glendower's house

'*Enter* HOTSPUR, WORCESTER, LORD MORTIMER,
and OWEN GLENDOWER', *carrying papers*

MORTIMER These promises are fair, the parties sure,
And our induction full of prosperous hope.

HOTSPUR Lord Mortimer, and cousin Glendower, will you sit
down? And uncle Worcester: a plague upon it, I have
forgot the map!

GLEND. No, here it is. Sit, cousin Percy, sit good cousin
Hotspur, for by that name as oft as Lancaster doth speak
of you, his cheek looks pale, and with a rising sigh he
wisheth you in heaven.   [*they sit*

HOTSPUR And you in hell, as oft as he hears Owen Glendower 10
spoke of.

GLEND. I cannot blame him: at my nativity
The front of heaven was full of fiery shapes,
Of burning cressets, and at my birth
The frame and huge foundation of the earth
Shaked like a coward.

HOTSPUR Why, so it would have done at the same season, if
your mother's cat had but kittened, though yourself
had never been born.

GLEND. I say the earth did shake, when I was born.   20

HOTSPUR And I say the earth was not of my mind,
If you suppose as fearing you it shook.

GLEND. The heavens were all on fire, the earth did tremble.

HOTSPUR O, then the earth shook to see the heavens on fire,
And not in fear of your nativity.
Diseaséd nature oftentimes breaks forth
In strange eruptions; oft the teeming earth
Is with a kind of colic pinched and vexed
By the imprisoning of unruly wind
Within her womb, which for enlargement striving   30
Shakes the old beldam earth, and topples down
Steeples and moss-grown towers. At your birth

Our grandam earth, having this distemperature,
In passion shook.

GLEND.   Cousin, of many men
I do not bear these crossings. Give me leave
To tell you once again that at my birth
The front of heaven was full of fiery shapes,
The goats ran from the mountains, and the herds
Were strangely clamorous to the frighted fields.
These signs have marked me extraordinary,   40
And all the courses of my life do show
I am not in the roll of common men.
Where is he living, clipped in with the sea
That chides the banks of England, Scotland, Wales,
Which calls me pupil or hath read to me?
And bring him out that is but woman's son
Can trace me in the tedious ways of art,
And hold me pace in deep experiments.

HOTSPUR   I think there's no man speaks better Welsh:
I'll to dinner.   [*he rises* 50

MORTIMER Peace, cousin Percy, you will make him mad.

GLEND.   I can call spirits from the vasty deep.

HOTSPUR   Why, so can I, or so can any man,
But will they come when you do call for them?

GLEND.   Why, I can teach you, cousin, to command the devil.

HOTSPUR   And I can teach thee, coz, to shame the devil,
By telling truth. Tell truth and shame the devil.
If thou have power to raise him, bring him hither,
And I'll be sworn I have power to shame him hence:
O, while you live, tell truth and shame the devil.   60

MORTIMER Come, come, no more of this unprofitable chat.

GLEND.   Three times hath Henry Bolingbroke made head
Against my power; thrice from the banks of Wye
And sandy-bottomed Severn have I sent him
Bootless home and weather-beaten back.

HOTSPUR   Home without boots, and in foul weather too!
How 'scapes he agues, in the devil's name?

GLEND.   Come, here's the map: shall we divide our right,
According to our threefold order ta'en?
                        [*the map is spread upon the table*

MORTIMER The archdeacon hath divided it   70
          Into three limits, very equally.
          England, from Trent to Severn hitherto,
          By south and east is to my part assigned:
          All westward, Wales beyond the Severn shore,
          And all the fertile land within that bound,
          To Owen Glendower: and, dear coz, to you
          The remnant northward, lying off from Trent.
          And our indentures tripartite are drawn,
          Which being sealéd interchangeably
          (A business that this night may execute),   80
          Tomorrow, cousin Percy, you and I
          And my good Lord of Worcester will set forth
          To meet your father and the Scottish power,
          As is appointed us, at Shrewsbury.
          My father Glendower is not ready yet,
          Nor shall we need his help these fourteen days.
          [*to Glendower*] Within that space you may have
                                             drawn together
          Your tenants, friends, and neighbouring gentlemen.
GLEND.   A shorter time shall send me to you, lords,
          And in my conduct shall your ladies come,   90
          From whom you now must steal and take no leave,
          For there will be a world of water shed
          Upon the parting of your wives and you.
HOTSPUR   [*studying the map*] Methinks, my moiety, north
                                             from Burton here,
          In quantity equals not one of yours.
          See how this river comes me cranking in,
          And cuts me from the best of all my land
          A huge half-moon, a monstrous cantle out.
          I'll have the current in this place dammed up,
          And here the smug and silver Trent shall run   100
          In a new channel, fair and evenly.
          It shall not wind with such a deep indent,
          To rob me of so rich a bottom here.
GLEND.   Not wind? It shall, it must – you see, it doth.
MORTIMER Yea, but
          Mark how he bears his course, and runs me up

With like advantage on the other side,
Gelding the opposéd continent as much
As on the other side it takes from you.

WORCESTER Yea, but a little charge will trench him here,   110
And on this north side win this cape of land,
And then he runs straight and even.

HOTSPUR I'll have it so, a little charge will do it.

GLEND. I'll not have it altered.

HOTSPUR   Will not you?

GLEND. No, nor you shall not.

HOTSPUR   Who shall say me nay?

GLEND. Why, that will I.

HOTSPUR Let me not understand you then, speak it in Welsh.

GLEND. I can speak English, lord, as well as you;
For I was trained up in the English court,
Where being but young I framéd to the harp   120
Many an English ditty, lovely well,
And gave the tongue a helpful ornament,
A virtue that was never seen in you.

HOTSPUR Marry,
And I am glad of it with all my heart!
I had rather be a kitten and cry mew
Than one of these same metre ballad-mongers.
I had rather hear a brazen canstick turned,
Or a dry wheel grate on the axle-tree,
And that would set my teeth nothing on edge,   130
Nothing so much as mincing poetry.
'Tis like the forced gait of a shuffling nag.

GLEND. Come, you shall have Trent turned.

HOTSPUR I do not care, I'll give thrice so much land
To any well-deserving friend:
But in the way of bargain, mark ye me,
I'll cavil on the ninth part of a hair.
Are the indentures drawn? Shall we be gone?

GLEND. The moon shines fair, you may away by night:
I'll haste the writer, and withal   140
Break with your wives of your departure hence.
I am afraid my daughter will run mad,
So much she doteth on her Mortimer.   [he goes out

MORTIMER Fie, cousin Percy! How you cross my father!

HOTSPUR I cannot choose. Sometime he angers me
With telling me of the moldwarp and the ant,
Of the dreamer Merlin and his prophecies,
And of a dragon and a finless fish,
A clip-winged griffin and a moulten raven,
A couching lion and a ramping cat,   150
And such a deal of skimble-skamble stuff
As puts me from my faith. I tell you what –
He held me last night at least nine hours
In reckoning up the several devils' names
That were his lackeys. I cried, 'hum', and 'well, go to',
But marked him not a word. O, he is as tedious
As a tired horse, a railing wife,
Worse than a smoky house; I had rather live
With cheese and garlic in a windmill, far,
Than feed on cates and have him talk to me   160
In any summer house in Christendom.

MORTIMER In faith, he is a worthy gentleman,
Exceedingly well read, and profited
In strange concealments, valiant as a lion,
And wondrous affable, and as bountiful
As mines of India. Shall I tell you, cousin?
He holds your temper in a high respect,
And curbs himself even of his natural scope,
When you come 'cross his humour, faith, he does.
I warrant you, that man is not alive   170
Might so have tempted him as you have done,
Without the taste of danger and reproof;
But do not use it oft, let me entreat you.

WORCESTER In faith, my lord, you are too wilful blame,
And since your coming hither have done enough
To put him quite beside his patience.
You must needs learn, lord, to amend this fault.
Though sometimes it show greatness, courage, blood –
And that's the dearest grace it renders you –
Yet oftentimes it doth present harsh rage,   180
Defect of manners, want of government,
Pride, haughtiness, opinion, and disdain,

The least of which haunting a nobleman
Loseth men's hearts, and leaves behind a stain
Upon the beauty of all parts besides,
Beguiling them of commendation.

HOTSPUR   Well, I am schooled: good manners be your speed!
Here come our wives, and let us take our leave.

'*Enter* GLENDOWER *with the* LADIES'

MORTIMER This is the deadly spite that angers me:
My wife can speak no English, I no Welsh.   190

GLEND.   My daughter weeps, she'll not part with you;
She'll be a soldier too, she'll to the wars.

MORTIMER Good father, tell her that she and my aunt Percy
Shall follow in your conduct speedily.

[*'Glendower speaks to her in Welsh,
and she answers him in the same'*

GLEND.   She is desperate here, a peevish self-willed harlotry, one
that no persuasion can do good upon.

[*She turns to Mortimer and 'speaks in Welsh'*

MORTIMER I understand thy looks. That pretty Welsh
Which thou pourest down from these swelling heavens
I am too perfect in, and but for shame
In such a parley should I answer thee.   200

[*'The lady' speaks 'again in Welsh'*

I understand thy kisses and thou mine,
And that's a feeling disputation;
But I will never be a truant, love,
Till I have learned thy language, for thy tongue
Makes Welsh as sweet as ditties highly penned,
Sung by a fair queen in a summer's bower,
With ravishing division, to her lute.

GLEND.   Nay, if you melt, then will she run mad.

[*'The lady speaks again in Welsh'*

MORTIMER O, I am ignorance itself in this!

GLEND.   She bids you on the wanton rushes lay you down,   210
And rest your gentle head upon her lap,
And she will sing the song that pleaseth you,
And on your eyelids crown the god of sleep,
Charming your blood with pleasing heaviness,

Making such difference 'twixt wake and sleep
As is the difference betwixt day and night,
The hour before the heavenly-harnessed team
Begins his golden progress in the east.

MORTIMER With all my heart I'll sit and hear her sing;
By that time will our book, I think, be drawn.   220

GLEND.   Do so,   [*Mortimer sits, and she with him*
And those musicians that shall play to you
Hang in the air a thousand leagues from hence,
And straight they shall be here. Sit and attend.

HOTSPUR Come, Kate, thou art perfect in lying down. Come,
quick, quick, that I may lay my head in thy lap.

LADY PERCY Go, ye giddy goose.

                                          [*'the music plays'*

HOTSPUR Now I perceive the devil understands Welsh,
And 'tis no marvel, he is so humorous.
By'r lady, he is a good musician.   230

LADY PERCY Then should you be nothing but musical, for you are
altogether governed by humours. Lie still, ye thief, and
hear the lady sing in Welsh.

HOTSPUR I had rather hear Lady, my brach, howl in Irish.

LADY PERCY Wouldst thou have thy head broken?

HOTSPUR No.

LADY PERCY Then be still.

HOTSPUR Neither – 'tis a woman's fault.

LADY PERCY Now God help thee!

HOTSPUR To the Welsh lady's bed.   240

LADY PERCY What's that?

HOTSPUR Peace! She sings.

                            [*'Here the lady sings a Welsh song'*

HOTSPUR Come, Kate, I'll have your song too.

LADY PERCY Not mine, in good sooth.

HOTSPUR Not yours, in good sooth! Heart! You swear like a
comfit-maker's wife – 'not you, in good sooth', and 'as
true as I live', and 'as God shall mend me', and 'as sure
as day';
And givest such sarcenet surety for thy oaths,
As if thou never walk'st further than Finsbury.   250
Swear me, Kate, like a lady as thou art,

A good mouth-filling oath, and leave 'in sooth',
And such protest of pepper-gingerbread,
To velvet-guards and Sunday citizens.
Come, sing.

LADY PERCY I will not sing.

HOTSPUR 'Tis the next way to turn tailor, or be red-breast
teacher. An the indentures be drawn, I'll away   within
these two hours; and so come in when ye will.   [he goes

GLEND. Come, come, Lord Mortimer, you are as slow   260
As hot Lord Percy is on fire to go.
By this our book is drawn. We'll but seal,
And then to horse immediately.

MORTIMER   With all my heart.
[they go

SCENE 2

London. A room in the palace

'*The* KING, PRINCE OF WALES, *and others*'

KING Lords, give us leave. The Prince of Wales and I
Must have some private conference. But be near
at hand,
For we shall presently have need of you.   [Lords go
I know not whether God will have it so
For some displeasing service I have done,
That, in his secret doom, out of my blood
He'll breed revengement and a scourge for me;
But thou dost in thy passages of life
Make me believe that thou art only marked
For the hot vengeance and the rod of heaven,   10
To punish my mistreadings. Tell me else,
Could such inordinate and low desires,
Such poor, such bare, such lewd, such mean attempts,
Such barren pleasures, rude society,
As thou art matched withal, and grafted to,
Accompany the greatness of thy blood,
And hold their level with thy princely heart?

PRINCE   So please your majesty, I would I could
              Quit all offences with as clear excuse
              As well as I am doubtless I can purge   20
              Myself of many I am charged withal.
              Yet such extenuation let me beg,
              As, in reproof of many tales devised,
              Which oft the ear of greatness needs must hear,
              By smiling pickthanks and base newsmongers,
              I may for some things true, wherein my youth
              Hath faulty wand'red and irregular,
              Find pardon on my true submission.

KING   God pardon thee! Yet let me wonder, Harry,
              At thy affections, which do hold a wing   30
              Quite from the flight of all thy ancestors.
              Thy place in council thou hast rudely lost,
              Which by thy younger brother is supplied,
              And art almost an alien to the hearts
              Of all the court and princes of my blood.
              The hope and expectation of thy time
              Is ruined, and the soul of every man
              Prophetically do forethink thy fall.
              Had I so lavish of my presence been,
              So common-hackneyed in the eyes of men,   40
              So stale and cheap to vulgar company,
              Opinion, that did help me to the crown,
              Had still kept loyal to possession,
              And left me in reputeless banishment,
              A fellow of no mark nor likelihood.
              By being seldom seen, I could not stir
              But, like a comet, I was wond'red at;
              That men would tell their children 'This is he';
              Others would say 'Where? Which is Bolingbroke?'
              And then I stole all courtesy from heaven,   50
              And dressed myself in such humility
              That I did pluck allegiance from men's hearts,
              Loud shouts and salutations from their mouths,
              Even in the presence of the crownéd king.
              Thus did I keep my person fresh and new,
              My presence like a robe pontifical,

Ne'er seen but wond'red at; and so my state,
Seldom but sumptuous, showéd like a feast,
And won by rareness such solemnity.
The skipping king, he ambled up and down   60
With shallow jesters and rash bavin wits,
Soon kindled and soon burnt; carded his state,
Mingled his royalty with cap'ring fools,
Had his great name profanéd with their scorns,
And gave his countenance, against his name,
To laugh at gibing boys, and stand the push
Of every beardless vain comparative;
Grew a companion to the common streets,
Enfeoffed himself to popularity;
That, being daily swallowed by men's eyes,   70
They surfeited with honey and began
To loathe the taste of sweetness, whereof a little
More than a little is by much too much.
So when he had occasion to be seen,
He was but as the cuckoo is in June,
Heard, not regarded; seen, but with such eyes
As, sick and blunted with community,
Afford no extraordinary gaze,
Such as is bent on sun-like majesty,
When it shines seldom in admiring eyes;   80
But rather drowsed and hung their eyelids down,
Slept in his face, and rend'red such aspect
As cloudy men use to their adversaries,
Being with his presence glutted, gorged, and full.
And in that very line, Harry, standest thou,
For thou hast lost thy princely privilege
With vile participation. Not an eye
But is a-weary of thy common sight,
Save mine, which hath desired to see thee more,
Which now doth that I would not have it do,   90
Make blind itself with foolish tenderness.

PRINCE   I shall hereafter, my thrice gracious lord,
Be more myself.

KING   For all the world
As thou art to this hour was Richard then,

When I from France set foot at Ravenspurgh,
And even as I was then is Percy now.
Now by my sceptre and my soul to boot,
He hath more worthy interest to the state
Than thou the shadow of succession.
For of no right, nor colour like to right,   100
He doth fill fields with harness in the realm,
Turns head against the lion's arméd jaws,
And, being no more in debt to years than thou,
Leads ancient lords and reverend bishops on
To bloody battles and to bruising arms.
What never-dying honour hath he got
Against renownéd Douglas! Whose high deeds,
Whose hot incursions and great name in arms
Holds from all soldiers chief majority,
And military title capital,   110
Through all the kingdoms that acknowledge Christ.
Thrice hath this Hotspur, Mars in swathling clothes,
This infant warrior, in his enterprises
Discomfited great Douglas, ta'en him once,
Enlargéd him and made a friend of him,
To fill the mouth of deep defiance up,
And shake the peace and safety of our throne.
And what say you to this? Percy, Northumberland,
The Archbishop's grace of York, Douglas, Mortimer,
Capitulate against us and are up.   120
But wherefore do I tell these news to thee?
Why, Harry, do I tell thee of my foes,
Which art my nearest and dearest enemy?
Thou that art like enough, through vassal fear,
Base inclination and the start of spleen,
To fight against me under Percy's pay,
To dog his heels and curtsy at his frowns,
To show how much thou art degenerate.
PRINCE   Do not think so, you shall not find it so;
And God forgive them that so much have swayed   130
Your majesty's good thoughts away from me!
I will redeem all this on Percy's head,
And in the closing of some glorious day

Be bold to tell you that I am your son,
When I will wear a garment all of blood,
And stain my favours in a bloody mask,
Which washed away shall scour my shame with it.
And that shall be the day, whene'er it lights,
That this same child of honour and renown,
This gallant Hotspur, this all-praiséd knight,   140
And your unthought-of Harry chance to meet.
For every honour sitting on his helm,
Would they were multitudes, and on my head
My shames redoubled! For the time will come,
That I shall make this northern youth exchange
His glorious deeds for my indignities.
Percy is but my factor, good my lord,
To engross up glorious deeds on my behalf,
And I will call him to so strict account
That he shall render every glory up,   150
Yea, even the slightest worship of his time,
Or I will tear the reckoning from his heart.
This, in the name of God, I promise here,
The which if He be pleased I shall perform,
I do beseech your majesty may salve
The long-grown wounds of my intemperature:
If not, the end of life cancels all bands,
And I will die a hundred thousand deaths
Ere break the smallest parcel of this vow.

KING   A hundred thousand rebels die in this;   160
Thou shalt have charge and sovereign trust herein.

Enter BLUNT

How now, good Blunt? Thy looks are full of speed.

BLUNT   So hath the business that I come to speak of.
Lord Mortimer of Scotland hath sent word
That Douglas and the English rebels met
The eleventh of this month at Shrewsbury.
A mighty and a fearful head they are,
If promises be kept on every hand,
As ever off'red foul play in a state.

KING   The Earl of Westmoreland set forth today,   170

With him my son, Lord John of Lancaster;
For this advertisement is five days old.
On Wednesday next, Harry, you shall set forward,
On Thursday, we ourselves will march. Our meeting
Is Bridgenorth; and, Harry, you shall march
Through Gloucestershire; by which account,
Our business valuéd, some twelve days hence
Our general forces at Bridgenorth shall meet.
Our hands are full of business, let's away;
Advantage feeds him fat while men delay.   180

[*they go*

SCENE 3

A room at the Boar's Head Tavern in Eastcheap; early morning

Enter FALSTAFF *(a truncheon hanging at his girdle) and* BARDOLPH

FALSTAFF Bardolph, am I not fallen away vilely since this last
action? Do I not bate? Do I not dwindle? Why, my
skin hangs about me like an old lady's loose gown, I
am withered like an old apple-John. Well, I'll repent,
and that suddenly, while I am in some liking. I shall be
out of heart shortly, and then I shall have no strength
to repent. An I have not forgotten what the inside of a
church is made of, I am a peppercorn, a brewer's horse.
The inside of a church! Company, villainous company,
hath been the spoil of me.   10

BARDOLPH Sir John, you are so fretful you cannot live long.

FALSTAFF Why, there is it: come, sing me a bawdy song, make
me merry. I was as virtuously given as a gentleman
need to be; virtuous enough, swore little, diced not
above seven times a week, went to a bawdy-house not
above once in a quarter of an hour, paid money that I
borrowed three or four times, lived well, and in good
compass: and now I live out of all order, out of all
compass.

BARDOLPH Why, you are so fat, Sir John, that you must needs be   20

out of all compass; out of all reasonable compass, Sir
John.

FALSTAFF   Do thou amend thy face, and I'll amend my life: thou
art our admiral, thou bearest the lantern in the poop,
but 'tis in the nose of thee: thou art the Knight of the
Burning Lamp.

BARDOLPH   Why, Sir John, my face does you no harm.

FALSTAFF   No, I'll be sworn – I make as good use of it as many a
man doth of a death's-head or a memento mori. I never
see thy face but I think upon hell-fire, and Dives that   30
lived in purple; for there he is in his robes, burning,
burning. If thou wert any way given to virtue, I would
swear by thy face; my oath should be, 'by this fire, that's
God's angel'. But thou art altogether given over; and
wert indeed, but for the light in thy face, the son of
utter darkness. When thou ran'st up Gad's Hill in the
night to catch my horse, if I did not think thou hadst
been an ignis fatuus or a ball of wildfire, there's no
purchase in money. O, thou art a perpetual triumph, an
everlasting bonfire-light! Thou hast saved me a thousand   40
marks in links and torches, walking with thee in the
night betwixt tavern and tavern: but the sack that thou
hast drunk me would have bought me lights as good
cheap at the dearest chandler's in Europe. I have maintained that salamander of yours with fire any time this
two and thirty years, God reward me for it!

BARDOLPH   'Sblood, I would my face were in your belly!

FALSTAFF   God-a-mercy! So should I be sure to be heart-burned.

HOSTESS *enters*

How now, Dame Partlet the hen! Have you inquired
yet who picked my pocket?   50

HOSTESS   Why, Sir John, what do you think, Sir John? Do you
think I keep thieves in my house? I have searched, I
have inquired, so has my husband, man by man, boy
by boy, servant by servant. The tithe of a hair was
never lost in my house before.

FALSTAFF   Ye lie, hostess – Bardolph was shaved, and lost many a
hair, and I'll be sworn my pocket was picked: go to,

you are a woman, go.

HOSTESS   Who, I? No, I defy thee: God's light, I was never
            called so in mine own house before.   60

FALSTAFF   Go to, I know you well enough.

HOSTESS   No, Sir John, you do not know me, Sir John. I know
            you, Sir John. You owe me money, Sir John, and now
            you pick a quarrel to beguile me of it. I bought you a
            dozen of shirts to your back.

FALSTAFF   Dowlas, filthy dowlas. I have given them away to
            bakers' wives. They have made bolters of them.

HOSTESS   Now, as I am a true woman, holland of eight shillings
            an ell! You owe money here besides, Sir John, for your
            diet and by-drinkings, and money lent you, four and   70
            twenty pound.

FALSTAFF   He had his part of it, let him pay.

HOSTESS   He? Alas, he is poor, he hath nothing.

FALSTAFF   How! Poor? Look upon his face. What call you rich?
            Let them coin his nose, let them coin his cheeks. I'll
            not pay a denier! What, will you make a younker of
            me? Shall I not take mine ease in mine inn but I shall
            have my pocket picked? I have lost a seal-ring of my
            grandfather's worth forty mark.

HOSTESS   O Jesu! I have heard the prince tell him, I know not   80
            how oft, that that ring was copper.

FALSTAFF   How! The prince is a Jack, a sneak-up. 'Sblood, an he
            were here, I would cudgel him like a dog, if he would
            say so.

               'Enter the PRINCE' and POINS, 'marching', single file;
            'FALSTAFF meets' them 'playing upon his truncheon like a fife.'
                      They march together round the room

FALSTAFF   How now, lad! Is the wind in that door, i'faith? Must
            we all march?

BARDOLPH   Yea, two and two, Newgate fashion.

HOSTESS   My lord, I pray you, hear me.

PRINCE   What say'st thou, Mistress Quickly? How doth thy
            husband? I love him well, he is an honest man.   90

HOSTESS   Good my lord, hear me.

FALSTAFF   Prithee, let her alone, and list to me.

PRINCE	What say'st thou, Jack?
FALSTAFF	The other night I fell asleep here, behind the arras, and had my pocket picked. This house is turned bawdy-house, they pick pockets.
PRINCE	What didst thou lose, Jack?
FALSTAFF	Wilt thou believe me, Hal? Three or four bonds of forty pound a-piece, and a seal-ring of my grandfather's.
PRINCE	A trifle, some eight-penny matter.
HOSTESS	So I told him, my lord, and I said I heard your grace say so: and, my lord, he speaks most vilely of you, like a foul-mouthed man as he is, and said he would cudgel you.
PRINCE	What! He did not?
HOSTESS	There's neither faith, truth, nor womanhood in me else.
FALSTAFF	There's no more faith in thee than in a stewed prune, nor no more truth in thee than in a drawn fox; and for womanhood, Maid Marian may be the deputy's wife of the ward to thee. Go, you thing, go.
HOSTESS	Say, what thing? What thing?
FALSTAFF	What thing? Why, a thing to thank God on.
HOSTESS	I am nothing to thank God on, I would thou shouldst know it. I am an honest man's wife, and setting thy knighthood aside, thou art a knave to call me so.
FALSTAFF	Setting thy womanhood aside, thou art a beast to say otherwise.
HOSTESS	Say, what beast, thou knave, thou?
FALSTAFF	What beast? Why, an otter.
PRINCE	An otter, Sir John! Why an otter?
FALSTAFF	Why? She's neither fish nor flesh, a man knows not where to have her.
HOSTESS	Thou art an unjust man in saying so, thou or any man knows where to have me, thou knave, thou!
PRINCE	Thou say'st true, hostess, and he slanders thee most grossly.
HOSTESS	So he doth you, my lord, and said this other day you ought him a thousand pound.
PRINCE	Sirrah, do I owe you a thousand pound?
FALSTAFF	A thousand pound, Hal? A million. Thy love is worth

Marginal line numbers: 100, 110, 120, 130

a million, thou owest me thy love.

HOSTESS   Nay, my lord, he called you Jack, and said he would
           cudgel you.

FALSTAFF   Did I, Bardolph?

BARDOLPH   Indeed, Sir John, you said so.

FALSTAFF   Yea, if he said my ring was copper.

PRINCE   I say 'tis copper. Darest thou be as good as thy word
           now?

FALSTAFF   Why, Hal, thou knowest, as thou art but man I dare,   140
           but as thou art prince I fear thee as I fear the roaring of
           the lion's whelp.

PRINCE   And why not as the lion?

FALSTAFF   The king himself is to be feared as the lion. Dost thou
           think I'll fear thee as I fear thy father? Nay, an I do, I
           pray God my girdle break.

PRINCE   O, if it should, how would thy guts fall about thy
           knees! But, sirrah, there's no room for faith, truth, nor
           honesty, in this bosom of thine – it is all filled up with
           guts and midriff. Charge an honest woman with picking   150
           thy pocket! Why, thou whoreson, impudent, embossed
           rascal, if there were anything in thy pocket but tavern-
           reckonings, memorandums of bawdy-houses, and one
           poor pennyworth of sugar-candy to make thee long
           winded – if thy pocket were enriched with any other
           injuries but these, I am a villain. And yet you will stand
           to it, you will not pocket up wrong! Art thou not
           ashamed?

FALSTAFF   Dost thou hear, Hal? Thou knowest in the state of
           innocency Adam fell, and what should poor Jack   170
           Falstaff do in the days of villainy? Thou seest I have
           more flesh than another man, and therefore more
           frailty. You confess then, you picked my pocket?

PRINCE   It appears so by the story.

FALSTAFF   Hostess, I forgive thee. Go, make ready breakfast, love
           thy husband, look to thy servants, cherish thy guests.
           Thou shalt find me tractable to any honest reason,
           thou seest I am pacified still. Nay, prithee, be gone.
           [Hostess goes] Now, Hal, to the news at court: for the
           robbery, lad, how is that answered?   180

PRINCE   O, my sweet beef, I must still be good angel to thee.
The money is paid back again.

FALSTAFF   O, I do not like that paying back, 'tis a double labour.

PRINCE   I am good friends with my father, and may do anything.

FALSTAFF   Rob me the exchequer the first thing thou doest, and
do it with unwashed hands too.

BARDOLPH Do, my lord.

PRINCE   I have procured thee, Jack, a charge of foot.

FALSTAFF   I would it had been of horse. Where shall I find one
that can steal well? O for a fine thief, of the age of two   190
and twenty or thereabouts! I am heinously unprovided.
Well, God be thanked for these rebels, they offend
none but the virtuous; I laud them, I praise them.

PRINCE   Bardolph –

BARDOLPH My lord.

PRINCE   Go bear this letter to Lord John of Lancaster, to my
brother John, this to my Lord of Westmoreland.
Go, Poins, to horse, to horse, for thou and I
Have thirty miles to ride yet ere dinner time.
Jack, meet me tomorrow in the Temple hall   200
At two o'clock in the afternoon.
There shalt thou know thy charge, and there receive
Money and order for their furniture.
The land is burning, Percy stands on high,
And either we or they must lower lie.
                        [he follows Bardolph and Poins

FALSTAFF   Rare words! Brave world! Hostess, my breakfast, come!
O, I could wish this tavern were my drum.
                                    [he goes

ACT 4 SCENE 1

A tent in the rebel camp near Shrewsbury

HOTSPUR, WORCESTER, *and* DOUGLAS

HOTSPUR	Well said, my noble Scot! If speaking truth	
	In this fine age were not thought flattery,	
	Such attribution should the Douglas have,	
	As not a soldier of this season's stamp	
	Should go so general current through the world.	
	By God, I cannot flatter, I do defy	
	The tongues of soothers, but a braver place	
	In my heart's love hath no man than yourself.	
	Nay, task me to my word, approve me, lord.	
DOUGLAS	Thou art the king of honour.	10
	No man so potent breathes upon the ground	
	But I will beard him.	
HOTSPUR	Do so, and 'tis well.	

'Enter one with letters'

	What letters hast thou there? — I can but thank you.	
MESSENGER	These letters come from your father.	
HOTSPUR	Letters from him! Why comes he not himself?	
MESSENGER	He cannot come, my lord, he is grievous sick.	
HOTSPUR	Zounds! How has he the leisure to be sick	
	In such a justling time? Who leads his power?	
	Under whose government come they along?	
MESSENGER	His letters bear his mind, not I, my lord.	20
WORCESTER	I prithee, tell me, doth he keep his bed?	
MESSENGER	He did, my lord, four days ere I set forth,	
	And at the time of my departure thence	
	He was much feared by his physicians.	
WORCESTER	I would the state of time had first been whole,	
	Ere he by sickness had been visited.	
	His health was never better worth than now.	
HOTSPUR	Sick now! Droop now! This sickness doth infect	
	The very life-blood of our enterprise,	
	'Tis catching hither, even to our camp.	30

He writes me here that inward sickness –
And that his friends by deputation could not
So soon be drawn, nor did he think it meet
To lay so dangerous and dear a trust
On any soul removed but on his own.
Yet doth he give us bold advertisement
That with our small conjunction we should on,
To see how fortune is disposed to us.
For as he writes there is no quailing now,
Because the king is certainly possessed   40
Of all our purposes. What say you to it?

WORCESTER Your father's sickness is a maim to us.

HOTSPUR A perilous gash, a very limb lopped off –
And yet, in faith, it is not. His present want
Seems more than we shall find it: were it good
To set the exact wealth of all our states
All at one cast? To set so rich a main
On the nice hazard of one doubtful hour?
It were not good, for therein should we read
The very bottom and the soul of hope,   50
The very list, the very utmost bound
Of all our fortunes.

DOUGLAS   Faith, and so we should.
Where now remains a sweet reversion,
We may boldly spend upon the hope of what
Is to come in.
A comfort of retirement lives in this.

HOTSPUR A rendezvous, a home to fly unto,
If that the devil and mischance look big
Upon the maidenhead of our affairs.

WORCESTER But yet I would your father had been here.   60
The quality and hair of our attempt
Brooks no division. It will be thought,
By some that know not why he is away,
That wisdom, loyalty, and mere dislike
Of our proceedings kept the earl from hence.
And think how such an apprehension
May turn the tide of fearful faction,
And breed a kind of question in our cause:

For well you know we of the off'ring side
Must keep aloof from strict arbitrement,   70
And stop all sight-holes, every loop from whence
The eye of reason may pry in upon us.
This absence of your father's draws a curtain
That shows the ignorant a kind of fear
Before not dreamt of.

HOTSPUR   You strain too far.
I rather of his absence make this use:
It lends a lustre and more great opinion,
A larger dare to our great enterprise,
Than if the earl were here; for men must think,
If we without his help can make a head   80
To push against a kingdom, with his help
We shall o'erturn it topsy-turvy down.
Yet all goes well, yet all our joints are whole.

DOUGLAS   As heart can think. There is not such a word
Spoke of in Scotland as this term of fear.

SIR RICHARD VERNON *enters the tent*

HOTSPUR   My cousin Vernon! Welcome, by my soul.
VERNON   Pray God, my news be worth a welcome, lord.
The Earl of Westmoreland, seven thousand strong,
Is marching hitherwards, with him Prince John.
HOTSPUR   No harm – what more?
VERNON   And further, I have learned,   90
The king himself in person is set forth,
Or hitherwards intended speedily,
With strong and mighty preparation.
HOTSPUR   He shall be welcome too: where is his son,
The nimble-footed madcap Prince of Wales,
And his comrades, that daffed the world aside,
And bid it pass?
VERNON   All furnished, all in arms;
All plumed like estridges that wing the wind,
Baited like eagles having lately bathed,
Glittering in golden coats like images,   100
As full of spirit as the month of May,
And gorgeous as the sun at midsummer,

Wanton as youthful goats, wild as young bulls.
I saw young Harry with his beaver on,
His cushes on his thighs, gallantly armed,
Rise from the ground like feathered Mercury,
And vaulted with such ease into his seat,
As if an angel dropped down from the clouds,
To turn and wind a fiery Pegasus,
And witch the world with noble horsemanship.   110

HOTSPUR   No more, no more! Worse than the sun in March,
This praise doth nourish agues. Let them come;
They come like sacrifices in their trim,
And to the fire-eyed maid of smoky war
All hot and bleeding will we offer them.
The mailéd Mars shall on his altar sit,
Up to the ears in blood. I am on fire
To hear this rich reprisal is so nigh,
And yet not ours. Come, let me taste my horse,
Who is to bear me like a thunderbolt   120
Against the bosom of the Prince of Wales.
Harry to Harry shall, hot horse to horse,
Meet and ne'er part till one drop down a corse.
O, that Glendower were come!

VERNON   There is more news.
I learned in Worcester, as I rode along,
He cannot draw his power this fourteen days.

DOUGLAS   That's the worst tidings that I hear of yet.

WORCESTER   Ay, by my faith, that bears a frosty sound.

HOTSPUR   What may the king's whole battle reach unto?

VERNON   To thirty thousand.

HOTSPUR   Forty let it be!   130
My father and Glendower being both away,
The powers of us may serve so great a day.
Come, let us take a muster speedily.
Doomsday is near; die all, die merrily.

DOUGLAS   Talk not of dying, I am out of fear
Of death or death's hand for this one half year.

                                         [they go

SCENE 2

A highway near Coventry

Enter FALSTAFF, *and* BARDOLPH

FALSTAFF Bardolph, get thee before to Coventry, fill me a bottle
of sack, our soldiers shall march through. We'll to
Sutton Co'fil' tonight.   [*he gives him a bottle*
BARDOLPH Will you give me money, captain?
FALSTAFF Lay out, lay out.
BARDOLPH This bottle makes an angel.
FALSTAFF An if it do, take it for thy labour; and if it make
twenty, take them all, I'll answer the coinage. Bid my
lieutenant Peto meet me at town's end.
BARDOLPH I will, captain. Farewell.   [*he goes* 10
FALSTAFF If I be not ashamed of my soldiers, I am a soused
gurnet. I have misused the king's press damnably. I
have got in exchange of a hundred and fifty soldiers
three hundred and odd pounds. I press me none but
good householders, yeomen's sons; inquire me out
contracted bachelors, such as had been asked twice on
the banns, such a commodity of warm slaves, as had as
lieve hear the devil as a drum, such as fear the report of
a caliver worse than a struck fowl or a hurt wild-duck.
I pressed me none but such toasts-and-butter, with 20
hearts in their bellies no bigger than pins' heads, and
they have bought out their services, and now my whole
charge consists of ancients, corporals, lieutenants,
gentlemen of companies – slaves as ragged as Lazarus in
the painted cloth, where the Glutton's dogs licked his
sores; and such as indeed were never soldiers, but discarded unjust serving-men, younger sons to younger
brothers, revolted tapsters, and ostlers trade-fallen, the
cankers of a calm world and a long peace, ten times
more dishonourable ragged than an old fazed ancient. 30
And such have I to fill up the rooms of them as have
bought out their services, that you would think that I
had a hundred and fifty tattered prodigals, lately come

from swine-keeping, from eating draff and husks. A mad fellow met me on the way, and told me I had unloaded all the gibbets and pressed the dead bodies. No eye hath seen such scarecrows. I'll not march through Coventry with them, that's flat: nay, and the villains march wide betwixt the legs as if they had gyves on, for indeed I had the most of them out of prison. 40 There's not a shirt and a half in all my company, and the half shirt is two napkins tacked together and thrown over the shoulders like a herald's coat without sleeves; and the shirt, to say the truth, stolen from my host at Saint Alban's or the red-nose innkeeper of Daventry. But that's all one; they'll find linen enough on every hedge.

PRINCE HENRY *and* WESTMORELAND *come up from behind*

PRINCE   How now, blown Jack? How now, quilt?

FALSTAFF   What, Hal? How now, mad wag? What a devil dost thou in Warwickshire? My good Lord of West- 50 moreland, I cry you mercy. I thought your honour had already been at Shrewsbury.

WEST'LAND   Faith, Sir John, 'tis more than time that I were there, and you too; but my powers are there already. The king, I can tell you, looks for us all; we must away all night.

FALSTAFF   Tut, never fear me, I am as vigilant as a cat to steal cream.

PRINCE   I think, to steal cream indeed, for thy theft hath already made thee butter. But tell me, Jack, whose fellows are these that come after?   60

FALSTAFF   Mine, Hal, mine.

PRINCE   I did never see such pitiful rascals.

FALSTAFF   Tut, tut, good enough to toss, food for powder, food for powder. They'll fill a pit as well as better; tush, man, mortal men, mortal men.

WEST'LAND   Ay, but, Sir John, methinks they are exceeding poor and bare, too beggarly.

FALSTAFF   Faith, for their poverty, I know not where they had that, and for their bareness I am sure they never learned that of me.   70

| PRINCE | No, I'll be sworn, unless you call three fingers in the ribs, bare. But, sirrah, make haste. Percy is already in the field.   [*he goes* |

FALSTAFF What, is the king encamped?

WEST'LAND He is, Sir John. I fear we shall stay too long.   [*he goes*

FALSTAFF Well,
          To the latter end of a fray and the beginning of a feast
          Fits a dull fighter and a keen guest.

                                                   [*he follows*

SCENE 3

The rebel camp near Shrewsbury

Enter HOTSPUR, WORCESTER, DOUGLAS, *and* VERNON

HOTSPUR We'll fight with him tonight.

WORCESTER   It may not be.

DOUGLAS You give him then advantage.

VERNON   Not a whit.

HOTSPUR Why say you so? Looks he not for supply?

VERNON So do we.

HOTSPUR   His is certain, ours is doubtful.

WORCESTER Good cousin, be advised, stir not tonight.

VERNON Do not, my lord.

DOUGLAS   You do not counsel well;
          You speak it out of fear and cold heart.

VERNON Do me no slander, Douglas. By my life,
          And I dare well maintain it with my life,
          If well-respected honour bid me on,   10
          I hold as little counsel with weak fear
          As you, my lord, or any Scot that this day lives.
          Let it be seen tomorrow in the battle
          Which of us fears.

DOUGLAS   Yea, or tonight.

VERNON   Content.

HOTSPUR Tonight, say I.

VERNON Come, come, it may not be. I wonder much,
          Being men of such great leading as you are,
          That you foresee not what impediments

Drag back our expedition. Certain horse
Of my cousin Vernon's are not yet come up;   20
Your uncle Worcester's horse came but today,
And now their pride and mettle is asleep,
Their courage with hard labour tame and dull,
That not a horse is half the half himself.

HOTSPUR So are the horses of the enemy
In general, journey-bated and brought low.
The better part of ours are full of rest.

WORCESTER The number of the king exceedeth ours.
For God's sake, cousin, stay till all come in.

                     [*'the trumpet sounds a parley'*

SIR WALTER BLUNT *enters*

BLUNT I come with gracious offers from the king,   30
If you vouchsafe me hearing and respect.

HOTSPUR Welcome, Sir Walter Blunt; and would to God,
You were of our determination!
Some of us love you well, and even those some
Envy your great deservings and good name,
Because you are not of our quality,
But stand against us like an enemy.

BLUNT And God defend but still I should stand so,
So long as out of limit and true rule
You stand against anointed majesty.   40
But to my charge. The king hath sent to know
The nature of your griefs, and whereupon
You conjure from the breast of civil peace
Such bold hostility, teaching his duteous land
Audacious cruelty. If that the king
Have any way your good deserts forgot,
Which he confesseth to be manifold,
He bids you name your griefs, and with all speed
You shall have your desires with interest,
And pardon absolute for yourself and these   50
Herein misled by your suggestion.

HOTSPUR The king is kind, and well we know the king
Knows at what time to promise, when to pay:
My father and my uncle and myself

Did give him that same royalty he wears:
And when he was not six and twenty strong,
Sick in the world's regard, wretched and low,
A poor unminded outlaw sneaking home,
My father gave him welcome to the shore;
And when he heard him swear and vow to God   60
He came but to be Duke of Lancaster,
To sue his livery and beg his peace
With tears of innocency and terms of zeal,
My father, in kind heart and pity moved,
Swore him assistance and performed it too.
Now when the lords and barons of the realm
Perceived Northumberland did lean to him,
The more and less came in with cap and knee,
Met him in boroughs, cities, villages,
Attended him on bridges, stood in lanes,   70
Laid gifts before him, proffered him their oaths,
Gave him their heirs as pages, followed him
Even at the heels in golden multitudes.
He presently, as greatness knows itself,
Steps me a little higher than his vow
Made to my father while his blood was poor
Upon the naked shore at Ravenspurgh;
And now, forsooth, takes on him to reform
Some certain edicts and some strait decrees
That lie too heavy on the commonwealth,   80
Cries out upon abuses, seems to weep
Over his country's wrongs; and by this face,
This seeming brow of justice, did he win
The hearts of all that he did angle for;
Proceeded further – cut me off the heads
Of all the favourites that the absent king
In deputation left behind him here,
When he was personal in the Irish war.

BLUNT   Tut, I came not to hear this.

HOTSPUR   Then to the point.
In short time after he deposed the king,   90
Soon after that deprived him of his life,
And in the neck of that tasked the whole state;

To make that worse, suffered his kinsman March
(Who is, if every owner were well placed,
Indeed his king) to be engaged in Wales,
There without ransom to lie forfeited;
Disgraced me in my happy victories,
Sought to entrap me by intelligence,
Rated mine uncle from the council-board,
In rage dismissed my father from the court,   100
Broke oath on oath, committed wrong on wrong,
And in conclusion drove us to seek out
This head of safety, and withal to pry
Into his title, the which we find
Too indirect for long continuance.

BLUNT   Shall I return this answer to the king?
HOTSPUR   Not so, Sir Walter. We'll withdraw awhile;
Go to the king, and let there be impawned
Some surety for a safe return again,
And in the morning early shall mine uncle   110
Bring him our purposes; and so farewell.
BLUNT   I would you would accept of grace and love.
HOTSPUR   And may be so we shall.
BLUNT   Pray God you do.

                              [they withdraw

SCENE 4

York. A room in the Archbishop's palace

The ARCHBISHOP OF YORK, *and* SIR MICHAEL

ARCH.   Hie, good Sir Michael, bear this sealéd brief
With wingéd haste to the lord marshal,
This to my cousin Scroop, and all the rest
To whom they are directed. If you knew
How much they do import, you would make haste.
SIR M.   My good lord,
I guess their tenour.
ARCH.   Like enough you do.
Tomorrow, good Sir Michael, is a day
Wherein the fortune of ten thousand men

Must bide the touch; for, sir, at Shrewsbury,   10
As I am truly given to understand,
The king with mighty and quick-raiséd power
Meets with Lord Harry: and I fear, Sir Michael,
What with the sickness of Northumberland,
Whose power was in the first proportion,
And what with Owen Glendower's absence thence,
Who with them was a rated sinew too,
And comes not in, o'er-ruled by prophecies,
I fear the power of Percy is too weak
To wage an instant trial with the king.   20

SIR M. Why, my good lord, you need not fear:
There is the Douglas and Lord Mortimer.

ARCH. No, Mortimer is not there.

SIR M. But there is Mordake, Vernon, Lord Harry Percy,
And there is my Lord of Worcester, and a head
Of gallant warriors, noble gentlemen.

ARCH. And so there is: but yet the king hath drawn
The special head of all the land together:
The Prince of Wales, Lord John of Lancaster,
The noble Westmoreland and warlike Blunt,   30
And many moe corrivals and dear men
Of estimation and command in arms.

SIR M. Doubt not, my lord, they shall be well opposed.

ARCH. I hope no less, yet needful 'tis to fear.
And, to prevent the worst, Sir Michael, speed:
For if Lord Percy thrive not, ere the king
Dismiss his power, he means to visit us,
For he hath heard of our confederacy;
And 'tis but wisdom to make strong against him.
Therefore, make haste. I must go write again   40
To other friends; and so farewell, Sir Michael.

[they go

ACT 5 SCENE I

The King's camp near Shrewsbury

Enter the KING, PRINCE HENRY, LORD JOHN OF LANCASTER,
SIR WALTER BLUNT, *and* FALSTAFF

KING How bloodily the sun begins to peer
   Above yon busky hill! The day looks pale
   At his distemp'rature.

PRINCE   The southern wind
   Doth play the trumpet to his purposes,
   And by his hollow whistling in the leaves
   Foretells a tempest and a blust'ring day.

KING Then with the losers let it sympathise,
   For nothing can seem foul to those that win.

            [*'the trumpet sounds'*

     Enter WORCESTER *and* VERNON

   How now, my Lord of Worcester! 'Tis not well
   That you and I should meet upon such terms 10
   As now we meet. You have deceived our trust,
   And made us doff our easy robes of peace,
   To crush our old limbs in ungentle steel.
   This is not well, my lord, this is not well.
   What say you to it? Will you again unknit
   This churlish knot of all-abhorréd war,
   And move in that obedient orb again
   Where you did give a fair and natural light,
   And be no more an exhaled meteor,
   A prodigy of fear, and a portent   20
   Of broachéd mischief to the unborn times?

WORCESTER Hear me, my liege:
   For mine own part, I could be well content
   To entertain the lag-end of my life
   With quiet hours; for I do protest
   I have not sought the day of this dislike.

KING You have not sought it! How comes it then?

FALSTAFF Rebellion lay in his way and he found it.

PRINCE   Peace, chewet, peace!
WORCESTER It pleased your majesty to turn your looks   30
           Of favour from myself and all our house;
           And yet I must remember you, my lord,
           We were the first and dearest of your friends.
           For you my staff of office did I break
           In Richard's time, and posted day and night
           To meet you on the way, and kiss your hand,
           When yet you were in place and in account
           Nothing so strong and fortunate as I.
           It was myself, my brother, and his son,
           That brought you home, and boldly did outdare   40
           The dangers of the time. You swore to us,
           And you did swear that oath at Doncaster,
           That you did nothing purpose 'gainst the state,
           Nor claim no further than your new-fall'n right,
           The seat of Gaunt, dukedom of Lancaster:
           To this we swore our aid. But in short space
           It rained down fortune show'ring on your head,
           And such a flood of greatness fell on you,
           What with our help, what with the absent king,
           What with the injuries of a wanton time,   50
           The seeming sufferances that you had borne,
           And the contrarious winds that held the king
           So long in his unlucky Irish wars
           That all in England did repute him dead:
           And from this swarm of fair advantages
           You took occasion to be quickly wooed
           To gripe the general sway into your hand,
           Forgot your oath to us at Doncaster,
           And being fed by us you used us so
           As that ungentle gull, the cuckoo's bird,   60
           Useth the sparrow – did oppress our nest,
           Grew by our feeding to so great a bulk
           That even our love durst not come near your sight
           For fear of swallowing; but with nimble wing
           We were enforced for safety sake to fly
           Out of your sight and raise this present head;
           Whereby we stand opposéd by such means

As you yourself have forged against yourself,
By unkind usage, dangerous countenance,
And violation of all faith and troth   70
Sworn to us in your younger enterprise.

KING   These things indeed you have articulate,
Proclaimed at market-crosses, read in churches,
To face the garment of rebellion
With some fine colour that may please the eye
Of fickle changelings and poor discontents,
Which gape and rub the elbow at the news
Of hurlyburly innovation.
And never yet did insurrection want
Such water-colours to impaint his cause,   80
Nor moody beggars starving for a time
Of pellmell havoc and confusion.

PRINCE   In both our armies there is many a soul
Shall pay full dearly for this encounter,
If once they join in trial. Tell your nephew,
The Prince of Wales doth join with all the world
In praise of Henry Percy. By my hopes,
This present enterprise set off his head,
I do not think a braver gentleman,
More active-valiant or more valiant-young,   90
More daring or more bold, is now alive
To grace this latter age with noble deeds.
For my part, I may speak it to my shame,
I have a truant been to chivalry,
And so I hear he doth account me too;
Yet this before my father's majesty –
I am content that he shall take the odds
Of his great name and estimation,
And will, to save the blood on either side,
Try fortune with him in a single fight.   100

KING   And, Prince of Wales, so dare we venture thee,
Albeit considerations infinite
Do make against it. No, good Worcester, no,
We love our people well; even those we love
That are misled upon your cousin's part.
And will they take the offer of our grace,

Both he, and they, and you, yea, every man
Shall be my friend again and I'll be his.
So tell your cousin, and bring me word
What he will do. But if he will not yield,   110
Rebuke and dread correction wait on us,
And they shall do their office. So, be gone;
We will not now be troubled with reply.
We offer fair, take it advisedly.

                              [Worcester and Vernon go

PRINCE   It will not be accepted, on my life.
The Douglas and the Hotspur both together
Are confident against the world in arms.

KING   Hence, therefore, every leader to his charge;
For on their answer will we set on them,
And God befriend us, as our cause is just!   120

              [they disperse; Falstaff plucks the Prince by the
                                     sleeve as he turns away

FALSTAFF   Hal, if thou see me down in the battle and bestride
me, so, 'tis a point of friendship.

PRINCE   Nothing but a colossus can do thee that friendship. Say
thy prayers, and farewell.

FALSTAFF   I would 'twere bed time, Hal, and all well.

PRINCE   Why, thou owest God a death.   *[he hurries off*

FALSTAFF   'Tis not due yet; I would be loath to pay him before his
day. What need I be so forward with him that calls not
on me? Well, 'tis no matter, honour pricks me on. Yea,
but how if honour prick me off when I come on? How 130
then? Can honour set to a leg? No. Or an arm? No. Or
take away the grief of a wound? No. Honour hath no
skill in surgery then? No. What is honour? A word.
What is in that word honour? What is that honour?
Air. A trim reckoning! Who hath it? He that died a-
Wednesday. Doth he feel it? No. Doth he hear it? No.
'Tis insensible then? Yea, to the dead. But will it not
live with the living? No. Why? Detraction will not
suffer it. Therefore I'll none of it. Honour is a mere
scutcheon – and so ends my catechism.   140

                                              [he goes

SCENE 2

A plain near the rebel camp

WORCESTER *and* VERNON *approach, returning from the King*

WORCESTER O no, my nephew must not know, Sir Richard,
    The liberal and kind offer of the king.
VERNON   'Twere best he did.
WORCESTER   Then are we all undone.
    It is not possible, it cannot be,
    The king should keep his word in loving us.
    He will suspect us still, and find a time
    To punish this offence in other faults.
    Supposition all our lives shall be stuck full
    Of eyes;
    For treason is but trusted like the fox,   10
    Who, ne'er so tame, so cherished and locked up,
    Will have a wild trick of his ancestors.
    Look how we can, or sad or merrily,
    Interpretation will misquote our looks,
    And we shall feed like oxen at a stall,
    The better cherished still the nearer death.
    My nephew's trespass may be well forgot,
    It hath the excuse of youth and heat of blood,
    And an adopted name of privilege –
    A hare-brained Hotspur, governed by a spleen.   20
    All his offences live upon my head
    And on his father's. We did train him on,
    And his corruption being ta'en from us,
    We as the spring of all shall pay for all.
    Therefore, good cousin, let not Harry know,
    In any case, the offer of the king.
VERNON Deliver what you will, I'll say 'tis so.
    Here comes your cousin.

        HOTSPUR *and* DOUGLAS, *come to meet them*

HOTSPUR My uncle is returned.
    Deliver up my Lord of Westmoreland.   30
    Uncle, what news?

WORCESTER. The king will bid you battle presently.

DOUGLAS Defy him by the Lord of Westmoreland.

HOTSPUR Lord Douglas, go you and tell him so.

DOUGLAS Marry, and shall, and very willingly.   [*he goes*

WORCESTER There is no seeming mercy in the king.

HOTSPUR Did you beg any? God forbid!

WORCESTER. I told him gently of our grievances,
   Of his oath-breaking – which he mended thus,
   By now forswearing that he is forsworn.   40
   He calls us rebels, traitors, and will scourge
   With haughty arms this hateful name in us.

DOUGLAS returns

DOUGLAS Arm, gentlemen, to arms! For I have thrown
   A brave defiance in King Henry's teeth,
   And Westmoreland that was engaged did bear it,
   Which cannot choose but bring him quickly on.

WORCESTER The Prince of Wales stepped forth before the king,
   And, nephew, challenged you to single fight.

HOTSPUR O would the quarrel lay upon our heads,
   And that no man might draw short breath today   50
   But I and Harry Monmouth! Tell me, tell me,
   How showed his tasking? Seemed it in contempt?

VERNON No, by my soul. I never in my life
   Did hear a challenge urged more modestly,
   Unless a brother should a brother dare
   To gentle exercise and proof of arms.
   He gave you all the duties of a man,
   Trimmed up your praises with a princely tongue,
   Spoke your deservings like a chronicle,
   Making you ever better than his praise   60
   By still dispraising praise valued with you;
   And, which became him like a prince indeed,
   He made a blushing cital of himself,
   And chid his truant youth with such a grace,
   As if he mast'red there a double spirit
   Of teaching and of learning instantly.
   There did he pause. But let me tell the world,
   If he outlive the envy of this day,

England did never owe so sweet a hope,
So much misconstrued in his wantonness.   70
HOTSPUR   Cousin, I think thou art enamouréd
Upon his follies. Never did I hear
Of any prince so wild a liberty.
But be he as he will, yet once ere night
I will embrace him with a soldier's arm,
That he shall shrink under my courtesy.
Arm, arm, with speed – and, fellows, soldiers, friends,
Better consider what you have to do
Than I, that have not well the gift of tongue,
Can lift your blood up with persuasion.   80

A messenger enters

MESSENGER My lord, here are letters for you.
HOTSPUR   I cannot read them now.
O gentlemen, the time of life is short!
To spend that shortness basely were too long,
If life did ride upon a dial's point,
Still ending at the arrival of an hour.
An if we live, we live to tread on kings,
If die, brave death, when princes die with us!
Now, for our consciences, the arms are fair,
When the intent of bearing them is just.   90

Another messenger enters

MESSENGER My lord, prepare, the king comes on apace.
HOTSPUR   I thank him that he cuts me from my tale,
For I profess not talking – only this,
Let each man do his best. And here draw I
A sword, whose temper I intend to stain
With the best blood that I can meet withal
In the adventure of this perilous day.
Now, Esperance! Percy! And set on.
Sound all the lofty instruments of war,
And by that music let us all embrace,   100
For, heaven to earth, some of us never shall
A second time do such a courtesy.
                [*'The trumpets sound.' 'They embrace'* and go

SCENE 3

'The King enters with his power' and marches past.
'Alarum to battle. Then enter DOUGLAS *and* SIR WALTER BLUNT'*
fighting; they pause

BLUNT	What is thy name, that in the battle thus
	Thou crossest me? What honour dost thou seek
	Upon my head?
DOUGLAS	Know then, my name is Douglas,
	And I do haunt thee in the battle thus
	Because some tell me that thou art a king.
BLUNT	They tell thee true.
DOUGLAS	The Lord of Stafford dear today hath bought
	Thy likeness, for instead of thee, King Harry,
	This sword hath ended him. So shall it thee,
	Unless thou yield thee as my prisoner.

                                            10

BLUNT   I was not born a yielder, thou proud Scot,
And thou shalt find a king that will revenge
Lord Stafford's death.

                         [*'They fight, Douglas kills Blunt'*

HOTSPUR *enters*

HOTSPUR	O Douglas, hadst thou fought at Holmedon thus,
	I never had triumphed upon a Scot.
DOUGLAS	All's done, all's won! Here breathless lies the king.
HOTSPUR	Where?
DOUGLAS	Here.
HOTSPUR	This, Douglas? No, I know this face full well.
	A gallant knight he was, his name was Blunt,
	Semblably furnished like the king himself.
DOUGLAS	A fool go with thy soul, whither it goes!
	A borrowed title hast thou bought too dear.
	Why didst thou tell me that thou wert a king?
HOTSPUR	The king hath many marching in his coats.
DOUGLAS	Now, by my sword, I will kill all his coats;
	I'll murder all his wardrobe, piece by piece,
	Until I meet the king.
HOTSPUR	Up, and away!

                                            20

Our soldiers stand full fairly for the day.

> *[they rejoin the forces*

'Alarum. Enter FALSTAFF, *solus'*

FALSTAFF   Though I could 'scape shot-free at London, I fear the   30
shot here; here's no scoring but upon the pate. Soft!
Who are you? Sir Walter Blunt – there's honour for
you! Here's no vanity! I am as hot as molten lead, and
as heavy too. God keep lead out of me! I need no more
weight than mine own bowels. I have led my raga-
muffins where they are peppered; there's not three of
my hundred and fifty left alive, and they are for the
town's end, to beg during life. But who comes here?

PRINCE HENRY *approaches*

PRINCE   What, stand'st thou idle here? Lend me thy sword.
Many a nobleman lies stark and stiff   40
Under the hoofs of vaunting enemies,
Whose deaths are yet unrevenged. I prithee, lend me
thy sword.

FALSTAFF   O Hal, I prithee, give me leave to breathe awhile. Turk
Gregory never did such deeds in arms as I have done
this day. I have paid Percy, I have made him sure.

PRINCE   He is, indeed, and living to kill thee. I prithee, lend
me thy sword.

FALSTAFF   Nay, before God, Hal, if Percy be alive, thou get'st not
my sword, but take my pistol if thou wilt.   50

PRINCE   Give it me. What, is it in the case?

FALSTAFF   Ay Hal, 'tis hot, 'tis hot. There's that will sack a city.

> *['The Prince draws it out and finds it to be a bottle of sack'*

PRINCE   What, is it a time to jest and dally now?

> *['he throws the bottle at him', and goes*

FALSTAFF   Well, if Percy be alive, I'll pierce him. If he do come
in my way, so. If he do not, if I come in his willingly,
let him make a carbonado of me. I like not such
grinning honour as Sir Walter hath. Give me life,
which if I can save, so; if not, honour comes unlooked
for, and there's an end.   *[he goes*

SCENE 4

'*Alarum, excursions. Enter the* KING, *the* PRINCE,
LORD JOHN OF LANCASTER, *and* EARL OF WESTMORELAND'

KING   I prithee,
            Harry, withdraw thyself, thou bleedest too much.
            Lord John of Lancaster, go you with him.

LANCASTER   Not I, my lord, unless I did bleed too.

PRINCE   I beseech your majesty, make up,
            Lest your retirement do amaze your friends.

KING   I will do so.
            My Lord of Westmoreland, lead him to his tent.

WEST'LAND   Come, my lord, I'll lead you to your tent.

PRINCE   Lead me, my lord? I do not need your help,   10
            And God forbid a shallow scratch should drive
            The Prince of Wales from such a field as this,
            Where stained nobility lies trodden on,
            And rebels' arms triumph in massacres!

LANCASTER   We breathe too long. Come, cousin Westmoreland,
            Our duty this way lies; for God's sake, come.
                    [*Lancaster and Westmoreland hurry forward*

PRINCE   By God, thou hast deceived me, Lancaster:
            I did not think thee lord of such a spirit.
            Before, I loved thee as a brother, John,
            But now, I do respect thee as my soul.   20

KING   I saw him hold Lord Percy at the point,
            With lustier maintenance than I did look for
            Of such an ungrown warrior.

PRINCE   O, this boy
            Lends mettle to us all!   [*he follows*

            DOUGLAS *appears from another part of the field*

DOUGLAS   Another king! They grow like Hydra's heads.
            I am the Douglas, fatal to all those
            That wear those colours on them. What art thou,
            That counterfeit'st the person of a king?

KING   The king himself, who, Douglas, grieves at heart
            So many of his shadows thou hast met,   30
            And not the very king. I have two boys

             Seek Percy and thyself about the field,
             But seeing thou fall'st on me so luckily
             I will assay thee: so, defend thyself.

DOUGLAS   I fear thou art another counterfeit,
             And yet in faith thou bear'st thee like a king;
             But mine I am sure thou art, whoe'er thou be,
             And thus I win thee.

                      ['*They fight. The King being in danger,*
                               enter Prince of Wales'

PRINCE   Hold up thy head, vile Scot, or thou art like
             Never to hold it up again! The spirits   40
             Of valiant Shirley, Stafford, Blunt, are in my arms.
             It is the Prince of Wales that threatens thee,
             Who never promiseth but he means to pay.

                          ['*they fight, Douglas flieth*'
             Cheerly, my lord, how fares your grace?
             Sir Nicholas Gawsey hath for succour sent,
             And so hath Clifton – I'll to Clifton straight.

KING   Stay, and breathe awhile.
             Thou hast redeemed thy lost opinion,
             And showed thou mak'st some tender of my life,
             In this fair rescue thou hast brought to me.   50

PRINCE   O God! They did me too much injury
             That ever said I heark'ned for your death.
             If it were so, I might have let alone
             The insulting hand of Douglas over you,
             Which would have been as speedy in your end
             As all the poisonous potions in the world,
             And saved the treacherous labour of your son.

KING   Make up to Clifton, I'll to Sir Nicholas Gawsey.

                                [*he goes*

                  HOTSPUR *enters*

HOTSPUR   If I mistake not, thou art Harry Monmouth.
PRINCE   Thou speak'st as if I would deny my name.   60
HOTSPUR   My name is Harry Percy.
PRINCE   Why, then I see
             A very valiant rebel of the name.
             I am the Prince of Wales, and think not, Percy,
             To share with me in glory any more:

Two stars keep not their motion in one sphere,
Nor can one England brook a double reign,
Of Harry Percy and the Prince of Wales.

HOTSPUR   Nor shall it, Harry, for the hour is come
To end the one of us; and would to God
Thy name in arms were now as great as mine!   70

PRINCE   I'll make it greater ere I part from thee,
And all the budding honours on thy crest
I'll crop, to make a garland for my head.

HOTSPUR   I can no longer brook thy vanities.   ['they fight'

FALSTAFF draws near

FALSTAFF   Well said, Hal! To it, Hal! Nay, you shall find no boy's
play here, I can tell you.

DOUGLAS returns; 'he fighteth with FALSTAFF', who 'falls down as if
he were dead'; he passes on. HOTSPUR is wounded, and falls

HOTSPUR   O Harry, thou hast robbed me of my youth!
I better brook the loss of brittle life
Than those proud titles thou hast won of me.
They wound my thoughts worse than thy sword
                                        my flesh.   80
But thought's the slave of life, and life time's fool,
And time that takes survey of all the world
Must have a stop. O, I could prophesy,
But that the earthy and cold hand of death
Lies on my tongue: no, Percy, thou art dust,
And food for –   [he dies

PRINCE   For worms, brave Percy. Fare thee well, great heart!
Ill-weaved ambition, how much art thou shrunk!
When that this body did contain a spirit,
A kingdom for it was too small a bound,   90
But now two paces of the vilest earth
Is room enough. This earth, that bears thee dead,
Bears not alive so stout a gentleman.
If thou wert sensible of courtesy,
I should not make so dear a show of zeal;
But let my favours hide thy mangled face.
                                [he covers Hotspur's face
And even in thy behalf I'll thank myself

For doing these fair rites of tenderness.
Adieu, and take thy praise with thee to heaven!
Thy ignominy sleep with thee in the grave,   100
But not remembered in thy epitaph!
                    [*'he spieth Falstaff on the ground'*
What! Old acquaintance! Could not all this flesh
Keep in a little life? Poor Jack, farewell!
I could have better spared a better man:
O, I should have a heavy miss of thee,
If I were much in love with vanity:
Death hath not struck so fat a deer today,
Though many dearer, in this bloody fray.
Embowelled will I see thee by and by;
Till then in blood by noble Percy lie.   [*he goes* 110

FALSTAFF   [*'riseth up'*] Embowelled! If thou embowel me today,
I'll give you leave to powder me and eat me too
tomorrow. 'Sblood, 'twas time to counterfeit, or that
hot termagant Scot had paid me, scot and lot too.
Counterfeit? I lie, I am no counterfeit. To die is to be a
counterfeit, for he is but the counterfeit of a man, who
hath not the life of a man: but to counterfeit dying,
when a man thereby liveth, is to be no counterfeit, but
the true and perfect image of life indeed. The better
part of valour is discretion, in the which better part I   120
have saved my life. Zounds, I am afraid of this gunpowder Percy, though he be dead. How, if he should
counterfeit too, and rise? By my faith, I am afraid he
would prove the better counterfeit. Therefore I'll make
him sure, yea, and I'll swear I killed him. Why may not
he rise as well as I? Nothing confutes me but eyes, and
nobody sees me: therefore, sirrah, [*stabs him*] with a
new wound in your thigh, come you along with me.
                    [*'he takes up Hotspur on his back'*

The PRINCE *and* LORD JOHN OF LANCASTER *return*

PRINCE   Come, brother John, full bravely hast thou fleshed
Thy maiden sword.

LANCASTER   But, soft! Whom have we here?   130
Did you not tell me this fat man was dead?

PRINCE   I did; I saw him dead,
                Breathless and bleeding on the ground. Art thou alive?
                Or is it fantasy that plays upon our eyesight?
                I prithee, speak. We will not trust our eyes,
                Without our ears. Thou art not what thou seem'st.

FALSTAFF   No, that's certain, I am not a double-man: but if I be
                not Jack Falstaff, then am I a Jack: there is Percy [*throws
                the body down*]. If your father will do me any honour, so;
                if not, let him kill the next Percy himself. I look to be   140
                either earl or duke, I can assure you.

PRINCE   Why, Percy I killed myself, and saw thee dead.

FALSTAFF   Didst thou? Lord, Lord, how this world is given to
                lying! I grant you I was down and out of breath, and so
                was he, but we rose both at an instant, and fought a
                long hour by Shrewsbury clock. If I may be believed,
                so: if not, let them that should reward valour bear the
                sin upon their own heads. I'll take it upon my death, I
                gave him this wound in the thigh. If the man were
                alive, and would deny it, zounds, I would make him   150
                eat a piece of my sword.

LANCASTER   This is the strangest tale that ever I heard.

PRINCE   This is the strangest fellow, brother John.
                Come, bring your luggage nobly on your back.

                                                      [*aside, to Falstaff*

                For my part, if a lie may do thee grace,
                I'll gild it with the happiest terms I have.

                                                      [*'a retreat is sounded'*

                The trumpet sounds retreat, the day is ours.
                Come, brother, let's to the highest of the field,
                To see what friends are living, who are dead.   [*they go*

FALSTAFF   I'll follow, as they say, for reward. He that rewards me,   160
                God reward him! If I do grow great, I'll grow less, for
                I'll purge, and leave sack, and live cleanly as a nobleman
                should do.

                                                      [*he goes*

SCENE 5

'The trumpets sound. Enter the KING, PRINCE OF WALES,
LORD JOHN OF LANCASTER, EARL OF WESTMORELAND,
         with WORCESTER *and* VERNON *prisoners'*

KING	Thus ever did rebellion find rebuke.
	Ill-spirited Worcester! Did not we send grace,
	Pardon and terms of love to all of you?
	And wouldst thou turn our offers contrary?
	Misuse the tenour of thy kinsman's trust?
	Three knights upon our party slain today,
	A noble earl and many a creature else,
	Had been alive this hour,
	If like a Christian thou hadst truly borne
	Betwixt our armies true intelligence.

                                                              10

WORCESTER What I have done my safety urged me to;
         And I embrace this fortune patiently,
         Since not to be avoided it falls on me.

KING   Bear Worcester to the death, and Vernon too:
         Other offenders we will pause upon.

                         [*Worcester and Vernon are led away*

         How goes the field?

PRINCE   The noble Scot, Lord Douglas, when he saw
         The fortune of the day quite turned from him,
         The noble Percy slain, and all his men
         Upon the foot of fear, fled with the rest;   20
         And falling from a hill, he was so bruised
         That the pursuers took him. At my tent
         The Douglas is; and I beseech your grace
         I may dispose of him.

KING   With all my heart.

PRINCE   Then, brother John of Lancaster, to you
         This honourable bounty shall belong.
         Go to the Douglas, and deliver him
         Up to his pleasure, ransomless and free.
         His valours shown upon our crests today
         Have taught us how to cherish such high deeds,   30
         Even in the bosom of our adversaries.

LANCASTER I thank your grace for this high courtesy,
        Which I shall give away immediately.
KING   Then this remains, that we divide our power.
        You, son John, and my cousin Westmoreland
        Towards York shall bend you with your dearest speed
        To meet Northumberland and the prelate Scroop,
        Who, as we hear, are busily in arms:
        Myself and you, son Harry, will towards Wales,
        To fight with Glendower and the Earl of March.   40
        Rebellion in this land shall lose his sway,
        Meeting the check of such another day,
        And since this business so fair is done,
        Let us not leave till all our own be won.

                                          [*they go*

HENRY IV Part 2

INTRODUCTION

Shakespeare seems to have written Part 2 of *Henry IV* straight after the success of the first play, during 1596–97. It was first published in 1600, and not reprinted until the folio edition of 1623. Structurally the play seems to recapitulate the events of the previous play. Hal's reconciliation with his father and his re-formed behaviour at Shrewsbury seem to have undergone a setback, and *2 Henry IV* sees him back in the taverns of Eastcheap, a thorn in the side of his father. Henry IV is still assailed by rebellion and threats to his sovereignty, and has not yet made his penitent pilgrimage to the Holy Land. Falstaff is still in the company of tavern associates, wheedling money and sack out of his friends, although in this play he spends relatively little time on-stage with Hal. This physical separation, following on the heavy hints in Part 1, further prepares the ground for the Prince's rejection of Falstaff at his accession to the throne. This play's similarity to its predecessor, and the popularity of Part 1, may suggest that *2 Henry IV is* a sequel analogous to the second part of a modern cinematic blockbuster, in which the formula which has proved to be successful is repeated, usually as a pale shadow of the original. On the other hand, Shakespeare has held back some crucial dramatic incidents, including the rejection of Falstaff and Hal's coronation as Henry V, which might easily have been compressed into a single play, suggesting that a second part had been intended from an early stage, rather than written in response to commercial demand. Whatever the circumstances of its com-position, however, *2 Henry IV* deserves attention, both as an individual and complete play, and as an important link in the sequence of history plays.

The inevitability of the rejection of Falstaff overshadows the

play. This long-awaited scene is the climax of the two plays'
depiction of Hal's progress from rakish Prince of Wales to respons-
ible king. While Falstaff is bragging to his old university friend, the
country justice Shallow, about how he will be favoured when his
protégé Hal ascends the throne, King Henry V, as he now is, is
making his regal pronouncements to the Lord Chief Justice and
other dignitaries. When he calls the Lord Chief Justice 'father'
(5.2.140), he has turned for ever from his Eastcheap father Falstaff.
With the crown he assumes a kind of majestic *gravitas*: 'Now call
we our high court of parliament, And let us choose such limbs of
noble counsel, That the great body of our state may go In equal
rank with the best governed nation' (5.2.134–36). His long appren-
ticeship is over, and, as he promised in *1 Henry IV*, he is ready to
take on his burden of office. Falstaff's eager preparations to meet
his 'tender lambkin' (5.3.109) are poignant and pathetic, and even
though his interests may be principally selfish, his humiliation by
his erstwhile companion is a painful end to the play: 'I know thee
not, old man. Fall to thy prayers' (5.5.47). Falstaff continues his
delusions, in his repeated belief that 'I shall be sent for soon at
night' (5.5.88–89). Falstaff, it seems, is the sacrifice for Hal's reformation, and it may be that this takes the lustre off King Henry's
triumphant coronation in the final scene. It is striking, too, that in
Henry's coronation, the audience is also distanced from him. We
can only wait, like Falstaff, for his train to pass by: the days of easy
dramatic intimacy with Prince Hal are gone, and in their place is
this formal, spectacular relation of monarch and subject. Now we,
too, are those onlookers marvelling at the rarely seen personage, as
Henry IV advised in *1 Henry IV*. Throughout the play, the warmth
of the comic relationships in the earlier part has cooled, and the
overall tone is much more muted, wistful, even bitter-sweet. The
scene in which Poins and Hal are found wearing leather jerkins and
waiting on the old reprobate at table does not have the same esprit
as the exuberant Gad's Hill escapade in *1 Henry IV*; the energy
which motivated those earlier pranks is diverted elsewhere, as the
hour of Hal's assumption of the role of king comes ever nearer.

   The weariness which marked some of Henry IV's speeches in the
previous play is here solidified into an atmosphere of exhausted
enervation around the sovereign, and the prospect of the king's
demise is imminent. His hold on this play is even more tenuous

than on Part 1, symbolised by his absence from the play's early scenes before his weakened appearance, 'in his nightgown', in Act 3 Scene 1. All his appearances in this play are marked by his physical debility. Images of sickness and disease are applied both to the monarch and to the realm. Warwick tells the king, 'Your majesty hath been this fortnight ill' (3.1.104), and the physical frailty of Henry is displayed as he faints in Act 4 Scene 4. The king's illness represents the wider sickness in the body politic. Henry describes 'the body of our kingdom' as 'foul', infected with 'rank diseases', and Warwick continued the imagery but with a more optimistic prognosis: 'It is but as a body yet distempered, Which to his former strength may be restored With good advice and little medicine' (3.1.38–43). The language of diagnosis and cure is also used at length by the Archbishop, who voices the cause of the sickness, the usurpation of Richard (4.1.54ff.). This vocabulary of political and royal disease is echoed in references to sickness, particularly venereal disease, in the Falstaff scenes; and the addition of characters named Mouldy and Wart helps to produce an overarching theme of infection and corruption – physical, material, and political.

Henry is full of the cares of office: 'Uneasy lies the head that wears a crown' (3.1.31). The golden circlet which seemed so high a prize for the aspirant Bolingbroke is a burden, as Henry's real anxieties about unrest in the kingdom combine with, or seem to be the punishment for, a troubled conscience. As the hour of Hal's inheritance approaches, there is a climactic scene in which he seems to wish for things to accelerate. In Act 4 Scene 5, the dying king sleeps with the crown on his pillow. His son picks up the treasure, apostrophising this 'polished peturbation! Golden care!' (4.5.23). Like his father and like Richard II before him, Hal recognises the cares and responsibilities of kingship. It has not been a sinecure for Henry IV. The king tells his son: 'God knows . . . By what by-paths and indirect crookt ways I met this crown, and I myself know well How troublesome it sate upon my head', and predicts, 'To thee it shall descend with better quiet' (4.5.183–87).

Where 1 Henry IV opened with the king's lengthy oration, Part 2 begins with the omniscient personification Rumour. The different forms of authority represented by these contrasting openings reveal much about the moods of their respective plays. In some respects, the introduction in *2 Henry IV* of Rumour 'painted full of tongues' anticipates the more thorough-going use of a chorus in *Henry V*, although here its role is confined to an expository introduction (the unidentified speaking voice of the Epilogue, in its colloquial prose and promise of dancing, seems altogether different). Rumour's remarks are largely redundant, as the first scene of the play demonstrates its insidious power through the serial second-hand reports of the outcome of the Battle of Shrewsbury. Rumour does, however, set a tone of suspicion and deceit which infuses much of the play. It is a world of 'surmises, jealousies, conjectures' (16), where the Archbishop's cry 'what trust is there in these times?' (1.3.100) sums up a prevailing mood. Falsified hopes – of victory, of preferment, of repayment, of defeat – spread through the play. Together with the imagery of disease and sickness, this theme creates a subdued mood. By contrast, the Epilogue is a predominantly comic device: there are epilogues to *As You Like It*, *A Midsummer Night's Dream* and *The Tempest* – although in all these examples the identity of the speaker is clear.

The play concludes with Prince John's prediction that 'ere this year expire, We bear our civil swords and native fire As far as France' (5.5.104–06). The Epilogue, too, whets our appetite for the next instalment of the historical saga: 'If you be not too much cloyed with fat meat, our humble author will continue the story, with Sir John in it, and make you merry with fair Katharine of France' (Epilogue, l. 26–29). Henry V, the long-awaited sovereign, has ascended his throne: there is now much weight of dramatic and political expectation on him.

The scene: England

CHARACTERS IN THE PLAY

RUMOUR, *the Presenter*
KING HENRY THE FOURTH
PRINCE HENRY, *afterwards crowned*
        King Henry V
PRINCE JOHN OF LANCASTER   } *sons to*
PRINCE HUMPHREY OF GLOUCESTER *King Henry IV*
PRINCE THOMAS OF CLARENCE

EARL OF WARWICK
EARL OF WESTMORELAND
EARL OF SURREY (*mute*)
EARL OF KENT (*mute*)   } *of the king's party*
GOWER
HARCOURT
SIR JOHN BLUNT (*mute*)
LORD CHIEF JUSTICE
A Servant to the Lord Chief Justice
EARL OF NORTHUMBERLAND
SCROOP, *Archbishop of York*
LORD MOWBRAY   } *opposites against*
LORD HASTINGS   *King Henry IV*
LORD BARDOLPH
SIR JOHN COLEVILLE
TRAVERS *and* MORTON, *retainers to Northumberland*
EDWARD POINS, *gentleman-in-waiting to Prince Henry*
FALSTAFF
BARDOLPH
PISTOL   } *irregular humourists*
PETO
A Page
SHALLOW   } *country justices*
SILENCE

DAVY, *servant to Shallow*
FRANCIS *and another drawer*
FANG *and* SNARE, *a sergeant and his yeoman*
MOULDY
SHADOW
WART } *country soldiers*
FEEBLE
BULLCALF

LADY NORTHUMBERLAND
LADY PERCY
HOSTESS QUICKLY
DOLL TEARSHEET

Lords and Attendants; a Porter, Beadles,
three Strewers of rushes

INDUCTION

Warkworth. Before the gate of Northumberland's castle

'Enter RUMOUR, *painted full of tongues'*

RUMOUR   Open your ears; for which of you will stop
The vent of hearing when loud Rumour speaks?
I from the orient to the drooping west,
Making the wind my post-horse, still unfold
The acts commencéd on this ball of earth.
Upon my tongues continual slanders ride,
The which in every language I pronounce,
Stuffing the ears of men with false reports.
I speak of peace while covert enmity
Under the smile of safety wounds the world: 10
And who but Rumour, who but only I,
Make fearful musters and prepared defence,
Whiles the big year, swoln with some other grief,
Is thought with child by the stern tyrant war,
And no such matter? Rumour is a pipe
Blown by surmises, jealousies, conjectures,
And of so easy and so plain a stop
That the blunt monster with uncounted heads,
The still-discordant wav'ring multitude,
Can play upon it. But what need I thus   20
My well-known body to anatomise
Among my household? Why is Rumour here?
I run before King Harry's victory,
Who in a bloody field by Shrewsbury
Hath beaten down young Hotspur and his troops,
Quenching the flame of bold rebellion,
Even with the rebels' blood. But what mean I
To speak so true at first? My office is
To noise abroad that Harry Monmouth fell
Under the wrath of noble Hotspur's sword,   30
And that the king before the Douglas' rage
Stooped his anointed head as low as death.

This have I rumoured through the peasant towns
Between that royal field of Shrewsbury
And this worm-eaten hold of ragged stone,
Where Hotspur's father, old Northumberland,
Lies crafty-sick. The posts come tiring on,
And not a man of them brings other news
Than they have learned of me. From Rumour's tongues
They bring smooth comforts false, worse than

                                         true wrongs.   40
                                           [he goes

ACT I SCENE I

'Enter the LORD BARDOLPH*'*

L. BARD.   Who keeps the gate here, ho?
                         [A Porter appears on the wall
                         Where is the earl?
PORTER   What shall I say you are?
L. BARD.   Tell thou the earl
That the Lord Bardolph doth attend him here.
PORTER   His lordship is walked forth into the orchard.
Please it your honour knock but at the gate,
And he himself will answer.

NORTHUMBERLAND *comes forth, hobbling upon a crutch*
and with his head muffled

L. BARD.   Here comes the earl.
NORTH.   What news, Lord Bardolph? Every minute now
Should be the father of some stratagem.
The times are wild; contention like a horse,
Full of high feeding, madly hath broke loose,   10
And bears down all before him.
L. BARD.   Noble earl,
I bring you certain news from Shrewsbury.
NORTH.   Good, an God will!
L. BARD.   As good as heart can wish:
The king is almost wounded to the death,
And in the fortune of my lord your son
Prince Harry slain outright, and both the Blunts

Killed by the hand of Douglas, young Prince John
And Westmoreland and Stafford fled the field,
And Harry Monmouth's brawn, the hulk Sir John,
Is prisoner to your son: O, such a day,   20
So fought, so followed, and so fairly won,
Came not till now to dignify the times,
Since Caesar's fortunes!

NORTH.   How is this derived?
Saw you the field? Came you from Shrewsbury?

L. BARD. I spake with one, my lord, that came from thence,
A gentleman well bred and of good name,
That freely rend'red me these news for true.

TRAVERS *approaches*

NORTH. Here comes my servant Travers, whom I sent
On Tuesday last to listen after news.

L. BARD. My lord, I overrode him on the way,   30
And he is furnished with no certainties
More than he haply may retail from me.

NORTH. Now, Travers, what good tidings comes with you?

TRAVERS My lord, Sir John Umfrevile turned me back
With joyful tidings, and, being better horsed,
Outrode me. After him came spurring hard
A gentleman, almost forspent with speed,
That stopped by me to breathe his bloodied horse.
He asked the way to Chester, and of him
I did demand what news from Shrewsbury.   40
He told me that rebellion had bad luck,
And that young Harry Percy's spur was cold:
With that he gave his able horse the head,
And bending forward struck his arméd heels
Against the panting sides of his poor jade
Up to the rowel-head, and starting so
He seemed in running to devour the way,
Staying no longer question.

NORTH.   Ha? Again!
Said he young Harry Percy's spur was cold?
Of Hotspur Coldspur? That rebellion   50
Had met ill luck?

L. BARD.   My lord, I'll tell you what —

If my young lord your son have not the day,
Upon mine honour, for a silken point
I'll give my barony. Never talk of it.

NORTH.   Why should that gentleman that rode by Travers
Give then such instances of loss?

L. BARD.   Who, he?
He was some hilding fellow, that had stol'n
The horse he rode on, and upon my life
Spoke at a venture. Look, here comes more news.

MORTON *enters*

NORTH.   Yea, this man's brow, like to a title-leaf,   60
Foretells the nature of a tragic volume.
So looks the strond whereon the imperious flood
Hath left a witnessed usurpation.
Say, Morton, didst thou come from Shrewsbury?

MORTON   I ran from Shrewsbury, my noble lord,
Where hateful death put on his ugliest mask
To fright our party.

NORTH.   How doth my son and brother?
Thou tremblest, and the whiteness in thy cheek
Is apter than thy tongue to tell thy errand.
Even such a man, so faint, so spiritless,   70
So dull, so dead in look, so woe-begone,
Drew Priam's curtain in the dead of night,
And would have told him half his Troy was burnt:
But Priam found the fire ere he his tongue,
And I my Percy's death ere thou report'st it.
This thou wouldst say, 'Your son did thus and thus,
Your brother thus; so fought the noble Douglas' —
Stopping my greedy ear with their bold deeds;
But in the end, to stop my ear indeed,
Thou hast a sigh to blow away this praise,   80
Ending with 'Brother, son, and all are dead.'

MORTON   Douglas is living, and your brother yet,
But for my lord your son —

NORTH.   Why, he is dead.
See what a ready tongue suspicion hath!
He that but fears the thing he would not know,
Hath by instinct knowledge from others' eyes

That what he feared is chancéd. Yet speak, Morton.
Tell thou an earl his divination lies,
And I will take it as a sweet disgrace,
And make thee rich for doing me such wrong.   90

MORTON   You are too great to be by me gainsaid;
Your spirit is too true, your fears too certain.

NORTH.   Yet, for all this, say not that Percy's dead.
I see a strange confession in thine eye;
Thou shak'st thy head, and hold'st it fear or sin
To speak a truth: if he be slain, say so.
The tongue offends not that reports his death,
And he doth sin that doth belie the dead,
Not he which says the dead is not alive.
Yet the first bringer of unwelcome news   100
Hath but a losing office, and his tongue
Sounds ever after as a sullen bell,
Remembered tolling a departing friend.

L. BARD.   I cannot think, my lord, your son is dead.

MORTON   I am sorry I should force you to believe
That which I would to God I had not seen;
But these mine eyes saw him in bloody state,
Rend'ring faint quittance, wearied and out-breathed,
To Harry Monmouth, whose swift wrath beat down
The never-daunted Percy to the earth,   110
From whence with life he never more sprung up.
In few, his death, whose spirit lent a fire
Even to the dullest peasant in his camp,
Being bruited once, took fire and heat away
From the best-tempered courage in his troops.
For from his mettle was his party steeled,
Which once in him abated, all the rest
Turned on themselves, like dull and heavy lead.
And as the thing that's heavy in itself
Upon enforcement flies with greatest speed,   120
So did our men, heavy in Hotspur's loss,
Lend to this weight such lightness with their fear,
That arrows fled not swifter toward their aim
Than did our soldiers, aiming at their safety,
Fly from the field. Then was that noble Worcester

Too soon ta'en prisoner; and that furious Scot,
The bloody Douglas, whose well-labouring sword
Had three times slain th' appearance of the king,
'Gan vail his stomach and did grace the shame
Of those that turned their backs, and in his flight,   130
Stumbling in fear, was took: the sum of all
Is that the king hath won, and hath sent out
A speedy power to encounter you, my lord,
Under the conduct of young Lancaster
And Westmoreland. This is the news at full.

NORTH. For this I shall have time enough to mourn.
In poison there is physic; and these news,
Having been well, that would have made me sick,
Being sick, have in some measure made me well:
And as the wretch whose fever-weak'ned joints,   140
Like strengthless hinges, buckle under life,
Impatient of his fit, breaks like a fire
Out of his keeper's arms; even so my limbs,
Weakened with grief, being now enraged with grief,
Are thrice themselves: hence therefore, thou
                                   nice crutch!
A scaly gauntlet now with joints of steel
Must glove this hand; and hence, thou sickly coif!
Thou art a guard too wanton for the head
Which princes, fleshed with conquest, aim to hit:
Now bind my brows with iron, and approach   150
The ragged'st hour that time and spite dare bring
To frown upon th'enraged Northumberland!
Let heaven kiss earth! Now let not Nature's hand
Keep the wild flood confined! Let order die!
And let this world no longer be a stage
To feed contention in a ling'ring act;
But let one spirit of the first-born Cain
Reign in all bosoms, that, each heart being set
On bloody courses, the rude scene may end,
And darkness be the burier of the dead!   160

L. BARD. This strainèd passion doth you wrong, my lord.

MORTON Sweet earl, divorce not wisdom from your honour.
The lives of all your loving complices

Lean on your health, the which, if you give o'er
To stormy passion, must perforce decay.
You cast th'event of war, my noble lord,
And summed the account of chance, before you said
'Let us make head': it was your presurmise,
That, in the dole of blows, your son might drop:
You knew he walked o'er perils, on an edge,   170
More likely to fall in than to get o'er:
You were advised his flesh was capable
Of wounds and scars, and that his forward spirit
Would lift him where most trade of danger ranged.
Yet did you say 'Go forth'; and none of this,
Though strongly apprehended, could restrain
The stiff-borne action: what hath then befall'n,
Or what hath this bold enterprise brought forth,
More than that being which was like to be?

L. BARD.   We all that are engagéd to this loss   180
Knew that we ventured on such dangerous seas
That if we wrought out life 'twas ten to one,
And yet we ventured for the gain proposed,
Choked the respect of likely peril feared,
And, since we are o'erset, venture again.
Come, we will all put forth body and goods.

MORTON   'Tis more than time: and, my most noble lord,
I hear for certain, and dare speak the truth,
The gentle Archbishop of York is up
With well-appointed powers; he is a man   190
Who with a double surety binds his followers.
My lord your son had only but the corpse,
But shadows and the shows of men, to fight:
For that same word, rebellion, did divide
The action of their bodies from their souls,
And they did fight with queasiness, constrained,
As men drink potions, that their weapons only
Seemed on our side; but, for their spirits and souls,
This word, rebellion, it had froze them up,
As fish are in a pond. But now the bishop   200
Turns insurrection to religion:
Supposed sincere and holy in his thoughts,

He's followed both with body and with mind;
And doth enlarge his rising with the blood
Of fair King Richard, scraped from Pomfret stones;
Derives from heaven his quarrel and his cause;
Tells them he doth bestride a bleeding land,
Gasping for life under great Bolingbroke;
And more and less do flock to follow him.

NORTH. I knew of this before: but, to speak truth,   210
This present grief had wiped it from my mind.
Go in with me, and counsel every man
The aptest way for safety and revenge.
Get posts and letters, and make friends with speed;
Never so few, and never yet more need.

                                                              [*they go*

SCENE 2

A street in London

Enter SIR JOHN FALSTAFF, *with 'his* PAGE,
bearing his sword and buckler'

FALSTAFF Sirrah, you giant, what says the doctor to my water?

PAGE He said, sir, the water itself was a good healthy water,
but for the party that owed it, he might have moe
diseases than he knew for.

FALSTAFF Men of all sorts take a pride to gird at me: the brain of
this foolish-compounded clay-man is not able to invent
anything that intends to laughter, more than I invent or
is invented on me. I am not only witty in myself, but
the cause that wit is in other men. I do here walk
before thee like a sow that hath overwhelmed all her   10
litter but one. If the prince put thee into my service for
any other reason than to set me off, why then I have no
judgement. Thou whoreson mandrake, thou art fitter
to be worn in my cap than to wait at my heels. I was
never manned with an agate till now: but I will inset
you neither in gold nor silver, but in vile apparel, and
send you back again to your master, for a jewel – the
juvenal, the prince your master, whose chin is not yet

fledge. I will sooner have a beard grow in the palm of
my hand than he shall get one off his cheek; and yet he   20
will not stick to say his face is a face royal: God may
finish it when he will, 'tis not a hair amiss yet: he may
keep it still at a face-royal, for a barber shall never earn
sixpence out of it; and yet he'll be crowing as if he had
writ man ever since his father was a bachelor. He may
keep his own grace, but he's almost out of mine, I can
assure him. What said Master Dommelton about the
satin for my short cloak and my slops?

PAGE   He said, sir, you should procure him better assurance
              than Bardolph; he would not take his band and yours,   30
              he liked not the security.

FALSTAFF   Let him be damned like the Glutton! Pray God his
              tongue be hotter! A whoreson Achitophel! A rascally
              yea-forsooth knave! To bear a gentleman in hand, and
              then stand upon security! The whoreson smooth-pates
              do now wear nothing but high shoes, and bunches of
              keys at their girdles, and if a man is through with them
              in honest taking-up, then they must stand upon secu-
              rity. I had as lief they would put ratsbane in my mouth
              as offer to stop it with security. I looked a' should have   40
              sent me two and twenty yards of satin, as I am a true
              knight, and he sends me 'security'. Well, he may sleep
              in security, for he hath the horn of abundance, and the
              lightness of his wife shines through it, and yet cannot
              he see, though he have his own lanthorn to light him.
              Where's Bardolph?

PAGE   He's gone into Smithfield to buy your worship a horse.

FALSTAFF   I bought him in Paul's, and he'll buy me a horse in
              Smithfield; an I could get me but a wife in the stews, I
              were manned, horsed, and wived.   50

                The LORD CHIEF JUSTICE *approaches, with a servant*

PAGE   Sir, here comes the nobleman that committed the
              prince for striking him about Bardolph.

FALSTAFF   Wait close, I will not see him.   [*hides*

CH. JUST.   What's he that goes there?

SERVANT   Falstaff, an't please your lordship.

CH. JUST. He that was in question for the robbery?

SERVANT   He, my lord. But he hath since done good service at
          Shrewsbury, and, as I hear, is now going with some
          charge to the Lord John of Lancaster.

CH. JUST. What, to York? Call him back again.   60

SERVANT   Sir John Falstaff!

FALSTAFF Boy, tell him I am deaf.

PAGE   You must speak louder, my master is deaf.

CH. JUST. I am sure he is, to the hearing of anything good. Go,
          pluck him by the elbow. I must speak with him.

SERVANT   Sir John!

FALSTAFF What! A young knave, and begging! Is there not wars?
          Is there not employment? Doth not the king lack sub-
          jects? Do not the rebels need soldiers? Though it be a
          shame to be on any side but one, it is worse shame to   70
          beg than to be on the worst side, were it worse than
          the name of rebellion can tell how to make it.

SERVANT   You mistake me, sir.

FALSTAFF Why, sir, did I say you were an honest man? Setting
          my knighthood and my soldiership aside, I had lied in
          my throat, if I had said so.

SERVANT   I pray you, sir, then set your knighthood and your
          soldiership aside, and give me leave to tell you, you lie
          in your throat, if you say I am any other than an
          honest man.   80

FALSTAFF I give thee leave to tell me so! I lay aside that which
          grows to me! If thou get'st any leave of me, hang me. If
          thou tak'st leave, thou wert better be hanged. You hunt
          counter, hence! Avaunt!

                              [the Lord Chief Justice comes up

SERVANT   [bows] Sir, my lord would speak with you.

CH. JUST. Sir John Falstaff, a word with you.

FALSTAFF My good lord! God give your lordship good time of
          day, I am glad to see your lordship abroad. I heard say
          your lordship was sick; I hope your lordship goes
          abroad by advice. Your lordship, though not clean past 90
          your youth, have yet some smack of age in you, some
          relish of the saltness of time, and I most humbly beseech
          your lordship to have a reverend care of your health.

CH. JUST.	Sir John, I sent for you before your expedition to Shrewsbury.
FALSTAFF	An't please your lordship, I hear his majesty is returned with some discomfort from Wales.
CH. JUST.	I talk not of his majesty. You would not come when I sent for you.
FALSTAFF	And I hear, moreover, his highness is fallen into this same whoreson apoplexy.
CH. JUST.	Well, God mend him! I pray you, let me speak with you.
FALSTAFF	This apoplexy, as I take it, is a kind of lethargy, an't please your lordship, a kind of sleeping in the blood, a whoreson tingling.
CH. JUST.	What tell you me of it? Be it as it is.
FALSTAFF	It hath it original from much grief, from study and perturbation of the brain. I have read the cause of his effects in Galen, it is a kind of deafness.
CH. JUST.	I think you are fallen into the disease, for you hear not what I say to you.
FALSTAFF	Very well, my lord, very well – rather, an't please you, it is the disease of not listening, the malady of not marking, that I am troubled withal.
CH. JUST.	To punish you by the heels would amend the attention of your ears, and I care not if I do become your physician.
FALSTAFF	I am as poor as Job, my lord, but not so patient. Your lordship may minister the potion of imprisonment to me, in respect of poverty, but how I should be your patient to follow your prescriptions, the wise may make some dram of a scruple, or indeed a scruple itself.
CH. JUST.	I sent for you, when there were matters against you for your life, to come speak with me.
FALSTAFF	As I was then advised by my learned counsel in the laws of this land service, I did not come.
CH. JUST.	Well, the truth is, Sir John, you live in great infamy.
FALSTAFF	He that buckles himself in my belt cannot live in less.
CH. JUST.	Your means are very slender, and your waste is great.
FALSTAFF	I would it were otherwise; I would my means were greater and my waist slenderer.

100

110

120

130

CH. JUST. You have misled the youthful prince.

FALSTAFF The young prince hath misled me. I am the fellow
with the great belly, and he my dog.

CH. JUST. Well, I am loath to gall a new-healed wound. Your
day's service at Shrewsbury hath a little gilded over your
night's exploit on Gad's Hill. You may thank th'unquiet
time for your quiet o'er-posting that action.

FALSTAFF My lord!   140

CH. JUST. But since all is well, keep it so: wake not a sleeping wolf.

FALSTAFF To wake a wolf is as bad as smell a fox.

CH. JUST. What, you are as a candle, the better part burnt out.

FALSTAFF A wassail candle, my lord – all tallow; if I did say of
wax, my growth would approve the truth.

CH. JUST. There is not a white hair on your face, but should have
his effect of gravity.

FALSTAFF His effect of gravy, gravy, gravy.

CH. JUST. You follow the young prince up and down, like his ill
angel.   150

FALSTAFF Not so, my lord; your ill angel is light, but I hope he
that looks upon me will take me without weighing.
And yet in some respects I grant I cannot go. I cannot
tell. Virtue is of so little regard in these costermongers'
times that true valour is turned bear-'ard: pregnancy is
made a tapster, and his quick wit wasted in giving
reckonings: all the other gifts appertinent to man, as the
malice of this age shapes them, are not worth a goose-
berry. You that are old consider not the capacities of us
that are young, you do measure the heat of our livers   160
with the bitterness of your galls; and we that are in the
vaward of our youth, I must confess, are wags too.

CH. JUST. Do you set down your name in the scroll of youth,
that are written down old with all the characters of
age? Have you not a moist eye? A dry hand? A yellow
cheek? A white beard? A decreasing leg? An increasing
belly? Is not your voice broken? Your wind short?
Your chin double? Your wit single? And every part
about you blasted with antiquity? And will you yet call
yourself young? Fie, fie, fie, Sir John!   170

FALSTAFF My lord, I was born about three of the clock in the afternoon, with a white head and something a round belly. For my voice, I have lost it with hallooing and singing of anthems. To approve my youth further, I will not: the truth is, I am only old in judgement and understanding; and he that will caper with me for a thousand marks, let him lend me the money, and have at him. For the box of the ear that the prince gave you, he gave it like a rude prince, and you took it like a sensible lord: I have checked him for it, and the young lion repents – [*aside*] marry, not in ashes and sackcloth, but in new silk and old sack.

CH. JUST. Well, God send the prince a better companion!

FALSTAFF God send the companion a better prince! I cannot rid my hands of him.

CH. JUST. Well, the king hath severed you: I hear you are going with Lord John of Lancaster against the Archbishop and the Earl of Northumberland.

FALSTAFF Yea, I thank your pretty sweet wit for it. [*louder*] But look you, pray, all you that kiss my lady Peace at home, that our armies join not in a hot day! For, by the Lord, I take but two shirts out with me, and I mean not to sweat extraordinarily: if it be a hot day, and I brandish anything but a bottle, I would I might never spit white again. There is not a dangerous action can peep out his head but I am thrust upon it. Well, I cannot last ever, but it was alway yet the trick of our English nation, if they have a good thing, to make it too common. If ye will needs say I am an old man, you should give me rest: I would to God my name were not so terrible to the enemy as it is. I were better to be eaten to death with a rust than to be scoured to nothing with perpetual motion.

CH. JUST. Well, be honest, be honest, and God bless your expedition!

FALSTAFF Will your lordship lend me a thousand pound to furnish me forth?

CH. JUST. Not a penny, not a penny; you are too impatient to bear crosses. Fare you well: commend me to my cousin Westmoreland.   [*he goes, the servant following*

FALSTAFF   If I do, fillip me with a three-man beetle. A man can
           no more separate age and covetousness than a' can part
           young limbs and lechery: but the gout galls the one,
           and the pox pinches the other; and so both the degrees
           prevent my curses. Boy!

PAGE   Sir?

FALSTAFF   What money is in my purse?

PAGE   Seven groats and two pence.

FALSTAFF   I can get no remedy against this consumption of the
           purse. Borrowing only lingers and lingers it out, but   220
           the disease is incurable. Go bear this letter to my Lord
           of Lancaster, this to the prince, this to the Earl of
           Westmoreland, and this to old Mistress Ursula, whom
           I have weekly sworn to marry since I perceived the
           first white hair of my chin: about it, you know where
           to find me. [*Page goes*] A pox of this gout! Or, a gout of
           this pox! For the one or the other plays the rogue with
           my great toe. 'Tis no matter if I do halt, I have the
           wars for my colour, and my pension shall seem the
           more reasonable. A good wit will make use of any-   230
           thing; I will turn diseases to commodity.

                                                           [*he goes*

SCENE 3

The Palace of the Archbishop of York

Enter the ARCHBISHOP OF YORK, HASTINGS, MOWBRAY,
and LORD BARDOLPH

ARCH.   Thus have you heard our cause and known our means,
           And, my most noble friends, I pray you all,
           Speak plainly your opinions of our hopes.
           And first, lord marshal, what say you to it?

MOWBRAY   I well allow the occasion of our arms,
           But gladly would be better satisfied
           How in our means we should advance ourselves
           To look with forehead bold and big enough
           Upon the power and puissance of the king.

HASTINGS   Our present musters grow upon the file   10

To five and twenty thousand men of choice;
And our supplies live largely in the hope
Of great Northumberland, whose bosom burns
With an incensèd fire of injuries.

L. BARD. The question then, Lord Hastings, standeth thus:
Whether our present five and twenty thousand
May hold up head without Northumberland.

HASTINGS With him, we may.

L. BARD.   Yea, marry, there's the point.
But if without him we be thought too feeble,
My judgement is, we should not step too far   20
Till we had his assistance by the hand.
For in a theme so bloody-faced as this
Conjecture, expectation, and surmise
Of aids incertain should not be admitted.

ARCH. Tis very true, Lord Bardolph, for indeed
It was young Hotspur's cause at Shrewsbury.

L. BARD. It was, my lord; who lined himself with hope,
Eating the air on promise of supply,
Flatt'ring himself in project of a power
Much smaller than the smallest of his thoughts;   30
And so, with great imagination
Proper to madmen, led his powers to death,
And, winking, leaped into destruction.

HASTINGS But, by your leave, it never yet did hurt
To lay down likelihoods and forms of hope.

L. BARD. Yes, if this present quality of war –
Indeed the instant action, a cause on foot –
Lives so in hope, as in an early spring
We see th'appearing buds; which to prove fruit
Hope gives not so much warrant as despair   ·   40
That frosts will bite them. When we mean to build,
We first survey the plot, then draw the model;
And when we see the figure of the house,
Then must we rate the cost of the erection;
Which if we find outweighs ability,
What do we then, but draw anew the model
In fewer offices, or at least desist
To build at all? Much more, in this great work

(Which is almost to pluck a kingdom down
And set another up) should we survey   50
The plot of situation and the model,
Consent upon a sure foundation,
Question surveyors, know our own estate,
How able such a work to undergo,
To weigh against his opposite; or else
We fortify in paper and in figures,
Using the names of men instead of men:
Like one that draws the model of an house
Beyond his power to build it; who, half through,
Gives o'er, and leaves his part-created cost   60
A naked subject to the weeping clouds,
And waste for churlish winter's tyranny.

HASTINGS   Grant that our hopes (yet likely of fair birth)
Should be stillborn, and that we now possessed
The utmost man of expectation,
I think we are a body strong enough,
Even as we are, to equal with the king.

L. BARD.   What, is the king but five and twenty thousand?

HASTINGS   To us no more, nay, not so much, Lord Bardolph.
For his divisions, as the times do brawl,   70
Are in three heads, one power against the French,
And one against Glendower; perforce a third
Must take up us: so is the unfirm king
In three divided, and his coffers sound
With hollow poverty and emptiness.

ARCH.   That he should draw his several strengths together
And come against us in full puissance,
Need not be dreaded.

HASTINGS   If he should do so,
He leaves his back unarmed, the French and Welsh
Baying him at the heels: never fear that.   80

L. BARD.   Who is it like should lead his forces hither?

HASTINGS   The Duke of Lancaster and Westmoreland:
Against the Welsh, himself and Harry Monmouth:
But who is substituted 'gainst the French,
I have no certain notice.

ARCH.   Let us on;

And publish the occasion of our arms.
The commonwealth is sick of their own choice,
Their over-greedy love hath surfeited:
An habitation giddy and unsure
Hath he that buildeth on the vulgar heart.   90
O thou fond many, with what loud applause
Didst thou beat heaven with blessing Bolingbroke,
Before he was what thou wouldst have him be!
And being now trimmed in thine own desires,
Thou, beastly feeder, art so full of him,
That thou provok'st thyself to cast him up.
So, so, thou common dog, didst thou disgorge
Thy glutton bosom of the royal Richard;
And now thou wouldst eat thy dead vomit up,
And howl'st to find it. What trust is in these times?   100
They that, when Richard lived, would have him die,
Are now become enamoured on his grave:
Thou, that threw'st dust upon his goodly head,
When through proud London he came sighing on
After th' admiréd heels of Bolingbroke,
Criest now, 'O earth, yield us that king again,
And take thou this!' O thoughts of men accursed!
Past and to come seems best; things present, worst.
MOWBRAY Shall we go draw our numbers, and set on?
HASTINGS We are time's subjects, and time bids be gone.   110
                                        [*they go*

ACT 2 SCENE 1

Eastcheap. Near the Boar's Head Tavern

Enter HOSTESS *with Sergeant* FANG

HOSTESS   Master Fang, have you entered the action?

FANG   It is entered.

HOSTESS   Where's your yeoman? Is't a lusty yeoman? Will a'
               stand to't?

FANG   Sirrah! Where's Snare?

HOSTESS   O Lord, ay, good Master Snare.

Yeoman SNARE *approaches*

SNARE   Here, here.

FANG   Snare, we must arrest Sir John Falstaff.

HOSTESS   Yea, good Master Snare, I have entered him and all.

SNARE   It may chance cost some of us our lives, for he will stab.   10

HOSTESS   Alas the day, take heed of him, he stabbed me in mine
               own house, most beastly in good faith. A' cares not
               what mischief he does, if his weapon be out. He will
               foin like any devil, he will spare neither man, woman,
               nor child.

FANG   If I can close with him, I care not for his thrust.

HOSTESS   No, nor I neither; I'll be at your elbow.

FANG   An I but fist him once, an a' come but within my vice –

HOSTESS   I am undone by his going. I warrant you, he's an
               infinitive thing upon my score. Good Master Fang,   20
               hold him sure; good Master Snare, let him not 'scape.
               A' comes continuantly to Pie-corner (saving your
               manhoods) to buy a saddle, and he is indited to dinner
               to the Lubber's head in Lumbert street, to Master
               Smooth's the silkman. I pray you, since my exion is
               entered, and my case so openly known to the world,
               let him be brought in to his answer. A hundred mark is
               a long one for a poor lone woman to bear, and I have
               borne, and borne, and borne, and have been fubbed
               off, and fubbed off, and fubbed off, from this day to   30
               that day, that it is a shame to be thought on. There is no

honesty in such dealing, unless a woman should be made
an ass, and a beast, to bear every knave's wrong.

SIR JOHN FALSTAFF, PAGE, *and* BARDOLPH *come along the street*

Yonder he comes, and that arrant malmsey-nose knave
Bardolph with him. Do your offices, do your offices,
Master Fang and Master Snare, do me, do me, do me
your offices.

FALSTAFF   How now? Whose mare's dead? What's the matter?

FANG   Sir John, I arrest you at the suit of Mistress Quickly.

FALSTAFF   Away, varlets! Draw, Bardolph, cut me off the villain's   40
            head; throw the quean in the channel.
                            [*Bardolph draws, and a scuffle ensues*

HOSTESS   Throw me in the channel? I'll throw thee in the chan-
            nel. Wilt thou? Wilt thou? Thou bastardly rogue!
            Murder, murder! Ah, thou honeysuckle villain! Wilt
            thou kill God's officers and the king's? Ah, thou
            honey-seed rogue! Thou art a honey-seed, a man-
            queller, and a woman-queller.

FALSTAFF   Keep them off, Bardolph.

FANG   A rescue! A rescue!   [*a crowd assembles*

HOSTESS   Good people, bring a rescue or two. [*the Page attacks*   50
            her] Thou wot, wot thou? Thou wot, wot ta? Do! Do,
            thou rogue! Do, thou hempseed!
                    [*she strikes at him and flees; Fang arrests Falstaff*

PAGE   [*pursuing*] Away, you scullion! You rampallian! You
            fustilarian! I'll tickle your catastrophe.

                '*Enter the* L. CHIEF JUSTICE *and his men*'

CH. JUST.   What is the matter? Keep the peace here, ho!

HOSTESS   Good my lord, be good to me. I beseech you, stand to
            me!

CH. JUST.   How, now, Sir John? What are you brawling here?
            Doth this become your place, your time and business?
            You should have been well on your way to York.   60
            Stand from him, fellow; wherefore hang'st upon him?

HOSTESS   O my most worshipful lord, an't please your grace, I
            am a poor widow of Eastcheap, and he is arrested at
            my suit.

CH. JUST.   For what sum?

HOSTESS   It is more than for some, my lord, it is for all, all I
have. He hath eaten me out of house and home, he
hath put all my substance into that fat belly of his. But
I will have some of it out again, or I will ride thee a-
nights like the mare.   70

FALSTAFF I think I am as like to ride the mare, if I have any
vantage of ground to get up.

CH. JUST. How comes this, Sir John? Fie! What man of good
temper would endure this tempest of exclamation? Are
you not ashamed to enforce a poor widow to so rough
a course to come by her own?

FALSTAFF What is the gross sum that I owe thee?

HOSTESS   Marry, if thou wert an honest man, thyself and the
money too. Thou didst swear to me upon a parcel-gilt
goblet, sitting in my Dolphin-chamber, at the round   80
table by a sea-coal fire, upon Wednesday in Wheeson
week, when the prince broke thy head for liking his
father to a singing-man of Windsor, thou didst swear
to me then, as I was washing thy wound, to marry me,
and make me my lady thy wife. Canst thou deny it?
Did not goodwife Keech, the butcher's wife, come in
then and call me gossip Quickly? Coming in to borrow
a mess of vinegar, telling us she had a good dish of
prawns, whereby thou didst desire to eat some,
whereby I told thee they were ill for a green wound? 90
And didst thou not, when she was gone down stairs,
desire me to be no more so familiarity with such poor
people, saying that ere long they should call me
madam? And didst thou not kiss me, and bid me fetch
thee thirty shillings? I put thee now to thy book-oath;
deny it if thou canst.

FALSTAFF My lord, this is a poor mad soul, and she says up and
down the town that her eldest son is like you. She hath
been in good case, and the truth is, poverty hath
distracted her. But for these foolish officers, I beseech 100
you I may have redress against them.

CH. JUST. Sir John, Sir John, I am well acquainted with your
manner of wrenching the true cause the false way: it is
not a confident brow, nor the throng of words that

come with such more than impudent sauciness from
you, can thrust me from a level consideration: you
have, as it appears to me, practised upon the easy-
yielding spirit of this woman, and made her serve your
uses both in purse and in person.

HOSTESS   Yea, in truth, my lord.   110

CH. JUST. Pray thee, peace. Pay her the debt you owe her, and
unpay the villainy you have done with her. The one
you may do with sterling money, and the other with
current repentance.

FALSTAFF   My lord, I will not undergo this sneap without reply.
You call honourable boldness impudent sauciness: if a
man will make curtsy and say nothing, he is virtuous.
No, my lord, my humble duty remembered, I will not
be your suitor. I say to you, I do desire deliverance
from these officers, being upon hasty employment in   120
the king's affairs.

CH. JUST. You speak as having power to do wrong. But answer
in th'effect of your reputation, and satisfy the poor
woman.

FALSTAFF   Come hither, hostess.   [he takes her aside

GOWER comes up with a letter

CH. JUST. Now, Master Gower, what news?

GOWER   The king, my lord, and Harry Prince of Wales
Are near at hand – the rest the paper tells.
                              [the Lord Chief Justice reads the letter

FALSTAFF   As I am a gentleman!

HOSTESS   Faith, you said so before.   130

FALSTAFF   As I am a gentleman. Come, no more words of it.

HOSTESS   By this heavenly ground I tread on, I must be fain to
pawn both my plate and the tapestry of my dining-
chambers.

FALSTAFF   Glasses, glasses, is the only drinking – and for thy walls,
a pretty slight drollery, or the story of the Prodigal, or
the German hunting, in waterwork, is worth a thousand
of these bed-hangers and these fly-bitten tapestries. Let
it be ten pound, if thou canst. Come, an 'twere not for
thy humours, there's not a better wench in England.   140

Go, wash thy face, and draw the action. Come, thou
must not be in this humour with me; dost not know
me? Come, come, I know thou wast set on to this.

HOSTESS   Pray thee, Sir John, let it be but twenty nobles. I' faith,
I am loath to pawn my plate, so God save me, la.

FALSTAFF   Let it alone, I'll make other shift; you'll be a fool still.

HOSTESS   Well, you shall have it, though I pawn my gown. I
hope you'll come to supper. You'll pay me all together?

FALSTAFF   Will I live? [*aside to Bardolph*] Go, with her, with her,
hook on, hook on.   150

HOSTESS   Will you have Doll Tearsheet meet you at supper?

FALSTAFF   No more words, let's have her.

> [*Hostess goes off with Bardolph,*
> *Officers and Page following*

CH. JUST.   [*to Gower*] I have heard better news.

FALSTAFF   What's the news, my lord?

CH. JUST.   [*to Gower*] Where lay the king tonight?

GOWER   At Basingstoke, my lord.

FALSTAFF   I hope, my lord, all's well. What is the news, my lord?

CH. JUST.   [*to Gower*] Come all his forces back?

GOWER   No, fifteen hundred foot, five hundred horse,
Are marched up to my lord of Lancaster,   160
Against Northumberland and the Archbishop.

FALSTAFF   Comes the king back from Wales, my noble lord?

CH. JUST.   [*to Gower*] You shall have letters of me presently.
Come, go along with me, good Master Gower.

> [*they turn to go*

FALSTAFF   My lord!

CH. JUST.   What's the matter?

FALSTAFF   [*to Gower*] Master Gower, shall I entreat you with me
to dinner?

GOWER   I must wait upon my good lord here, I thank you,
good Sir John.   170

CH. JUST.   Sir John, you loiter here too long, being you are to
take soldiers up in counties as you go.

FALSTAFF   [*to Gower*] Will you sup with me, Master Gower?

CH. JUST.   What foolish master taught you these manners, Sir
John?

FALSTAFF Master Gower, if they become me not, he was a fool
that taught them me. [*to the L. Chief Justice*] This is the
right fencing grace, my lord, tap for tap, and so part
fair.

CH. JUST. Now the Lord lighten thee! Thou art a great fool.   180

[*they go*]

SCENE 2

London. A room in the Prince's house

Enter PRINCE HENRY *and* POINS, *newly arrived from Wales*

PRINCE Before God, I am exceeding weary.

POINS Is't come to that? I had thought weariness durst not
have attached one of so high blood.

PRINCE Faith, it does me, though it discolours the complexion
of my greatness to acknowledge it. Doth it not show
vilely in me to desire small beer?

POINS Why, a prince should not be so loosely studied as to
remember so weak a composition.

PRINCE Belike then my appetite was not princely got, for, by
my troth, I do now remember the poor creature, small 10
beer. But indeed these humble considerations make
me out of love with my greatness. What a disgrace is it
to me to remember thy name! Or to know thy face tomorrow! Or to take note how many pair of silk
stockings thou hast, viz. these, and those that were thy
peach-coloured ones! Or to bear the inventory of thy
shirts – as, one for superfluity, and another for use! But
that the tennis-court keeper knows better than I, for it
is a low ebb of linen with thee when thou keepest not
racket there, as thou hast not done a great while, 20
because the rest of thy low countries have made a shift
to eat up thy holland: and God knows whether those
that bawl out the ruins of thy linen shall inherit his
kingdom: but the midwives say the children are not in
the fault, whereupon the world increases and kindreds
are mightily strengthened.

POINS   How ill it follows, after you have laboured so hard, you should talk so idly! Tell me, how many good young princes would do so, their fathers being so sick as yours at this time is?   30

PRINCE   Shall I tell thee one thing, Poins?

POINS   Yes, faith, and let it be an excellent good thing.

PRINCE   It shall serve among wits of no higher breeding than thine.

POINS   Go to. I stand the push of your one thing that you will tell.

PRINCE   Marry, I tell thee, it is not meet that I should be sad now my father is sick; albeit I could tell to thee, as to one it pleases me for fault of a better to call my friend, I could be sad, and sad indeed too.   40

POINS   Very hardly, upon such a subject.

PRINCE   By this hand, thou thinkest me as far in the devil's book as thou and Falstaff for obduracy and persistency. Let the end try the man. But I tell thee, my heart bleeds inwardly that my father is so sick, and keeping such vile company as thou art hath in reason taken from me all ostentation of sorrow.

POINS   The reason?

PRINCE   What wouldst thou think of me if I should weep?

POINS   I would think thee a most princely hypocrite.   50

PRINCE   It would be every man's thought, and thou art a blessed fellow to think as every man thinks; never a man's thought in the world keeps the road-way better than thine: every man would think me an hypocrite indeed. And what accites your most worshipful thought to think so?

POINS   Why, because you have been so lewd, and so much engraffed to Falstaff.

PRINCE   And to thee.

POINS   By this light, I am well spoke on, I can hear it with   60
         mine own ears. The worst that they can say of me is that I am a second brother, and that I am a proper fellow of my hands, and those two things I confess I cannot help. By the mass, here comes Bardolph.

'Enter BARDOLPH, *and* PAGE'

PRINCE	And the boy that I gave Falstaff. A' had him from me Christian, and look if the fat villain have not transformed him ape.
BARDOLPH	God save your grace!
PRINCE	And yours, most noble Bardolph!
POINS	Come, you virtuous ass, you bashful fool, must you be 70 blushing? Wherefore blush you now? What a maidenly man-at-arms are you become? Is't such a matter to get a pottle-pot's maidenhead?
PAGE	A' calls me e'en now, my lord, through a red lattice, and I could discern no part of his face from the window. At last I spied his eyes, and methought he had made two holes in the ale-wife's new petticoat and so peeped through.
PRINCE	Has not the boy profited?
BARDOLPH	Away, you whoreson upright rabbit, away! 80
PAGE	Away, you rascally Althaea's dream, away!
PRINCE	Instruct us, boy. What dream, boy?
PAGE	Marry, my lord, Althaea dreamt she was delivered of a fire-brand, and therefore I call him her dream.
PRINCE	A crown's worth of good interpretation. There 'tis, boy.

[gives him money

POINS	O that this blossom could be kept from cankers! Well, there is sixpence to preserve thee.
BARDOLPH	An you do not make him be hanged among you, the gallows shall have wrong.
PRINCE	And how doth thy master, Bardolph? 90
BARDOLPH	Well, my lord. He heard of your grace's coming to town. There's a letter for you.

[the Prince opens and reads

POINS	Delivered with good respect. And how doth the martlemas, your master?
BARDOLPH	In bodily health, sir.
POINS	Marry, the immortal part needs a physician, but that moves not him. Though that be sick, it dies not.
PRINCE	I do allow this wen to be as familiar with me as my dog; and he holds his place, for look you how he writes.

[he shows the superscription

POINS   'John Falstaff, knight' – Every man must know that as 100
          oft as he has occasion to name himself: even like those
          that are kin to the king, for they never prick their
          finger but they say, 'There's some of the king's blood
          spilt.' 'How comes that?' says he, that takes upon him
          not to conceive. The answer is as ready as a borrower's
          cap, 'I am the king's poor cousin, sir.'

PRINCE   Nay, they will be kin to us, or they will fetch it from
          Japhet. But the letter: [*reads*] 'Sir John Falstaff, knight,
          to the son of the king nearest his father, Harry Prince
          of Wales, greeting.'   110

POINS   Why, this is a certificate.

PRINCE   Peace! [*reads*] 'I will imitate the honourable Romans in
          brevity.'

POINS   He sure means brevity in breath, short-winded.

PRINCE   [*reads*] 'I commend me to thee, I commend thee, and I
          leave thee. Be not too familiar with Poins; for he
          misuses thy favours so much that he swears thou art to
          marry his sister Nell. Repent at idle times as thou
          may'st, and so farewell.

              'Thine, by yea and no, which is as much as to say as 120
              thou usest him, JACK FALSTAFF with my familiars,
              JOHN with my brothers and sisters, and SIR JOHN
              with all Europe.'

POINS   My lord, I'll steep this letter in sack, and make him eat it.

PRINCE   That's to make him eat twenty of his words. But do
          you use me thus, Ned? Must I marry your sister?

POINS   God send the wench no worse fortune! But I never
          said so.

PRINCE   Well, thus we play the fools with the time, and the
          spirits of the wise sit in the clouds and mock us. Is 130
          your master here in London?

BARDOLPH Yea, my lord.

PRINCE   Where sups he? Doth the old boar feed in the old
          frank?

BARDOLPH At the old place, my lord, in Eastcheap.

PRINCE   What company?

PAGE   Ephesians, my lord, of the old church.

PRINCE   Sup any women with him?

PAGE   None, my lord, but old Mistress Quickly and Mistress
Doll Tearsheet.   140

PRINCE   What pagan may that be?

PAGE   A proper gentlewoman, sir, and a kinswoman of my
master's.

PRINCE   Even such kin as the parish heifers are to the town
bull. Shall we steal upon them, Ned, at supper?

POINS   I am your shadow, my lord, I'll follow you.

PRINCE   Sirrah, you boy, and Bardolph, no word to your master
that I am yet come to town. [*he gives them money*]
There's for your silence.

BARDOLPH   I have no tongue, sir.   150

PAGE   And for mine, sir, I will govern it.

PRINCE   Fare you well; go. [*Bardolph and the Page go*] This Doll
Tearsheet should be some road.

POINS   I warrant you, as common as the way between Saint
Albans and London.

PRINCE   How might we see Falstaff bestow himself tonight in
his true colours, and not ourselves be seen?

POINS   Put on two leathern jerkins and aprons, and wait upon
him at his table as drawers.

PRINCE   From a god to a bull? A heavy descension! It was 160
Jove's case. From a prince to a prentice? A low transformation! That shall be mine. For in everything the
purpose must weigh with the folly. Follow me, Ned.

                                               [*they go*

SCENE 3

Warkworth. Before the Castle

Enter NORTHUMBERLAND, LADY NORTHUMBERLAND,
and LADY PERCY

NORTH.   I pray thee, loving wife, and gentle daughter,
Give even way unto my rough affairs.
Put not you on the visage of the times,
And be like them to Percy troublesome.

LADY N. I have given over, I will speak no more.
        Do what you will, your wisdom be your guide.
NORTH. Alas, sweet wife, my honour is at pawn,
        And, but my going, nothing can redeem it.
LADY PERCY O yet, for God's sake, go not to these wars!
        The time was, father, that you broke your word,   10
        When you were more endeared to it than now;
        When your own Percy, when my heart's dear Harry,
        Threw many a northward look to see his father
        Bring up his powers – but he did long in vain.
        Who then persuaded you to stay at home?
        There were two honours lost, yours and your son's.
        For yours, the God of heaven brighten it!
        For his, it stuck upon him, as the sun
        In the grey vault of heaven, and by his light
        Did all the chivalry of England move   20
        To do brave acts. He was indeed the glass
        Wherein the noble youth did dress themselves.
        He had no legs that practised not his gait;
        And speaking thick, which nature made his blemish,
        Became the accents of the valiant;
        For those that could speak low and tardily
        Would turn their own perfection to abuse,
        To seem like him: so that in speech, in gait,
        In diet, in affections of delight,
        In military rules, humours of blood,   30
        He was the mark and glass, copy and book,
        That fashioned others. And him, O wondrous him!
        O miracle of men! Him did you leave,
        Second to none, unseconded by you,
        To look upon the hideous god of war
        In disadvantage, to abide a field
        Where nothing but the sound of Hotspur's name
        Did seem defensible: so you left him.
        Never, O never, do his ghost the wrong
        To hold your honour more precise and nice   40
        With others than with him! Let them alone:
        The marshal and the archbishop are strong:
        Had my sweet Harry had but half their numbers,

Today might I, hanging on Hotspur's neck,
Have talked of Monmouth's grave.

NORTH.   Beshrew your heart,
Fair daughter, you do draw my spirits from me
With new lamenting ancient oversights.
But I must go and meet with danger there,
Or it will seek me in another place,
And find me worse provided.

LADY N.   O, fly to Scotland,   50
Till that the nobles and the arméd commons
Have of their puissance made a little taste.

LADY PERCY If they get ground and vantage of the king,
Then join you with them, like a rib of steel,
To make strength stronger; but, for all our loves,
First let them try themselves. So did your son:
He was so suffered, so came I a widow,
And never shall have length of life enough
To rain upon remembrance with mine eyes,
That it may grow and sprout as high as heaven,   60
For recordation to my noble husband.

NORTH.   Come, come, go in with me. 'Tis with my mind
As with the tide swelled up unto his height,
That makes a still-stand, running neither way.
Fain would I go to meet the archbishop,
But many thousand reasons hold me back.
I will resolve for Scotland! There am I,
Till time and vantage crave my company.

                                        [they go

                    SCENE 4

        London. The Boar's Head Tavern in Eastcheap

        FRANCIS laying the table: enter another Drawer

FRANCIS   What the devil hast thou brought there – apple-johns?
Thou knowest Sir John cannot endure an apple-john.

2 DRAWER Mass, thou say'st true. The prince once set a dish of
apple-johns before him, and told him there were five
more Sir Johns, and putting off his hat, said, 'I will

now take my leave of these six dry, round, old, withered knights.' It angered him to the heart. But he hath
forgot that.

FRANCIS   Why then, cover and set them down, and see if thou
canst find out Sneak's noise. Mistress Tearsheet would   10
fain hear some music.

2 DRAWER   Dispatch. The room where they supped is too hot,
they'll come in straight.

FRANCIS   Sirrah, here will be the prince and Master Poins anon,
and they will put on two of our jerkins and aprons,
and Sir John must not know of it. Bardolph hath
brought word.

2 DRAWER   By the mass, here will be old utis. It will be an excellent stratagem.

FRANCIS   I'll see if I can find out Sneak.   [*he goes*   20

HOSTESS *and* DOLL TEARSHEET *enter*

HOSTESS   I'faith, sweetheart, methinks now you are in an excellent good temperality: your pulsidge beats as extraordinarily as heart would desire, and your colour, I
warrant you, is as red as any rose, in good truth, la!
But, i'faith, you have drunk too much canaries, and
that's a marvellous searching wine, and it perfumes the
blood ere one can say 'What's this?' How do you now?

DOLL   [*faintly*] Better than I was: hem!   [*they sit*

HOSTESS   Why, that's well said; a good heart's worth gold. Lo,
here comes Sir John.   30

FALSTAFF *enters, singing*

FALSTAFF   '*When Arthur first in court*' – [*to the drawer, aside*] Empty
the jordan – '*and was a worthy king*'. [2 DRAWER *goes out*]
How now, Mistress Doll?

HOSTESS   Sick of a calm, yea, good faith.

FALSTAFF   So is all her sect. An they be once in a calm, they are
sick.

DOLL   A pox damn you, you muddy rascal, is that all the
comfort you give me?

FALSTAFF   You make fat rascals, Mistress Doll.

DOLL   I make them! Gluttony and diseases make them. I   40
make them not.

FALSTAFF If the cook help to make the gluttony, you help to
make the diseases, Doll. We catch of you, Doll, we
catch of you. Grant that, my poor virtue, grant that.

DOLL Yea, joy, our chains and our jewels.

FALSTAFF 'Your brooches, pearls, and ouches.' For to serve
bravely is to come halting off, you know – to come off
the breach with his pike bent bravely, and to surgery
bravely, to venture upon the charged chambers
bravely –   50

DOLL Hang yourself, you muddy conger, hang yourself!

HOSTESS By my troth, this is the old fashion! You two never
meet but you fall to some discord. You are both, i'
good troth, as rheumatic as two dry toasts, you cannot
one bear with another's confirmities. [to Doll] What the
good-year! One must bear, and that must be you; you
are the weaker vessel, as they say, the emptier vessel.

DOLL Can a weak empty vessel bear such a huge full hogs-
head? There's a whole merchant's venture of Bourd–
eaux stuff in him; you have not seen a hulk better   60
stuffed in the hold. Come, I'll be friends with thee,
Jack. Thou art going to the wars, and whether I shall
ever see thee again or no, there is nobody cares.

FRANCIS *returns*

FRANCIS Sir, Ancient Pistol's below, and would speak with you.

DOLL Hang him, swaggering rascal! Let him not come
hither. It is the foul-mouth'dst rogue in England.

HOSTESS If he swagger, let him not come here. No, by my faith,
I must live among my neighbours. I'll no swaggerers, I
am in good name and fame with the very best. Shut
the door, there comes no swaggerers here; I have not   70
lived all this while to have swaggering now – shut the
door, I pray you.

FALSTAFF Dost thou hear, hostess?

HOSTESS Pray ye, pacify yourself, Sir John. There comes no
swaggerers here.

FALSTAFF Dost thou hear? It is mine ancient.

HOSTESS Tilly-fally, Sir John, ne'er tell me: an your ancient
swagger, a' comes not in my doors. I was before Master
Tisick, the debuty, t'other day, and (as he said to me) –

'twas no longer ago than Wednesday last – 'I'good 80
faith, neighbour Quickly,' says he – Master Dumb, our
minister, was by then – 'Neighbour Quickly (says he)
receive those that are civil, for (said he) you are in an ill
name'; now a' said so, I can tell whereupon: 'for (says
he) you are an honest woman, and well thought on,
therefore take heed what guests you receive: receive
(says he) no swaggering companions.' There comes
none here. You would bless you to hear what he said:
no, I'll no swaggerers.

FALSTAFF   He's no swaggerer, hostess – a tame cheater, i'faith. You 90
may stroke him as gently as a puppy greyhound. He'll
not swagger with a Barbary hen, if her feathers turn
back in any show of resistance. Call him up, drawer.
                                            [*Francis goes out*

HOSTESS   Cheater, call you him? I will bar no honest man my
house, nor no cheater, but I do not love swaggering,
by my troth. I am the worse, when one says swagger:
feel, masters, how I shake, look you, I warrant you.

DOLL   So you do, hostess.

HOSTESS   Do I? Yea, in very truth, do I, an 'twere an aspen leaf.
I cannot abide swaggerers.   100

        PISTOL, BARDOLPH, *and* PAGE *enter*

PISTOL   God save you, Sir John!

FALSTAFF   Welcome, Ancient Pistol. Here, Pistol, I charge you
with a cup of sack. Do you discharge upon mine hostess.
                            [*filling and reaching out to him*

PISTOL   I will discharge upon her, Sir John, with two bullets.

FALSTAFF   She is pistol-proof, sir; you shall not hardly offend her.

HOSTESS   Come, I'll drink no proofs, nor no bullets. I'll drink no
more than will do me good, for no man's pleasure, I.

PISTOL   Then to you, Mistress Dorothy, I will charge you.
                                        [*he raises the cup*

DOLL   Charge me! I scorn you, scurvy companion. What! You
poor, base, rascally, cheating, lack-linen mate! Away, 110
you mouldy rogue, away! I am meat for your master.

PISTOL   I know you, Mistress Dorothy.

DOLL   Away, you cut-purse rascal! You filthy bung, away! By
this wine, I'll thrust my knife in your mouldy chaps,

an you play the saucy cuttle with me. Away, you
bottle-ale rascal! You basket-hilt stale juggler, you!
Since when, I pray you, sir? God's light, with two
points on your shoulder? Much!

PISTOL   God let me not live, but I will murder your ruff for this.

FALSTAFF   No more, Pistol. I would not have you go off here.   120
Discharge yourself of our company, Pistol.

HOSTESS   No, good Captain Pistol, not here, sweet captain.

DOLL   Captain! Thou abominable damned cheater, art thou
not ashamed to be called captain? An captains were of
my mind, they would truncheon you out, for taking
their names upon you before you have earned them.
You a captain! You slave, for what? For tearing a poor
whore's ruff in a bawdy-house. He a captain! Hang
him, rogue! He lives upon mouldy stewed prunes and
dried cakes. A captain! God's light, these villains will   130
make the word as odious as the word 'occupy', which
was an excellent good word before it was ill sorted:
therefore captains had need look to't.

BARDOLPH   Pray thee, go down, good ancient.

FALSTAFF   Hark thee hither, Mistress Doll.   [they go aside

PISTOL   Not I. I tell thee what, Corporal Bardolph, I could tear
her. I'll be revenged of her.

PAGE   Pray thee, go down.

PISTOL   I'll see her damned first – to Pluto's damned lake, by
this hand, to th'infernal deep, with Erebus and tortures   140
vile also. Hold hook and line, say I. Down! Down,
dogs! Down, faitors! Have we not Hiren here?
                                          [he draws his sword

HOSTESS   Good Captain Peesel, be quiet – 'tis very late, i'faith –
I beseek you now, aggravate your choler.

PISTOL   These be good humours, indeed!
                                        Shall pack-horses
And hollow pampered jades of Asia,
Which cannot go but thirty mile a day,
Compare with Caesars and with Cannibals
And Trojant Greeks? Nay, rather damn them with
King Cerberus, and let the welkin roar.   150
Shall we fall foul for toys?

HOSTESS   By my troth, captain, these are very bitter words.
BARDOLPH Be gone, good ancient: this will grow to a brawl anon.
PISTOL   Die men, like dogs! Give crowns like pins! Have we not
          Hiren here?
HOSTESS   O' my word, captain, there's none such here. What
          the good-year! Do you think, I would deny her? For
          God's sake, be quiet.
PISTOL   Then, feed, and be fat, my fair Calipolis.
          Come, give's some sack.   160
          'Si fortune me tormente, sperato me contento.'
          Fear we broadsides? No, let the fiend give fire.
          Give me some sack – and, sweetheart, lie thou there.
                                      [laying down his sword
          Come we to full points here? And are etceteras nothings?
FALSTAFF Pistol, I would be quiet.
PISTOL   Sweet knight, I kiss thy neaf. What! We have seen the
          seven stars.
DOLL   For God's sake, thrust him down stairs. I cannot endure
          such a fustian rascal.
PISTOL   Thrust him down stairs! Know we not Galloway nags? 170
FALSTAFF Quoit him down, Bardolph, like a shove-groat shilling.
          Nay, an a' do nothing but speak nothing, a' shall be
          nothing here.
BARDOLPH Come, get you down stairs.
PISTOL   What! Shall we have incision? Shall we imbrue?
                                      [he snatches up his sword
          Then death rock me asleep, abridge my doleful days!
          Why then, let grievous, ghastly, gaping wounds
          Untwind the Sisters Three! Come, Atropos, I say!
                                      [he offers to fight
HOSTESS   Here's goodly stuff toward!
FALSTAFF Give me my rapier, boy.   180
DOLL   I pray thee, Jack, I pray thee, do not draw.
FALSTAFF [draws] Get you down stairs.
                              [Bardolph forces Pistol back;
                               Falstaff follows behind
HOSTESS   Here's a goodly tumult! I'll forswear keeping house,
          afore I'll be in these tirrits and frights. So! Murder, I

warrant now. Alas, alas! Put up your naked weapons,
put up your naked weapons.

> [*Bardolph pushes Pistol through the door,*
> *and goes after; Falstaff returns*

DOLL   I pray thee, Jack, be quiet, the rascal's gone. Ah, you
        whoreson little valiant villain, you.

HOSTESS   Are you not hurt i'the groin? Methought a' made a
        shrewd thrust at your belly.   190

BARDOLPH returns

FALSTAFF   Have you turned him out-a-doors?

BARDOLPH   Yea, sir. The rascal's drunk, you have hurt him, sir,
        i'th shoulder.

FALSTAFF   A rascal! To brave me!

DOLL   Ah, you sweet little rogue, you! Alas, poor ape, how
        thou sweat'st! Come, let me wipe thy face, come on,
        you whoreson chops: ah, rogue! I'faith, I love thee.
        Thou art as valorous as Hector of Troy, worth five of
        Agamemnon, and ten times better than the Nine
        Worthies. Ah, villain!   200

FALSTAFF   A rascally slave! I will toss the rogue in a blanket.

DOLL   Do, an thou darest for thy heart. An thou dost, I'll
        canvass thee between a pair of sheets.

Musicians enter

PAGE   The music is come, sir.

FALSTAFF   Let them play. Play, sirs. Sit on my knee, Doll. A rascal
        bragging slave! The rogue fled from me like quick-
        silver.

DOLL   I'faith, and thou follow'dst him like a church. Thou
        whoreson little tidy Bartholomew boar-pig, when wilt
        thou leave fighting a days and foining a nights, and   210
        begin to patch up thine old body for heaven?

Enter behind, the PRINCE and POINS, disguised like Drawers

FALSTAFF   Peace, good Doll! Do not speak like a death's-head, do
        not bid me remember mine end.

DOLL   Sirrah, what humour's the prince of?

FALSTAFF   A good shallow young fellow, a' would have made a
        good pantler, a' would ha' chipped bread well.

DOLL   They say, Poins has a good wit.

FALSTAFF   He a good wit? Hang him, baboon! His wit's as thick
            as Tewkesbury mustard, there's no more conceit in
            him than is in a mallet.   220

DOLL   Why does the prince love him so, then?

FALSTAFF   Because their legs are both of a bigness, and a' plays at
            quoits well, and eats conger and fennel, and drinks off
            candles' ends for flap-dragons, and rides the wild-mare
            with the boys, and jumps upon joined-stools, and
            swears with a good grace, and wears his boots very
            smooth like unto the Sign of the Leg, and breeds no
            bate with telling of discreet stories; and such other
            gambol faculties a' has that show a weak mind and an
            able body, for the which the prince admits him: for the 230
            prince himself is such another, the weight of a hair will
            turn the scales between their avoirdupois.

                                          [*she strokes his head*

PRINCE   Would not this nave of a wheel have his ears cut off?

POINS   Let's beat him before his whore.

PRINCE   Look, whether the withered elder hath not his poll
            clawed like a parrot.

POINS   Is it not strange that desire should so many years out-
            live performance?

FALSTAFF   Kiss me, Doll.   [*they kiss*

PRINCE   Saturn and Venus this year in conjunction! What says 240
            th' almanac to that?

POINS   And look whether the fiery Trigon, his man, be not
            lisping to his master's old tables, his note-book, his
            counsel-keeper.

FALSTAFF   Thou dost give me flattering busses.

DOLL   By my troth, I kiss thee with a most constant heart.

FALSTAFF   I am old, I am old.

DOLL   I love thee better than I love e'er a scurvy young boy
            of them all.

FALSTAFF   What stuff wilt have a kirtle of? I shall receive money o' 250
            Thursday – shalt have a cap tomorrow. A merry song,
            come! A' grows late, we'll to bed. Thou't forget me
            when I am gone.

DOLL   By my troth, thou't set me a-weeping, an thou say'st so. Prove that ever I dress myself handsome till thy return. Well, hearken a' th' end.

FALSTAFF   Some sack, Francis.

PRINCE }
POINS }   Anon, anon, sir.   [*they hurry forward*

FALSTAFF   [*starts up*] Ha! A bastard son of the king's? And art not thou Poins his brother?   260

PRINCE   Why, thou globe of sinful continents, what a life dost thou lead?

FALSTAFF   A better than thou. I am a gentleman, thou art a drawer.

PRINCE   Very true, sir, and I come to draw you out by the ears.

HOSTESS   O, the Lord preserve thy good grace! By my troth, welcome to London. Now the Lord bless that sweet face of thine! O Jesu, are you come from Wales?

FALSTAFF   Thou whoreson mad compound of majesty, by this light flesh and corrupt blood, thou art welcome.   270

DOLL   How! You fat fool, I scorn you.

POINS   My lord, he will drive you out of your revenge, and turn all to a merriment, if you take not the heat.

PRINCE   You whoreson candle-mine, you, how vilely did you speak of me even now, before this honest, virtuous, civil gentlewoman!

HOSTESS   God's blessing of your good heart! And so she is, by my troth.

FALSTAFF   Didst thou hear me?

PRINCE   Yea, and you knew me, as you did when you ran away   280 by Gad's Hill. You knew I was at your back, and spoke it on purpose to try my patience.

FALSTAFF   No, no, no, not so; I did not think thou wast within hearing.

PRINCE   I shall drive you then to confess the wilful abuse, and then I know how to handle you.

FALSTAFF   No abuse, Hal, o' mine honour, no abuse.

PRINCE   Not! To dispraise me, and call me pantler and bread-chipper and I know not what?

FALSTAFF   No abuse, Hal.   290

POINS   No abuse?

FALSTAFF   No abuse, Ned, i'th' world, honest Ned, none. I

dispraised him before the wicked, that the wicked
might not fall in love with thee: in which doing, I
have done the part of a careful friend and a true
subject, and thy father is to give me thanks for it. No
abuse, Hal; none, Ned, none; no, faith, boys, none.

PRINCE   See now, whether pure fear and entire cowardice doth
not make thee wrong this virtuous gentlewoman, to
close with us. Is she of the wicked? Is thine hostess   300
here of the wicked? Or is thy boy of the wicked? Or
honest Bardolph, whose zeal burns in his nose, of the
wicked?

POINS   Answer, thou dead elm, answer.

FALSTAFF   The fiend hath pricked down Bardolph irrecoverable,
and his face is Lucifer's privy-kitchen, where he doth
nothing but roast malt-worms. For the boy, there is a
good angel about him, but the devil blinds him too.

PRINCE   For the women?

FALSTAFF   For one of them, she's in hell already, and burns poor   310
souls. For th' other, I owe her money, and whether
she be damned for that I know not.

HOSTESS   No, I warrant you.

FALSTAFF   No, I think thou art not. I think thou art quit for that.
Marry, there is another indictment upon thee, for
suffering flesh to be eaten in thy house, contrary to
the law, for the which I think thou wilt howl.

HOSTESS   All victuallers do so. What's a joint of mutton or two
in a whole Lent?

PRINCE   You, gentlewoman –   320

DOLL   What says your grace?

FALSTAFF   His grace says that which his flesh rebels against.

                              [*a knocking is heard*

HOSTESS   Who knocks so loud at door? Look to th' door there,
Francis.

PETO *enters*

PRINCE   Peto, how now? What news?

PETO   The king your father is at Westminster,
And there are twenty weak and wearied posts
Come from the north, and as I came along

I met and overtook a dozen captains,
Bare-headed, sweating, knocking at the taverns,   330
And asking every one for Sir John Falstaff.

PRINCE   By heaven, Poins, I feel me much to blame,
So idly to profane the precious time,
When tempest of commotion, like the south
Borne with black vapour, doth begin to melt,
And drop upon our bare unarméd heads.
Give me my sword and cloak. Falstaff, good night.
                    [*Prince, Poins, Peto, and Bardolph hasten away*

FALSTAFF   Now comes in the sweetest morsel of the night, and
we must hence and leave it unpicked. [*more knocking
heard*] More knocking at the door.   340

                    BARDOLPH *returns*

How now? What's the matter?

BARDOLPH   You must away to court, sir, presently;
A dozen captains stay at door for you.

FALSTAFF   [*to the* PAGE] Pay the musicians, sirrah. Farewell hostess,
farewell Doll. You see, my good wenches, how men
of merit are sought after. The undeserver may sleep,
when the man of action is called on. Farewell, good
wenches: if I be not sent away post, I will see you
again ere I go.

DOLL   I cannot speak. If my heart be not ready to burst — 350
well, sweet Jack, have a care of thyself.

FALSTAFF   Farewell, farewell.
                    [*he goes out with Bardolph*

HOSTESS   Well, fare thee well. I have known thee these twenty-
nine years, come peascod-time, but an honester and
truer-hearted man — well, fare thee well.

BARDOLPH   [*at the door*] Mistress Tearsheet!

HOSTESS   What's the matter?

BARDOLPH   Bid Mistress Tearsheet come to my master.

HOSTESS   O run, Doll, run, run, good Doll.

BARDOLPH   Come!   360

HOSTESS   She comes blubbered.

BARDOLPH   Yea, will you come, Doll?
                    [*they go*

ACT 3 SCENE I

The palace at Westminster; past midnight

'Enter the KING *in his nightgown', with a Page*

KING   Go call the Earls of Surrey and of Warwick:
But, ere they come, bid them o'er-read these letters,
And well consider of them – make good speed.
                           [the Page goes
How many thousand of my poorest subjects
Are at this hour asleep! O sleep, O gentle sleep,
Nature's soft nurse, how have I frighted thee,
That thou no more wilt weigh my eyelids down,
And steep my senses in forgetfulness?
Why rather, sleep, liest thou in smoky cribs,
Upon uneasy pallets stretching thee,   10
And hushed with buzzing night-flies to thy slumber,
Than in the perfumed chambers of the great,
Under the canopies of costly state,
And lulled with sound of sweetest melody?
O thou dull god, why li'st thou with the vile
In loathsome beds, and leav'st the kingly couch
A watch-case or a common 'larum-bell?
Wilt thou upon the high and giddy mast
Seal up the ship-boy's eyes and rock his brains
In cradle of the rude imperious surge,   20
And in the visitation of the winds,
Who take the ruffian billows by the top,
Curling their monstrous heads, and hanging them
With deafing clamour in the slippery clouds,
That, with the hurly, death itself awakes?
Canst thou, O partial sleep, give thy repose
To the wet sea-boy in an hour so rude,
And in the calmest and most stillest night,
With all appliances and means to boot,
Deny it to a king? Then, happy low, lie down!   30
Uneasy lies the head that wears a crown.

'Enter WARWICK, SURREY *and* SIR JOHN BLUNT*'*

WARWICK Many good morrows to your majesty!

KING Is it good morrow, lords?

WARWICK 'Tis one o'clock, and past.

KING Why then, good morrow to you all, my lords.
Have you read o'er the letters that I sent you?

WARWICK We have, my liege.

KING Then you perceive the body of our kingdom,
How foul it is: what rank diseases grow,
And with what danger, near the heart of it.   40

WARWICK It is but as a body yet distempered,
Which to his former strength may be restored
With good advice and little medicine.
My Lord Northumberland will soon be cooled.

KING O God! That one might read the book of fate,
And see the revolution of the times
Make mountains level, and the continent,
Weary of solid firmness, melt itself
Into the sea! And, other times, to see
The beachy girdle of the ocean   50
Too wide for Neptune's hips; how chances mock
And changes fill the cup of alteration
With divers liquors! O, if this were seen,
The happiest youth, viewing his progress through,
What perils passed, what crosses to ensue,
Would shut the book, and sit him down and die.
'Tis not ten years gone
Since Richard and Northumberland, great friends,
Did feast together, and in two years after
Were they at wars: it is but eight years since   60
This Percy was the man nearest my soul;
Who like a brother toiled in my affairs,
And laid his love and life under my foot;
Yea, for my sake, even to the eyes of Richard
Gave him defiance. But which of you was by –
You, cousin Nevil, as I may remember –   [*to Warwick*
When Richard, with his eye brimful of tears,
Then checked and rated by Northumberland,

Did speak these words, now proved a prophecy?
'Northumberland, thou ladder by the which   70
My cousin Bolingbroke ascends my throne' –
Though then, God knows, I had no such intent,
But that necessity so bowed the state,
That I and greatness were compelled to kiss.
'The time shall come,' thus did he follow it,
'The time will come, that foul sin, gathering head,
Shall break into corruption': so went on,
Foretelling this same time's condition,
And the division of our amity.

WARWICK   There is a history in all men's lives,   80
Figuring the natures or the times deceased:
The which observed, a man may prophesy,
With a near aim, of the main chance of things
As yet not come to life, who in their seeds
And weak beginnings lie intreasuréd.
Such things become the hatch and brood of time;
And by the necessary form of this
King Richard might create a perfect guess
That great Northumberland, then false to him,
Would of that seed grow to a greater falseness,   90
Which should not find a ground to root upon,
Unless on you.

KING   Are these things then necessities?
Then let us meet them like necessities.
And that same word even now cries out on us:
They say the bishop and Northumberland
Are fifty thousand strong.

WARWICK   It cannot be, my lord.
Rumour doth double, like the voice and echo,
The numbers of the feared. Please it your grace
To go to bed: upon my soul, my lord,
The powers that you already have sent forth   100
Shall bring this prize in very easily:
To comfort you the more, I have received
A certain instance that Glendower is dead.
Your majesty hath been this fortnight ill,
And these unseasoned hours perforce must add

Unto your sickness.

KING   I will take your counsel.
And were these inward wars once out of hand,
We would, dear lords, unto the Holy Land.

[they go

SCENE 2

Before Justice Shallow's house in Gloucestershire

Enter SHALLOW *and* SILENCE, *meeting;* MOULDY, SHADOW,
WART, FEEBLE, BULLCALF *and servants, behind*

SHALLOW Come on, come on, come on, give me your hand, sir,
give me your hand, sir! An early stirrer, by the rood.
[they shake hands] And how doth my good cousin
Silence?

SILENCE Good morrow, good cousin Shallow.

SHALLOW And how doth my cousin, your bedfellow? And your
fairest daughter and mine, my god-daughter Ellen?

SILENCE Alas, a black ousel, cousin Shallow.

SHALLOW By yea and no, sir, I dare say my cousin William is
become a good scholar. He is at Oxford still, is he not? 10

SILENCE Indeed, sir, to my cost.

SHALLOW A' must then to the inns o' court shortly: I was once of
Clement's Inn, where I think they will talk of mad
Shallow yet.

SILENCE You were called 'lusty Shallow' then, cousin.

SHALLOW By the mass, I was called anything, and I would have
done any thing indeed too, and roundly too. There was
I, and little John Doit of Staffordshire, and black George
Barnes, and Francis Pickbone, and Will Squele a
Cots'ole man – you had not four such swinge-bucklers 20
in all the inns o' court again: and I may say to you, we
knew where the bona-robas were, and had the best of
them all at commandment. Then was Jack Falstaff (now
Sir John) a boy, and page to Thomas Mowbray, Duke of
Norfolk.

SILENCE This Sir John, cousin, that comes hither anon about
soldiers?

SHALLOW   The same Sir John, the very same. I see him break
           Scoggin's head at the court-gate, when a' was a crack,
           not thus high: and the very same day did I fight with one   30
           Sampson Stockfish, a fruiterer, behind Gray's Inn. Jesu,
           Jesu, the mad days that I have spent! And to see how
           many of my old acquaintance are dead!

SILENCE   We shall all follow, cousin.

SHALLOW   Certain, 'tis certain, very sure, very sure. Death, as the
           Psalmist saith, is certain to all, all shall die. How a good
           yoke of bullocks at Stamford fair?

SILENCE   By my troth, I was not there.

SHALLOW   Death is certain. Is old Double of your town living yet?

SILENCE   Dead, sir.   40

SHALLOW   Jesu, Jesu, dead! A' drew a good bow – and dead! A'
           shot a fine shoot: John a Gaunt loved him well, and
           betted much money on his head. Dead! A' would have
           clapped i'th' clout at twelve score, and carried you a
           forehand shaft a fourteen and fourteen and a half, that
           it would have done a man's heart good to see. How a
           score of ewes now?

SILENCE   Thereafter as they be, a score of good ewes may be
           worth ten pounds.

SHALLOW   And is old Double dead!   50

           'Enter BARDOLPH, *and one with him'*

SILENCE   Here come two of Sir John Falstaff's men, as I think.

SHALLOW   Good morrow, honest gentlemen.

BARDOLPH   I beseech you, which is Justice Shallow?

SHALLOW   I am Robert Shallow, sir, a poor esquire of this county,
           and one of the king's justices of the peace. What is
           your good pleasure with me?

BARDOLPH   My captain, sir, commends him to you; my captain,
           Sir John Falstaff, a tall gentleman, by heaven, and a
           most gallant leader.

SHALLOW   He greets me well, sir. I knew him a good backsword   60
           man. How doth the good knight? May I ask how my
           lady his wife doth?

BARDOLPH   Sir, pardon! A soldier is better accommodated than
           with a wife.

SHALLOW It is well said, in faith, sir, and it is well said indeed too.
Better accommodated! It is good, yea, indeed, is it.
Good phrases are surely, and ever were, very com-
mendable. Accommodated: it comes of 'accommodo' –
very good, a good phrase.

BARDOLPH Pardon sir, I have heard the word. Phrase call you it? 70
By this day, I know not the phrase, but I will maintain
the word with my sword to be a soldier-like word, and
a word of exceeding good command, by heaven. Accommodated, that is, when a man is, as they say,
accommodated, or when a man is being whereby a'
may be thought to be accommodated – which is an
excellent thing.

Enter FALSTAFF

SHALLOW It is very just. Look, here comes good Sir John. Give
me your good hand, give me your worship's good
hand. By my troth, you like well, and bear your years 80
very well. Welcome, good Sir John.

[they shake hands

FALSTAFF I am glad to see you well, good Master Robert Shallow.
Master Surecard, as I think?

SHALLOW No Sir John, it is my cousin Silence, in commission
with me.

FALSTAFF Good Master Silence, it well befits you should be of
the Peace.

SILENCE Your good worship is welcome.

FALSTAFF Fie! This is hot weather, gentlemen. Have you provided
me here half a dozen sufficient men?   90

SHALLOW Marry, have we, sir. Will you sit?

FALSTAFF *[sits]* Let me see them, I beseech you.

SHALLOW Where's the roll? Where's the roll? Where's the roll?
Let me see, let me see, let me see. So, so, so, so, so, so,
so. Yea, marry, sir. Rafe Mouldy! Let them appear as I
call, let them do so, let them do so. Let me see, where
is Mouldy?

MOULDY Here, an't please you.

SHALLOW What think you, Sir John? A good-limbed fellow,
young, strong, and of good friends.   100

FALSTAFF Is thy name Mouldy?

MOULDY Yea, an't please you.

FALSTAFF 'Tis the more time thou wert used.

SHALLOW Ha, ha, ha! Most excellent, i'faith! Things that are mouldy lack use: very singular good! In faith, well said, Sir John, very well said.

FALSTAFF Prick him.

MOULDY I was pricked well enough before, and you could have let me alone. My old dame will be undone now for one to do her husbandry and her drudgery. You need 110 not to have pricked me, there are other men fitter to go out than I.

FALSTAFF Go to. Peace, Mouldy, you shall go. Mouldy, it is time you were spent.

MOULDY Spent!

SHALLOW Peace, fellow, peace – stand aside. Know you where you are? For th' other, Sir John: let me see – Simon Shadow!

FALSTAFF Yea, marry, let me have him to sit under. He's like to be a cold soldier. 120

SHALLOW Where's Shadow?

SHADOW Here, sir.

FALSTAFF Shadow, whose son art thou?

SHADOW My mother's son, sir.

FALSTAFF Thy mother's son! Like enough, and thy father's shadow. So the son of the female is the shadow of the male: it is often so, indeed, but much of the father's substance!

SHALLOW Do you like him, Sir John?

FALSTAFF Shadow will serve for summer. Prick him, for we have 130 a number of shadows to fill up the muster-book.

SHALLOW Thomas Wart!

FALSTAFF Where's he?

WART Here, sir.

FALSTAFF Is thy name Wart?

WART Yea, sir.

FALSTAFF Thou art a very ragged wart.

SHALLOW Shall I prick him, Sir John?

FALSTAFF It were superfluous, for his apparel is built up on his

back, and the whole frame stands upon pins: prick him 140
no more.

SHALLOW Ha, ha, ha! You can do it, sir, you can do it. I commend
you well. Francis Feeble!

FEEBLE Here, sir.

SHALLOW What trade art thou, Feeble?

FEEBLE A woman's tailor, sir.

SHALLOW Shall I prick him, sir?

FALSTAFF You may – but if he had been a man's tailor, he'd ha'
pricked you. Wilt thou make as many holes in an
enemy's battle as thou hast done in a woman's petti- 150
coat?

FEEBLE I will do my good will, sir; you can have no more.

FALSTAFF Well said, good woman's tailor! Well said, courageous
Feeble! Thou wilt be as valiant as the wrathful dove or
most magnanimous mouse. Prick the woman's tailor:
well, Master Shallow, deep, Master Shallow.

FEEBLE I would Wart might have gone, sir.

FALSTAFF I would thou wert a man's tailor, that thou mightst
mend him and make him fit to go. I cannot put him to
a private soldier, that is the leader of so many thou- 160
sands. Let that suffice, most forcible Feeble.

FEEBLE It shall suffice, sir.

FALSTAFF I am bound to thee, reverend Feeble. Who is next?

SHALLOW Peter Bullcalf o' th' green!

FALSTAFF Yea, marry, let's see Bullcalf.

BULLCALF Here, sir.

FALSTAFF 'Fore God, a likely fellow! Come, prick me Bullcalf,
till he roar again.

BULLCALF O Lord! Good my lord captain –

FALSTAFF What, dost thou roar before thou art pricked? 170

BULLCALF O Lord, sir! I am a diseased man.

FALSTAFF What disease hast thou?

BULLCALF A whoreson cold, sir, a cough, sir, which I caught
with ringing in the king's affairs upon his coronation-
day, sir.

FALSTAFF Come, thou shalt go to the wars in a gown, we will
have away thy cold, and I will take such order that thy
friends shall ring for thee. Is here all?

SHALLOW   Here is two more called than your number. You must
          have but four here, sir. And so, I pray you, go in with 180
          me to dinner.

FALSTAFF Come, I will go drink with you, but I cannot tarry
          dinner. I am glad to see you, by my troth, Master
          Shallow.

SHALLOW   O Sir John, do you remember since we lay all night in
          the windmill in Saint George's field?

FALSTAFF No more of that, good Master Shallow, no more of
          that.

SHALLOW   Ha, 'twas a merry night. And is Jane Nightwork alive?

FALSTAFF She lives, Master Shallow.   190

SHALLOW   She never could away with me.

FALSTAFF Never, never; she would always say she could not
          abide Master Shallow.

SHALLOW   By the mass, I could anger her to th' heart. She was
          then a bona-roba. Doth she hold her own well?

FALSTAFF Old, old, Master Shallow.

SHALLOW   Nay, she must be old, she cannot choose but be old.
          Certain she's old, and had Robin Nightwork by old
          Nightwork before I came to Clement's Inn.

SILENCE   That's fifty-five year ago.   200

SHALLOW   Ha, cousin Silence, that thou hadst seen that that this
          knight and I have seen! Ha, Sir John, said I well?

FALSTAFF We have heard the chimes at midnight, Master Shallow.

SHALLOW   That we have, that we have, that we have; in faith, Sir
          John, we have. Our watchword was 'Hem, boys!'
          Come, let's to dinner, come, let's to dinner. Jesus, the
          days that we have seen! Come, come.

                    [he leads Falstaff in; Silence follows

BULLCALF Good Master Corporate Bardolph, stand my friend,
          and here's four Harry ten shillings in French crowns
          for you. In very truth, sir, I had as lief be hanged, sir, 210
          as go. And yet for mine own part, sir, I do not care,
          but rather because I am unwilling, and for mine own
          part have a desire to stay with my friends; else, sir, I
          did not care for mine own part so much.

BARDOLPH Go to, stand aside.

MOULDY   And, good Master Corporal Captain, for my old dame's sake, stand my friend. She has nobody to do any thing about her when I am gone, and she is old and cannot help herself. You shall have forty, sir.

[he shows him a shilling

BARDOLPH Go to, stand aside.   220

FEEBLE By my troth, I care not; a man can die but once, we owe God a death, I'll ne'er bear a base mind. An't be my dest'ny, so; an't be not, so. No man's too good to serve's prince, and let it go which way it will, he that dies this year is quit for the next.

BARDOLPH Well said! Th'art a good fellow.

FEEBLE Faith, I'll bear no base mind.

FALSTAFF *and the* JUSTICES *return*

FALSTAFF Come, sir, which men shall I have?

SHALLOW Four of which you please.

BARDOLPH Sir, a word with you. I have three pound to free   230
Mouldy and Bullcalf.

FALSTAFF Go to, well.

SHALLOW Come, Sir John, which four will you have?

FALSTAFF Do you choose for me.

SHALLOW Marry then, Mouldy, Bullcalf, Feeble, and Shadow.

FALSTAFF Mouldy and Bullcalf! For you, Mouldy, stay at home till you are past service: and for your part, Bullcalf, grow till you come unto it: I will none of you.

SHALLOW Sir John, Sir John, do not yourself wrong; they are your likeliest men, and I would have you served with   240
the best.

FALSTAFF Will you tell me, Master Shallow, how to choose a man? Care I for the limb, the thews, the stature, bulk, and big assemblance of a man? Give me the spirit, Master Shallow. Here's Wart, you see what a ragged appearance it is, a' shall charge you and discharge you with the motion of a pewterer's hammer, come off and on swifter than he that gibbets on the brewer's bucket. And this same half-faced fellow, Shadow – give me this man. He presents no mark to the enemy, the foeman   250
may with as great aim level at the edge of a penknife. And for a retreat, how swiftly will this Feeble, the

woman's tailor, run off! O, give me the spare men, and
spare me the great ones. Put me a caliver into Wart's
hand, Bardolph.   [*he does so*

BARDOLPH Hold, Wart, traverse! Thus, thus, thus.

FALSTAFF Come, manage me your caliver. So, very well, go to,
very good, exceeding good. O, give me always a little,
lean, old, chopt, bald shot. Well said, i'faith, Wart,
th'art a good scab. Hold, there's a tester for thee.   260

SHALLOW He is not his craft's master, he doth not do it right. I
remember at Mile-end Green, when I lay at Clement's
Inn – I was then Sir Dagonet in Arthur's show – there
was a little quiver fellow, and a' would manage you his
piece thus, and a' would about and about, and come
you in, and come you in: 'rah-tah-tah,' would a' say;
'bounce', would a' say; and away again would a' go,
and again would a' come: I shall ne'er see such a
fellow.

FALSTAFF These fellows will do well, Master Shallow. God keep   270
you, Master Silence, I will not use many words with
you. Fare you well, gentlemen both. I thank you. I
must a dozen mile to-night. Bardolph, give the soldiers
coats.

SHALLOW Sir John, the Lord bless you! God prosper your affairs!
God send us peace! At your return, visit our house, let
our old acquaintance be renewed. Peradventure I will
with ye to the court.

FALSTAFF 'Fore God, would you would, Master Shallow.

SHALLOW Go to, I have spoke at a word. God keep you.   280

FALSTAFF Fare you well, gentle gentlemen. [*Shallow and Silence go
in*] On, Bardolph; lead the men away. [*Bardolph marches
them off*] As I return, I will fetch off these justices. I do
see the bottom of Justice Shallow. Lord, Lord, how
subject we old men are to this vice of lying! This same
starved justice hath done nothing but prate to me of
the wildness of his youth, and the feats he hath done
about Turnbull Street – and every third word a lie,
duer paid to the hearer than the Turk's tribute. I do
remember him at Clement's Inn, like a man made after   290
supper of a cheese-paring. When a' was naked, he was

for all the world like a forked radish, with a head
fantastically carved upon it with a knife. A' was so
forlorn, that his dimensions to any thick sight were
invisible. A' was the very genius of famine, yet lecher-
ous as a monkey, and the whores called him mandrake.
A' came ever in the rearward of the fashion, and sung
those tunes to the overscutched huswives that he heard
the carmen whistle, and sware they were his fancies or
his good-nights. And now is this Vice's dagger become   300
a squire, and talks as familiarly of John a Gaunt as if he
had been sworn brother to him, and I'll be sworn a'
ne'er saw him but once in the Tilt-yard, and then he
burst his head for crowding among the marshal's men. I
saw it, and told John a Gaunt he beat his own name, for
you might have trussed him and all his apparel into an
eel-skin – the case of a treble hautboy was a mansion for
him, a court. And now has he land and beefs! Well, I'll
be acquainted with him if I return, and 't shall go hard
but I'll make him a philosopher's two stones to me. If   310
the young dace be a bait for the old pike, I see no
reason in the law of nature but I may snap at him. Let
time shape, and there an end.

                                      [he goes off

ACT 4 SCENE 1

Gaultree Forest, Yorkshire

The ARCHBISHOP OF YORK, MOWBRAY,
HASTINGS, LORD BARDOLPH *and others*

ARCH.	What is this forest called?
HASTINGS	'Tis Gaultree Forest, an't shall please your grace.
ARCH.	Here stand, my lords, and send discoverers forth
	To know the numbers of our enemies.
HASTINGS	We have sent forth already.
ARCH.	'Tis well done.

My friends and brethren in these great affairs,
I must acquaint you that I have received
New-dated letters from Northumberland,
Their cold intent, tenour, and substance thus:
Here doth he wish his person, with such powers   10
As might hold sortance with his quality,
The which he could not levy; whereupon
He is retired, to ripe his growing fortunes,
To Scotland, and concludes in hearty prayers
That your attempts may overlive the hazard
And fearful meeting of their opposite.

MOWBRAY Thus do the hopes we have in him touch ground
And dash themselves to pieces.

A Messenger comes up

HASTINGS   Now, what news?

MESSENGER West of this forest, scarcely off a mile,
In goodly form comes on the enemy,   20
And by the ground they hide I judge their number
Upon or near the rate of thirty thousand.

MOWBRAY The just proportion that we gave them out.
Let us sway on and face them in the field.

WESTMORELAND, *with attendant officers, is seen approaching*

ARCH. What well-appointed leader fronts us here?
MOWBRAY I think it is my Lord of Westmoreland.

WEST'LAND Health and fair greeting from our general,
The prince, Lord John and Duke of Lancaster.
ARCH. Say on, my Lord of Westmoreland, in peace.
What doth concern your coming?
WEST'LAND   Then, my lord,   30
Unto your grace do I in chief address
The substance of my speech. If that rebellion
Came like itself, in base and abject routs,
Led on by bloody youth, guarded with rags,
And countenanced by boys and beggary;
I say, if damned commotion so appeared
In his true, native and most proper shape,
You, reverend father, and these noble lords
Had not been here, to dress the ugly form
Of base and bloody insurrection   40
With your fair honours. You, lord Archbishop,
Whose see is by a civil peace maintained,
Whose beard the silver hand of peace hath touched,
Whose learning and good letters peace hath tutored,
Whose white investments figure innocence,
The dove and very blessed spirit of peace,
Wherefore do you so ill translate yourself
Out of the speech of peace that bears such grace,
Into the harsh and boist'rous tongue of war?
Turning your books to graves, your ink to blood,   50
Your pens to lances, and your tongue divine
To a loud trumpet and a point of war?
ARCH. Wherefore do I this? So the question stands.
Briefly to this end: we are all diseased,
And with our surfeiting and wanton hours
Have brought ourselves into a burning fever,
And we must bleed for it: of which disease
Our late king, Richard, being infected, died.
But, my most noble Lord of Westmoreland,
I take not on me here as a physician,   60
Nor do I as an enemy to peace
Troop in the throngs of military men;
But rather show awhile like fearful war,

To diet rank minds, sick of happiness,
And purge the obstructions, which begin to stop
Our very veins of life. Hear me more plainly.
I have in equal balance justly weighed
What wrongs our arms may do, what wrongs we suffer,
And find our griefs heavier than our offences.
We see which way the stream of time doth run,   70
And are enforced from our most quiet shore
By the rough torrent of occasion,
And have the summary of all our griefs,
When time shall serve, to show in articles;
Which long ere this we offered to the king,
And might by no suit gain our audience:
When we are wronged and would unfold our griefs,
We are denied access unto his person
Even by those men that most have done us wrong.
The dangers of the days but newly gone,   80
Whose memory is written on the earth
With yet appearing blood, and the examples
Of every minute's instance, present now,
Hath put us in these ill-beseeming arms;
Not to break peace or any branch of it,
But to establish here a peace indeed,
Concurring both in name and quality.

WEST'LAND When ever yet was your appeal denied?
Wherein have you been gallèd by the king?
What peer hath been suborned to grate on you,   90
That you should seal this lawless bloody book
Of forged rebellion with a seal divine,
And consecrate commotion's bitter edge?

ARCH. My brother general, the commonwealth,
To brother born an household cruelty,
I make my quarrel in particular.

WEST'LAND There is no need of any such redress,
Or if there were, it not belongs to you.

MOWBRAY Why not to him in part, and to us all
That feel the bruises of the days before,   100
And suffer the condition of these times
To lay a heavy and unequal hand

Upon our honours?

WEST'LAND   O my good Lord Mowbray,
Construe the times to their necessities,
And you shall say, indeed, it is the time,
And not the king, that doth you injuries.
Yet for your part, it not appears to me,
Either from the king, or in the present time,
That you should have an inch of any ground
To build a grief on: were you not restored   110
To all the Duke of Norfolk's signories,
Your noble and right well remembered father's?

MOWBRAY What thing, in honour, had my father lost,
That need to be revived and breathed in me?
The king that loved him, as the state stood then,
Was force perforce compelled to banish him:
And then that Henry Bolingbroke and he,
Being mounted and both rouséd in their seats,
Their neighing coursers daring of the spur,
Their arméd staves in charge, their beavers down,   120
Their eyes of fire sparkling through sights of steel,
And the loud trumpet blowing them together,
Then, then, when there was nothing could have stayed
My father from the breast of Bolingbroke,
O, when the king did throw his warder down –
His own life hung upon the staff he threw –
Then threw he down himself and all their lives
That by indictment and by dint of sword
Have since miscarried under Bolingbroke.

WEST'LAND You speak, Lord Mowbray, now you know not what. 130
The Earl of Hereford was reputed then
In England the most valiant gentleman.
Who knows on whom fortune would then have smiled?
But if your father had been victor there,
He ne'er had borne it out of Coventry:
For all the country in a general voice
Cried hate upon him; and all their prayers and love
Were set on Hereford, whom they doted on,
And blessed and graced indeed more than the king.
But this is mere digression from my purpose.   140

Here come I from our princely general
To know your griefs, to tell you from his grace
That he will give you audience, and wherein
It shall appear that your demands are just
You shall enjoy them, everything set off
That might so much as think you enemies.

MOWBRAY But he hath forced us to compel this offer,
And it proceeds from policy, not love.

WEST'LAND Mowbray, you overween to take it so:
This offer comes from mercy, not from fear.   150
For, lo! Within a ken our army lies,
Upon mine honour, all too confident
To give admittance to a thought of fear.
Our battle is more full of names than yours,
Our men more perfect in the use of arms,
Our armour all as strong, our cause the best;
Then reason will our hearts should be as good:
Say you not then our offer is compelled.

MOWBRAY Well, by my will, we shall admit no parley.

WEST'LAND That argues but the shame of your offence: 160
A rotten case abides no handling.

HASTINGS Hath the Prince John a full commission,
In very ample virtue of his father,
To hear and absolutely to determine
Of what conditions we shall stand upon?

WEST'LAND That is intended in the general's name.
I muse you make so slight a question.

ARCH. Then take, my Lord of Westmoreland, this schedule,
For this contains our general grievances.
Each several article herein redressed,   170
All members of our cause, both here and hence,
That are insinewed to this action,
Acquitted by a true substantial form,
And present execution of our wills
To us and to our purposes confined,
We come within our awful banks again,
And knit our powers to the arm of peace.

WEST'LAND This will I show the general. Please you, lords,
In sight of both our battles we may meet;

	And either end in peace, which God so frame!	180
	Or to the place of diff'rence call the swords
	Which must decide it.

ARCH.   My lord, we will do so.

[*Westmoreland departs with his men*

MOWBRAY There is a thing within my bosom tells me
That no conditions of our peace can stand.

HASTINGS Fear you not that: if we can make our peace
Upon such large terms and so absolute
As our conditions shall consist upon,
Our peace shall stand as firm as rocky mountains.

MOWBRAY Yea, but our valuation shall be such,
That every slight and false-derivéd cause,   190
Yea, every idle, nice and wanton reason,
Shall to the king taste of this action;
That were our royal faiths martyrs in love,
We shall be winnowed with so rough a wind
That even our corn shall seem as light as chaff,
And good from bad find no partition.

ARCH.   No, no, my lord. Note this – the king is weary
Of dainty and such picking grievances;
For he hath found to end one doubt by death
Revives two greater in the heirs of life.   200
And therefore will he wipe his tables clean,
And keep no tell-tale to his memory
That may repeat and history his loss
To new remembrance; for full well he knows
He cannot so precisely weed this land
As his misdoubts present occasion:
His foes are so enrooted with his friends,
That plucking to unfix an enemy,
He doth unfasten so and shake a friend.
So that this land, like an offensive wife   210
That hath enragéd him on to offer strokes,
As he is striking, holds his infant up,
And hangs resolved correction in the arm
That was upreared to execution.

HASTINGS Besides, the king hath wasted all his rods
On late offenders, that he now doth lack

The very instruments of chastisement;
So that his power, like to a fangless lion,
May offer, but not hold.

ARCH.   'Tis very true,
And therefore be assured, my good lord marshal,   220
If we do now make our atonement well,
Our peace will, like a broken limb united,
Grow stronger for the breaking.

MOWBRAY   Be it so.
Here is returned my Lord of Westmoreland.

                    WESTMORELAND *comes in again*

WEST'LAND The prince is here at hand. Pleaseth your lordship
To meet his grace just distance 'tween our armies?
MOWBRAY Your grace of York, in God's name then set forward.
ARCH.   Before, and greet his grace. My lord, we come.

                                SCENE 2

                    Another part of the forest

From one side enter MOWBRAY, *the* ARCHBISHOP OF YORK, HASTINGS
and others; from the other, PRINCE JOHN OF LANCASTER,
                    WESTMORELAND *and officers*

PR. JOHN You are well encountered here, my cousin Mowbray.
Good day to you, gentle lord archbishop,
And so to you, Lord Hastings, and to all.
My Lord of York, it better showed with you
When that your flock, assembled by the bell,
Encircled you to hear with reverence
Your exposition on the holy text,
Than now to see you here an iron man talking,
Cheering a rout of rebels with your drum,
Turning the word to sword, and life to death.   10
That man that sits within a monarch's heart,
And ripens in the sunshine of his favour,
Would he abuse the countenance of the king,
Alack, what mischiefs might he set abroach
In shadow of such greatness! With you, lord bishop,
It is even so. Who hath not heard it spoken

How deep you were within the books of God?
To us the speaker in his parliament,
To us th'imagined voice of God himself,
The very opener and intelligencer   20
Between the grace, the sanctities of heaven
And our dull workings. O, who shall believe
But you misuse the reverence of your place,
Employ the countenance and grace of heaven,
As a false favourite doth his prince's name,
In deeds dishonourable? You have ta'en up,
Under the counterfeited zeal of God,
The subjects of His substitute, my father,
And both against the peace of heaven and him,
Have here up-swarmed them.

ARCH.   Good my Lord of Lancaster,   30
I am not here against your father's peace,
But as I told my Lord of Westmoreland,
The time misordered doth, in common sense,
Crowd us and crush us to this monstrous form,
To hold our safety up. I sent your grace
The parcels and particulars of our grief,
The which hath been with scorn shoved from the court,
Whereon this hydra son of war is born,
Whose dangerous eyes may well be charmed asleep
With grant of our most just and right desires,   40
And true obedience, of this madness cured,
Stoop tamely to the foot of majesty.

MOWBRAY If not, we ready are to try our fortunes
To the last man.

HASTINGS   And though we here fall down,
We have supplies to second our attempt:
If they miscarry, theirs shall second them,
And so success of mischief shall be born,
And heir from heir shall hold this quarrel up,
Whiles England shall have generation.

PR. JOHN You are too shallow, Hastings, much too shallow,   50
To sound the bottom of the after-times.

WEST'LAND Pleaseth your grace to answer them directly
How far forth you do like their articles?

PR. JOHN   I like them all, and do allow them well,
           And swear here, by the honour of my blood,
           My father's purposes have been mistook,
           And some about him have too lavishly
           Wrested his meaning and authority.
           My lord, these griefs shall be with speed redressed;
           Upon my soul, they shall. If this may please you,   60
           Discharge your powers unto their several counties,
           As we will ours, and here between the armies
           Let's drink together friendly and embrace,
           That all their eyes may bear those tokens home
           Of our restoréd love and amity.
                              [attendants bring up a table with
                                   flagons of wine and cups therein
ARCH.   I take your princely word for these redresses.
PR. JOHN   I give it you, and will maintain my word.
           And thereupon I drink unto your grace.
                                        [they drink together
HASTINGS   Go, captain, and deliver to the army
           This news of peace. Let them have pay, and part.   70
           I know it will well please them. Hie thee, captain!
                                        [an officer goes
ARCH.   To you, my noble Lord of Westmoreland.
WEST'LAND I pledge your grace, and if you knew what pains
           I have bestowed to breed this present peace,
           You would drink freely: but my love to ye
           Shall show itself more openly hereafter.
ARCH.   I do not doubt you.
WEST'LAND   I am glad of it.   [they drink
           Health to my lord and gentle cousin, Mowbray.
MOWBRAY   You wish me health in very happy season,
           For I am on the sudden something ill.   80
ARCH.   Against ill chances men are ever merry,
           But heaviness foreruns the good event.
WEST'LAND Therefore be merry, coz, since sudden sorrow
           Serves to say thus, 'some good thing comes tomorrow.'
ARCH.   Believe me, I am passing light in spirit.
MOWBRAY   So much the worse, if your own rule be true.
                                        [shouts heard

PR. JOHN   The word of peace is rendered. Hark, how they shout!
MOWBRAY   This had been cheerful after victory.
ARCH.   A peace is of the nature of a conquest,   90
            For then both parties nobly are subdued,
            And neither party loser.
PR. JOHN   Go, my lord,
            And let our army be dischargéd too. [*Westmoreland goes*
            And, good my lord, so please you, let our trains
            March by us, that we may peruse the men
            We should have coped withal.
ARCH.   Go, good Lord Hastings,
            And, ere they be dismissed, let them march by.
                                               [*Hastings goes*
PR. JOHN   I trust, lords, we shall lie tonight together.

                    WESTMORELAND *returns*

            Now, cousin, wherefore stands our army still?
WEST'LAND The leaders, having charge from you to stand,
            Will not go off until they hear you speak.   100
PR. JOHN   They know their duties.

                    HASTINGS *returns*

HASTINGS   My lord, our army is dispersed already:
            Like youthful steers unyoked, they take their courses
            East, west, north, south; or like a school broke up,
            Each hurries toward his home and sporting-place.
WEST'LAND Good tidings, my Lord Hastings; for the which
            I do arrest thee, traitor, of high treason.
            And you, lord archbishop, and you, Lord Mowbray,
            Of capital treason I attach you both.
                              [*they are placed under guard*
MOWBRAY   Is this proceeding just and honourable?   110
WEST'LAND Is your assembly so?
ARCH.   Will you thus break your faith?
PR. JOHN   I pawned thee none.
            I promised you redress of these same grievances
            Whereof you did complain, which by mine honour
            I will perform with a most Christian care.
            But, for you, rebels, look to taste the due

Meet for rebellion and such acts as yours.
Most shallowly did you these arms commence,
Fondly brought here and foolishly sent hence.
Strike up our drums, pursue the scattered stray;   120
God, and not we, hath safely fought today.
Some guard these traitors to the block of death,
Treason's true bed and yielder up of breath.

[they march away

SCENE 3

*'Alarum. Excursions.' Skirmishes between Prince John's soldiers and
parties of rebels in flight.* FALSTAFF *comes up and encounters one*
COLEVILE; *they make ready to fight*

FALSTAFF   What's your name, sir? Of what condition are you,
and of what place?

COLEVILE   I am a knight, sir, and my name is Colevile of the
Dale.

FALSTAFF   Well then, Colevile is your name, a knight is your
degree, and your place the dale: Colevile shall be still
your name, a traitor your degree, and the dungeon
your place – a place deep enough, so shall you be still
Colevile of the Dale.

COLEVILE   Are not you Sir John Falstaff?   10

FALSTAFF   As good a man as he, sir, whoe'er I am. Do ye yield, sir?
Or shall I sweat for you? If I do sweat, they are the
drops of thy lovers, and they weep for thy death. Therefore rouse up fear and trembling, and do observance to
my mercy.

COLEVILE   [*kneels*] I think you are Sir John Falstaff, and in that
thought yield me.

FALSTAFF   I have a whole school of tongues in this belly of mine,
and not a tongue of them all speaks any other word
but my name. An I had but a belly of any indifferency,   20
I were simply the most active fellow in Europe: my
womb, my womb, my womb undoes me. Here comes
our general.

PRINCE JOHN OF LANCASTER, WESTMORELAND,
BLUNT *and others return*

PR. JOHN   The heat is past, follow no further now.
   Call in the powers, good cousin Westmoreland.
             [*Westmoreland goes*
   Now, Falstaff, where have you been all this while?
   When everything is ended, then you come:
   These tardy tricks of yours will, on my life,
   One time or other break some gallows' back.

FALSTAFF   I would be sorry, my lord, but it should be thus: I never 30
knew yet but rebuke and check was the reward of valour.
Do you think me a swallow, an arrow, or a bullet? Have
I, in my poor and old motion, the expedition of
thought? I have speeded hither with the very extremest
inch of possibility. I have foundered nine score and odd
posts, and here, travel-tainted as I am, have, in my pure
and immaculate valour, taken Sir John Colevile of the
Dale, a most furious knight and valorous enemy. But
what of that? He saw me, and yielded, that I may justly
say, with the hook-nosed fellow of Rome, 'I came, saw 40
and overcame.'

PR. JOHN   It was more of his courtesy than your deserving.

FALSTAFF   I know not. Here he is, and here I yield him. And I
beseech your grace, let it be booked with the rest of
this day's deeds; or by the Lord, I will have it in a
particular ballad else, with mine own picture on the
top on't, Colevile kissing my foot: to the which course
if I be enforced, if you do not all show like gilt two-
pences to me, and I in the clear sky of fame o'ershine
you as much as the full moon doth the cinders of the 50
element, which show like pins' heads to her, believe
not the word of the noble: therefore let me have right,
and let desert mount.

PR. JOHN   Thine's too heavy to mount.

FALSTAFF   Let it shine then.

PR. JOHN   Thine's too thick to shine.

FALSTAFF   Let it do something, my good lord, that may do me
good, and call it what you will.

PR. JOHN   Is thy name Colevile?

COLEVILE	It is, my lord.	60

PR. JOHN   A famous rebel art thou, Colevile.

FALSTAFF   And a famous true subject took him.

COLEVILE   I am, my lord, but as my betters are
That led me hither. Had they been ruled by me,
You should have won them dearer than you have.

FALSTAFF   I know not how they sold themselves, but thou like a
kind fellow gavest thyself away gratis, and I thank thee
for thee.

WESTMORELAND returns

PR. JOHN   Now, have you left pursuit?

WEST'LAND   Retreat is made and execution stayed.   70

PR. JOHN   Send Colevile with his confederates
To York, to present execution.
Blunt, lead him hence, and see you guard him sure.
[they lead Colevile away
And now dispatch we toward the court, my lords:
I hear the king my father is sore sick.
Our news shall go before us to his majesty,
Which, cousin, you shall bear to comfort him,
And we with sober speed will follow you.

FALSTAFF   My lord, I beseech you, give me leave to go through
Gloucestershire: and, when you come to court, stand   80
my good lord, pray, in your good report.

PR. JOHN   Fare you well, Falstaff. I, in my condition,
Shall better speak of you than you deserve.   [he goes

FALSTAFF   I would you had but the wit, 'twere better than your
dukedom. Good faith, this same young sober-blooded
boy doth not love me, nor a man cannot make him
laugh – but that's no marvel, he drinks no wine.
There's never none of these demure boys come to any
proof, for thin drink doth so over-cool their blood, and
making many fish-meals, that they fall into a kind of   90
male green-sickness, and then when they marry they
get wenches. They are generally fools and cowards,
which some of us should be too, but for inflammation.
A good sherris-sack hath a twofold operation in it. It
ascends me into the brain, dries me there all the foolish
and dull and crudy vapours which environ it, makes it

apprehensive, quick, forgetive, full of nimble, fiery, and
delectable shapes; which delivered o'er to the voice, the
tongue, which is the birth, becomes excellent wit. The
second property of your excellent sherris is the warm-   100
ing of the blood, which before, cold and settled, left
the liver white and pale, which is the badge of pusilla-
nimity and cowardice; but the sherris warms it and
makes it course from the inwards to the parts extremes.
It illumineth the face, which as a beacon gives warning
to all the rest of this little kingdom, man, to arm. And
then the vital commoners, and inland petty spirits,
muster me all to their captain, the heart; who, great
and puffed up with this retinue, doth any deed of
courage; and this valour comes of sherris. So that skill   110
in the weapon is nothing without sack, for that sets it
a-work; and learning a mere hoard of gold kept by a
devil, till sack commences it and sets it in act and use.
Hereof comes it that Prince Harry is valiant, for the
cold blood he did naturally inherit of his father he hath,
like lean, sterile and bare land, manured, husbanded and
tilled with excellent endeavour of drinking good and
good store of fertile sherris, that he is become very hot
and valiant. If I had a thousand sons, the first humane
principle I would teach them should be, to forswear   120
thin potations, and to addict themselves to sack.

BARDOLPH enters

How now, Bardolph?

BARDOLPH The army is dischargéd all and gone.

FALSTAFF Let them go. I'll through Gloucestershire, and there
will I visit Master Robert Shallow, esquire. I have him
already tempering between my finger and my thumb,
and shortly will I seal with him. Come away.

[they go

SCENE 4

Westminster. The Jerusalem chamber

Enter the KING, PRINCE THOMAS OF CLARENCE,
PRINCE HUMPHREY OF GLOUCESTER, WARWICK, KENT *and others*

KING	Now, lords, if God doth give successful end
	To this debate that bleedeth at our doors,
	We will our youth lead on to higher fields,
	And draw no swords but what are sanctified.
	Our navy is addressed, our power collected,
	Our substitutes in absence well invested,
	And everything lies level to our wish.
	Only we want a little personal strength;
	And pause us till these rebels now afoot
	Come underneath the yoke of government.

WARWICK Both which we doubt not but your majesty
        Shall soon enjoy.

KING   Humphrey, my son of Gloucester,
        Where is the prince your brother?

GLO'STER I think he's gone to hunt, my lord, at Windsor.

KING And how accompanied?

GLO'STER   I do not know, my lord.

KING Is not his brother, Thomas of Clarence, with him?

GLO'STER No, my good lord, he is in presence here.

CLARENCE What would my lord and father?

KING Nothing but well to thee, Thomas of Clarence.
        How chance thou art not with the prince thy brother?
        He loves thee, and thou dost neglect him, Thomas.
        Thou hast a better place in his affection
        Than all thy brothers: cherish it, my boy,
        And noble offices thou mayst effect
        Of mediation after I am dead,
        Between his greatness and thy other brethren.
        Therefore, omit him not, blunt not his love,
        Nor lose the good advantage of his grace
        By seeming cold or careless of his will.
        For he is gracious, if he be observed:

He hath a tear for pity, and a hand
Open as day for melting charity.
Yet notwithstanding, being incensed, he's flint,
As humorous as winter, and as sudden
As flaws congealéd in the spring of day:
His temper, therefore, must be well observed.
Chide him for faults, and do it reverently,
When you perceive his blood inclined to mirth:
But, being moody, give him line and scope,
Till that his passions, like a whale on ground,   40
Confound themselves with working. Learn
                                    this, Thomas,
And thou shalt prove a shelter to thy friends,
A hoop of gold to bind thy brothers in,
That the united vessel of their blood,
Mingled with venom of suggestion,
(As, force perforce, the age will pour it in)
Shall never leak, though it do work as strong
As aconitum or rash gunpowder.

CLARENCE I shall observe him with all care and love.

KING   Why art thou not at Windsor with him, Thomas?   50

CLARENCE He is not there today, he dines in London.

KING   And how accompanied? Canst thou tell that?

CLARENCE With Poins, and other his continual followers.

KING   Most subject is the fattest soil to weeds,
And he, the noble image of my youth,
Is overspread with them! Therefore my grief
Stretches itself beyond the hour of death.
The blood weeps from my heart when I do shape,
In forms imaginary, th'unguided days
And rotten times that you shall look upon,   60
When I am sleeping with my ancestors.
For when his headstrong riot hath no curb,
When rage and hot blood are his counsellors,
When means and lavish manners meet together,
O, with what wings shall his affections fly
Towards fronting peril and opposed decay!

WARWICK My gracious lord, you look beyond him quite:
The prince but studies his companions

Like a strange tongue, wherein, to gain the language,
'Tis needful that the most immodest word   70
Be looked upon and learned; which once attained,
Your highness knows, comes to no further use
But to be known and hated. So, like gross terms,
The prince will in the perfectness of time
Cast off his followers, and their memory
Shall as a pattern or a measure live,
By which his grace must mete the lives of other,
Turning past evils to advantages.

KING   'Tis seldom when the bee doth leave her comb
In the dead carrion.   80

WESTMORELAND enters

                    Who's here? Westmoreland?

WEST'LAND Health to my sovereign, and new happiness
Added to that that I am to deliver!
Prince John your son doth kiss your grace's hand:
Mowbray, the Bishop Scroop, Hastings and all
Are brought to the correction of your law;
There is not now a rebel's sword unsheathed,
But Peace puts forth her olive everywhere.
The manner how this action hath been borne
Here at more leisure may your highness read,
With every course in his particular.   90

KING   O Westmoreland, thou art a summer bird,
Which ever in the haunch of winter sings
The lifting up of day. Look – here's more news.

HARCOURT enters

HARCOURT From enemies heaven keep your majesty,
And when they stand against you, may they fall
As those that I am come to tell you of!
The Earl Northumberland and the Lord Bardolph,
With a great power of English and of Scots,
Are by the shrieve of Yorkshire overthrown.
The manner and true order of the fight,   100
This packet, please it you, contains at large.

KING   And wherefore should these good news make me sick?
Will Fortune never come with both hands full,

But mete her fair words still in foulest terms?
She either gives a stomach and no food –
Such are the poor, in health; or else a feast
And takes away the stomach – such are the rich,
That have abundance and enjoy it not.
I should rejoice now at this happy news,
And now my sight fails, and my brain is giddy.   110
O me! Come near me now, I am much ill.

He swoons falling to the floor; the princes run to him

GLO'STER   Comfort, your majesty!
CLARENCE   O my royal father!
WEST'LAND My sovereign lord, cheer up yourself, look up!
WARWICK   Be patient, princes. You do know these fits
Are with his highness very ordinary.
Stand from him, give him air, he'll straight be well.
CLARENCE No, no, he cannot long hold out these pangs.
Th'incessant care and labour of his mind
Hath wrought the mure, that should confine it in,
So thin that life looks through and will break out.   120
GLO'STER   The people fear me, for they do observe
Unfathered heirs and loathly births of nature.
The seasons change their manners, as the year
Had found some months asleep and leaped them over.
CLARENCE The river hath thrice flowed, no ebb between,
And the old folk, time's doting chronicles,
Say it did so a little time before
That our great-grandsire, Edward, sicked and died.
WARWICK   Speak lower, princes, for the king recovers.
GLO'STER   This apoplexy will certain be his end.   130
KING   I pray you, take me up, and bear me hence
Into some other chamber: softly, pray.

                                [they carry him out

SCENE 5

Another chamber

The KING *on a bed;* CLARENCE, GLOUCESTER, WARWICK
and others in attendance

KING   Let there be no noise made, my gentle friends,
          Unless some dull and favourable hand
          Will whisper music to my weary spirit.

WARWICK   Call for the music in the other room.

KING   Set me the crown upon my pillow here.

CLARENCE His eye is hollow, and he changes much.

PRINCE HENRY *enters in haste*

WARWICK   Less noise, less noise!   [*he places the crown*

PRINCE   Who saw the Duke of Clarence?

CLARENCE I am here, brother, full of heaviness.

PRINCE   How now! Rain within doors, and none abroad!
          How doth the king?   10

GLOSTER   Exceeding ill.

PRINCE   Heard he the good news yet? Tell it him.

GLOSTER   He altered much upon the hearing it.

PRINCE   If he be sick with joy, he'll recover without physic.

WARWICK   Not so much noise, my lords. Sweet prince,
                                          speak low;
          The king your father is disposed to sleep.

CLARENCE Let us withdraw into the other room.

WARWICK   Will't please your grace to go along with us?

PRINCE   No, I will sit and watch here by the king.
                                          [*they go out*
          Why doth the crown lie there upon his pillow,   20
          Being so troublesome a bedfellow?
          O polished perturbation! Golden care!
          That keep'st the ports of slumber open wide
          To many a watchful night! Sleep with it now?
          Yet not so sound and half so deeply sweet
          As he whose brow with homely biggen bound
          Snores out the watch of night. O majesty!
          When thou dost pinch thy bearer, thou dost sit

Like a rich armour worn in heat of day,
That scald'st with safety. By his gates of breath   30
There lies a downy feather which stirs not:
Did he suspire, that light and weightless down
Perforce must move. My gracious lord! My father!
This sleep is sound indeed, this is a sleep
That from this golden rigol hath divorced
So many English kings. Thy due from me
Is tears and heavy sorrows of the blood,
Which nature, love, and filial tenderness,
Shall, O dear father, pay thee plenteously.
My due from thee is this imperial crown,   40
Which, as immediate from thy place and blood,
Derives itself to me. [*he sets it on his head*] Lo,
                                        where it sits,
Which God shall guard! And put the world's
                                        whole strength
Into one giant arm, it shall not force
This lineal honour from me: this from thee
Will I to mine leave, as 'tis left to me.
                    [*he kneels a moment, and then departs*

KING   [*stirs*] Warwick! Gloucester! Clarence!

        WARWICK *and the young princes return in haste*

CLARENCE Doth the king call?
WARWICK What would your majesty? How fares your grace?
KING Why did you leave me here alone, my lords?   50
CLARENCE We left the prince my brother here, my liege,
        Who undertook to sit and watch by you.
KING The Prince of Wales! Where is he? Let me see him:
        He is not here.
WARWICK This door is open, he is gone this way.
GLO'STER He came not through the chamber where we stayed.
KING Where is the crown? Who took it from my pillow?
WARWICK When we withdrew, my liege, we left it here.
KING The prince hath ta'en it hence: go, seek him out.
        Is he so hasty that he doth suppose   60
        My sleep my death?
        Find him, my Lord of Warwick. Chide him hither.
                                        [*Warwick departs*

This part of his conjoins with my disease,
And helps to end me. See, sons, what things you are!
How quickly nature falls into revolt
When gold becomes her object!
For this the foolish over-careful fathers
Have broke their sleep with thoughts,
Their brains with care, their bones with industry;
For this they have engrosséd and piled up   70
The cank'red heaps of strange-achievéd gold;
For this they have been thoughtful to invest
Their sons with arts and martial exercises.
When, like the bee, culling from every flower
The virtuous sweets,
Our thighs with wax, our mouths with honey packed,
We bring it to the hive; and, like the bees,
Are murdered for our pains. This bitter taste
Yields his engrossments to the ending father.

               WARWICK *returns*

Now, where is he that will not stay so long   80
Till his friend sickness have determined me?
WARWICK My lord, I found the prince in the next room,
Washing with kindly tears his gentle cheeks,
With such a deep demeanour in great sorrow,
That tyranny, which never quaffed but blood,
Would, by beholding him, have washed his knife
With gentle eye-drops. He is coming hither.
KING   But wherefore did he take away the crown?

               The PRINCE *enters with the crown*

Lo, where he comes. Come hither to me, Harry.
Depart the chamber, leave us here alone.   90
                              [*Warwick and the rest leave*
PRINCE   I never thought to hear you speak again.
KING   Thy wish was father, Harry, to that thought.
I stay too long by thee, I weary thee.
Dost thou so hunger for mine empty chair
That thou wilt needs invest thee with my honours
Before thy hour be ripe? O foolish youth!
Thou seek'st the greatness that will overwhelm thee.

Stay but a little, for my cloud of dignity
Is held from falling with so weak a wind
That it will quickly drop: my day is dim.   100
Thou hast stol'n that which after some few hours
Were thine without offence; and at my death
Thou hast sealed up my expectation.
Thy life did manifest thou lov'dst me not,
And thou wilt have me die assured of it.
Thou hid'st a thousand daggers in thy thoughts,
Whom thou hast whetted on thy stony heart,
To stab at half an hour of my life.
What, canst thou not forbear me half an hour?
Then get thee gone and dig my grave thyself,   110
And bid the merry bells ring to thine ear
That thou art crownéd, not that I am dead:
Let all the tears that should bedew my hearse
Be drops of balm to sanctify thy head.
Only compound me with forgotten dust,
Give that which gave thee life unto the worms,
Pluck down my officers, break my decrees,
For now a time is come to mock at form:
Harry the Fifth is crowned. Up, vanity!
Down, royal state! All you sage counsellors, hence!   120
And to the English court assemble now
From every region apes of idleness!
Now, neighbour confines, purge you of your scum:
Have you a ruffian that will swear, drink, dance,
Revel the night, rob, murder and commit
The oldest sins the newest kind of ways?
Be happy, he will trouble you no more:
England shall double gild his treble guilt,
England shall give him office, honour, might.
For the fifth Harry from curbed licence plucks   130
The muzzle of restraint, and the wild dog
Shall flesh his tooth on every innocent.
O my poor kingdom! Sick with civil blows
When that my care could not withhold thy riots,
What wilt thou do when riot is thy care?
O, thou wilt be a wilderness again,

Peopled with wolves, thy old inhabitants!

PRINCE   O pardon me, my liege! But for my tears,
The moist impediments unto my speech,
I had forestalled this dear and deep rebuke,   140
Ere you with grief had spoke and I had heard
The course of it so far. There is your crown;
And He that wears the crown immortally
Long guard it yours! If I affect it more
Than as your honour and as your renown,
Let me no more from this obedience rise,
Which my most inward true and duteous spirit
Teacheth this prostrate and exterior bending!
God witness with me, when I here came in,
And found no course of breath within your majesty,   150
How cold it struck my heart! If I do feign,
O, let me in my present wildness die,
And never live to show th'incredulous world
The noble change that I have purposéd.
Coming to look on you, thinking you dead –
And dead almost, my liege, to think you were –
I spake unto this crown as having sense,
And thus upbraided it: 'The care on thee depending
Hath fed upon the body of my father;
Therefore, thou best of gold art worst of gold.   160
Other, less fine in carat, is more precious,
Preserving life in med'cine potable:
But thou, most fine, most honoured, most renowned,
Hast eat thy bearer up.' Thus, my most royal liege,
Accusing it, I put it on my head,
To try with it, as with an enemy
That had before my face murdered my father,
The quarrel of a true inheritor.
But if it did infect my blood with joy,
Or swell my thoughts to any strain of pride,   170
If any rebel or vain spirit of mine
Did with the least affection of a welcome
Give entertainment to the might of it,
Let God for ever keep it from my head,
And make me as the poorest vassal is,

That doth with awe and terror kneel to it!

KING O my son!
God put it in thy mind to take it hence,
That thou mightst win the more thy father's love,
Pleading so wisely in excuse of it.   180
Come hither, Harry, sit thou by my bed,
And hear, I think, the very latest counsel
That ever I shall breathe. God knows, my son,
By what by-paths and indirect crookt ways
I met this crown, and I myself know well
How troublesome it sate upon my head:
To thee it shall descend with better quiet,
Better opinion, better confirmation;
For all the soil of the achievement goes
With me into the earth. It seemed in me   190
But as an honour snatched with boist'rous hand,
And I had many living to upbraid
My gain of it by their assistances,
Which daily grew to quarrel and to bloodshed,
Wounding supposéd peace. All these bold fears
Thou see'st with peril I have answeréd:
For all my reign hath been but as a scene
Acting that argument; and now my death
Changes the mood: for what in me was purchased,
Falls upon thee in a more fairer sort;   200
So thou the garland wear'st successively.
Yet, though thou stand'st more sure than I could do,
Thou art not firm enough, since griefs are green,
And all my friends, which thou must make thy friends,
Have but their stings and teeth newly ta'en out;
By whose fell working I was first advanced,
And by whose power I well might lodge a fear
To be again displaced: which to avoid,
I cut them off; and had a purpose now
To lead out many to the Holy Land,   210
Lest rest and lying still might make them look
Too near unto my state. Therefore, my Harry,
Be it thy course to busy giddy minds
With foreign quarrels; that action hence borne out

May waste the memory of the former days.
More would I, but my lungs are wasted so
That strength of speech is utterly denied me.
How I came by the crown, O God, forgive!
And grant it may with thee in true peace live!

PRINCE   My gracious liege,   220
You won it, wore it, kept it, gave it me.
Then plain and right must my possession be,
Which I with more than with a common pain
'Gainst all the world will rightfully maintain.

Enter PRINCE JOHN OF LANCASTER, WARWICK, *and others*

KING   Look, look, here comes my John of Lancaster.
PR. JOHN Health, peace, and happiness to my royal father!
KING   Thou bring'st me happiness and peace, son John,
But health, alack, with youthful wings is flown
From this bare withered trunk: upon thy sight
My worldly business makes a period.   230
Where is my Lord of Warwick?

PRINCE   My Lord of Warwick!
KING   Doth any name particular belong
Unto the lodging where I first did swoon?

WARWICK 'Tis called Jerusalem, my noble lord.
KING   Laud be to God! Even there my life must end.
It hath been prophesied to me many years,
I should not die but in Jerusalem;
Which vainly I supposed the Holy Land.
But bear me to that chamber, there I'll lie:
In that Jerusalem shall Harry die.   240

                                 [they carry him out

ACT 5 SCENE 1

Gloucestershire. Shallow's house

SHALLOW *enters, bringing in* FALSTAFF; BARDOLPH *and Page follow*

SHALLOW   By cock and pie, sir, you shall not away tonight. What, Davy, I say!

FALSTAFF   You must excuse me, Master Robert Shallow.

SHALLOW   I will not excuse you, you shall not be excused, excuses shall not be admitted, there is no excuse shall serve, you shall not be excused. Why, Davy!

DAVY *comes from within*

DAVY   Here, sir.

SHALLOW   Davy, Davy, Davy, Davy, let me see, Davy, let me see, Davy, let me see – yea, marry, William cook, bid him come hither. Sir John, you shall not be excused.   10

DAVY   Marry, sir, thus: those precepts cannot be served. And, again, sir, shall we sow the hade land with wheat?

SHALLOW   With red wheat, Davy. But for William cook, are there no young pigeons?

DAVY   Yes, sir. Here is now the smith's note for shoeing and plough-irons.

SHALLOW   Let it be cast and paid. Sir John, you shall not be excused.

DAVY   Now, sir, a new link to the bucket must needs be had: and, sir, do you mean to stop any of William's wages,   20 about the sack he lost the other day at Hinckley fair?

SHALLOW   A' shall answer it. Some pigeons, Davy, a couple of short-legged hens, a joint of mutton, and any pretty little tine kickshaws, tell William cook.

DAVY   Doth the man of war stay all night, sir?

SHALLOW   Yes, Davy. I will use him well. A friend i' th' court is better than a penny in purse. Use his men well, Davy, for they are arrant knaves, and will backbite.

DAVY   No worse than they are backbitten, sir, for they have marvellous foul linen.   30

SHALLOW   Well conceited, Davy. About thy business, Davy.

DAVY   I beseech you, sir, to countenance William Visor of
         Woncot against Clement Perkes o' th' hill.

SHALLOW There is many complaints, Davy, against that Visor.
         That Visor is an arrant knave, on my knowledge.

DAVY   I grant your worship, that he is a knave, sir; but yet,
         God forbid, sir, but a knave should have some counte-
         nance at his friend's request. An honest man, sir, is able
         to speak for himself, when a knave is not. I have
         served your worship truly, sir, this eight years, and if I   40
         cannot once or twice in a quarter bear out a knave
         against an honest man, I have but a very little credit
         with your worship. The knave is mine honest friend,
         sir; therefore, I beseech your worship, let him be
         countenanced.

SHALLOW Go to, I say he shall have no wrong. Look so about,
         Davy. [*Davy goes*]. Where are you, Sir John? Come,
         come, come, off with your boots. Give me your hand,
         Master Bardolph.

BARDOLPH I am glad to see your worship.   50

SHALLOW I thank thee with all my heart, kind Master Bardolph –
         [*to the Page*] and welcome, my tall fellow. Come, Sir
         John.   [*he goes in*

FALSTAFF I'll follow you, good Master Robert Shallow. Bardolph,
         look to our horses. [*Bardolph goes out, with the Page*] If I
         were sawed into quantities, I should make four dozen
         of such bearded hermits' staves as Master Shallow. It is
         a wonderful thing to see the semblable coherence of his
         men's spirits and his. They, by observing of him, do bear
         themselves like foolish justices; he, by conversing with   60
         them, is turned into a justice-like serving-man. Their
         spirits are so married in conjunction, with the partici-
         pation of society, that they flock together in consent,
         like so many wild geese. If I had a suit to Master
         Shallow, I would humour his men with the imputation
         of being near their master: if to his men, I would curry
         with Master Shallow that no man could better com-
         mand his servants. It is certain that either wise bearing or
         ignorant carriage is caught, as men take diseases, one of
         another: therefore, let men take heed of their company.   70

I will devise matter enough out of this Shallow to keep
Prince Harry in continual laughter the wearing out of
six fashions, which is four terms, or two actions; and a'
shall laugh without intervallums. O, it is much that a lie
with a slight oath, and a jest with a sad brow, will do
with a fellow that never had the ache in his shoulders!
O, you shall see him laugh till his face be like a wet
cloak ill laid up!

SHALLOW   [*within*] Sir John!
FALSTAFF   I come, Master Shallow. I come, Master Shallow.   80

[*he goes in*

SCENE 2

Westminster. A room in the palace

WARWICK *and the* LORD CHIEF JUSTICE *meeting*

WARWICK   How now, my lord chief justice? Whither away?
CH. JUST.   How doth the king?
WARWICK   Exceeding well, his cares are now all ended.
CH. JUST.   I hope, not dead.
WARWICK   He's walked the way of nature,
And to our purposes he lives no more.
CH. JUST.   I would his majesty had called me with him:
The service that I truly did his life
Hath left me open to all injuries.
WARWICK   Indeed, I think the young king loves you not.
CH. JUST.   I know he doth not, and do arm myself   10
To welcome the condition of the time,
Which cannot look more hideously upon me
Than I have drawn it in my fantasy.

Enter PRINCE JOHN, CLARENCE, GLOUCESTER,
WESTMORELAND, *and others*

WARWICK   Here come the heavy issue of dead Harry.
O, that the living Harry had the temper
Of he, the worst of these three gentlemen!
How many nobles then should hold their places,
That must strike sail to spirits of vile sort!

CH. JUST.	O God, I fear all will be overturned!
PR. JOHN	Good morrow, cousin Warwick, good morrow. 20
GLO'STER CLARENCE	} Good morrow, cousin.
PR. JOHN	We meet like men that had forgot to speak.
WARWICK	We do remember, but our argument Is all too heavy to admit much talk.
PR. JOHN	Well, peace be with him that hath made us heavy!
CH. JUST.	Peace be with us, lest we be heavier!
GLO'STER	O good my lord, you have lost a friend, indeed, And I dare swear you borrow not that face Of seeming sorrow: it is sure your own.
PR. JOHN	Though no man be assured what grace to find, 30 You stand in coldest expectation. I am the sorrier, would 'twere otherwise.
CLARENCE	Well, you must now speak Sir John Falstaff fair, Which swims against your stream of quality.
CH. JUST.	Sweet princes, what I did, I did in honour, Led by th'impartial conduct of my soul; And never shall you see that I will beg A ragged and forestalled remission. If truth and upright innocency fail me, I'll to the king my master that is dead, 40 And tell him who hath sent me after him.
WARWICK	Here comes the prince.

'Enter the PRINCE and BLUNT'

CH. JUST.	Good morrow, and God save your majesty!
PRINCE	This new and gorgeous garment, majesty, Sits not so easy on me as you think. Brothers, you mix your sadness with some fear: This is the English, not the Turkish court, Not Amurath an Amurath succeeds, But Harry Harry! Yet be sad, good brothers, For by my faith, it very well becomes you; 50 Sorrow so royally in you appears That I will deeply put the fashion on, And wear it in my heart: why then, be sad, But entertain no more of it, good brothers,

Than a joint burden laid upon us all.
For me, by heaven, I bid you be assured,
I'll be your father and your brother too.
Let me but bear your love, I'll bear your cares:
Yet weep that Harry's dead, and so will I;
But Harry lives that shall convert those tears　　　　60
By number into hours of happiness.

PR. JOHN, etc. We hope no otherwise from your majesty.

PRINCE You all look strangely on me –
[*to the Lord Chief Justice*]　　　　　and you most.
You are, I think, assured I love you not.

CH. JUST. I am assured, if I be measured rightly,
Your majesty hath no just cause to hate me.

PRINCE No!
How might a prince of my great hopes forget
So great indignities you laid upon me?
What! Rate, rebuke, and roughly send to prison　　　　70
Th'immediate heir of England! Was this easy?
May this be washed in Lethe, and forgotten?

CH. JUST. I then did use the person of your father;
The image of his power lay then in me,
And, in th'administration of his law,
Whiles I was busy for the commonwealth,
Your highness pleaséd to forget my place,
The majesty and power of law and justice,
The image of the king whom I presented,
And struck me in my very seat of judgement;　　　　80
Whereon, as an offender to your father,
I gave bold way to my authority,
And did commit you. If the deed were ill,
Be you contented, wearing now the garland,
To have a son set your decrees at nought,
To pluck down Justice from your awful bench,
To trip the course of law and blunt the sword
That guards the peace and safety of your person?
Nay more, to spurn at your most royal image,
And mock your workings in a second body?　　　　90
Question your royal thoughts, make the case yours;
Be now the father and propose a son,

Hear your own dignity so much profaned,
See your most dreadful laws so loosely slighted,
Behold yourself so by a son disdained;
And then imagine me taking your part,
And in your power soft silencing your son:
After this cold considerance, sentence me;
And as you are a king speak in your state
What I have done that misbecame my place,   100
My person, or my liege's sovereignty.

PRINCE   You are right, Justice, and you weigh this well.
Therefore still bear the balance and the sword;
And I do wish your honours may increase,
Till you do live to see a son of mine
Offend you, and obey you, as I did.
So shall I live to speak my father's words:
'Happy am I, that have a man so bold,
That dares do justice on my proper son;
And not less happy, having such a son,   110
That would deliver up his greatness so
Into the hands of Justice.' You did commit me:
For which, I do commit into your hand
Th'unstainéd sword that you have used to bear;
With this remembrance, that you use the same
With the like bold, just, and impartial spirit
As you have done 'gainst me. There is my hand.
You shall be as a father to my youth,
My voice shall sound as you do prompt mine ear,
And I will stoop and humble my intents   120
To your well-practised wise directions.
And, princes all, believe me, I beseech you,
My father is gone wild into his grave.
For in his tomb lie my affections,
And with his spirits sadly I survive,
To mock the expectation of the world,
To frustrate prophecies, and to raze out
Rotten opinion, who hath writ me down
After my seeming. The tide of blood in me
Hath proudly flowed in vanity till now: 130
Now doth it turn and ebb back to the sea,

Where it shall mingle with the state of floods,
And flow henceforth in formal majesty.
Now call we our high court of parliament,
And let us choose such limbs of noble counsel,
That the great body of our state may go
In equal rank with the best governed nation,
That war, or peace, or both at once, may be
As things acquainted and familiar to us:
In which you, father, shall have foremost hand. 　　　140
　　　　　　　　　　　　　　[to the Lord Chief Justice
Our coronation done, we will accite,
As I before remembered, all our state.
And, God consigning to my good intents,
No prince nor peer shall have just cause to say,
God shorten Harry's happy life one day.

　　　　　　　　　　　　　　　　　　　　　[they go

SCENE 3

Gloucestershire. The orchard behind Justice SHALLOW's *house*

SHALLOW *and* FALSTAFF, *followed by* SILENCE, BARDOLPH,
PAGE *and* DAVY, *come from within*

SHALLOW　Nay, you shall see my orchard, where, in an arbour,
we will eat a last year's pippin of my own graffing,
with a dish of caraways, and so forth – come, cousin
Silence – and then to bed.

FALSTAFF　'Fore God, you have here a goodly dwelling and a rich.

SHALLOW　Barren, barren, barren. Beggars all, beggars all, Sir
John – marry, good air. Spread, Davy, spread, Davy,
well said, Davy.

　　　　　　　　　　　　[Davy sets dishes upon the tables

FALSTAFF　This Davy serves you for good uses, he is your serving-
man and your husband. 　　　　　　　　　　　　　10

SHALLOW　A good varlet, a good varlet, a very good varlet, Sir
John. By the mass, I have drunk too much sack at
supper: a good varlet. Now sit down, now sit down;
come, cousin.

　　　　　　　　　[Shallow, Falstaff and Silence sit at a table

SILENCE   Ah, sirrah! Quoth-a, we shall
          [*sings*]   Do nothing but eat, and make good cheer,
                      And praise God for the merry year,
                      When flesh is cheap and females dear,
                      And lusty lads roam here and there
                              So merrily,   20
                      And ever among so merrily.

FALSTAFF There's a merry heart! Good Master Silence,
          I'll give you a health for that anon.

SHALLOW   Give Master Bardolph some wine, Davy.

DAVY   Sweet sir, sit — I'll be with you anon; Most sweet sir,
          sit; master page, good master page, sit. Proface! What
          you want in meat, we'll have in drink: but you must
          bear; the heart's all.   [*he goes in*

SHALLOW   Be merry, Master Bardolph, and my little soldier there,
          be merry.   30

SILENCE   [*sings*]   Be merry, be merry, my wife has all,
                      For women are shrews, both short and tall,
                      'Tis merry in hall when beards wag all,
                              And welcome merry Shrove-tide.
                      Be merry, be merry.

FALSTAFF I did not think Master Silence had been a man of this
          mettle.

SILENCE   Who, I? I have been merry twice and once ere now.

                      DAVY *returns*

DAVY   There's a dish of leather-coats for you.
                                      [*sets them before Bardolph*

SHALLOW   Davy!   40

DAVY   Your worship! I'll be with you straight. [*to Bardolph*] A
          cup of wine, sir?

SILENCE   [*sings*]   A cup of wine, that's brisk and fine,
                      And drink unto thee, leman mine,
                              And a merry heart lives long-a.

FALSTAFF Well said, Master Silence.

SILENCE   An we shall be merry, now comes in the sweet o' th'
          night.

FALSTAFF [*toasts him*] Health and long life to you, Master Silence.

SILENCE   [*sings*]   Fill the cup and let it come,   50
                      I'll pledge you a mile to the bottom.

SHALLOW   Honest Bardolph, welcome [*toasts him*]. If thou want'st
           anything, and wilt not call, beshrew thy heart. Welcome,
           my little tine thief [*to the Page*], and welcome indeed
           too. I'll drink to Master Bardolph, and to all the caballeros
           about London.

DAVY   I hope to see London once ere I die.

BARDOLPH   An I might see you there, Davy –

SHALLOW   By the mass, you'll crack a quart together, ha? Will you
           not, Master Bardolph?   60

BARDOLPH   Yea, sir, in a pottle-pot.

SHALLOW   By God's liggens, I thank thee. The knave will stick by
           thee, I can assure thee that. A' will not out, a'; 'tis true
           bred!

BARDOLPH   And I'll stick by him, sir.

SHALLOW   Why, there spoke a king. Lack nothing, be merry.
           [*knocking at the door*] Look who's at door there. Ho!
           Who knocks?   [*Davy goes within*

           Silence drinks a bumper to Falstaff

FALSTAFF   Why, now you have done me right.

SILENCE   [*sings*]   Do me right,   70
                        And dub me knight,
                           Samingo.
           Is't not so?

FALSTAFF   'Tis so.

SILENCE   Is't so? Why then, say an old man can do somewhat.

           DAVY *returns, with* PISTOL *following*

DAVY   An't please your worship, there's one Pistol come from
           the court with news.

FALSTAFF   From the court? Let him come in. How now, Pistol?

PISTOL   Sir John, God save you.

FALSTAFF   What wind blew you hither, Pistol?   80

PISTOL   Not the ill wind which blows no man to good.
           Sweet knight, thou art now one of the greatest men
           in this realm.

SILENCE   By'r lady, I think a' be – but goodman Puff of Barson.

PISTOL   Puff!
           Puff i'thy teeth, most recreant coward base!
           Sir John, I am thy Pistol and thy friend,

And helter-skelter have I rode to thee;
And tidings do I bring and lucky joys
And golden times and happy news of price.   90

FALSTAFF I pray thee now, deliver them like a man of this world.

PISTOL A foutre for the world and worldlings base!
I speak of Africa and golden joys.

FALSTAFF O base Assyrian knight, what is thy news?
Let King Cophetua know the truth thereof.

SILENCE [sings]   And Robin Hood, Scarlet and John.

PISTOL Shall dunghill curs confront the Helicons?
And shall good news be baffled?
Then, Pistol, lay thy head in Furies' lap.

SHALLOW Honest gentleman, I know not your breeding.   100

PISTOL Why then, lament therefore.

SHALLOW Give me pardon, sir. If, sir, you come with news from
the court, I take it there's but two ways, either to utter
them or conceal them. I am, sir, under the king, in some
authority.

PISTOL Under which king, Besonian? Speak, or die.

SHALLOW Under King Harry.

PISTOL   Harry the Fourth? Or Fifth?

SHALLOW Harry the Fourth.

PISTOL   A foutre for thine office!
Sir John, thy tender lambkin now is king;
Harry the Fifth's the man: I speak the truth.   110
When Pistol lies, do this; and fig me, like
The bragging Spaniard.

FALSTAFF   What! Is the old king dead?

PISTOL As nail in door! The things I speak are just.

FALSTAFF Away, Bardolph, saddle my horse. Master Robert
Shallow, choose what office thou wilt in the land, 'tis
thine: Pistol, I will double-charge thee with dignities.

BARDOLPH O joyful day!
I would not take a knighthood for my fortune.

PISTOL What! I do bring good news?

FALSTAFF [to Davy] Carry Master Silence to bed. Master Shallow,   120
my Lord Shallow: be what thou wilt, I am Fortune's
steward. Get on thy boots, we'll ride all night. O, sweet
Pistol [they embrace]. Away, Bardolph. [Bardolph goes]

Come, Pistol, utter more to me, and withal devise
something to do thyself good. Boot, boot, Master
Shallow! I know the young king is sick for me. Let us
take any man's horses – the laws of England are at my
commandment. Blessed are they that have been my
friends, and woe to my lord chief justice!

PISTOL   Let vultures vile seize on his lungs also!   130
'Where is the life that late I led?' say they:
Why, here it is; welcome these pleasant days.

                                    [*they go*

SCENE 4

A street in London

Enter BEADLES, *dragging in* HOSTESS QUICKLY *and* DOLL TEARSHEET

HOSTESS   No, thou arrant knave! I would to God that I might
die, that I might have thee hanged. Thou hast drawn
my shoulder out of joint.

1 BEADLE   The constables have delivered her over to me, and she
shall have whipping-cheer enough, I warrant her.
There hath been a man or two lately killed about her.

DOLL   Nut-hook, nut-hook, you lie. [*he strikes her*] Come on,
I'll tell thee what, thou damned tripe-visaged rascal, an
the child I go with do miscarry, thou wert better thou
hadst struck thy mother, thou paper-faced villain.   10

HOSTESS   O the Lord, that Sir John were come! He would make
this a bloody day to somebody: but I pray God the
fruit of her womb miscarry!

1 BEADLE   If it do, you shall have a dozen of cushions again – you
have but eleven now. Come, I charge you both go
with me, for the man is dead that you and Pistol beat
amongst you.

DOLL   I'll tell you what, you thin man in a censer, I will have
you as soundly swinged for this – you blue-bottle
rogue, you filthy famished correctioner, if you be not   20
swinged, I'll forswear half-kirtles.

1 BEADLE   Come, come, you she knight-errant, come.

HOSTESS   O God, that right should thus overcome might! Well,
           of sufferance comes ease.

DOLL   Come, you rogue, come, bring me to a justice.

HOSTESS   Ay come, you starved bloodhound.

DOLL   Goodman death! Goodman bones!

HOSTESS   Thou atomy, thou!

DOLL   Come, you thin thing; come, you rascal!

1 BEADLE   Very well!   30

                              [*they drag them away to prison*

                              SCENE 5

                A public place near Westminster Abbey

                     '*Enter strewers of rushes*'

1 STREWER More rushes, more rushes.

2 STREWER The trumpets have sounded twice.

3 STREWER 'Twill be two o'clock ere they come from the coron-
           ation. Dispatch, dispatch.   [*they pass on*

     '*Trumpets sound*'; '*the King and his train*' *pass in procession,*
      FALSTAFF, SHALLOW, PISTOL, BARDOLPH, *and the* PAGE *approach*

FALSTAFF   Stand here by me, Master Robert Shallow, I will make
           the king do you grace. I will leer upon him as a' comes
           by, and do but mark the countenance that he will
           give me.

PISTOL   God bless thy lungs, good knight.

FALSTAFF   Come here, Pistol, stand behind me. [*to Shallow*] O, if I   10
           had had time to have made new liveries, I would have
           bestowed the thousand pound I borrowed of you. But
           'tis no matter, this poor show doth better, this doth
           infer the zeal I had to see him.

SHALLOW   It doth so.

FALSTAFF   It shows my earnestness of affection –

PISTOL   It doth so.

FALSTAFF   My devotion –

PISTOL   It doth, it doth, it doth.

FALSTAFF   As it were, to ride day and night, and not to deliberate,   20
           not to remember, not to have patience to shift me –

SHALLOW	It is best, certain.
FALSTAFF	But to stand stained with travel, and sweating with desire to see him, thinking of nothing else, putting all affairs else in oblivion, as if there were nothing else to be done but to see him.
PISTOL	'Tis 'semper idem', for 'obsque hoc nihil est'. 'Tis 'all in every part'.
SHALLOW	'Tis so, indeed.

PISTOL   My knight, I will inflame thy noble liver,   30
            And make thee rage.
            Thy Doll, and Helen of thy noble thoughts,
            Is in base durance and contagious prison,
            Haled thither
            By most mechanical and dirty hand:
            Rouse up revenge from ebon den with fell
                                        Alecto's snake,
            For Doll is in: Pistol speaks nought but truth.
FALSTAFF   I will deliver her.   [trumpets heard, and a great shout
PISTOL   There roared the sea, and trumpet-clangor sounds.

'The KING *and his train', with* LORD CHIEF JUSTICE,
come from the Abbey

FALSTAFF   God save thy grace, King Hal! My royal Hal!   40
PISTOL   The heavens thee guard and keep, most royal imp of fame!
FALSTAFF   God save thee, my sweet boy!
KING   My lord chief justice, speak to that vain man.
CH. JUST.   Have you your wits? Know you what 'tis you speak?
FALSTAFF   My king! My Jove! I speak to thee, my heart!
KING   I know thee not, old man. Fall to thy prayers.
            How ill white hairs become a fool and jester!
            I have long dreamed of such a kind of man,
            So surfeit-swelled, so old, and so profane;   50
            But, being awaked, I do despise my dream.
            Make less thy body hence, and more thy grace;
            Leave gormandising, know the grave doth gape
            For thee thrice wider than for other men.
            Reply not to me with a fool-born jest:
            Presume not that I am the thing I was,

For God doth know, so shall the world perceive,
That I have turned away my former self;
So will I those that kept me company.
When thou dost hear I am as I have been,   60
Approach me, and thou shalt be as thou wast,
The tutor and the feeder of my riots:
Till then, I banish thee, on pain of death,
As I have done the rest of my misleaders,
Not to come near our person by ten mile.
For competence of life I will allow you,
That lack of means enforce you not to evils.
And as we hear you do reform yourselves,
We will, according to your strengths and qualities,
Give you advancement. Be it your charge, my lord,   70
To see performed the tenour of my word.
Set on.   [*the procession passes on*

FALSTAFF   Master Shallow, I owe you a thousand pound.

SHALLOW   Yea, marry, Sir John, which I beseech you to let me
            have home with me.

FALSTAFF   That can hardly be, Master Shallow. Do not you
            grieve at this. I shall be sent for in private to him; look
            you, he must seem thus to the world. Fear not your
            advancements: I will be the man yet that shall make
            you great.   80

SHALLOW   I cannot perceive how, unless you give me your doublet,
            and stuff me out with straw. I beseech you, good Sir
            John, let me have five hundred of my thousand.

FALSTAFF   Sir, I will be as good as my word. This that you heard
            was but a colour.

SHALLOW   A colour that I fear you will die in, Sir John.

FALSTAFF   Fear no colours, go with me to dinner. Come Lieu-
            tenant Pistol, come, Bardolph. I shall be sent for soon
            at night.

          PRINCE JOHN *returns with the* LORD CHIEF JUSTICE *and officers*

CH. JUST.   [*to the officers*] Go carry Sir John Falstaff to the Fleet;   90
            Take all his company along with him.
                                  [*they arrest Falstaff and his party*

FALSTAFF   My lord, my lord —

CH. JUST. I cannot now speak. I will hear you soon.
         Take them away.
PISTOL   'Si fortuna me tormenta, spero me contenta.'
                           [the officers lead them off
PR. JOHN I like this fair proceeding of the king's.
         He hath intent his wonted followers
         Shall all be very well provided for;
         But all are banished till their conversations
         Appear more wise and modest to the world.   100
CH. JUST. And so they are.
PR. JOHN The king hath called his parliament, my lord.
CH. JUST. He hath.
PR. JOHN I will lay odds that, ere this year expire,
         We bear our civil swords and native fire
         As far as France. I heard a bird so sing,
         Whose music, to my thinking, pleased the king.
         Come, will you hence?
                                 [they go

EPILOGUE

First my fear, then my curtsy, last my speech. My fear
is your displeasure, my curtsy my duty, and my speech
to beg your pardons. If you look for a good speech
now, you undo me, for what I have to say is of mine
own making, and what indeed I should say will, I
doubt, prove mine own marring: but to the purpose,
and so to the venture. Be it known to you, as it is very
well, I was lately here in the end of a displeasing play,
to pray your patience for it and to promise you a
better. I meant indeed to pay you with this; which, if   10
like an ill venture it come unluckily home, I break,
and you, my gentle creditors, lose. Here I promised
you I would be, and here I commit my body to your
mercies. Bate me some, and I will pay you some, and,
as most debtors do, promise you infinitely: and so I
kneel down before you; but, indeed, to pray for the
Queen.

If my tongue cannot entreat you to acquit me, will
you command me to use my legs? And yet that were
but light payment, to dance out of your debt. But a   20
good conscience will make any possible satisfaction,
and so would I. All the gentlewomen here have for-
given me; if the gentlemen will not, then the
gentlemen do not agree with the gentlewomen, which
was never seen before in such an assembly.

One word more, I beseech you. If you be not too
much cloyed with fat meat, our humble author will
continue the story, with Sir John in it, and make you
merry with fair Katharine of France; where, for any-
thing I know, Falstaff shall die of a sweat, unless already   30
a' be killed with your hard opinions; for Oldcastle died
a martyr, and this is not the man. My tongue is weary.
When my legs are too, I will bid you good night.

HENRY V

INTRODUCTION

It is possible to date *Henry V* with an accuracy unusual in the Shakespearean canon, because of a contemporary allusion in the Chorus to Act 5. The speech encourages the audience to imagine the victorious Henry's triumphant return to London and his reception by the citizens, and draws a comparison with another returning hero:

> As, by a lower but loving likelihood,
> Were now the general of our gracious empress,
> As in good time he may, from Ireland coming,
> Bringing rebellion broachéd on his sword,
> How many would the peaceful city quit,
> To welcome him!   (5.Chorus 29–34)

The 'gracious empress' is, of course, Queen Elizabeth, and her 'general' is the Earl of Essex, whose military expedition – widely predicted to end the long-running war in Ireland – left London in the spring of 1599. The play seems to preserve the short period in mid-1599 when hopes for the success of his enterprise were still alive; within months it was known that the much-vaunted campaign had ended in ignominious defeat. If the reference to Ireland dates the play to the summer months of 1599 it also hints at the background of its first performances. London in 1599 was preoccupied by war, especially, but not exclusively, in Ireland. Musters of troops and horse, and requisitioning of food and supplies, kept military conflict in the forefront of audience consciousness, as a continuing drain on individual and national resources. The historian R. B. Outhwaite has dubbed the war with Ireland 'England's Vietnam'. Thus, the play's account of a glorious and decisive triumph in France, when a plucky English army led

by a charismatic military king were in the minority but still
victorious, would have had an obvious appeal in a London
wearied by an ongoing and seemingly unwinnable war. Like
glossy, extravagant Hollywood musicals in the Depression, *Henry V*
was a distraction, wish-fulfilment – a dramatic experience in
which, unlike real life, victory was assured. This element of the
play's representation of battle and its warrior king has frequently
appealed to audiences at different historical points, and the history
of the play in performance has long been associated with times of
national adversity. Laurence Olivier's stirring film of the play,
made during the Second World War and dedicated to those
fighting in it, is only the most accessible version in the play's
history of co-option to different political and patriotic agendas.

There is indeed much tub-thumping patriotism in the play. The
French are suitably proud and haughty, the English outnumbered
but valiant. National stereotypes, the accented voices of Jamy,
Macmorris and Fluellen, suggest an anachronistic 'United Kingdom' of soldiers drawn together under the inspiring young English
king. 'Cry "God for Harry, England, and St George" ' (3.1.34)
sums up the play's appeal to nationalistic sentiment. Whereas in the
earlier plays of the historical sequence, England is variously described as a 'pelting farm' (*Richard II*) or a cannibalistic mother
'daub[ing] her lips with her own children's blood' (*1 Henry IV*),
here it is brave and true, represented by plucky soldiery and a bluff
warrior-king who cannot speak French. In *Richard II* England was
an unpruned garden running to wilderness: here it is France which
is 'wanting the scythe, all uncorrected, rank' (5.2.50). *Henry V* is
also a play which explicitly demands our imaginative sympathy and
efforts. The Chorus's admission of the limitations of theatre opens
the play, bidding its audience to 'piece out our imperfections with
your thoughts' (23), 'For 'tis your thoughts that now must deck
our kings' (28). While these acts of imagination might be thought
to be common to all theatre – earlier history plays which similarly
require an audience to supply imaginary troops and horses, and to
accept that the stage represents geographically separate locations,
do not feel the need to invoke them so explicitly – the Chorus adds
an epic dimension to the events portrayed in *Henry V*. Its speeches
are full of pride and excitement – 'now sits Expectation in the air'
(2.Chorus 8) – and their eloquent, elevated diction and non-realist

style serve to heighten the dramatic tension. The Chorus proclaims Henry 'the mirror of all Christian kings' (2.Chorus 6), a 'royal captain' whose looks bring comfort to his wretched soldiers with 'A little touch of Harry in the night' (4.Chorus 29, 47). Henry himself is pious, seeking the church's support for the campaign in France and giving the Agincourt victory to God, 'for it is none but thine' (4.8.113). In his soliloquy before the battle he meditates on the burden of kingship: 'O hard condition Twin-born with greatness' (4.1.223–24), and prays that God will not take this opportunity to punish him for the sin of his father: 'think not upon the fault My father made in compassing the crown!' (4.1.283–84). He is decisive and scrupulous: the traitors are swiftly dispatched, and Bardolph, one of the prince's erstwhile drinking companions now caught stealing from a church, is also executed without sentiment. He promises brotherhood and fellowship for those who fight with him, and money and a passage home for those who would not. He is an attractively clumsy wooer in Act 5, where he ruefully displays his lack of facility in French. This long scene, and the humour of their linguistic mismatch, shifts the play from historical epic into comedy, a genre defined by its resolution in marriage.

But there is another side to Henry's character, and it is not simply the more cynical attitude to patriotism and warfare in the late twentieth century which has discovered in the play a distinct counter to its ostensible celebrations. It can be read and performed as a play extremely suspicious of warfare, patriotic rhetoric and charismatic leadership. The Archbishop makes it clear that the Church will encourage the war with France for its own purposes, and the play begins in an atmosphere of political intrigue and manipulation. The muddled exposition of the Salic law in Act 1 Scene 2 has been seen by some critics of the play to undermine any legal claim Henry might have to France, presenting the war instead as political expediency. On his sickbed, Henry IV had advised his son to 'busy giddy minds With foreign quarrels' (2 Henry II, 4.5. 213–14), and certainly Henry V is able to channel the aggression which dogged his father's reign in the form of civil war into opposition to an external foe. Before the walls of Harfleur, Henry delivers a speech which is bloodthirsty and brutal, repeatedly promising to 'mow . . . like grass Your fair fresh virgins, and your flowering infants' (3.3.13–14); and he orders the killing of the French prisoners in a fit of anger and revenge. War is not all glorious speeches and the victory of good (us) over bad (them) – the Boy's answer to Pistol's singing of 'immortal fame' as a prize of war is touching in its simple truth: 'Would I were in an alehouse in London! I would give all my fame for a pot of ale, and safety' (3.2.11–12). The play does not include Falstaff, as the epilogue to *2 Henry IV* had promised, save in the account of his death, and his absence is a noticeable feature of the play. Henry's speeches urging on his men would have been very different with Falstaff's amoral commentary: his speech from *1 Henry IV* on the windiness of the word 'honour', for example, would have been extremely subversive before Agincourt. *Henry V* is a play which cannot allow for a dissident voice, particularly not one which would steal the limelight. Going incognito among his soldiers, Henry does not hear what he would like, and far from moving around in easy fellowship, he hears unanswerable criticism of the king, and picks a fight with Williams which he later slides onto Fluellen. Finally, the play cannot rest on its laurels. No sooner has Henry won France, and as a prize of war, Princess Katharine, than the Epilogue reminds us of what happened next:

> Henry the Sixth, in infant bands crowned king
> Of France and England, did this king succeed:
> Whose state so many had the managing,
> That they lost France, and made his England bleed.
>
> (Epilogue 9–12)

History does not stay still, and this longer historical perspective which closes the play rather reduces Henry's achievement in France. The glorious victory – be it Henry's, England's or God's – is only momentary. Shakespeare was too astute to write simple propaganda, and the Epilogue to *Henry V* means that the play concludes on a note of sadness and defeat, rather than triumph. The sequence of histories has reached the point at which it began – the Henry VI plays, which were Shakespeare's first plays on English history. The cyclical nature of historical and Shakespearean chronology is clearly established.

The scene: first England, then France

CHARACTERS IN THE PLAY

Chorus
KING HENRY THE FIFTH
HUMPHREY, DUKE OF GLOUCESTER ⎫
JOHN OF LANCASTER, DUKE OF BEDFORD ⎬ *brothers to*
THOMAS OF LANCASTER, DUKE OF CLARENCE ⎭ *the king*
DUKE OF EXETER, *uncle to the king*
DUKE OF YORK, *cousin to the king, formerly Aumerle*
EARLS OF SALISBURY, WESTMORELAND, *and* WARWICK
ARCHBISHOP OF CANTERBURY
BISHOP OF ELY
EARL OF CAMBRIDGE
LORD SCROOP
SIR THOMAS GREY
SIR THOMAS ERPINGHAM, GOWER, FLUELLEN,
    MACMORRIS, JAMY, *officers in King Henry's army*
BATES, COURT, WILLIAMS, *soldiers in the same*
PISTOL, NYM, BARDOLPH
BOY
Herald
CHARLES *the Sixth, King of France*
LEWIS, *the Dauphin*
DUKES OF BURGUNDY, ORLEANS, BRITAINE *and* BOURBON
The Constable of France
RAMBURES *and* GRANDPRÉ, *French Lords*
Governor of Harfleur
MONTJOY, *a French herald*
Ambassadors to the King of England

ISABEL, *Queen of France*
KATHARINE, *daughter to Charles and Isabel*
ALICE, *a lady attending upon her*
HOSTESS, *formerly Mrs Quickly, now Pistol's wife*

Lords, Ladies, Officers, French and English Soldiers,
    Messengers, and Attendants

HENRY V

I. PROLOGUE

Enter CHORUS

CHORUS   O for a Muse of fire, that would ascend
The brightest heaven of invention:
A kingdom for a stage, princes to act,
And monarchs to behold the swelling scene.
Then should the warlike Harry, like himself,
Assume the port of Mars, and at his heels,
Leashed in like hounds, should Famine, Sword, and Fire
Crouch for employment. But pardon, gentles all,
The flat unraiséd spirits that hath dared
On this unworthy scaffold to bring forth   10
So great an object. Can this cockpit hold
The vasty fields of France? Or may we cram
Within this wooden O the very casques
That did affright the air at Agincourt?
O, pardon! Since a crooked figure may
Attest in little place a million;
And let us, ciphers to this great accompt,
On your imaginary forces work.
Suppose within the girdle of these walls
Are now confined two mighty monarchies,   20
Whose high uprearéd and abutting fronts
The perilous narrow ocean parts asunder.
Piece out our imperfections with your thoughts:
Into a thousand parts divide one man,
And make imaginary puissance.
Think, when we talk of horses, that you see them
Printing their proud hoofs i'th'receiving earth:
For 'tis your thoughts that now must deck our kings,
Carry them here and there; jumping o'er times,
Turning th'accomplishment of many years   30
Into an hour-glass: for the which supply,

Admit me Chorus to this history;
Who prologue-like your humble patience pray,
Gently to hear, kindly to judge, our play.

['*exit*'

ACT I SCENE I

London. An antechamber in the King's palace

Enter the ARCHBISHOP OF CANTERBURY *and the* BISHOP OF ELY

CANT'BURY My lord, I'll tell you – that self bill is urged,
Which in th' eleventh year of the last king's reign
Was like, and had indeed against us passed,
But that the scambling and unquiet time
Did push it out of farther question.
ELY But how, my lord, shall we resist it now?
CANT'BURY It must be thought on. If it pass against us,
We lose the better half of our possession:
For all the temporal lands which men devout
By testament have given to the Church   10
Would they strip from us; being valued thus –
As much as would maintain, to the king's honour,
Full fifteen earls, and fifteen hundred knights,
Six thousand and two hundred good esquires;
And, to relief of lazars and weak age,
Of indigent faint souls past corporal toil,
A hundred almshouses right well supplied;
And to the coffers of the king beside,
A thousand pounds by th'year: thus runs the bill.
ELY This would drink deep.
CANT'BURY   'Twould drink the cup and all. 20
ELY But what prevention?
CANT'BURY The king is full of grace and fair regard,
and a true lover of the holy Church.
ELY The courses of his youth promised it not.
CANT'BURY The breath no sooner left his father's body,
But that his wildness, mortified in him,
Seemed to die too: yea, at that very moment,
Consideration like an angel came,

And whipped th' offending Adam out of him;
Leaving his body as a Paradise,   30
T'envelop and contain celestial spirits.
Never was such a sudden scholar made:
Never came reformation in a flood,
With such a heady currance, scouring faults:
Nor never Hydra-headed wilfulness
So soon did lose his seat, and all at once,
As in this king.

ELY   We are blessèd in the change.

CANT'BURY Hear him but reason in divinity;
And, all-admiring, with an inward wish
You would desire the king were made a prelate: 40
Hear him debate of commonwealth affairs;
You would say it hath been all in all his study:
List his discourse of war; and you shall hear
A fearful battle rendered you in music.
Turn him to any cause of policy,
The Gordian knot of it he will unloose,
Familiar as his garter: that, when he speaks,
The air, a chartered libertine, is still,
And the mute wonder lurketh in men's ears,
To steal his sweet and honeyed sentences: 50
So that the art and practic part of life
Must be the mistress to this theoric;
Which is a wonder, how his grace should glean it,
Since his addiction was to courses vain,
His companies unlettered, rude, and shallow,
His hours filled up with riots, banquets, sports;
And never noted in him any study,
Any retirement, any sequestration
From open haunts and popularity.

ELY   The strawberry grows underneath the nettle,   60
And wholesome berries thrive and ripen best
Neighboured by fruit of baser quality:
And so the prince obscured his contemplation
Under the veil of wildness, which, no doubt,
Grew like the summer grass, fastest by night,
Unseen, yet crescive in his faculty.

CANT'BURY It must be so; for miracles are ceased:
          And therefore we must needs admit the means
          How things are perfected.
ELY   But, my good lord,
          How now for mitigation of this bill   70
          Urged by the commons? Doth his majesty
          Incline to it, or no?
CANT'BURY   He seems indifferent;
          Or rather swaying more upon our part
          Than cherishing th' exhibiters against us:
          For I have made an offer to his majesty,
          Upon our spiritual convocation,
          And in regard of causes now in hand,
          Which I have opened to his grace at large,
          As touching France, to give a greater sum
          Than ever at one time the clergy yet   80
          Did to his predecessors part withal.
ELY   How did this offer seem received, my lord?
CANT'BURY With good acceptance of his majesty:
          Save that there was not time enough to hear,
          As I perceived his grace would fain have done,
          The severals and unhidden passages
          Of his true titles to some certain dukedoms,
          And generally to the crown and seat of France
          Derived from Edward, his great-grandfather.
ELY   What was th' impediment that broke this off?   90
CANT'BURY The French ambassador upon that instant
          Craved audience; and the hour, I think, is come
          To give him hearing: is it four o'clock?
ELY   It is.
CANT'BURY Then go we in, to know his embassy:
          Which I could with a ready guess declare,
          Before the Frenchman speak a word of it.
ELY   I'll wait upon you, and I long to hear it.

                                              [they go

SCENE 2

The Presence-chamber in the palace

Enter the KING, GLOUCESTER, BEDFORD, EXETER, WARWICK,
WESTMORELAND *and attendants*

KING Where is my gracious Lord of Canterbury?
EXETER Not here in presence.
KING   Send for him, good uncle.
WEST'LAND Shall we call in th'ambassador, my liege?
KING Not yet, my cousin: we would be resolved,
    Before we hear him, of some things of weight
    That task our thoughts, concerning us and France.

The ARCHBISHOP OF CANTERBURY *and the* BISHOP OF ELY
enter and make obeisance

CANT'BURY God and his angels guard your sacred throne,
    And make you long become it!
KING   Sure, we thank you.
    My learnéd lord, we pray you to proceed,
    And justly and religiously unfold
    Why the law Salic that they have in France   10
    Or should or should not bar us in our claim.
    And God forbid, my dear and faithful lord,
    That you should fashion, wrest, or bow your reading,
    Or nicely charge your understanding soul
    With opening titles miscreate, whose right
    Suits not in native colours with the truth:
    For God doth know how many now in health
    Shall drop their blood in approbation
    Of what your reverence shall incite us to.
    Therefore take heed how you impawn our person, 20
    How you awake our sleeping sword of war;
    We charge you in the name of God, take heed:
    For never two such kingdoms did contend
    Without much fall of blood, whose guiltless drops
    Are every one a woe, a sore complaint
    'Gainst him whose wrongs gives edge unto the swords
    That makes such waste in brief mortality.
    Under this conjuration, speak, my lord:

For we will hear, note, and believe in heart,   30
That what you speak is in your conscience washed
As pure as sin with baptism.
CANT'BURY Then hear me, gracious sovereign, and you peers,
That owe yourselves, your lives, and services
To this imperial throne. There is no bar
To make against your highness' claim to France,
But this which they produce from Pharamond:
'In terram Salicam mulieres ne succedant' –
'No woman shall succeed in Salic land':
Which Salic land the French unjustly gloze   40
To be the realm of France, and Pharamond
The founder of this law and female bar.
Yet their own authors faithfully affirm
That the land Salic is in Germany,
Between the floods of Sala and of Elbe:
Where Charles the Great, having subdued the Saxons,
There left behind and settled certain French:
Who holding in disdain the German women
For some dishonest manners of their life,
Established then this law – to wit, no female   50
Should be inheritrix in Salic land:
Which Salic, as I said, 'twixt Elbe and Sala,
Is at this day in Germany called Meisen.
Then doth it well appear the Salic law
Was not deviséd for the realm of France;
Nor did the French possess the Salic land
Until four hundred one and twenty years
After defunction of King Pharamond,
Idly supposed the founder of this law,
Who died within the year of our redemption   60
Four hundred twenty-six: and Charles the Great
Subdued the Saxons, and did seat the French
Beyond the river Sala, in the year
Eight hundred five. Besides, their writers say,
King Pepin, which deposéd Childeric,
Did, as heir general, being descended
Of Blithild, which was daughter to King Clothair,
Make claim and title to the crown of France.

Hugh Capet also, who usurped the crown
Of Charles the duke of Lorraine, sole heir male   70
Of the true line and stock of Charles the Great,
To find his title with some shows of truth,
Though in pure truth it was corrupt and naught,
Conveyed himself as th'heir to th'Lady Lingare,
Daughter to Charlemain, who was the son
To Lewis the emperor, and Lewis the son
Of Charles the Great: also King Lewis the tenth,
Who was sole heir to the usurper Capet,
Could not keep quiet in his conscience,
Wearing the crown of France, till satisfied   80
That fair Queen Isabel, his grandmother,
Was lineal of the Lady Ermengare,
Daughter to Charles the foresaid duke of Lorraine:
By the which marriage the line of Charles the Great
Was reunited to the crown of France.
So that, as clear as is the summer's sun,
King Pepin's title and Hugh Capet's claim,
King Lewis his satisfaction, all appear
To hold in right and title of the female:
So do the kings of France unto this day.   90
Howbeit they would hold up this Salic law
To bar your highness claiming from the female,
And rather choose to hide them in a net
Than amply to imbare their crooked titles,
Usurped from you and your progenitors.

KING   May I with right and conscience make this claim?

CANT'BURY   The sin upon my head, dread sovereign!
For in the book of Numbers is it writ,
When the man dies, let the inheritance
Descend unto the daughter. Gracious lord,   100
Stand for your own, unwind your bloody flag,
Look back into your mighty ancestors.
Go, my dread lord, to your great-grandsire's tomb,
From whom you claim; invoke his warlike spirit,
And your great-uncle's, Edward the Black Prince,
Who on the French ground played a tragedy,
Making defeat on the full power of France,

Whiles his most mighty father on a hill
Stood smiling to behold his lion's whelp
Forage in blood of French nobility. 110
O noble English, that could entertain
With half their forces the full pride of France,
And let another half stand laughing by,
All out of work and cold for action!

ELY   Awake remembrance of these valiant dead,
And with your puissant arm renew their feats.
You are their heir, you sit upon their throne:
The blood and courage that renownèd them
Runs in your veins: and my thrice-puissant liege
Is in the very May-morn of his youth, 120
Ripe for exploits and mighty enterprises.

EXETER   Your brother kings and monarchs of the earth
Do all expect that you should rouse yourself,
As did the former lions of your blood.

WEST'LAND   They know your grace hath cause, and means, and might;
So hath your highness: never king of England
Had nobles richer, and more loyal subjects,
Whose hearts have left their bodies here in England,
And lie pavilioned in the fields of France.

CANT'BURY   O let their bodies follow, my dear liege, 130
With blood and sword and fire, to win your right:
In aid whereof, we of the spiritualty
Will raise your highness such a mighty sum
As never did the clergy at one time
Bring in to any of your ancestors.

KING   We must not only arm t'invade the French,
But lay down our proportions to defend
Against the Scot, who will make road upon us
With all advantages.

CANT'BURY   They of those marches, gracious sovereign, 140
Shall be a wall sufficient to defend
Our inland from the pilfering borderers.

KING   We do not mean the coursing snatchers only,
But fear the main intendment of the Scot,
Who hath been still a giddy neighbour to us:
For you shall read that my great-grandfather

Never went with his forces into France,
But that the Scot on his unfurnished kingdom
Came pouring like the tide into a breach,
With ample and brim fulness of his force,   150
Galling the gleanéd land with hot assays,
Girding with grievous siege castles and towns:
That England, being empty of defence,
Hath shook and trembled at th'ill neighbourhood.

CANT'BURY She hath been then more feared than harmed, my liege:
For hear her but exampled by herself:
When all her chivalry hath been in France,
And she a mourning widow of her nobles,
She hath herself not only well defended,
But taken and impounded as a stray   160
The King of Scots; whom she did send to France,
To fill King Edward's fame with prisoner kings,
And make her chronicle as rich with praise
As is the ooze and bottom of the sea
With sunken wrack and sumless treasuries.

ELY   But there's a saying very old and true:
                 'If that you will France win,
                    Then with Scotland first begin.'
             For once the eagle England being in prey,
             To her unguarded nest the weasel Scot   170
             Comes sneaking, and so sucks her princely eggs,
             Playing the mouse in absence of the cat,
             To 'tame and havoc more than she can eat.

EXETER   It follows then the cat must stay at home.
             Yet that is but a crushed necessity,
             Since we have locks to safeguard necessaries,
             And pretty traps to catch the petty thieves.
             While that the arméd hand doth fight abroad
             Th'advised head defends itself at home:
             For government, though high, and low, and lower,   180
             Put into parts, doth keep in one consent,
             Congreeing in a full and natural close,
             Like music.

CANT'BURY   Therefore doth heaven divide
             The state of man in divers functions,

Setting endeavour in continual motion;
To which is fixéd, as an aim or butt,
Obedience: for so work the honey-bees,
Creatures that by a rule in nature teach
The act of order to a peopled kingdom.
They have a king and officers of sorts: 190
Where some, like magistrates, correct at home,
Others, like merchants, venture trade abroad:
Others, like soldiers, arméd in their stings
Make boot upon the summer's velvet buds:
Which pillage they with merry march bring home
To the tent-royal of their emperor:
Who, busied in his majesty, surveys
The singing masons building roofs of gold,
The civil citizens kneading up the honey,
The poor mechanic porters crowding in   200
Their heavy burdens at his narrow gate,
The sad-eyed justice, with his surly hum,
Delivering o'er to executors pale
The lazy yawning drone. I this infer,
That many things, having full reference
To one consent, may work contrariously:
As many arrows looséd several ways
Come to one mark;
As many several ways meet in one town;
As many fresh streams meet in one salt sea;   210
As many lines close in the dial's centre;
So may a thousand actions, once afoot,
End in one purpose, and be all well borne
Without defeat. Therefore to France, my liege.
Divide your happy England into four,
Whereof take you one quarter into France,
And you withal shall make all Gallia shake.
If we, with thrice such powers left at home,
Cannot defend our own doors from the dog,
Let us be worried, and our nation lose   220
The name of hardiness and policy.

KING   Call in the messengers sent from the Dauphin.
                                        [*attendants go forth*

Now are we well resolved, and by God's help
And yours, the noble sinews of our power,
France being ours, we'll bend it to our awe,
Or break it all to pieces. Or there we'll sit,
Ruling in large and ample empery
O'er France and all her almost kingly dukedoms,
Or lay these bones in an unworthy urn,
Tombless, with no remembrance over them.   230
Either our history shall with full mouth
Speak freely of our acts, or else our grave,
Like Turkish mute, shall have a tongueless mouth,
Not worshipped with a waxen epitaph.

'Enter Ambassadors of France'

Now are we well prepared to know the pleasure
Of our fair cousin Dauphin: for we hear
Your greeting is from him, not from the king.

1 AMBASS. May't please your majesty to give us leave
Freely to render what we have in charge:
Or shall we sparingly show you far off   240
The Dauphin's meaning and our embassy?

KING We are no tyrant, but a Christian king,
Unto whose grace our passion is as subject
As is our wretches fettered in our prisons;
Therefore with frank and with uncurbéd plainness
Tell us the Dauphin's mind.

1 AMBASS.   Thus then, in few.
Your highness, lately sending into France,
Did claim some certain dukedoms, in the right
Of your great predecessor, King Edward the Third.
In answer of which claim, the prince our master   250
Says that you savour too much of your youth,
And bids you be advised there's nought in France
That can be with a nimble galliard won:
You cannot revel into dukedoms there.
He therefore sends you, meeter for your spirit,
This tun of treasure; and, in lieu of this,
Desires you let the dukedoms that you claim
Hear no more of you. This the Dauphin speaks.

KING   What treasure, uncle?
EXETER   [*opening the barrel*]   Tennis-balls, my liege.
KING   We are glad the Dauphin is so pleasant with us.   260
              His present and your pains we thank you for.
              When we have matched our rackets to these balls,
              We will in France, by God's grace, play a set
              Shall strike his father's crown into the hazard.
              Tell him he hath made a match with such a wrangler
              That all the courts of France will be disturbed
              With chases. And we understand him well,
              How he comes o'er us with our wilder days,
              Not measuring what use we made of them.
              We never valued this poor seat of England,   270
              And therefore, living hence, did give ourself
              To barbarous licence: as 'tis ever common
              That men are merriest when they are from home.
              But tell the Dauphin I will keep my state,
              Be like a king, and show my sail of greatness,
              When I do rouse me in my throne of France.
              For that I have laid by my majesty,
              And plodded like a man for working-days:
              But I will rise there with so full a glory
              That I will dazzle all the eyes of France,   280
              Yea, strike the Dauphin blind to look on us.
              And tell the pleasant prince this mock of his
              Hath turned his balls to gun-stones, and his soul
              Shall stand sore chargéd for the wasteful vengeance
              That shall fly with them: for many a thousand widows
              Shall this his mock mock out of their dear husbands;
              Mock mothers from their sons, mock castles down:
              And some are yet ungotten and unborn
              That shall have cause to curse the Dauphin's scorn.
              But this lies all within the will of God,   290
              To whom I do appeal, and in whose name,
              Tell you the Dauphin, I am coming on,
              To venge me as I may, and to put forth
              My rightful hand in a well-hallowed cause.
              So get you hence in peace; and tell the Dauphin
              His jest will savour but of shallow wit,

When thousands weep more than did laugh at it.
Convey them with safe conduct. Fare you well.

['Exeunt Ambassadors'

EXETER   This was a merry message.

KING   We hope to make the sender blush at it.   300
Therefore, my lords, omit no happy hour
That may give furth'rance to our expedition:
For we have now no thought in us but France,
Save those to God, that run before our business.
Therefore let our proportions for these wars
Be soon collected, and all things thought upon
That may with reasonable swiftness add
More feathers to our wings: for, God before,
We'll chide this Dauphin at his father's door.
Therefore let every man now task his thought,   310
That this fair action may on foot be brought.

[he rises and departs, the rest following

2. PROLOGUE

'Flourish. Enter CHORUS*'*

CHORUS   Now all the youth of England are on fire,
And silken dalliance in the wardrobe lies:
Now thrive the armourers, and honour's thought
Reigns solely in the breast of every man.
They sell the pasture now, to buy the horse;
Following the mirror of all Christian kings,
With wingéd heels, as English Mercuries.
For now sits Expectation in the air,
And hides a sword, from hilts unto the point,
With crowns imperial, crowns and coronets,   10
Promised to Harry and his followers.
The French, advised by good intelligence
Of this most dreadful preparation,
Shake in their fear, and with pale policy
Seek to divert the English purposes.
O England! Model to thy inward greatness,
Like little body with a mighty heart:
What might'st thou do, that honour would thee do,
Were all thy children kind and natural!
But see, thy fault France hath in thee found out,   20
A nest of hollow bosoms, which he fills
With treacherous crowns: and three corrupted men,
One, Richard Earl of Cambridge, and the second,
Henry Lord Scroop of Masham, and the third,
Sir Thomas Grey, knight of Northumberland,
Have for the gilt of France (O guilt indeed!)
Confirmed conspiracy with fearful France;
And by their hands this grace of kings must die,
If hell and treason hold their promises,
Ere he take ship for France, and in Southampton.   30
Linger your patience on, and we'll digest
Th'abuse of distance, force a play:
The sum is paid, the traitors are agreed,
The king is set from London, and the scene

Is now transported, gentles, to Southampton.
There is the playhouse now, there must you sit,
And thence to France shall we convey you safe,
And bring you back, charming the narrow seas
To give you gentle pass; for if we may,
We'll not offend one stomach with our play.   40
But till the king come forth, and not till then,
Unto Southampton do we shift our scene.

['exit']

ACT 2 SCENE I

London. A street

NYM *and* BARDOLPH *meeting*

BARDOLPH Well met, Corporal Nym.

NYM Good morrow, Lieutenant Bardolph.

BARDOLPH What, are Ancient Pistol and you friends yet?

NYM For my part, I care not. I say little: but when time shall
serve, there shall be smiles – but that shall be as it may.
I dare not fight, but I will wink and hold out mine
iron: it is a simple one, but what though? It will toast
cheese, and it will endure cold, as another man's sword
will, and there's an end.

BARDOLPH I will bestow a breakfast to make you friends, and we'll   10
be all three sworn brothers to France: let't be so, good
Corporal Nym.

NYM Faith, I will live so long as I may, that's the certain of it;
and when I cannot live any longer, I will do as I may.
That is my rest, that is the rendezvous of it.

BARDOLPH It is certain, corporal, that he is married to Nell
Quickly, and certainly she did you wrong, for you
were troth-plight to her.

NYM I cannot tell. Things must be as they may: men may
sleep, and they may have their throats about them at   20
that time, and some say knives have edges. It must be as
it may; though patience be a tired mare, yet she will
plod. There must be conclusions – well, I cannot tell.

Ancient PISTOL *and the* HOSTESS *approach*

BARDOLPH Here comes Ancient Pistol and his wife: good corporal,
be patient here.

NYM How now, mine host Pistol!

PISTOL Base tike, call'st thou me host?
Now by this hand I swear I scorn the term:
Nor shall my Nell keep lodgers.

HOSTESS No, by my troth, not long: for we cannot lodge and 30
board a dozen or fourteen gentlewomen that live
honestly by the prick of their needles, but it will be
thought we keep a bawdy-house straight. [*Nym draws
his sword*] O well-a-day, Lady, if he be not hewn now,
we shall see wilful adultery and murder committed.

BARDOLPH Good lieutenant, good corporal, offer nothing here.

NYM Pish!

PISTOL Pish for thee, Iceland dog! Thou prick-eared cur of
Iceland!

HOSTESS Good Corporal Nym, show thy valour, and put up your 40
sword.

NYM Will you shog off? I would have you solus.
                              [*he sheathes his sword*

PISTOL 'Solus', egregious dog? O viper vile!
The 'solus' in thy most marvellous face,
The 'solus' in thy teeth, and in thy throat,
And in thy hateful lungs, yea in thy maw, perdy –
And, which is worse, within thy nasty mouth!
I do retort the 'solus' in thy bowels,
For I can take, and Pistol's cock is up,
And flashing fire will follow.   50

NYM I am not Barbason, you cannot conjure me. I have an
humour to knock you indifferently well. If you grow
foul with me, Pistol, I will scour you with my rapier,
as I may, in fair terms. If you would walk off, I would
prick your guts a little in good terms, as I may, and
that's the humour of it.

PISTOL O braggart vile, and damnéd furious wight,
The grave doth gape, and doting death is near,
Therefore exhale!   [*they both draw*

BARDOLPH [*also drawing*] Hear me, hear me what I say: he that 60

           strikes the first stroke, I'll run him up to the hilts, as I
           am a soldier.

PISTOL   An oath of mickle might, and fury shall abate.

                                       [they sheathe

           Give me thy fist, thy fore-foot to me give:
           Thy spirits are most tall.

NYM   I will cut thy throat one time or other in fair terms,
           that is the humour of it.

PISTOL   'Couple a gorge',
           That is the word. I thee defy again.
           O hound of Crete, think'st thou my spouse to get?   70
           No, to the spital go,
           And from the powdering-tub of infamy
           Fetch forth the lazar kite of Cressid's kind,
           Doll Tearsheet she by name, and her espouse.
           I have, and I will hold, the quondam Quickly
           For the only she: and – pauca, there's enough.
           Go to.

                    'Enter the BOY*'*

BOY   Mine host Pistol, you must come to my master, and
           you, hostess: he is very sick, and would to bed. Good
           Bardolph, put thy face between his sheets, and do the   80
           office of a warming-pan: faith, he's very ill.

BARDOLPH Away, you rogue.   *[the Boy runs off*

HOSTESS   By my troth, he'll yield the crow a pudding one of
           these days. The king has killed his heart. Good husband,
           come home presently.   *[Hostess follows the Boy*

BARDOLPH Come, shall I make you two friends? We must to
           France together: why the devil should we keep knives
           to cut one another's throats?

PISTOL   Let floods o'erswell, and fiends for food howl on!

NYM   You'll pay me the eight shillings I won of you at   90
           betting?

PISTOL   Base is the slave that pays.

NYM   That now I will have: that's the humour of it.

PISTOL   As manhood shall compound: push home. *[they 'draw'*

BARDOLPH By this sword, he that makes the first thrust, I'll kill
           him: by this sword, I will.

PISTOL   Sword is an oath, and oaths must have their course.

BARDOLPH Corporal Nym, an thou wilt be friends, be friends; an
            thou wilt not, why then, be enemies with me too:
            prithee put up.   100

NYM   I shall have my eight shillings I won of you at betting?

PISTOL   A noble shalt thou have, and present pay,
            And liquor likewise will I give to thee,
            And friendship shall combine, and brotherhood.
            I'll live by Nym, and Nym shall live by me.
            Is not this just? For I shall sutler be
            Unto the camp, and profits will accrue.
            Give me thy hand.   [they sheathe again

NYM   I shall have my noble?

PISTOL   In cash, most justly paid.   110

NYM   Well, then, that's the humour of 't.   [they strike hands

                        HOSTESS returns

HOSTESS   As ever you come of women, come in quickly to Sir
            John. Ah, poor heart! He is so shaked of a burning
            quotidian tertian, that it is most lamentable to behold.
            Sweet men, come to him.

NYM   The king hath run bad humours on the knight, that's
            the even of it.

PISTOL   Nym, thou hast spoke the right,
            His heart is fracted and corroborate.

NYM   The king is a good king, but it must be as it may: he 120
            passes some humours and careers.

PISTOL   Let us condole the knight; for, lambkins, we will live.
                                                            [they go

                            SCENE 2

                Southampton. A council-chamber

            'Enter EXETER, BEDFORD, and WESTMORELAND'

BEDFORD   'Fore God, his grace is bold to trust these traitors.

EXETER   They shall be apprehended by and by.

WEST'LAND   How smooth and even they do bear themselves,
            As if allegiance in their bosoms sat,

	Crownéd with faith, and constant loyalty.
BEDFORD	The king hath note of all that they intend,
	By interception which they dream not of.
EXETER	Nay, but the man that was his bedfellow,
	Whom he hath dulled and cloyed with gracious

favours —

| | That he should for a foreign purse so sell | 10 |
| | His sovereign's life to death and treachery! | |

Trumpets sound. 'Enter the KING, SCROOP, CAMBRIDGE,
and GREY', *with attendants*

KING	Now sits the wind fair, and we will aboard.
	My Lord of Cambridge, and my kind Lord of Masham,
	And you, my gentle knight, give me your thoughts.
	Think you not that the powers we bear with us
	Will cut their passage through the force of France,
	Doing the execution and the act
	For which we have in head assembled them?
SCROOP	No doubt, my liege, if each man do his best.
KING	I doubt not that, since we are well persuaded

20

	We carry not a heart with us from hence,
	That grows not in a fair consent with ours;
	Nor leave not one behind, that doth not wish
	Success and conquest to attend on us.
CAMB.	Never was monarch better feared and loved
	Than is your majesty; there's not, I think, a subject
	That sits in heart-grief and uneasiness
	Under the sweet shade of your government.
GREY	True: those that were your father's enemies
	Have steeped their galls in honey, and do serve you

30

	With hearts create of duty and of zeal.
KING	We therefore have great cause of thankfulness,
	And shall forget the office of our hand
	Sooner than quittance of desert and merit,
	According to the weight and worthiness.
SCROOP	So service shall with steeléd sinews toil,
	And labour shall refresh itself with hope
	To do your grace incessant services.
KING	We judge no less. Uncle of Exeter,

	Enlarge the man committed yesterday, 40

Enlarge the man committed yesterday,   40
That railed against our person: we consider
It was excess of wine that set him on,
And on his more advice we pardon him.

SCROOP   That's mercy, but too much security:
Let him be punished, sovereign, lest example
Breed, by his sufferance, more of such a kind.

KING   O let us yet be merciful.

CAMB.   So may your highness, and yet punish too.

GREY   Sir,
You show great mercy if you give him life,   50
After the taste of much correction.

KING   Alas, your too much love and care of me
Are heavy orisons 'gainst this poor wretch.
If little faults, proceeding on distemper,
Shall not be winked at, how shall we stretch our eye
When capital crimes, chewed, swallowed, and digested,
Appear before us? We'll yet enlarge that man,
Though Cambridge, Scroop, and Grey, in their
                                                    dear care
And tender preservation of our person
Would have him punished. And now to our
                            French causes: [*he takes up papers* 60
Who are the late commissioners?

CAMB.   I one, my lord.
Your highness bade me ask for it today.

SCROOP   So did you me, my liege.

GREY   And I, my royal sovereign.

KING   [*delivering the papers*] Then, Richard, Earl of Cambridge,
                                        there is yours:
There yours, Lord Scroop of Masham: and, sir knight,
Grey of Northumberland, this same is yours.
Read them, and know I know your worthiness.
My Lord of Westmoreland, and uncle Exeter,   70
We will aboard tonight. Why, how now, gentlemen?
What see you in those papers, that you lose
So much complexion? Look ye how they change:
Their cheeks are paper. Why, what read you there,
That have so cowarded and chased your blood

Out of appearance?

CAMB.   I do confess my fault,
And do submit me to your highness' mercy.

GREY
SCROOP }   To which we all appeal.

KING   The mercy that was quick in us but late,
By your own counsel is suppressed and killed.   80
You must not dare, for shame, to talk of mercy,
For your own reasons turn into your bosoms,
As dogs upon their masters, worrying you.
See you, my princes, and my noble peers,
These English monsters: my Lord of Cambridge here,
You know how apt our love was to accord
To furnish him with all appertinents
Belonging to his honour; and this man
Hath for a few light crowns lightly conspired
And sworn unto the practices of France   90
To kill us here in Hampton. To the which
This knight, no less for bounty bound to us
Than Cambridge is, hath likewise sworn. But O,
What shall I say to thee, Lord Scroop, thou cruel,
Ingrateful, savage, and inhuman creature?
Thou that didst bear the key of all my counsels,
That knew'st the very bottom of my soul,
That almost mightst have coined me into gold
Wouldst thou have practised on me for thy use.
May it be possible, that foreign hire   100
Could out of thee extract one spark of evil
That might annoy my finger? 'Tis so strange,
That though the truth of it stands off as gross
As black on white, my eye will scarcely see it.
Treason and murder ever kept together,
As two yoke-devils sworn to either's purpose,
Working so grossly in a natural cause,
That admiration did not whoop at them.
But thou, 'gainst all proportion, didst bring in
Wonder to wait on treason and on murder: 110
And whatsoever cunning fiend it was
That wrought upon thee so preposterously,

Hath got the voice in hell for excellence.
All other devils that suggest by treasons
Do hotch and bungle up damnation,
With patches, colours, and with forms being fetched
From glist'ring semblances of piety:
But he that tempered thee, bade thee stand up,
Gave thee no instance why thou shouldst do treason,
Unless to dub thee with the name of traitor.   120
If that same demon that hath gulled thee thus
Should with his lion gait walk the whole world,
He might return to vasty Tartar back,
And tell the legions, 'I can never win
A soul so easy as that Englishman's.'
O, how hast thou with jealousy infected
The sweetness of affiance? Show men dutiful?
Why, so didst thou. Seem they grave and learnéd?
Why, so didst thou. Come they of noble family?
Why, so didst thou. Seem they religious?   130
Why, so didst thou. Or are they spare in diet,
Free from gross passion, or of mirth, or anger,
Constant in spirit, not swerving with the blood,
Garnished and decked in modest complement,
Not working with the eye without the ear,
And but in purgéd judgement trusting neither?
Such and so finely bolted didst thou seem:
And thus thy fall hath left a kind of blot,
To mark the full-fraught man and best indued
With some suspicion. I will weep for thee: 140
For this revolt of thine, methinks, is like
Another fall of man. Their faults are open;
Arrest them to the answer of the law,
And God acquit them of their practices.

EXETER   I arrest thee of high treason, by the name of Richard
              Earl of Cambridge.
              I arrest thee of high treason, by the name of Henry
              Lord Scroop of Masham.
              I arrest thee of high treason, by the name of Thomas
              Grey, knight of Northumberland.   150

SCROOP   Our purposes God justly hath discovered,

And I repent my fault more than my death;
Which I beseech your highness to forgive,
Although my body pay the price of it.

CAMB.   For me, the gold of France did not seduce,
Although I did admit it as a motive,
The sooner to effect what I intended:
But God be thankéd for prevention,
Which I in sufferance heartily will rejoice,
Beseeching God, and you, to pardon me.   160

GREY   Never did faithful subject more rejoice
At the discovery of most dangerous treason,
Than I do at this hour joy o'er myself,
Prevented from a damnéd enterprise;
My fault, but not my body, pardon, sovereign.

KING   God quit you in his mercy! Hear your sentence.
You have conspired against our royal person,
Joined with an enemy proclaimed, and from his coffers
Received the golden earnest of our death:
Wherein you would have sold your king to slaughter,   170
His princes and his peers to servitude,
His subjects to oppression and contempt,
And his whole kingdom into desolation.
Touching our person, seek we no revenge,
But we our kingdom's safety must so tender,
Whose ruin you have sought, that to her laws
We do deliver you. Get you therefore hence,
Poor miserable wretches, to your death:
The taste whereof God of his mercy give
You patience to endure, and true repentance   180
Of all your dear offences. Bear them hence.
        [*Exeunt* CAMBRIDGE, SCROOP, *and* GREY, *guarded*
Now, lords, for France: the enterprise whereof
Shall be to you as us, like glorious.
We doubt not of a fair and lucky war,
Since God so graciously hath brought to light
This dangerous treason lurking in our way
To hinder our beginnings. We doubt not now
But every rub is smoothéd on our way.
Then forth, dear countrymen: let us deliver

Our puissance into the hand of God,   190
Putting it straight in expedition.
Cheerly to sea, the signs of war advance:
No king of England, if not king of France.

[*'Flourish'; they go*

SCENE 3

London. Before a tavern

Enter PISTOL, HOSTESS, NYM, BARDOLPH, *and* BOY

HOSTESS Prithee, honey-sweet husband, let me bring thee to
Staines.

PISTOL No: for my manly heart doth earn.
Bardolph, be blithe; Nym, rouse thy vaunting veins;
Boy, bristle thy courage up: for Falstaff he is dead,
And we must earn therefore.

BARDOLPH Would I were with him, wheresome'er he is, either in
heaven or in hell!

HOSTESS Nay sure, he's not in hell: he's in Arthur's bosom, if
ever man went to Arthur's bosom: a' made a finer end, 10
and went away an it had been any christom child: a'
parted e'en just between twelve and one, e'en at the
turning o'th'tide: for after I saw him fumble with the
sheets, and play with flowers, and smile upon his finger's
end, I knew there was but one way: for his nose was as
sharp as a pen, and a' babbled of green fields. 'How
now, Sir John?' quoth I. 'What, man! Be o' good
cheer': so a' cried out, 'God, God, God!' three or four
times: now I, to comfort him, bid him a' should not
think of God; I hoped there was no need to trouble 20
himself with any such thoughts yet: so a' bade me lay
more clothes on his feet: I put my hand into the bed,
and felt them, and they were as cold as any stone: then
I felt to his knees, and so up'ard and up'ard, and all was
as cold as any stone.

NYM They say he cried out of sack.

HOSTESS Ay, that a' did.

BARDOLPH   And of women.

HOSTESS   Nay, that a' did not.

BOY   Yes, that a' did, and said they were devils incarnate.   30

HOSTESS   A' could never abide carnation – 'twas a colour he never
liked.

BOY   A' said once, the devil would have him about women.

HOSTESS   A' did in some sort, indeed, handle women: but then
he was rheumatic, and talked of the whore of Babylon.

BOY   Do you not remember a' saw a flea stick upon Bardolph's nose, and a' said it was a black soul burning in
hell?

BARDOLPH   Well, the fuel is gone that maintained that fire: that's
all the riches I got in his service.   40

NYM   Shall we shog? The king will be gone from Southampton.

PISTOL   Come, let's away. My love, give me thy lips.
Look to my chattels and my movables:
Let senses rule: the word is 'Pitch and pay'.
Trust none:
For oaths are straws, men's faiths are wafer-cakes,
And Holdfast is the only dog, my duck.
Therefore, Caveto be thy counsellor.
Go, clear thy crystals. Yoke-fellows in arms,   50
Let us to France, like horse-leeches, my boys,
To suck, to suck, the very blood to suck!

BOY   And that's but unwholesome food, they say.

PISTOL   Touch her soft mouth, and march.

BARDOLPH   Farewell, hostess.   *[kissing her*

NYM   I cannot kiss, that is the humour of it: but adieu.

PISTOL   Let housewifery appear: keep close, I thee command.

HOSTESS   Farewell: adieu.

                                               [they march off

SCENE 4

The French King's palace

'*Flourish. Enter the* FRENCH KING, *the* DAUPHIN, *the Dukes of*
BERRI *and* BRITAINE', *the* CONSTABLE, *and others*

FR. KING Thus comes the English with full power upon us,
 And more than carefully it us concerns
 To answer royally in our defences.
 Therefore the Dukes of Berri and of Britaine,
 Of Brabant and of Orleans, shall make forth,
 And you, Prince Dauphin, with all swift dispatch
 To line and new repair our towns of war
 With men of courage and with means defendant:
 For England his approaches makes as fierce
 As waters to the sucking of a gulf.   10
 It fits us then to be as provident
 As fear may teach us, out of late examples
 Left by the fatal and neglected English
 Upon our fields.

DAUPHIN   My most redoubted father,
 It is most meet we arm us 'gainst the foe:
 For peace itself should not so dull a kingdom,
 Though war nor no known quarrel were in question,
 But that defences, musters, preparations,
 Should be maintained, assembled, and collected,
 As were a war in expectation.   20
 Therefore I say 'tis meet we all go forth
 To view the sick and feeble parts of France:
 And let us do it with no show of fear,
 No, with no more than if we heard that England
 Were busied with a Whitsun morris-dance:
 For, my good liege, she is so idly kinged,
 Her sceptre so fantastically borne
 By a vain, giddy, shallow, humorous youth,
 That fear attends her not.

CONSTABLE   O peace, Prince Dauphin!
 You are too much mistaken in this king: 30

Question your grace the late ambassadors,
With what great state he heard their embassy,
How well supplied with noble counsellors,
How modest in exception; and, withal,
How terrible in constant resolution:
And you shall find his vanities forespent
Were but the outside of the Roman Brutus,
Covering discretion with a coat of folly;
As gardeners do with ordure hide those roots
That shall first spring, and be most delicate.   40

DAUPHIN Well, 'tis not so, my lord high constable.
But though we think it so, it is no matter.
In cases of defence, 'tis best to weigh
The enemy more mighty than he seems,
So the proportions of defence are filled:
Which, of a weak and niggardly projection,
Doth like a miser spoil his coat with scanting
A little cloth.

FR. KING   Think we King Harry strong:
And, princes, look you strongly arm to meet him.
The kindred of him hath been fleshed upon us,   50
And he is bred out of that bloody strain,
That haunted us in our familiar paths.
Witness our too much memorable shame,
When Cressy battle fatally was struck,
And all our princes captived, by the hand
Of that black name, Edward, Black Prince of Wales:
Whiles that his mountain sire, on mountain standing
Up in the air, crowned with the golden sun,
Saw his heroical seed, and smiled to see him
Mangle the work of nature, and deface   60
The patterns that by God and by French fathers
Had twenty years been made. This is a stem
Of that victorious stock: and let us fear
The native mightiness and fate of him.

'Enter a MESSENGER*'*

MESSENGER Ambassadors from Harry King of England
Do crave admittance to your majesty.

FR. KING We'll give them present audience. Go, and bring them.

[the Messenger departs, with certain lords

You see this chase is hotly followed, friends.

DAUPHIN Turn head, and stop pursuit: for coward dogs
Most spend their mouths, when what they seem
to threaten 70
Runs far before them. Good my sovereign,
Take up the English short, and let them know
Of what a monarchy you are the head:
Self-love, my liege, is not so vile a sin
As self-neglecting.

Re-enter lords, with EXETER *and his train*

FR. KING   From our brother of England?

EXETER From him, and thus he greets your majesty.
He wills you, in the name of God Almighty,
That you divest yourself, and lay apart
The borrowed glories that by gift of heaven,
By law of nature, and of nations, 'longs 80
To him and to his heirs, namely, the crown,
And all wide-stretchéd honours, that pertain
By custom, and the ordinance of times,
Unto the crown of France: that you may know
'Tis no sinister, nor no awkward claim,
Picked from the worm-holes of long-vanished days,
Nor from the dust of old oblivion raked,
He sends you this most memorable line, *[gives a paper*
In every branch truly demonstrative,
Willing you overlook this pedigree. 90
And when you find him evenly derived
From his most famed of famous ancestors,
Edward the Third, he bids you then resign
Your crown and kingdom, indirectly held
From him the native and true challenger.

FR. KING Or else what follows?

EXETER Bloody constraint: for if you hide the crown
Even in your hearts, there will he rake for it.
Therefore in fierce tempest is he coming,
In thunder and in earthquake, like a Jove: 100

That, if requiring fail, he will compel.
And bids you, in the bowels of the Lord,
Deliver up the crown, and to take mercy
On the poor souls, for whom this hungry war
Opens his vasty jaws: and on your head
Turning the widows' tears, the orphans' cries,
The dead men's blood, the pining maidens' groans,
For husbands, fathers, and betrothéd lovers,
That shall be swallowed in this controversy.
This is his claim, his threatening, and my message:　110
Unless the Dauphin be in presence here;
To whom expressly I bring greeting too.

FR. KING　For us, we will consider of this further:
Tomorrow shall you bear our full intent
Back to our brother of England.

DAUPHIN　　　　　　　　　　　　For the Dauphin,
I stand here for him: what to him from England?

EXETER　Scorn and defiance, slight regard, contempt,
And anything that may not misbecome
The mighty sender, doth he prize you at.
Thus says my king: an if your father's highness　120
Do not, in grant of all demands at large,
Sweeten the bitter mock you sent his majesty,
He'll call you to so hot an answer of it,
That caves and womby vaultages of France
Shall chide your trespass, and return your mock
In second accent of his ordinance.

DAUPHIN　Say, if my father render fair return,
It is against my will; for I desire
Nothing but odds with England. To that end,
As matching to his youth and vanity,　130
I did present him with the Paris-balls.

EXETER　He'll make your Paris Louvre shake for it,
Were it the mistress-court of mighty Europe.
And, be assured, you'll find a difference,
As we his subjects have in wonder found,
Between the promise of his greener days,
And these he masters now; now he weighs time
Even to the utmost grain: that you shall read

In your own losses, if he stay in France.

FR. KING Tomorrow shall you know our mind at full.   140

[*'Flourish'*

EXETER Dispatch us with all speed, lest that our king
Come here himself to question our delay;
For he is footed in this land already.

FR. KING You shall be soon dispatched, with fair conditions.
A night is but small breath, and little pause,
To answer matters of this consequence.

[*they go*

3. PROLOGUE

'Flourish. Enter CHORUS*'*

CHORUS Thus with imagined wing our swift scene flies,
In motion of no less celerity
Than that of thought. Suppose that you have seen
The well-appointed king at Hampton pier
Embark his royalty, and his brave fleet
With silken streamers the young Phoebus fanning.
Play with your fancies: and in them behold,
Upon the hempen tackle, ship-boys climbing;
Hear the shrill whistle, which doth order give
To sounds confused: behold the threaden sails,   10
Borne with th'invisible and creeping wind,
Draw the huge bottoms through the furrowed sea,
Breasting the lofty surge. O, do but think
You stand upon the rivage, and behold
A city on th'inconstant billows dancing:
For so appears this fleet majestical,
Holding due course to Harfleur. Follow, follow!
Grapple your minds to sternage of this navy,
And leave your England as dead midnight, still,
Guarded with grandsires, babies, and old women,   20
Either past or not arrived to pith and puissance.
For who is he, whose chin is but enriched
With one appearing hair, that will not follow
These culled and choice-drawn cavaliers to France?
Work, work your thoughts, and therein see a siege:
Behold the ordinance on their carriages,
With fatal mouths gaping on girded Harfleur.
Suppose th'ambassador from the French comes back:
Tells Harry that the king doth offer him
Katharine his daughter, and with her, to dowry,   30
Some petty and unprofitable dukedoms.
The offer likes not: and the nimble gunner
With linstock now the devilish cannon touches,
                              [*'Alarum, and chambers go off'*

And down goes all before them. Still be kind,
And eke out our performance with your mind.

[*'exit'*]

ACT 3 SCENE 1

France. Before the gates 'at Harfleur'

'Alarum'. 'Enter the KING, EXETER, BEDFORD, *and* GLOUCESTER*',
followed by soldiers with 'scaling ladders'*

KING   Once more unto the breach, dear friends, once more;
              Or close the wall up with our English dead.
              In peace, there's nothing so becomes a man,
              As modest stillness, and humility.
              But when the blast of war blows in our ears,
              Then imitate the action of the tiger:
              Stiffen the sinews, conjure up the blood,
              Disguise fair nature with hard-favoured rage.
              Then lend the eye a terrible aspect:
              Let it pry through the portage of the head,   10
              Like the brass cannon: let the brow o'erwhelm it
              As fearfully as doth a gallèd rock
              O'erhang and jutty his confounded base,
              Swilled with the wild and wasteful ocean.
              Now set the teeth, and stretch the nostril wide,
              Hold hard the breath, and bend up every spirit
              To his full height! On, on, you noblest English,
              Whose blood is fet from fathers of war-proof:
              Fathers, that like so many Alexanders,
              Have in these parts from morn till even fought,   20
              And sheathed their swords for lack of argument.
              Dishonour not your mothers: now attest
              That those whom you called fathers did beget you!
              Be copy now to men of grosser blood,
              And teach them how to war! And you, good yeomen,
              Whose limbs were made in England, show us here
              The mettle of your pasture; let us swear,
              That you are worth your breeding – which I doubt not:

For there is none of you so mean and base,
That hath not noble lustre in your eyes.   30
I see you stand like greyhounds in the slips,
Straining upon the start. The game's afoot:
Follow your spirit; and upon this charge,
Cry, 'God for Harry, England, and Saint George!'

> [*They pass forward to the breach.*
> *'Alarum, and chambers go off'*

SCENE 2

'NYM, BARDOLPH, PISTOL,' *and the* 'BOY' *come up*

BARDOLPH On, on, on, on, on! To the breach, to the breach!

NYM Pray thee, corporal, stay, the knocks are too hot: and
for mine own part, I have not a case of lives: the
humour of it is too hot, that is the very plain-song of it.

PISTOL The plain-song is most just, for humours do abound.
Knocks go and come, God's vassals drop and die:
> And sword and shield,
> In bloody field,
> Doth win immortal fame.

BOY Would I were in an alehouse in London! I would give 10
all my fame for a pot of ale, and safety.

PISTOL And I:
> If wishes would prevail with me,
> My purpose should not fail with me;
> But thither would I hie.

BOY
> As duly,
> But not as truly,
> As bird doth sing on bough.

FLUELLEN *marches up with troops*

FLUELLEN Up to the breach, you dogs; avaunt, you cullions!

PISTOL Be merciful, great duke, to men of mould: 20
Abate thy rate, abate thy manly rage;
Abate thy rage, great duke!
Good bawcock, bate thy rage: use lenity, sweet chuck!

NYM These be good humours. Your honour wins bad
humours.   [*Fluellen drives them forward with his men*

BOY   [*stealing forth*] As young as I am, I have observed these
      three swashers: I am boy to them all three, but all they
      three, though they would serve me, could not be man
      to me; for indeed three such antics do not amount to a
      man. For Bardolph, he is white-livered and red-faced; 30
      by the means whereof a' faces it out, but fights not: for
      Pistol, he hath a killing tongue, and a quiet sword; by
      the means whereof a' breaks words, and keeps whole
      weapons: for Nym, he hath heard that men of few
      words are the best men, and therefore he scorns to say
      his prayers, lest a' should be thought a coward: but his
      few bad words are matched with as few good deeds;
      for a' never broke any man's head but his own, and
      that was against a post, when he was drunk. They will
      steal anything, and call it purchase. Bardolph stole a 40
      lute-case, bore it twelve leagues, and sold it for three
      half-pence. Nym and Bardolph are sworn brothers in
      filching: and in Calais they stole a fire-shovel. I knew
      by that piece of service, the men would carry coals.
      They would have me as familiar with men's pockets as
      their gloves or their handkerchers: which makes much
      against my manhood, if I should take from another's
      pocket, to put into mine; for it is plain pocketing up of
      wrongs. I must leave them, and seek some better serv-
      ice: their villany goes against my weak stomach, and 50
      therefore I must cast it up.   [*he goes*

                   FLUELLEN *returns with* GOWER

GOWER   Captain Fluellen, you must come presently to the
        mines; the Duke of Gloucester would speak with you.

FLUELLEN   To the mines? Tell you the duke, it is not so good to
        come to the mines: for look you, the mines is not
        according to the disciplines of the war; the concavities
        of it is not sufficient: for look you, th'athversary − you
        may discuss unto the duke − look you, is digt himself
        four yard under the counter-mines: by Cheshu, I think
        a' will plow up all, if there is not better directions.   60

GOWER   The Duke of Gloucester, to whom the order of the
        siege is given, is altogether directed by an Irishman, a
        very valiant gentleman, i'faith.

FLUELLEN	It is Captain Macmorris, is it not?
GOWER	I think it be.
FLUELLEN	By Cheshu, he is an ass, as in the world; I will verify as much in his beard. He has no more directions in the true disciplines of the wars, look you, of the Roman disciplines, than is a puppy-dog.

'Enter MACMORRIS *and* CAPTAIN JAMY*'*

GOWER	Here a' comes, and the Scots captain, Captain Jamy, with him.
FLUELLEN	Captain Jamy is a marvellous falorous gentleman, that is certain, and of great expedition and knowledge in th'ancient wars, upon my particular knowledge of his directions: by Cheshu, he will maintain his argument as well as any military man in the world, in the disciplines of the pristine wars of the Romans.
JAMY	I say gud-day, Captain Fluellen.
FLUELLEN	God-den to your worship, good Captain James.
GOWER	How now, Captain Macmorris, have you quit the mines? Have the pioners given o'er?
MACMOR.	By Chrish, la, tish ill done: the work ish give over, the trompet sound the retreat. By my hand I swear, and my father's soul, the work ish ill done: it ish give over: I would have blowed up the town, so Chrish save me, la, in an hour. O tish ill done, tish ill done: by my hand, tish ill done!
FLUELLEN	Captain Macmorris, I beseech you now, will you voutsafe me, look you, a few disputations with you, as partly touching or concerning the disciplines of the war, the Roman wars, in the way of argument, look you, and friendly communication: partly to satisfy my opinion, and partly for the satisfaction, look you, of my mind: as touching the direction of the military discipline, that is the point.
JAMY	It sall be vary gud, gud feith, gud captains bath, and I sall quit you with gud leve, as I may pick occasion: that sall I, marry.
MACMOR.	It is no time to discourse, so Chrish save me: the day is hot, and the weather, and the wars, and the king, and

Line numbers: 70, 80, 90, 100

the dukes. It is no time to discourse, the town is beseeched: an the trumpet call us to the breach, and we talk, and, be Chrish, do nothing, 'tis shame for us all. So God sa' me, 'tis shame to stand still, it is shame, by my hand: an there is throats to be cut, and works to be done, and there ish nothing done, so Chrish sa' me, la!

JAMY   By the mess, ere these eyes of mine take themselves to slomber, ay'll de gude service, or ay'll lig i'th'grund for it; ay, or go to death: and ay'll pay't as valorously as I may, that sal I suerly do, that is the breff and the long. 110 Mary, I wad full fain hear some question 'tween you tway.

FLUELLEN   Captain Macmorris, I think, look you, under your correction, there is not many of your nation –

MACMOR.   Of my nation! What ish my nation? Ish a villain, and a bastard, and a knave, and a rascal – What ish my nation? Who talks of my nation?

FLUELLEN   Look you, if you take the matter otherwise than is meant, Captain Macmorris, peradventure I shall think you do not use me with that affability as in discretion 120 you ought to use me, look you, being as good a man as yourself, both in the disciplines of war, and in the derivation of my birth, and in other particularities.

MACMOR.   I do not know you so good a man as myself: so Chrish save me, I will cut off your head.

GOWER   Gentlemen both, you will mistake each other.

JAMY   Ah! That's a foul fault.

              'A parley' sounded from the walls

GOWER   The town sounds a parley.

FLUELLEN   Captain Macmorris, when there is more better opportunity to be required, look you, I will be so bold as to 130 tell you I know the disciplines of war: and there is an end.

                                [they stand aside

SCENE 3

The GOVERNOR *and some* CITIZENS *appear upon the walls.*
'Enter the King and all his train before the gates'

KING How yet resolves the governor of the town?
    This is the latest parle we will admit:
    Therefore to our best mercy give yourselves,
    Or, like to men proud of destruction,
    Defy us to our worst; for, as I am a soldier,
    A name that in my thoughts becomes me best,
    If I begin the battery once again,
    I will not leave the half-achieved Harfleur
    Till in her ashes she lie buriéd.
    The gates of mercy shall be all shut up,   10
    And the fleshed soldier, rough and hard of heart,
    In liberty of bloody hand, shall range
    With conscience wide as hell, mowing like grass
    Your fresh fair virgins, and your flowering infants.
    What is it then to me, if impious war,
    Arrayed in flames like to the prince of fiends,
    Do with his smirched complexion all fell feats
    Enlinked to waste and desolation?
    What is't to me, when you yourselves are cause,
    If your pure maidens fall into the hand   20
    Of hot and forcing violation?
    What rein can hold licentious wickedness,
    When down the hill he holds his fierce career?
    We may as bootless spend our vain command
    Upon th'enragéd soldiers in their spoil,
    As send precepts to the leviathan
    To come ashore. Therefore, you men of Harfleur,
    Take pity of your town and of your people,
    Whiles yet my soldiers are in my command,
    Whiles yet the cool and temperate wind of grace 30
    O'erblows the filthy and contagious clouds
    Of heady murder, spoil, and villainy.
    If not, why, in a moment look to see
    The blind and bloody soldier with foul hand

Defile the locks of your shrill-shrieking daughters:
Your fathers taken by the silver beards,
And their most reverend heads dashed to the walls:
Your naked infants spitted upon pikes,
Whiles the mad mothers with their howls confused
Do break the clouds; as did the wives of Jewry,   40
At Herod's bloody-hunting slaughtermen.
What say you? Will you yield, and this avoid?
Or, guilty in defence, be thus destroyed?

GOVERNOR Our expectation hath this day an end:
The Dauphin, whom of succours we entreated,
Returns us that his powers are yet not ready
To raise so great a siege. Therefore, great king,
We yield our town and lives to thy soft mercy:
Enter our gates, dispose of us and ours,
For we no longer are defensible.   50

KING Open your gates. Come, uncle Exeter,
Go you and enter Harfleur; there remain,
And fortify it strongly 'gainst the French:
Use mercy to them all. For us, dear uncle,
The winter coming on, and sickness growing
Upon our soldiers, we will retire to Calais.
Tonight in Harfleur will we be your guest;
Tomorrow for the march are we addrest.

[*'Flourish'. The King and his forces 'enter the town'*]

SCENE 4

Rouen. The French King's palace

The Princess KATHARINE *and* ALICE, *'an old Gentlewoman', and other
ladies-in-waiting*

KATHARINE Alice, tu as été en Angleterre, et tu bien parles le
langage.

ALICE Un peu, madame.

KATHARINE Je te prie, m'enseignez: il faut que j'apprenne à parler.
Comment appelez-vous la main en anglais?

ALICE La main? Elle est appelée de hand.

KATHARINE De hand. Et les doigts?

ALICE　　　Les doigts? Ma foi, j'oublie les doigts; mais je me
　　　　　　souviendrai. Les doigts? Je pense qu'ils sont appelés de
　　　　　　fingres: oui, de fingres.　　　　　　　　　　　　　10

KATHARINE　La main, de hand: les doigts, de fingres. Je pense que je
　　　　　　suis le bon écolier. J'ai gagné deus mots d'anglais
　　　　　　vitement. Comment appelez-vous les ongles?

ALICE　　　Les ongles? Nous les appelons de nails.

KATHARINE　De nails. Ecoutez; dites moi si je parle bien: de hand,
　　　　　　de fingres, et de nails.

ALICE　　　C'est bien dit, madame; il est fort bon anglais.

KATHARINE　Dites moi l'anglais pour le bras.

ALICE　　　De arm, madame.

KATHARINE　Et le coude.　　　　　　　　　　　　　　　　　　20

ALICE　　　D' elbow.

KATHARINE　D' elbow. Je m'en fais la répétition de tous les mots
　　　　　　que vous m'avez appris dès à présent.

ALICE　　　Il est trop difficile, madame, comme je pense.

KATHARINE　Excusez-moi, Alice; écoutez: d' hand, de fingre, de
　　　　　　nails, d' arma, de bilbow.

ALICE　　　D' elbow, madame.

KATHARINE　O Seigneur Dieu, je m'en oublie! D' elbow. Comment
　　　　　　appelez-vous le col?

ALICE　　　De nick, madame.　　　　　　　　　　　　　　　30

KATHARINE　De nick. Et le menton?

ALICE　　　De chin.

KATHARINE　De sin. Le col, de nick: le menton, de sin.

ALICE　　　Oui. Sauf votre honneur, en vérité, vous prononcez les
　　　　　　mots aussi droit que les natifs d'Angleterre.

KATHARINE　Je ne doute point d'apprendre, par la grace de Dieu, et
　　　　　　en peu de temps.

ALICE　　　N'avez vous pas déjà oublié ce que je vous ai enseigné?

KATHARINE　Non, je reciterai à vous promptement: d' hand, de
　　　　　　fingre, de mails –　　　　　　　　　　　　　　40

ALICE　　　De nails, madame.

KATHARINE　De nails, de arm, de ilbow.

ALICE　　　Sauf votre honneur, d' elbow.

KATHARINE　Ainsi dis-je: d' elbow, de nick, et de sin. Comment
　　　　　　appelez-vous le pied et la robe?

ALICE　　　Le foot, madame, et le coun.

KATHARINE Le foot, et le coun? O Seigneur Dieu! Ils sont mots de
son mauvais, corruptible, gros, et impudique, et non
pour les dames d'honneur d'user: je ne voudrais
prononcer ces mots devant les seigneurs de France pour 50
tout le monde. Foh! Le foot et le coun. Néanmoins, je
reciterai une autre fois ma leçon ensemble: d' hand, de
fingre, de nailes, d' arm, d' elbow, de nick, de sin, de
foot, le coun.

ALICE   Excellent, madame!

KATHARINE C'est assez pour une fois: allons-nous à dîner.

[*they go*

SCENE 5

'*Enter the* KING *of France, the* DAUPHIN,' *the* DUKE OF BRITAINE,
'*the* CONSTABLE *of France, and others*'

FR. KING   'Tis certain he hath passed the river Somme.

CONSTABLE And if he be not fought withal, my lord,
Let us not live in France: let us quit all,
And give our vineyards to a barbarous people.

DAUPHIN   O Dieu vivant! Shall a few sprays of us,
The emptying of our fathers' luxury,
Our scions, put in wild and savage stock,
Spirt up so suddenly into the clouds,
And overlook their grafters?

BRITAINE   Normans, but bastard Normans, Norman bastards!   10
Mort Dieu! Ma vie! If they march along
Unfought withal, but I will sell my dukedom,
To buy a slobbery and a dirty farm
In that nook-shotten isle of Albion.

CONSTABLE Dieu de batailles! Where have they this mettle?
Is not their climate foggy, raw, and dull?
On whom, as in despite, the sun looks pale,
Killing their fruit with frowns. Can sodden water,
A drench for sur-reined jades, their barley broth,
Decoct their cold blood to such valiant heat?   20
And shall our quick blood, spirited with wine,
Seem frosty? O, for honour of our land,
Let us not hang like roping icicles

Upon our houses' thatch, whiles a more frosty people
Sweat drops of gallant youth in our rich fields –
Poor we may call them in their native lords.

DAUPHIN   By faith and honour,
Our madams mock at us, and plainly say
Our mettle is bred out, and they will give
Their bodies to the lust of English youth,   30
To new-store France with bastard warriors.

BRITAINE They bid us to the English dancing-schools,
And teach lavoltas high, and swift corantos,
Saying our grace is only in our heels,
And that we are most lofty runaways.

FR. KING Where is Montjoy the herald? Speed him hence,
Let him greet England with our sharp defiance.
Up, princes, and with spirit of honour edged
More sharper than your swords, hie to the field:
Charles Delabreth, high constable of France,   40
You Dukes of Orleans, Bourbon, and of Berri,
Alençon, Brabant, Bar, and Burgundy,
Jacques Chatillon, Rambures, Vaudemont,
Beaumont, Grandpré, Roussi, and Faulconbridge,
Foix, Lestrake, Bouciqualt, and Charolois,
High dukes, great princes, barons, lords, and knights;
For your great seats now quit you of great shames.
Bar Harry England, that sweeps through our land
With pennons painted in the blood of Harfleur:
Rush on his host, as doth the melted snow   50
Upon the valleys, whose low vassal seat
The Alps doth spit and void his rheum upon.
Go down upon him, you have power enough;
And in a chariot, captive into Rouen
Bring him our prisoner.

CONSTABLE   This becomes the great.
Sorry am I his numbers are so few,
His soldiers sick and famished in their march:
For I am sure, when he shall see our army,
He'll drop his heart into the sink of fear,
And for achievement offer us his ransom.   60

FR. KING Therefore, lord constable, haste on Montjoy,

And let him say to England, that we send
To know what willing ransom he will give.
Prince Dauphin, you shall stay with us in Rouen.
DAUPHIN   Not so, I do beseech your majesty.
FR. KING   Be patient, for you shall remain with us.
Now forth, lord constable and princes all,
And quickly bring us word of England's fall.

                                                    [*they go*

SCENE 6

The English camp in Picardy

The English and Welsh captains, GOWER *and* FLUELLEN, *meeting*

GOWER   How now, Captain Fluellen! Come you from the
bridge?
FLUELLEN   I assure you, there is very excellent services committed
at the pridge.
GOWER   Is the Duke of Exeter safe?
FLUELLEN   The Duke of Exeter is as magnanimous as Agamem—
non, and a man that I love and honour with my soul,
and my heart, and my duty, and my live, and my
living, and my uttermost power. He is not – God be
praised and blessed! – any hurt in the world, but keeps   10
the pridge most valiantly, with excellent discipline.
There is an ancient lieutenant there at the pridge, I
think in my very conscience he is as valiant a man as
Mark Antony, and he is a man of no estimation in the
world, but I did see him do as gallant service.
GOWER   What do you call him?
FLUELLEN   He is called Ancient Pistol.
GOWER   I know him not.

                    PISTOL *is seen approaching*

FLUELLEN   Here is the man.
PISTOL   Captain, I thee beseech to do me favours: 20
The Duke of Exeter doth love thee well.
FLUELLEN   Ay, I praise God, and I have merited some love at his
hands.

PISTOL   Bardolph, a soldier firm and sound of heart,
And of buxom valour, hath, by cruel fate,
And giddy Fortune's furious fickle wheel,
That goddess blind,
That stands upon the rolling restless stone —

FLUELLEN   By your patience, Ancient Pistol: Fortune is painted
blind, with a muffler afore her eyes, to signify to you that   30
Fortune is blind; and she is painted also with a wheel, to
signify to you, which is the moral of it, that she is
turning and inconstant, and mutability, and variation:
and her foot, look you, is fixed upon a spherical stone,
which rolls, and rolls, and rolls: in good truth, the poet
makes a most excellent description of it: Fortune is an
excellent moral.

PISTOL   Fortune is Bardolph's foe, and frowns on him:
For he hath stolen a pax, and hangéd must a' be —
A damnéd death!   40
Let gallows gape for dog, let man go free,
And let not hemp his windpipe suffocate:
But Exeter hath given the doom of death,
For pax of little price.
Therefore go speak, the duke will hear thy voice;
And let not Bardolph's vital thread be cut
With edge of penny cord, and vile reproach.
Speak, captain, for his life, and I will thee requite.

FLUELLEN   Ancient Pistol, I do partly understand your meaning.

PISTOL   Why then, rejoice therefore.   50

FLUELLEN   Certainly, ancient, it is not a thing to rejoice at: for if,
look you, he were my brother, I would desire the
duke to use his good pleasure, and put him to execution; for discipline ought to be used.

PISTOL   Die and be damned! And figo for thy friendship!

FLUELLEN   It is well.

PISTOL   [bites his thumb] The fig of Spain!   [he goes

FLUELLEN   Very good.

GOWER   Why, this is an arrant counterfeit rascal, I remember
him now: a bawd, a cutpurse.   60

FLUELLEN   I'll assure you, a' uttered as prave words at the pridge
as you shall see in a summer's day: but it is very well

what he has spoke to me, that is well, I warrant you, when time is serve.

GOWER   Why, 'tis a gull, a fool, a rogue, that now and then goes to the wars, to grace himself at his return into London, under the form of a soldier. And such fellows are perfect in the great commanders' names, and they will learn you by rote where services were done; at such and such a sconce, at such a breach, at such a convoy: who 70 came off bravely, who was shot, who disgraced, what terms the enemy stood on; and this they con perfectly in the phrase of war, which they trick up with new-tuned oaths: and what a beard of the general's cut, and a horrid suit of the camp, will do among foaming bottles, and ale-washed wits, is wonderful to be thought on. But you must learn to know such slanders of the age, or else you may be marvellously mistook.

FLUELLEN   I tell you what, Captain Gower: I do perceive he is not the man that he would gladly make show to the 80 world he is: if I find a hole in his coat, I will tell him my mind. [*Drum heard*] Hark you, the king is coming, and I must speak with him from the pridge.

'Drum and colours. Enter King' HENRY, GLOUCESTER,
'and his poor soldiers'

FLUELLEN   God pless your majesty!

KING   How now, Fluellen, cam'st thou from the bridge?

FLUELLEN   Ay, so please your majesty. The Duke of Exeter has very gallantly maintained the pridge; the French is gone off, look you, and there is gallant and most prave passages: marry, th'athversary was have possession of the pridge, but he is enforced to retire, and the Duke of 90 Exeter is master of the pridge. I can tell your majesty, the duke is a prave man.

KING   What men have you lost, Fluellen?

FLUELLEN   The perdition of th'athversary hath been very great, reasonable great: marry, for my part, I think the duke hath lost never a man, but one that is like to be executed for robbing a church, one Bardolph, if your majesty know the man: his face is all bubukles and

whelks, and knobs, and flames afire, and his lips blows
at his nose, and it is like a coal of fire, sometimes plue, 100
and sometimes red; but his nose is executed, and his
fire's out.

KING We would have all such offenders so cut off: and we
give express charge that in our marches through the
country there be nothing compelled from the villages;
nothing taken but paid for; none of the French upbraided or abused in disdainful language; for when
lenity and cruelty play for a kingdom, the gentler
gamester is the soonest winner.

A 'tucket' sounds. MONTJOY *approaches*

MONTJOY You know me by my habit. 110
KING Well then, I know thee: what shall I know of thee?
MONTJOY My master's mind.
KING Unfold it.
MONTJOY Thus says my king. Say thou to Harry of England,
Though we seemed dead, we did but sleep: advantage
is a better soldier than rashness. Tell him, we could
have rebuked him at Harfleur, but that we thought not
good to bruise an injury till it were full ripe. Now we
speak upon our cue, and our voice is imperial: England shall repent his folly, see his weakness, and admire 120
our sufferance. Bid him therefore consider of his ransom, which must proportion the losses we have borne,
the subjects we have lost, the disgrace we have digested; which in weight to re-answer, his pettiness
would bow under. For our losses, his exchequer is too
poor; for th'effusion of our blood, the muster of his
kingdom too faint a number; and for our disgrace, his
own person kneeling at our feet, but a weak and
worthless satisfaction. To this add defiance: and tell
him, for conclusion, he hath betrayed his followers, 130
whose condemnation is pronounced. So far my king
and master; so much my office.

KING What is thy name? I know thy quality.
MONTJOY Montjoy.
KING Thou dost thy office fairly. Turn thee back,
And tell thy king I do not seek him now,

But could be willing to march on to Calais
Without impeachment: for, to say the sooth,
Though 'tis no wisdom to confess so much
Unto an enemy of craft and vantage,   140
My people are with sickness much enfeebled,
My numbers lessened: and those few I have,
Almost no better than so many French;
Who when they were in health, I tell thee, herald,
I thought upon one pair of English legs
Did march three Frenchmen. Yet forgive me, God,
That I do brag thus! This your air of France
Hath blown that vice in me. I must repent.
Go therefore, tell thy master here I am;
My ransom is this frail and worthless trunk;   150
My army, but a weak and sickly guard:
Yet, God before, tell him we will come on,
Though France himself, and such another neighbour,
Stand in our way. There's for thy labour, Montjoy.
                                    [*he gives a purse of gold*
Go bid thy master well advise himself.
If we may pass, we will: if we be hindered,
We shall your tawny ground with your red blood
Discolour. And so, Montjoy, fare you well.
The sum of all our answer is but this:
We would not seek a battle as we are,   160
Nor, as we are, we say we will not shun it.
So tell your master.

MONTJOY I shall deliver so. Thanks to your highness.
                                    [*he bows low and departs*

GLO'STER I hope they will not come upon us now.

KING We are in God's hand, brother, not in theirs.
March to the bridge, it now draws toward night;
Beyond the river we'll encamp ourselves,
And on tomorrow bid them march away.
                                                    [*they go*

SCENE 7

A tent in the French camp, near Agincourt

'Enter the CONSTABLE OF FRANCE, *the Lord* RAMBURES,
ORLEANS, DAUPHIN, *with others*'

CONSTABLE Tut! I have the best armour of the world: would it
    were day!

ORLEANS You have an excellent armour: but let my horse have
    his due.

CONSTABLE It is the best horse of Europe.

ORLEANS Will it never be morning?

DAUPHIN My Lord of Orleans, and my Lord High Constable,
    you talk of horse and armour?

ORLEANS You are as well provided of both as any prince in the
    world.   10

DAUPHIN What a long night is this! I will not change my horse
    with any that treads but on four pasterns. Ça, ha! He
    bounds from the earth, as if his entrails were hairs: le
    cheval volant, the Pegasus, chez les narines de feu!
    When I bestride him, I soar, I am a hawk: he trots the
    air: the earth sings when he touches it: the basest horn
    of his hoof is more musical than the pipe of Hermes.

ORLEANS He's of the colour of the nutmeg.

DAUPHIN And of the heat of the ginger. It is a beast for Perseus:
    he is pure air and fire; and the dull elements of earth   20
    and water never appear in him, but only in patient
    stillness while his rider mounts him. He is indeed a
    horse, and all other jades you may call beasts.

CONSTABLE Indeed, my lord, it is a most absolute and excellent
    horse.

DAUPHIN It is the prince of palfreys: his neigh is like the bidding
    of a monarch, and his countenance enforces homage.

ORLEANS No more, cousin.

DAUPHIN Nay, the man hath no wit that cannot, from the rising
    of the lark to the lodging of the lamb, vary deserved   30
    praise on my palfrey: it is a theme as fluent as the sea:
    turn the sands into eloquent tongues, and my horse is

argument for them all: 'tis a subject for a sovereign to reason on, and for a sovereign's sovereign to ride on: and for the world, familiar to us and unknown, to lay apart their particular functions and wonder at him. I once writ a sonnet in his praise, and began thus, 'Wonder of nature' –

ORLEANS   I have heard a sonnet begin so to one's mistress.

DAUPHIN   Then did they imitate that which I composed to my   40
courser, for my horse is my mistress.

ORLEANS   Your mistress bears well.

DAUPHIN   Me well, which is the prescript praise and perfection of a good and particular mistress.

CONSTABLE   Nay, for methought yesterday your mistress shrewdly shook your back.

DAUPHIN   So perhaps did yours.

CONSTABLE   Mine was not bridled.

DAUPHIN   O then belike she was old and gentle, and you rode like a kern of Ireland, your French hose off, and in   50
your strait strossers.

CONSTABLE   You have good judgement in horsemanship.

DAUPHIN   Be warned by me then: they that ride so, and ride not warily, fall into foul bogs. I had rather have my horse to my mistress.

CONSTABLE   I had as lief have my mistress a jade.

DAUPHIN   I tell thee, constable, my mistress wears his own hair.

CONSTABLE   I could make as true a boast as that, if I had a sow to my mistress.

DAUPHIN   'Le chien est retourné à son propre vomissement, et la   60
truie lavée au bourbier': thou mak'st use of anything.

CONSTABLE   Yet do I not use my horse for my mistress, or any such proverb so little kin to the purpose.

RAMBURES   My lord constable, the armour that I saw in your tent tonight, are those stars or suns upon it?

CONSTABLE   Stars, my lord.

DAUPHIN   Some of them will fall tomorrow, I hope.

CONSTABLE   And yet my sky shall not want.

DAUPHIN   That may be, for you bear a many superfluously, and 'twere more honour some were away.   70

CONSTABLE   Ev'n as your horse bears your praises, who would trot
         as well, were some of your brags dismounted.

DAUPHIN   Would I were able to load him with his desert! Will it
         never be day? I will trot tomorrow a mile, and my way
         shall be paved with English faces.

CONSTABLE   I will not say so, for fear I should be faced out of my
         way: but I would it were morning, for I would fain be
         about the ears of the English.

RAMBURES   Who will go to hazard with me for twenty prisoners?

CONSTABLE   You must first go yourself to hazard, ere you have them.   80

DAUPHIN   'Tis midnight, I'll go arm myself.   [*he leaves the tent*

ORLEANS   The Dauphin longs for morning.

RAMBURES   He longs to eat the English.

CONSTABLE   I think he will eat all he kills.

ORLEANS   By the white hand of my lady, he's a gallant prince.

CONSTABLE   Swear by her foot, that she may tread out the oath.

ORLEANS   He is simply the most active gentleman of France.

CONSTABLE   Doing is activity, and he will still be doing.

ORLEANS   He never did harm, that I heard of.

CONSTABLE   Nor will do none tomorrow: he will keep that good   90
         name still.

ORLEANS   I know him to be valiant.

CONSTABLE   I was told that, by one that knows him better than you.

ORLEANS   What's he?

CONSTABLE   Marry, he told me so himself, and he said he cared not
         who knew it.

ORLEANS   He needs not, it is no hidden virtue in him.

CONSTABLE   By my faith, sir, but it is: never anybody saw it, but his
         lackey: 'tis a hooded valour, and when it appears, it
         will bate.   100

ORLEANS   Ill will never said well.

CONSTABLE   I will cap that proverb with 'There is flattery in friend-
         ship.'

ORLEANS   And I will take up that with 'Give the devil his due.'

CONSTABLE   Well placed: there stands your friend for the devil.
         Have at the very eye of that proverb with 'A pox of
         the devil.'

ORLEANS   You are the better at proverbs, by how much 'A fool's
         bolt is soon shot.'

CONSTABLE You have shot over.   110
ORLEANS   'Tis not the first time you were overshot.

'Enter a MESSENGER*'*

MESSENGER My Lord High Constable, the English lie within fif-
           teen hundred paces of your tents.
CONSTABLE Who hath measured the ground?
MESSENGER The lord Grandpré.
CONSTABLE A valiant and most expert gentleman. Would it were
           day! Alas, poor Harry of England! He longs not for the
           dawning, as we do.
ORLEANS   What a wretched and peevish fellow is this King of
           England, to mope with his fat-brained followers so far 120
           out of his knowledge!
CONSTABLE If the English had any apprehension, they would run
           away.
ORLEANS   That they lack: for if their heads had any intellectual
           armour, they could never wear such heavy head-
           pieces.
RAMBURES   That island of England breeds very valiant creatures;
           their mastiffs are of unmatchable courage.
ORLEANS   Foolish curs, that run winking into the mouth of a
           Russian bear, and have their heads crushed like rotten 130
           apples! You may as well say, that's a valiant flea that
           dare eat his breakfast on the lip of a lion.
CONSTABLE Just, just: and the men do sympathise with the mastiffs
           in robustious and rough coming on, leaving their wits
           with their wives: and then give them great meals of
           beef, and iron and steel; they will eat like wolves, and
           fight like devils.
ORLEANS   Ay, but these English are shrewdly out of beef.
CONSTABLE Then shall we find tomorrow they have only stomachs
           to eat, and none to fight. Now is it time to arm: come, 140
           shall we about it?
ORLEANS   It is now two o'clock: but, let me see, by ten
           We shall have each a hundred Englishmen.

                                              [*they go out*

4. PROLOGUE

Enter 'CHORUS'

CHORUS   Now entertain conjecture of a time
When creeping murmur and the poring dark
Fills the wide vessel of the universe.
From camp to camp, through the foul womb of night
The hum of either army stilly sounds,
That the fixed sentinels almost receive
The secret whispers of each other's watch.
Fire answers fire, and through their paly flames
Each battle sees the other's umbered face.
Steed threatens steed, in high and boastful neighs   10
Piercing the night's dull ear: and from the tents
The armourers, accomplishing the knights,
With busy hammers closing rivets up,
Give dreadful note of preparation.
The country cocks do crow, the clocks do toll,
And the third hour of drowsy morning name.
Proud of their numbers, and secure in soul,
The confident and over-lusty French
Do the low-rated English play at dice;
And chide the cripple tardy-gaited night,   20
Who like a foul and ugly witch doth limp
So tediously away. The poor condemnéd English,
Like sacrifices, by their watchful fires
Sit patiently, and inly ruminate
The morning's danger: and their gesture sad,
Investing lank-lean cheeks, and war-worn coats,
Presenteth them unto the gazing moon
So many horrid ghosts. O now, who will behold
The royal captain of this ruined band
Walking from watch to watch, from tent to tent,   30
Let him cry, 'Praise and glory on his head!'
For forth he goes, and visits all his host,
Bids them good morrow with a modest smile,
And calls them brothers, friends, and countrymen.
Upon his royal face there is no note,

How dread an army hath enrounded him;
Nor doth he dedicate one jot of colour
Unto the weary and all-watchéd night:
But freshly looks, and over-bears attaint
With cheerful semblance, and sweet majesty: 40
That every wretch, pining and pale before,
Beholding him, plucks comfort from his looks.
A largess universal, like the sun,
His liberal eye doth give to every one,
Thawing cold fear, that mean and gentle all
Behold, as may unworthiness define,
A little touch of Harry in the night.
And so our scene must to the battle fly:
Where – O for pity! – we shall much disgrace,
With four or five most vile and ragged foils,   50
Right ill-disposed, in brawl ridiculous,
The name of Agincourt: yet sit and see,
Minding true things by what their mock'ries be.

                                  ['*Exit*'

ACT 4 SCENE 1

The English camp at Agincourt. Before dawn

KING HENRY, BEDFORD, *and* GLOUCESTER

KING   Gloucester, 'tis true that we are in great danger;
The greater therefore should our courage be.
Good morrow, brother Bedford. God Almighty!
There is some soul of goodness in things evil,
Would men observingly distil it out.
For our bad neighbour makes us early stirrers,
Which is both healthful, and good husbandry.
Besides, they are our outward consciences
And preachers to us all, admonishing
That we should dress us fairly for our end.   10
Thus may we gather honey from the weed,
And make a moral of the devil himself.

ERPINGHAM *comes up*

Good morrow, old Sir Thomas Erpingham:

A good soft pillow for that good white head
Were better than a churlish turf of France.

ERPING. Not so, my liege: this lodging likes me better,
Since I may say 'Now lie I like a king.'

KING   'Tis good for men to love their present pains,
Upon example – so the spirit is eased:
And when the mind is quickened, out of doubt   20
The organs, though defunct and dead before,
Break up their drowsy grave, and newly move
With casted slough and fresh legerity.
Lend me thy cloak, Sir Thomas. Brothers both,
Commend me to the princes in our camp;
Do my good morrow to them, and anon
Desire them all to my pavilion.

GLOSTER We shall, my liege.

ERPING. Shall I attend your grace?

KING   No, my good knight:
Go with my brothers to my lords of England: 30
I and my bosom must debate awhile,
And then I would no other company.

ERPING. The Lord in heaven bless thee, noble Harry!

KING   God-a-mercy, old heart! Thou speak'st cheerfully.

                          [*they take leave of the King*

                PISTOL *enters*

PISTOL Qui va là?

KING   A friend.

PISTOL Discuss unto me, art thou officer,
Or art thou base, common, and popular?

KING   I am a gentleman of a company.

PISTOL Trail'st thou the puissant pike?   40

KING   Even so: what are you?

PISTOL As good a gentleman as the emperor.

KING   Then you are a better than the king.

PISTOL The king's a bawcock, and a heart of gold,
A lad of life, an imp of fame,
Of parents good, of fist most valiant:
I kiss his dirty shoe, and from heart-string
I love the lovely bully. What is thy name?

KING	Harry le Roy.
PISTOL	Le Roy? A Cornish name: art thou of Cornish crew? 50
KING	No, I am a Welshman.
PISTOL	Know'st thou Fluellen?
KING	Yes.
PISTOL	Tell him I'll knock his leek about his pate Upon Saint Davy's day.
KING	Do not you wear your dagger in your cap that day, lest he knock that about yours.
PISTOL	Art thou his friend?
KING	And his kinsman too.
PISTOL	The figo for thee then! 60
KING	I thank you: God be with you!
PISTOL	My name is Pistol called. [he goes
KING	It sorts well with your fierceness.

The King withdraws a little; FLUELLEN *and* GOWER *enter*

GOWER	Captain Fluellen!
FLUELLEN	So! In the name of Jesu Christ, speak fewer. It is the greatest admiration in the universal world, when the true and ancient prerogatifes and laws of the wars is not kept: if you would take the pains but to examine the wars of Pompey the Great, you shall find, I warrant you, that there is no tiddle taddle nor pibble pabble in 70 Pompey's camp: I warrant you, you shall find the ceremonies of the wars, and the cares of it, and the forms of it, and the sobriety of it, and the modesty of it, to be otherwise.
GOWER	Why, the enemy is loud, you hear him all night.
FLUELLEN	If the enemy is an ass and a fool, and a prating coxcomb, is it meet, think you, that we should also, look you, be an ass and a fool, and a prating coxcomb? In your own conscience now?
GOWER	I will speak lower. 80
FLUELLEN	I pray you, and beseech you, that you will.

                                      [*they depart*

KING	Though it appear a little out of fashion, There is much care and valour in this Welshman.

'Three soldiers, JOHN BATES, ALEXANDER COURT,
and MICHAEL WILLIAMS*', come up*

COURT Brother John Bates, is not that the morning which breaks yonder?

BATES I think it be: but we have no great cause to desire the approach of day.

WILLIAMS We see yonder the beginning of the day, but I think we shall never see the end of it. Who goes there?

KING A friend.   90

WILLIAMS Under what captain serve you?

KING Under Sir Thomas Erpingham.

WILLIAMS A good old commander, and a most kind gentleman: I pray you, what thinks he of our estate?

KING Even as men wracked upon a sand, that look to be washed off the next tide.

BATES He hath not told his thought to the king?

KING No: nor it is not meet he should: for, though I speak it to you, I think the king is but a man, as I am: the violet smells to him as it doth to me; the element shows to 100 him as it doth to me; all his senses have but human conditions: his ceremonies laid by, in his nakedness he appears but a man; and though his affections are higher mounted than ours, yet, when they stoop, they stoop with the like wing: therefore, when he sees reason of fears, as we do, his fears, out of doubt, be of the same relish as ours are: yet, in reason, no man should possess him with any appearance of fear, lest he, by showing it, should dishearten his army.

BATES He may show what outward courage he will: but I 110 believe, as cold a night as 'tis, he could wish himself in Thames up to the neck; and so I would he were, and I by him, at all adventures, so we were quit here.

KING By my troth, I will speak my conscience of the king: I think he would not wish himself anywhere but where he is.

BATES Then I would he were here alone; so should he be sure to be ransomed, and a many poor men's lives saved.

KING I dare say you love him not so ill, to wish him here alone: howsoever you speak this to feel other men's 120 minds. Methinks I could not die anywhere so contented as in the king's company; his cause being just, and his quarrel honourable.

WILLIAMS That's more than we know.

BATES Ay, or more than we should seek after; for we know enough, if we know we are the king's subjects: if his cause be wrong, our obedience to the king wipes the crime of it out of us.

WILLIAMS But if the cause be not good, the king himself hath a heavy reckoning to make, when all those legs, and 130 arms, and heads, chopped off in a battle, shall join together at the latter day, and cry all 'We died at such a place'; some swearing, some crying for a surgeon; some upon their wives, left poor behind them; some upon the debts they owe; some upon their children rawly left. I am afeard there are few die well, that die in a battle: for how can they charitably dispose of anything, when blood is their argument? Now, if these men do not die well, it will be a black matter for the king, that led them to it; who to disobey were against 140 all proportion of subjection.

KING So, if a son that is by his father sent about merchandise do sinfully miscarry upon the sea, the imputation of his wickedness, by your rule, should be imposed upon his father that sent him: or if a servant, under his master's command, transporting a sum of money, be assailed by robbers, and die in many irreconciled iniquities, you may call the business of the master the author of the servant's damnation. But this is not so: the king is not bound to answer the particular endings of his soldiers, 150 the father of his son, nor the master of his servant; for they purpose not their death, when they purpose their services. Besides, there is no king, be his cause never so spotless, if it come to the arbitrement of swords, can try it out with all unspotted soldiers: some, peradventure, have on them the guilt of premeditated and contrived murder; some, of beguiling virgins with the broken seals of perjury; some, making the wars their bulwark, that have before gored the gentle bosom of

peace with pillage and robbery. Now, if these men 160
have defeated the law, and outrun native punishment,
though they can outstrip men, they have no wings to
fly from God. War is His beadle, war is His vengeance:
so that here men are punished, for before breach of the
king's laws, in now the king's quarrel: where they
feared the death, they have borne life away; and where
they would be safe, they perish. Then if they die
unprovided, no more is the king guilty of their damnation than he was before guilty of those impieties for
the which they are now visited. Every subject's duty is 170
the king's, but every subject's soul is his own. Therefore should every soldier in the wars do as every sick
man in his bed, wash every mote out of his conscience: and dying so, death is to him advantage; or
not dying, the time was blessedly lost, wherein such
preparation was gained: and in him that escapes, it
were not sin to think that, making God so free an offer,
He let him outlive that day, to see His greatness, and to
teach others how they should prepare.

WILLIAMS 'Tis certain, every man that dies ill, the ill upon his 180
own head, the king is not to answer it.

BATES I do not desire he should answer for me, and yet I
determine to fight lustily for him.

KING I myself heard the king say he would not be ransomed.

WILLIAMS Ay, he said so, to make us fight cheerfully: but when
our throats are cut, he may be ransomed, and we ne'er
the wiser.

KING If I live to see it, I will never trust his word after.

WILLIAMS You pay him then! That's a perilous shot out of an
elder-gun, that a poor and a private displeasure can do 190
against a monarch! You may as well go about to turn
the sun to ice, with fanning in his face with a peacock's
feather. You'll never trust his word after! Come, 'tis a
foolish saying.

KING Your reproof is something too round: I should be
angry with you, if the time were convenient.

WILLIAMS Let it be a quarrel between us, if you live.

KING I embrace it.

WILLIAMS   How shall I know thee again?

KING   Give me any gage of thine, and I will wear it in my   200
           bonnet: then, if ever thou dar'st acknowledge it, I will
           make it my quarrel.

WILLIAMS   Here's my glove: give me another of thine.

KING   There.

WILLIAMS   This will I also wear in my cap: if ever thou come to
           me and say, after tomorrow, 'This is my glove', by this
           hand I will take thee a box on the ear.

KING   If ever I live to see it, I will challenge it.

WILLIAMS   Thou dar'st as well be hanged.

KING   Well, I will do it, though I take thee in the king's   210
           company.

WILLIAMS   Keep thy word: fare thee well.

BATES   Be friends, you English fools, be friends; we have
           French quarrels enow, if you could tell how to reckon.

KING   Indeed, the French may lay twenty French crowns to
           one, they will beat us, for they bear them on their
           shoulders: but it is no English treason to cut French
           crowns, and tomorrow the king himself will be a
           clipper.   [the soldiers go their way
           Upon the king! Let us our lives, our souls,   220
           Our debts, our careful wives,
           Our children, and our sins, lay on the king!
           We must bear all. O hard condition,
           Twin-born with greatness, subject to the breath
           Of every fool, whose sense no more can feel
           But his own wringing! What infinite heart's ease
           Must kings neglect that private men enjoy!
           And what have kings, that privates have not too,
           Save ceremony, save general ceremony?
           And what art thou, thou idol Ceremony?   230
           What kind of god art thou, that suffer'st more
           Of mortal griefs than do thy worshippers?
           What are thy rents? What are thy comings in?
           O Ceremony, show me but thy worth!
           What is thy soul of adoration?
           Art thou aught else but place, degree, and form,
           Creating awe and fear in other men?

Wherein thou art less happy, being feared,
Than they in fearing.
What drink'st thou oft, instead of homage sweet,   240
But poisoned flattery? O, be sick, great greatness,
And bid thy ceremony give thee cure!
Thinkst thou the fiery fever will go out
With titles blown from adulation?
Will it give place to flexure and low bending?
Canst thou, when thou command'st the beggar's knee,
Command the health of it? No, thou proud dream,
That play'st so subtly with a king's repose.
I am a king that find thee: and I know,
'Tis not the balm, the sceptre, and the ball,   250
The sword, the mace, the crown imperial,
The intertissued robe of gold and pearl,
The farcéd title running 'fore the king,
The throne he sits on: nor the tide of pomp
That beats upon the high shore of this world:
No, not all these, thrice-gorgeous ceremony,
Not all these, laid in bed majestical,
Can sleep so soundly as the wretched slave:
Who, with a body filled, and vacant mind,
Gets him to rest, crammed with distressful bread;   260
Never sees horrid night, the child of hell:
But, like a lackey, from the rise to set,
Sweats in the eye of Phoebus; and all night
Sleeps in Elysium: next day, after dawn,
Doth rise, and help Hyperion to his horse,
And follows so the ever-running year
With profitable labour to his grave:
And, but for ceremony, such a wretch,
Winding up days with toil, and nights with sleep,
Had the fore-hand and vantage of a king.   270
The slave, a member of the country's peace,
Enjoys it; but in gross brain little wots
What watch the king keeps to maintain the peace,
Whose hours the peasant best advantages.

ERPINGHAM *returns*

ERPING.   My lord, your nobles, jealous of your absence,
            Seek through your camp to find you.
KING   Good old knight,
            Collect them all together at my tent:
            I'll be before thee.
ERPING.   I shall do't, my lord.   [*he goes*
KING   O God of battles, steel my soldiers' hearts,
            Possess them not with fear: take from them now   280
            The sense of reck'ning, or th'opposéd numbers
            Pluck their hearts from them. Not today, O Lord,
            O, not today, think not upon the fault
            My father made in compassing the crown!
            I Richard's body have interréd new,
            And on it have bestowed more contrite tears,
            Than from it issued forcéd drops of blood.
            Five hundred poor I have in yearly pay,
            Who twice a day their withered hands hold up
            Toward heaven, to pardon blood: and I have built   290
            Two chantries, where the sad and solemn priests
            Sing still for Richard's soul. More will I do:
            Though all that I can do is nothing worth;
            Since that my penitence comes after all,
            Imploring pardon.

                    GLOUCESTER *returns*

GLO'STER   My liege!
KING   My brother Gloucester's voice? Ay:
            I know thy errand, I will go with thee:
            The day, my friends, and all things stay for me.
                                                        [*they go*

SCENE 2

The French camp

The DAUPHIN, ORLEANS, RAMBURES, *and others enter*

ORLEANS   The sun doth gild our armour. Up, my lords!
DAUPHIN   Montez à cheval! My horse! Varlet! Laquais! Ha!
ORLEANS   O brave spirit!
DAUPHIN   Via! Les eaux et la terre!
ORLEANS   Rien puis? L'air et le feu?
DAUPHIN   Ciel! Cousin Orleans.

CONSTABLE *enters*

Now, my lord Constable?
CONSTABLE Hark how our steeds for present service neigh.
DAUPHIN   Mount them, and make incision in their hides,
That their hot blood may spin in English eyes,   10
And dout them with superfluous courage, ha!
RAMBURES   What, will you have them weep our horses' blood?
How shall we then behold their natural tears?

'Enter MESSENGER'

MESSENGER The English are embattled, you French peers.
CONSTABLE To horse, you gallant princes, straight to horse!
Do but behold yon poor and starvéd band,
And your fair show shall suck away their souls,
Leaving them but the shales and husks of men.
There is not work enough for all our hands,
Scarce blood enough in all their sickly veins,   20
To give each naked curtle-axe a stain,
That our French gallants shall today draw out,
And sheathe for lack of sport. Let us but blow on them,
The vapour of our valour will o'erturn them.
'Tis positive 'gainst all exceptions, lords,
That our superfluous lackeys, and our peasants,
Who in unnecessary action swarm
About our squares of battle, were enow
To purge this field of such a hilding foe;
Though we upon this mountain's basis by   30
Took stand for idle speculation:

But that our honours must not. What's to say?
A very little little let us do,
And all is done. Then let the trumpets sound
The tucket sonance, and the note to mount:
For our approach shall so much dare the field,
That England shall couch down in fear, and yield.

'Enter GRANDPRÉ*'*

GRANDPRÉ Why do you stay so long, my lords of France?
Yon island carrions, desperate of their bones,
Ill-favouredly become the morning field: 40
Their ragged curtains poorly are let loose,
And our air shakes them passing scornfully.
Big Mars seems bankrout in their beggared host,
And faintly through a rusty beaver peeps.
The horsemen sit like fixéd candlesticks,
With torch-staves in their hand: and their poor jades
Lob down their heads, dropping the hides and hips,
The gum down-roping from their pale-dead eyes,
And in their pale dull mouths the gimmaled bit
Lies foul with chawed-grass, still and motionless.   50
And their executors, the knavish crows,
Fly o'er them all, impatient for their hour.
Description cannot suit itself in words,
To demonstrate the life of such a battle,
In life so lifeless as it shows itself.

CONSTABLE They have said their prayers, and they stay for death.
DAUPHIN Shall we go send them dinners, and fresh suits,
And give their fasting horses provender,
And after fight with them?

CONSTABLE I stay but for my guidon: to the field!   60
I will the banner from a trumpet take,
And use it for my haste. Come, come away!
The sun is high, and we outwear the day.

[they go

SCENE 3

The English camp; before the KING'S *pavilion*

'*Enter* GLOUCESTER, BEDFORD, EXETER, ERPINGHAM *with all his host:*
SALISBURY *and* WESTMORELAND', *with others*

GLO'STER	Where is the king?
BEDFORD	The king himself is rode to view their battle.
WEST'LAND	Of fighting men they have full three-score thousand.
EXETER	There's five to one, besides they all are fresh.
SALISBURY	God's arm strike with us! 'Tis a fearful odds.

          God bye you, princes all; I'll to my charge:
          If we no more meet till we meet in heaven,
          Then joyfully, my noble Lord of Bedford,
          My dear Lord Gloucester, and my good Lord Exeter,
          And my kind kinsman, warriors all, adieu!   10

BEDFORD	Farewell, good Salisbury, and good luck go with thee!
EXETER	Farewell, kind lord; fight valiantly today:

          And yet I do thee wrong, to mind thee of it,
          For thou art framed of the firm truth of valour.

                                [*Salisbury goes*

BEDFORD	He is as full of valour as of kindness,

          Princely in both.

The KING *approaches*

WEST'LAND	O that we now had here

          But one ten thousand of those men in England,
          That do no work today!

KING	What's he that wishes so?

          My cousin Westmoreland? No, my fair cousin:
          If we are marked to die, we are enow   20
          To do our country loss: and if to live,
          The fewer men, the greater share of honour.
          God's will, I pray thee wish not one man more.
          By Jove, I am not covetous for gold,
          Nor care I who doth feed upon my cost:
          It earns me not if men my garments wear;
          Such outward things dwell not in my desires.
          But if it be a sin to covet honour,

I am the most offending soul alive.
No, faith, my coz, wish not a man from England: 30
God's peace, I would not lose so great an honour,
As one man more, methinks, would share from me,
For the best hope I have. O, do not wish one more:
Rather proclaim it, Westmoreland, through my host,
That he which hath no stomach to this fight,
Let him depart, his passport shall be made,
And crowns for convoy put into his purse:
We would not die in that man's company
That fears his fellowship, to die with us.
This day is called the feast of Crispian: 40
He that outlives this day, and comes safe home,
Will stand a tip-toe when this day is named,
And rouse him at the name of Crispian.
He that shall see this day, and live old age,
Will yearly on the vigil feast his neighbours,
And say, 'Tomorrow is Saint Crispian.'
Then will he strip his sleeve, and show his scars,
And say, 'These wounds I had on Crispin's day.'
Old men forget; yet all shall be forgot,
But he'll remember, with advantages,   50
What feats he did that day. Then shall our names,
Familiar in his mouth as household words,
Harry the King, Bedford and Exeter,
Warwick and Talbot, Salisbury and Gloucester,
Be in their flowing cups freshly remembered.
This story shall the good man teach his son:
And Crispin Crispian shall ne'er go by,
From this day to the ending of the world,
But we in it shall be rememberéd;
We few, we happy few, we band of brothers: 60
For he today that sheds his blood with me
Shall be my brother: be he ne'er so vile,
This day shall gentle his condition.
And gentlemen in England, now a-bed,
Shall think themselves accursed they were not here;
And hold their manhoods cheap, whiles any speaks
That fought with us upon Saint Crispin's day.

SALISBURY *returns*

SALISBURY My sovereign lord, bestow yourself with speed:
The French are bravely in their battles set,
And will with all expedience charge on us.   70
KING All things are ready, if our minds be so.
WEST'LAND Perish the man whose mind is backward now!
KING Thou dost not wish more help from England, coz?
WEST'LAND God's will, my liege, would you and I alone,
Without more help, could fight this royal battle!
KING Why, now thou hast unwished five thousand men:
Which likes me better than to wish us one.
You know your places: God be with you all!

A 'tucket' sounds and MONTJOY *approaches*

MONTJOY Once more I come to know of thee, King Harry,
If for thy ransom thou wilt now compound,   80
Before thy most assuréd overthrow:
For certainly thou art so near the gulf,
Thou needs must be englutted. Besides, in mercy,
The Constable desires thee thou wilt mind
Thy followers of repentance; that their souls
May make a peaceful and a sweet retire
From off these fields: where, wretches, their poor bodies
Must lie and fester.
KING   Who hath sent thee now?
MONTJOY The Constable of France.
KING I pray thee bear my former answer back: 90
Bid them achieve me, and then sell my bones.
Good God! Why should they mock poor fellows thus?
The man that once did sell the lion's skin
While the beast lived, was killed with hunting him.
A many of our bodies shall no doubt
Find native graves: upon the which, I trust,
Shall witness live in brass of this day's work.
And those that leave their valiant bones in France,
Dying like men, though buried in your dunghills,
They shall be famed: for there the sun shall greet them,   100
And draw their honours reeking up to heaven,
Leaving their earthly parts to choke your clime,

The smell whereof shall breed a plague in France.
Mark then abounding valour in our English:
That being dead, like to the bullet's crazing
Break out into a second course of mischief,
Killing in relapse of mortality.
Let me speak proudly: tell the Constable
We are but warriors for the working-day:
Our gayness and our gilt are all besmirched   110
With rainy marching in the painful field.
There's not a piece of feather in our host –
Good argument, I hope, we will not fly –
And time hath worn us into slovenry.
But, by the mass, our hearts are in the trim:
And my poor soldiers tell me yet ere night
They'll be in fresher robes, or they will pluck
The gay new coats o'er the French soldiers' heads,
And turn them out of service. If they do this –
As, if God please, they shall – my ransom then   120
Will soon be levied. Herald, save thou thy labour:
Come thou no more for ransom, gentle herald;
They shall have none, I swear, but these my joints:
Which if they have, as I will leave 'em them,
Shall yield them little, tell the Constable.

MONTJOY   I shall, King Harry. And so fare thee well:
Thou never shalt hear herald any more.   [*he goes*

KING   I fear thou wilt once more come again for a ransom.

The DUKE OF YORK *comes up*

YORK   My lord, most humbly on my knee I beg   130
The leading of the vaward.

KING   Take it, brave York. Now soldiers, march away;
And how thou pleasest, God, dispose the day!
          [*they march off*

SCENE 4

The field of battle

'Alarum. Excursions. Enter PISTOL, FRENCH SOLDIER,*' and* 'BOY'

PISTOL   Yield, cur!

FR. SOLD.   Je pense que vous êtes le gentilhomme de bonne qualité.

PISTOL   Qualtitie! Calen o custure me! Art thou a gentleman?
               What is thy name? Discuss.

FR. SOLD.   O Seigneur Dieu!

PISTOL   O, Signieur Dew should be a gentleman:
               Perpend my words, O Signieur Dew, and mark:
               O Signieur Dew, thou diest on point of fox,
               Except, O signieur, thou do give to me
               Egregious ransom.   10

FR. SOLD.   O, prenez miséricorde! Ayez pitié de moi!

PISTOL   Moy shall not serve, I will have forty moys:
               Or I will fetch thy rim out at thy throat,
               In drops of crimson blood.

FR. SOLD.   Est-il impossible d'échapper la force de ton bras?

PISTOL   Brass, cur?
               Thou damnéd and luxurious mountain goat,
               Offer'st me brass?

FR. SOLD.   O pardonnez moi!

PISTOL   Say'st thou me so? Is that a ton of moys?   20
               Come hither, boy, ask me this slave in French
               What is his name.

BOY   Écoutez: comment êtes-vous appelé?

FR. SOLD.   Monsieur le Fer.

BOY   He says his name is Master Fer.

PISTOL   Master Fer! I'll fer him, and firk him, and ferret him:
               discuss the same in French unto him.

BOY   I do not know the French for fer, and ferret, and firk.

PISTOL   Bid him prepare, for I will cut his throat.

FR. SOLD.   Que dit-il, monsieur?   30

BOY   Il me commande à vous dire que vous faites vous prêt,
               car ce soldat ici est disposé tout à cette heure de couper
               votre gorge.

PISTOL   Owy, cuppele gorge, permafoy,

Peasant, unless thou give me crowns, brave crowns;
Or mangled shalt thou be by this my sword.

FR. SOLD. O, je vous supplie, pour l'amour de Dieu, me pardonner! Je suis le gentilhomme de bonne maison,
gardez ma vie, et je vous donnerai deux cents écus.

PISTOL   What are his words?   40

BOY   He prays you to save his life, he is a gentleman of a
good house, and for his ransom he will give you two
hundred crowns.

PISTOL   Tell him my fury shall abate, and I
The crowns will take.

FR. SOLD. Petit monsieur, que dit-il?

BOY   Encore qu'il est contre son jurement de pardonner
aucun prisonnier: néanmoins, pour les écus que vous
l'avez promis, il est content à vous donner la liberté, le
franchisement.   50

FR. SOLD. Sur mes genous je vous donne mille remercîments, et
je m'estime heureux que je suis tombé entre les mains
d'un chevalier, je pense, le plus brave, vaillant, et très
distingué seigneur d'Angleterre.

PISTOL   Expound unto me, boy.

BOY   He gives you upon his knees a thousand thanks, and
he esteems himself happy that he hath fallen into the
hands of one, as he thinks, the most brave, valorous,
and thrice-worthy signieur of England.

PISTOL   As I suck blood, I will some mercy show. Follow me! 60
                                                [*Pistol goes*

BOY   Suivez-vous le grand capitaine!
                                    [*the French soldier follows*
I did never know so full a voice issue from so empty a
heart: but the saying is true, 'The empty vessel makes
the greatest sound.' Bardolph and Nym had ten times
more valour than this roaring devil i'th'old play, that
every one may pare his nails with a wooden dagger,
and they are both hanged, and so would this be, if he
durst steal any thing adventurously. I must stay with
the lackeys with the luggage of our camp; the French
might have a good prey of us, if he knew of it, for   70
there is none to guard it but boys.   [*he goes*

SCENE 5

'Enter CONSTABLE, ORLEANS, BOURBON, DAUPHIN, *and* RAMBURES' *in flight*

CONSTABLE   O diable!

ORLEANS   O Seigneur! Le jour est perdu, tout est perdu!

DAUPHIN   Mort Dieu! Ma vie! All is confounded, all!
      Reproach and everlasting shame
      Sits mocking in our plumes.   [*'a short alarum'*
      O méchante fortune! Do not run away.

CONSTABLE   Why, all our ranks are broke.

DAUPHIN   O perdurable shame! Let's stab ourselves:
      Be these the wretches that we played at dice for?

ORLEANS   Is this the king we sent to for his ransom?   10

BOURBON   Shame, and eternal shame, nothing but shame!
      Let us die in harness: once more back again,
      And he that will not follow Bourbon now,
      Let him go hence, and with his cap in hand
      Like a base pandar hold the chamber-door,
      Whilst by a slave, no gentler than my dog,
      His fairest daughter is contaminated.

CONSTABLE   Disorder, that hath spoiled us, friend us now!
      Let us on heaps go offer up our lives.

ORLEANS   We are enow yet living in the field   20
      To smother up the English in our throngs,
      If any order might be thought upon.

BOURBON   The devil take order now! I'll to the throng;
      Let life be short, else shame will be too long.
                         [*they return to the field*

SCENE 6

'Alarum. Enter the KING *and his train, with prisoners',*
EXETER *and others*

KING   Well have we done, thrice-valiant countrymen,
            But all's not done – yet keep the French the field.

EXETER   The Duke of York commends him to your majesty.

KING   Lives he, good uncle? Thrice within this hour
            I saw him down; thrice up again, and fighting,
            From helmet to the spur all blood he was.

EXETER   In which array, brave soldier, doth he lie,
            Larding the plain: and by his bloody side,
            Yoke-fellow to his honour-owing wounds,
            The noble Earl of Suffolk also lies.   10
            Suffolk first died, and York, all haggled over,
            Comes to him, where in gore he lay insteeped,
            And takes him by the beard, kisses the gashes
            That bloodily did yawn upon his face,
            And cries aloud, 'Tarry, my cousin Suffolk!
            My soul shall thine keep company to heaven:
            Tarry, sweet soul, for mine, then fly abreast:
            As in this glorious and well-foughten field
            We kept together in our chivalry.'
            Upon these words I came, and cheered him up;   20
            He smiled me in the face, raught me his hand,
            And, with a feeble gripe, says, 'Dear my lord,
            Commend my service to my sovereign.'
            So did he turn, and over Suffolk's neck
            He threw his wounded arm, and kissed his lips,
            And so espoused to death, with blood he sealed
            A testament of noble-ending love:
            The pretty and sweet manner of it forced
            Those waters from me which I would have stopped,
            But I had not so much of man in me,   30
            And all my mother came into mine eyes,
            And gave me up to tears.

KING   I blame you not,
            For, hearing this, I must perforce compound

With mistful eyes, or they will issue too.　　　　['*alarum*'
But hark! What new alarum is this same?
The French have reinforced their scattered men:
Then every soldier kill his prisoners,
Give the word through.

　　　　　　　　　　　　　　　　　　　　　　　[*they go*

SCENE 7

'*Enter* FLUELLEN *and* GOWER'

FLUELLEN　Kill the poys and the luggage! 'Tis expressly against the
law of arms, 'tis as arrant a piece of knavery, mark you
now, as can be offert. In your conscience now, is it not?

GOWER　'Tis certain there's not a boy left alive, and the cowardly rascals that ran from the battle ha' done this
slaughter: besides, they have burned and carried away
all that was in the king's tent, wherefore the king most
worthily hath caused every soldier to cut his prisoner's
throat. O, 'tis a gallant king!

FLUELLEN　Ay, he was porn at Monmouth, Captain Gower: what call　10
you the town's name where Alexander the pig was born?

GOWER　Alexander the Great.

FLUELLEN　Why, I pray you, is not pig great? The pig, or the great,
or the mighty, or the huge, or the magnanimous, are all
one reckonings, save the phrase is a little variations.

GOWER　I think Alexander the Great was born in Macedon; his
father was called Philip of Macedon, as I take it.

FLUELLEN　I think it is in Macedon where Alexander is porn: I tell
you, captain, if you look in the maps of the 'orld, I
warrant you sall find, in the comparisons between　20
Macedon and Monmouth, that the situations, look you,
is both alike. There is a river in Macedon, and there is
also moreover a river at Monmouth, it is called Wye at
Monmouth: but it is out of my prains what is the name
of the other river: but 'tis all one, 'tis alike as my fingers
is to my fingers, and there is salmons in both. If you
mark Alexander's life well, Harry of Monmouth's life is
come after it indifferent well, for there is figures in all

things. Alexander, God knows, and you know, in his
rages, and his furies, and his wraths, and his cholers, and   30
his moods, and his displeasures, and his indignations,
and also being a little intoxicates in his prains, did in his
ales and his angers, look you, kill his best friend Cleitus.

GOWER   Our king is not like him in that, he never killed any of
          his friends.

FLUELLEN It is not well done, mark you now, to take the tales
          out of my mouth, ere it is made and finished. I speak
          but in the figures and comparisons of it: as Alexander
          killed his friend Cleitus, being in his ales and his cups;
          so also Harry Monmouth, being in his right wits and   40
          his good judgements, turned away the fat knight with
          the great-belly doublet: he was full of jests, and gipes,
          and knaveries, and mocks, I have forgot his name.

GOWER   Sir John Falstaff.

FLUELLEN That is he: I'll tell you, there is good men porn at
          Monmouth.

GOWER   Here comes his majesty.

> '*Alarum. Enter* KING HARRY *and* BOURBON *with prisoners'*,
> *meeting* WARWICK, GLOUCESTER, EXETER, *heralds*
> *and soldiers,* WILLIAMS *among them.* '*Flourish*'

KING   I was not angry since I came to France
          Until this instant. Take a trumpet, herald,
          Ride thou unto the horsemen on yon hill: 50
          If they will fight with us, bid them come down,
          Or void the field: they do offend our sight.
          If they'll do neither, we will come to them,
          And make them skirr away, as swift as stones
          Enforcéd from the old Assyrian slings:
          Besides, we'll cut the throats of those we have,
          And not a man of them that we shall take
          Shall taste our mercy. Go and tell them so.

                                              [*a herald goes*

                    MONTJOY *approaches*

EXETER   Here comes the herald of the French, my liege.

GLO'STER His eyes are humbler than they used to be.   60

KING   How now, what means this, herald? Know'st thou not

That I have fined these bones of mine for ransom?
Com'st thou again for ransom?

MONTJOY   No, great king:
I come to thee for charitable licence,
That we may wander o'er this bloody field,
To book our dead, and then to bury them,
To sort our nobles from our common men.
For many of our princes – woe the while! –
Lie drowned and soaked in mercenary blood:
So do our vulgar drench their peasant limbs   70
In blood of princes, and their wounded steeds
Fret fetlock deep in gore, and with wild rage
Yerk out their arméd heels at their dead masters,
Killing them twice. O, give us leave, great king,
To view the field in safety, and dispose
Of their dead bodies.

KING   I tell thee truly, herald,
I know not if the day be ours or no,
For yet a many of your horsemen peer,
And gallop o'er the field.

MONTJOY   The day is yours.

KING   Praiséd be God, and not our strength, for it!   80
What is this castle called that stands hard by?

MONTJOY   They call it Agincourt.

KING   Then call we this the field of Agincourt,
Fought on the day of Crispin Crispianus.

FLUELLEN   Your grandfather of famous memory, an't please your
majesty, and your great-uncle Edward the Plack Prince
of Wales, as I have read in the chronicles, fought a
most prave pattle here in France.

KING   They did, Fluellen.

FLUELLEN   Your majesty says very true: if your majesties is re-   90
membered of it, the Welshmen did good service in a
garden where leeks did grow, wearing leeks in their
Monmouth caps, which your majesty know to this hour
is an honourable badge of the service: and I do believe
your majesty takes no scorn to wear the leek upon Saint
Tavy's day.

KING   I wear it for a memorable honour:

For I am Welsh, you know, good countryman.

FLUELLEN   All the water in Wye cannot wash your majesty's
Welsh plood out of your pody, I can tell you that: 100
God pless it, and preserve it, as long as it pleases his
grace, and his majesty too!

KING   Thanks, good my countryman.

FLUELLEN   By Jeshu, I am your majesty's countryman, I care not
who know it: I will confess it to all the 'orld, I need
not to be ashamed of your majesty, praised be God, so
long as your majesty is an honest man.

KING   God keep me so! Our heralds go with him:
Bring me just notice of the numbers dead
On both our parts.   [*heralds depart with Montjoy*
Call yonder fellow hither.   110

EXETER   Soldier, you must come to the king.

KING   Soldier, why wear'st thou that glove in thy cap?

WILLIAMS   An't please your majesty, 'tis the gage of one that I
should fight withal if he be alive.

KING   An Englishman?

WILLIAMS   An't please your majesty, a rascal that swaggered with
me last night: who, if a' live and ever dare to challenge
this glove, I have sworn to take him a box o'th'ear: or
if I can see my glove in his cap – which he swore, as
he was a soldier, he would wear if alive – I will strike it   120
out soundly.

KING   What think you, Captain Fluellen, is it fit this soldier
keep his oath?

FLUELLEN   He is a craven and a villain else, an't please your
majesty, in my conscience.

KING   It may be his enemy is a gentleman of great sort, quite
from the answer of his degree.

FLUELLEN   Though he be as good a gentleman as the devil is, as
Lucifer and Belzebub himself, it is necessary, look your
grace, that he keep his vow and his oath: if he be   130
perjured, see you now, his reputation is as arrant a
villain and a Jack-sauce as ever his black shoe trod upon
God's ground and his earth, in my conscience, la!

KING   Then keep thy vow, sirrah, when thou meet'st the fellow.

WILLIAMS   So I will, my liege, as I live.

KING	Who serv'st thou under?
WILLIAMS	Under Captain Gower, my liege.
FLUELLEN	Gower is a good captain, and is good knowledge and literatured in the wars.
KING	Call him hither to me, soldier. 140
WILLIAMS	I will, my liege. *[he goes*
KING	Here, Fluellen, wear thou this favour for me, and stick it in thy cap: when Alençon and myself were down together, I plucked this glove from his helm: if any man challenge this, he is a friend to Alençon, and an enemy to our person; if thou encounter any such, apprehend him, an thou dost me love.
FLUELLEN	Your grace does me as great honours as can be desired in the hearts of his subjects: I would fain see the man that has but two legs that shall find himself aggriefed at 150 this glove; that is all: but I would fain see it once, an please God of his grace that I might see.
KING	Know'st thou Gower?
FLUELLEN	He is my dear friend, an please you.
KING	Pray thee, go seek him, and bring him to my tent.
FLUELLEN	I will fetch him. *[he goes*
KING	My Lord of Warwick, and my brother Gloucester,
	Follow Fluellen closely at the heels.
	The glove which I have given him for a favour
	May haply purchase him a box o'th'ear. 160
	It is the soldier's: I by bargain should
	Wear it myself. Follow, good cousin Warwick:
	If that the soldier strike him, as I judge
	By his blunt bearing he will keep his word,
	Some sudden mischief may arise of it:
	For I do know Fluellen valiant,
	And, touched with choler, hot as gunpowder,
	And quickly will return an injury.
	Follow, and see there be no harm between them.
	Go you with me, uncle of Exeter. 170
	[they go

SCENE 8

Before King Henry's pavilion

GOWER *and* WILLIAMS *in conversation*

WILLIAMS   I warrant it is to knight you, captain.

FLUELLEN *approaches*

FLUELLEN   God's will, and his pleasure, captain, I beseech you
now, come apace to the king: there is more good
toward you, peradventure, than is in your knowledge
to dream of.

WILLIAMS   [*points to his own bonnet*] Sir, know you this glove?

FLUELLEN   Know the glove? I know the glove is a glove.

WILLIAMS   [*points to Fluellen's cap*] I know this, and thus I challenge it.
                                                        [*'strikes him'*

FLUELLEN   'Sblood, an arrant traitor as any's in the universal
world, or in France, or in England.   10

GOWER   How now, sir? You villain!

WILLIAMS   Do you think I'll be forsworn?

FLUELLEN   Stand away, Captain Gower, I will give treason his
payment into plows, I warrant you.

WILLIAMS   I am no traitor.

FLUELLEN   That's a lie in thy throat. I charge you in his majesty's
name, apprehend him; he's a friend of the Duke
Alençon's.

WARWICK *and* GLOUCESTER *enter, with the* KING
and EXETER *following*

WARWICK   How now, how now, what's the matter?

FLUELLEN   My Lord of Warwick, here is, praised be God for it, a   20
most contagious treason come to light, look you, as you
shall desire in a summer's day. Here is his majesty.

KING   Now now, what's the matter?

FLUELLEN   My liege, here is a villain and a traitor, that, look your
grace, has struck the glove which your majesty is take
out of the helmet of Alençon.

WILLIAMS   My liege, this was my glove, here is the fellow of it:
and he that I gave it to in change promised to wear it

              in his cap: I promised to strike him, if he did: I met
this man with my glove in his cap, and I have been as   30
good as my word.

FLUELLEN   Your majesty, hear now, saving your majesty's manhood, what an arrant, rascally, beggarly, lousy knave it is:
I hope your majesty is pear me testimony and witness,
and will avouchment, that this is the glove of Alençon,
that your majesty is give me, in your conscience now.

KING   Give me thy glove, soldier; look, here is the fellow of it:
'Twas I indeed thou promised'st to strike,
And thou hast given me most bitter terms.

FLUELLEN   An please your majesty, let his neck answer for it, if   40
there is any martial law in the world.

KING   How canst thou make me satisfaction?

WILLIAMS   All offences, my lord, come from the heart: never
came any from mine that might offend your majesty.

KING   It was ourself thou didst abuse.

WILLIAMS   Your majesty came not like yourself: you appeared to
me but as a common man; witness the night, your
garments, your lowliness: and what your highness
suffered under that shape, I beseech you take it for
your own fault, and not mine: for had you been as I   50
took you for, I made no offence; therefore I beseech
your highness pardon me.

KING   Here, uncle Exeter, fill this glove with crowns,
And give it to this fellow. Keep it, fellow,
And wear it for an honour in thy cap,
Till I do challenge it. Give him the crowns:
And, captain, you must needs be friends with him.

FLUELLEN   By this day and this light, the fellow has mettle enough
in his belly. Hold, there is twelve-pence for you, and I
pray you to serve God, and keep you out of prawls and   60
prabbles, and quarrels and dissensions, and I warrant you
it is the better for you.

WILLIAMS   I will none of your money.

FLUELLEN   It is with a good will: I can tell you it will serve you to
mend your shoes: come, wherefore should you be so
pashful? Your shoes is not so good: 'tis a good silling, I
warrant you, or I will change it.

An English Herald returns from the battlefield

KING   Now, herald, are the dead numbered?

HERALD   Here is the number of the slaughtered French.

                               [he delivers a paper

KING   What prisoners of good sort are taken, uncle?   70

EXETER   Charles Duke of Orleans, nephew to the king,
           John Duke of Bourbon, and Lord Bouciqualt:
           Of other lords and barons, knights and squires,
           Full fifteen hundred, besides common men.

KING   This note doth tell me of ten thousand French
           That in the field lie slain: of princes, in this number,
           And nobles bearing banners, there lie dead
           One hundred twenty-six: added to these,
           Of knights, esquires, and gallant gentlemen,
           Eight thousand and four hundred: of the which,   80
           Five hundred were but yesterday dubbed knights.
           So that, in these ten thousand they have lost,
           There are but sixteen hundred mercenaries:
           The rest are princes, barons, lords, knights, squires,
           And gentlemen of blood and quality.
           The names of those their nobles that lie dead –
           Charles Delabreth, high constable of France,
           Jaques of Chatillon, admiral of France,
           The master of the cross-bows, Lord Rambures,
           Great Master of France, the brave Sir Guichard Dolphin,   90
           John Duke of Alençon, Anthony Duke of Brabant,
           The brother to the Duke of Burgundy,
           And Edward Duke of Bar: of lusty earls,
           Grandpré and Roussi, Faulconbridge and Foix,
           Beaumont and Marle, Vaudemont and Lestrake.
           Here was a royal fellowship of death!
           Where is the number of our English dead?

                      [the herald presents another paper

           Edward the Duke of York, the Earl of Suffolk,
           Sir Richard Kikely, Davy Gam, esquire;
           None else of name: and, of all other men,   100
           But five and twenty. O God, thy arm was here:
           And not to us, but to thy arm alone,
           Ascribe we all: when, without stratagem,

But in plain shock, and even play of battle,
Was ever known so great and little loss,
On one part and on th'other? Take it, God,
For it is none but thine!

EXETER   'Tis wonderful!

KING   Come, go we in procession to the village:
And be it death proclaiméd through our host
To boast of this or take that praise from God   110
Which is his only.

FLUELLEN   Is it not lawful, an please your majesty, to tell how many
is killed?

KING   Yes, captain: but with this acknowledgement,
That God fought for us.

FLUELLEN   Yes, my conscience, he did us great good.

KING   Do we all holy rites:
Let there be sung 'Non nobis' and 'Te Deum',
The dead with charity enclosed in clay:
And then to Calais, and to England then,   120
Where ne'er from France arrived more happy men.

                                 [*they go*

5. PROLOGUE

'Enter CHORUS*'*

CHORUS   Vouchsafe to those that have not read the story,
That I may prompt them: and of such as have,
I humbly pray them to admit th'excuse
Of time, of numbers, and due course of things,
Which cannot in their huge and proper life
Be here presented. Now we bear the king
Toward Calais: grant him there; there seen,
Heave him away upon your wingéd thoughts,
Athwart the sea: behold the English beach
Pales in the flood with men, with wives, and boys,   10
Whose shouts and claps out-voice the
                                deep-mouthed sea,
Which like a mighty whiffler 'fore the king
Seems to prepare his way: so let him land,
And solemnly see him set on to London.
So swift a pace hath thought, that even now
You may imagine him upon Blackheath:
Where that his lords desire him to have borne
His bruiséd helmet, and his bended sword
Before him through the city: he forbids it,
Being free from vainness and self-glorious pride;   20
Giving full trophy, signal, and ostent,
Quite from himself, to God. But now behold,
In the quick forge and working-house of thought,
How London doth pour out her citizens:
The mayor and all his brethren in best sort,
Like to the senators of th'antique Rome,
With the plebeians swarming at their heels,
Go forth and fetch their conqu'ring Caesar in:
As, by a lower but loving likelihood,
Were now the general of our gracious empress,   30
As in good time he may, from Ireland coming,
Bringing rebellion broachéd on his sword,
How many would the peaceful city quit,

To welcome him! Much more, and much more cause,
Did they this Harry. Now in London place him;
As yet the lamentation of the French
Invites the King of England's stay at home,
The emperor's coming in behalf of France,
To order peace between them; and omit
All the occurrences, whatever chanced,   40
Till Harry's back-return again to France:
There must we bring him; and myself have played
The interim, by rememb'ring you 'tis past.
Then brook abridgement, and your eyes advance,
After your thoughts, straight back again to France.

[*'Exit'*

ACT 5 SCENE 1

France. The English camp

enter GOWER *and* FLUELLEN

GOWER Nay, that's right. But why wear you your leek today?
Saint Davy's day is past.

FLUELLEN There is occasions and causes why and wherefore in all
things: I will tell you, ass my friend, Captain Gower;
the rascally, scauld, beggarly, lousy, pragging knave
Pistol, which you and yourself, and all the world, know
to be no petter than a fellow, look you now, of no
merits – he is come to me, and prings me pread and salt
yesterday, look you, and bid me eat my leek: it was in a
place where I could not breed no contention with him;   10
but I will be so bold as to wear it in my cap till I see
him once again, and then I will tell him a little piece of
my desires.

PISTOL *enters*

GOWER Why, here he comes, swelling like a turkey-cock.

FLUELLEN 'Tis no matter for his swellings, nor his turkey-cocks.
God pless you, Ancient Pistol! You scurvy lousy
knave, God pless you.

PISTOL Ha! Art thou bedlam? Dost thou thirst, base Troyan,

To have me fold up Parca's fatal web?

Hence! I am qualmish at the smell of leek.   20

FLUELLEN I peseech you heartily, scurvy lousy knave, at my desires, and my requests, and my petitions, to eat, look you, this leek; because, look you, you do not love it, nor your affections, and your appetites, and your digestions does not agree with it, I would desire you to eat it.

PISTOL Not for Cadwallader and all his goats.

FLUELLEN There is one goat for you. [*'strikes him'*] Will you be so good, scauld knave, as eat it?

PISTOL Base Troyan, thou shalt die.

FLUELLEN You say very true, scauld knave, when God's will is: I   30 will desire you to live in the mean time, and eat your victuals: come, there is sauce for it. [*striking him again*] You called me yesterday mountain-squire, but I will make you today a squire of low degree. [*he knocks him down*] I pray you fall to – if you can mock a leek, you can eat a leek.

GOWER Enough, captain, you have astonished him.

FLUELLEN I say, I will make him eat some part of my leek, or I will peat his pate four days: bite, I pray you, it is good for your green wound, and your ploody coxcomb.   40

[*he thrusts the leek between his teeth*

PISTOL Must I bite?

FLUELLEN Yes certainly, and out of doubt, and out of question too, and ambiguities.

PISTOL By this leek, I will most horribly revenge – I eat and eat, I swear.

FLUELLEN Eat; I pray you, will you have some more sauce to your leek? There is not enough leek to swear by.

[*he beats him again*

PISTOL Quiet thy cudgel, thou dost see I eat.

FLUELLEN Much good do you, scauld knave, heartily. [*releases Pistol*] Nay, pray you throw none away, the skin is good   50 for your broken coxcomb; when you take occasions to see leeks hereafter, I pray you mock at 'em, that is all.

PISTOL Good.

FLUELLEN Ay, leeks is good. Hold you, there is a groat to heal your pate.

PISTOL   Me a groat!

FLUELLEN   Yes verily, and in truth you shall take it, or I have another leek in my pocket, which you shall eat.

PISTOL   I take thy groat in earnest of revenge.

FLUELLEN   If I owe you anything, I will pay you in cudgels: you 60 shall be a woodmonger, and buy nothing of me but cudgels. God bye you, and keep you, and heal your pate.   [*he goes*

PISTOL   All hell shall stir for this.

GOWER   Go, go, you are a counterfeit cowardly knave: will you mock at an ancient tradition, began upon an honourable respect, and worn as a memorable trophy of predeceased valour, and dare not avouch in your deeds any of your words? I have seen you gleeking and galling at this gentleman twice or thrice. You thought, 70 because he could not speak English in the native garb, he could not therefore handle an English cudgel: you find it otherwise, and henceforth let a Welsh correction teach you a good English condition – fare ye well.

                                                   [*he goes*

PISTOL   Doth Fortune play the huswife with me now?
News have I that my Doll is dead i'th'spital
O' malady of France,
And there my rendezvous is quite cut off.
Old I do wax, and from my weary limbs
Honour is cudgelled. Well, bawd I'll turn,   80
And something lean to cutpurse of quick hand.
To England will I steal, and there I'll steal:
And patches will I get unto these cudgelled scars,
And swear I got them in the Gallia wars.

                                                   [*he goes*

SCENE 2

France. A royal palace

'Enter, at one door, KING HENRY, EXETER, BEDFORD, WARWICK, *and other Lords; at another,* QUEEN ISABEL, *the'* FRENCH 'KING', *the Princess* KATHARINE, ALICE, *and other Ladies,* '*the* DUKE OF BURGUNDY, *and other French'*

KING	Peace to this meeting, wherefore we are met!
	Unto our brother France, and to our sister,
	Health and fair time of day: joy and good wishes
	To our most fair and princely cousin Katharine:
	And, as a branch and member of this royalty,
	By whom this great assembly is contrived,
	We do salute you, Duke of Burgundy;
	And, princes French, and peers, health to you all!
FR. KING	Right joyous are we to behold your face,
	Most worthy brother England, fairly met: 10
	So are you, princes English, every one.
ISABEL	So happy be the issue, brother England,
	Of this good day, and of this gracious meeting,
	As we are now glad to behold your eyes,
	Your eyes which hitherto have borne in them
	Against the French, that met them in their bent,
	The fatal balls of murdering basilisks.
	The venom of such looks, we fairly hope,
	Have lost their quality, and that this day
	Shall change all griefs and quarrels into love. 20
KING	To cry amen to that, thus we appear.
ISABEL	You English princes all, I do salute you.
BURGUNDY	My duty to you both, on equal love.
	Great kings of France and England, that I have laboured
	With all my wits, my pains, and strong endeavours,
	To bring your most imperial majesties
	Unto this bar and royal interview,
	Your mightiness on both parts best can witness.
	Since then my office hath so far prevailed,
	That face to face, and royal eye to eye, 30
	You have congreeted, let it not disgrace me,

If I demand before this royal view,
What rub, or what impediment there is,
Why that the naked, poor, and mangled Peace,
Dear nurse of arts, plenties, and joyful births,
Should not in this best garden of the world,
Our fertile France, put up her lovely visage?
Alas, she hath from France too long been chased,
And all her husbandry doth lie on heaps,
Corrupting in it own fertility.   40
Her vine, the merry cheerer of the heart,
Unprunéd, dies: her hedges even-pleached,
Like prisoners wildly overgrown with hair,
Put forth disordered twigs: her fallow leas
The darnel, hemlock, and rank fumitory
Doth root upon, while that the coulter rusts,
That should deracinate such savagery:
The even mead, that erst brought sweetly forth
The freckled cowslip, burnet, and green clover,
Wanting the scythe, all uncorrected, rank,   50
Conceives by idleness, and nothing teems
But hateful docks, rough thistles, kecksies, burs,
Losing both beauty and utility;
And as our vineyards, fallows, meads, and hedges,
Defective in their natures, grow to wildness,
Even so our houses, and ourselves, and children,
Have lost, or do not learn, for want of time,
The sciences that should become our country;
But grow like savages, as soldiers will,
That nothing do but meditate on blood,   60
To swearing, and stern looks, diffused attire,
And everything that seems unnatural.
Which to reduce into our former favour,
You are assembled: and my speech entreats,
That I may know the let, why gentle Peace
Should not expel these inconveniences,
And bless us with her former qualities.
KING   If, Duke of Burgundy, you would the peace,
Whose want gives growth to th'imperfections
Which you have cited, you must buy that peace   70

                    With full accord to all our just demands,
                    Whose tenours and particular effects
                    You have, enscheduled briefly, in your hands.
BURGUNDY   The king hath heard them: to the which, as yet,
                    There is no answer made.
KING   Well then: the peace, which you before so urged,
                    Lies in his answer.
FR. KING   I have but with a cursitory eye
                    O'erglanced the articles: pleaseth your grace
                    To appoint some of your council presently   80
                    To sit with us once more, with better heed
                    To resurvey them, we will suddenly
                    Pass our accept and peremptory answer
KING   Brother, we shall. Go, uncle Exeter,
                    And brother Clarence, and you, brother Gloucester,
                    Warwick, and Huntingdon, go with the king,
                    And take with you free power, to ratify,
                    Augment, or alter, as your wisdoms best
                    Shall see advantageable for our dignity,
                    Anything in or out of our demands,   90
                    And we'll consign thereto. Will you, fair sister,
                    Go with the princes, or stay here with us?
ISABEL   Our gracious brother, I will go with them:
                    Haply a woman's voice may do some good,
                    When articles too nicely urged be stood on.
KING   Yet leave our cousin Katharine here with us;
                    She is our capital demand, comprised
                    Within the fore-rank of our articles.
ISABEL   She hath good leave.   [All depart but King Henry,
                                                                    Katharine, and Alice
KING   Fair Katharine, and most fair,
                    Will you vouchsafe to teach a soldier terms,
                    Such as will enter at a lady's ear,   100
                    And plead his love-suit to her gentle heart?
KATHARINE Your majesty shall mock at me, I cannot speak your
                    England.
KING   O fair Katharine, if you will love me soundly with
                    your French heart, I will be glad to hear you confess it

	brokenly with your English tongue. Do you like me, Kate?	
KATHARINE	Pardonnez moi, I cannot tell vat is 'like me'.	
KING	An angel is like you, Kate, and you are like an angel.	
KATHARINE	Que dit-il? Que je suis semblable à les anges?	110
ALICE	Oui, vraiment, sauf votre grace, ainsi dit-il.	
KING	I said so, dear Katharine, and I must not blush to affirm it.	
KATHARINE	O bon Dieu! Les langues des hommes sont pleines de tromperies.	
KING	What says she, fair one? That the tongues of men are full of deceits?	
ALICE	Oui, dat de tongues of de mans is be full of deceits: dat is de princess.	
KING	The princess is the better Englishwoman. I'faith, Kate, my wooing is fit for thy understanding; I am glad thou canst speak no better English, for, if thou couldst, thou wouldst find me such a plain king, that thou wouldst think I had sold my farm to buy my crown. I know no ways to mince it in love, but directly to say 'I love you'; then if you urge me farther than to say 'Do you in faith?' I wear out my suit. Give me your answer, i'faith do, and so clap hands, and a bargain: how say you, lady?	120
KATHARINE	Sauf votre honneur, me understand vell.	130
KING	Marry, if you would put me to verses, or to dance for your sake, Kate, why, you undid me: for the one, I have neither words nor measure; and for the other, I have no strength in measure, yet a reasonable measure in strength. If I could win a lady at leap-frog, or by vaulting into my saddle with my armour on my back, under the correction of bragging be it spoken, I should quickly leap into a wife: or if I might buffet for my love, or bound my horse for her favours, I could lay on like a butcher, and sit like a jack-an-apes, never off. But before God, Kate, I cannot look greenly, nor gasp out my eloquence, nor I have no cunning in protestation; only downright oaths, which I never use till urged, nor never break for urging. If thou canst love a fellow of	140

this temper, Kate, whose face is not worth sun-burning, that never looks in his glass for love of anything he sees there, let thine eye be thy cook. I speak to thee plain soldier: if thou canst love me for this, take me; if not, to say to thee that I shall die is true; but for thy 150 love, by the Lord, no: yet I love thee too. And while thou liv'st, dear Kate, take a fellow of plain and uncoined constancy, for he perforce must do thee right, because he hath not the gift to woo in other places: for these fellows of infinite tongue, that can rhyme themselves into ladies' favours, they do always reason themselves out again. What! A speaker is but a prater, a rhyme is but a ballad; a good leg will fall, a straight back will stoop, a black beard will turn white, a curled pate will grow bald, a fair face will wither, a 160 full eye will wax hollow: but a good heart, Kate, is the sun and the moon, or rather the sun and not the moon; for it shines bright, and never changes, but keeps his course truly. If thou would have such a one, take me! And take me, take a soldier: take a soldier, take a king. And what say'st thou then to my love? Speak, my fair, and fairly, I pray thee.

KATHARINE Is it possible dat I sould love de enemy of France?

KING   No, it is not possible you should love the enemy of France, Kate; but, in loving me, you should love the 170 friend of France: for I love France so well that I will not part with a village of it; I will have it all mine: and, Kate, when France is mine, and I am yours, then yours is France, and you are mine.

KATHARINE I cannot tell vat is dat.

KING   No, Kate? I will tell thee in French, which I am sure will hang upon my tongue like a new-married wife about her husband's neck, hardly to be shook off. Je quand sur le possession de France, et quand vous avez le possession de moi — let me see, what then? Saint 180 Dennis be my speed — donc votre est France, et vous êtes mienne. It is as easy for me, Kate, to conquer the kingdom, as to speak so much more French: I shall never move thee in French, unless it be to laugh at me.

KATHARINE Sauf votre honneur, le français que vous parlez, il est meilleur que l'anglais lequel je parle.

KING No, faith, is't not, Kate: but thy speaking of my tongue, and I thine, most truly falsely, must needs be granted to be much at one. But, Kate, dost thou understand thus much English? Canst thou love me? 190

KATHARINE I cannot tell.

KING Can any of your neighbours tell, Kate? I'll ask them. Come, I know thou lovest me: and at night, when you come into your closet, you'll question this gentlewoman about me; and I know, Kate, you will to her dispraise those parts in me that you love with your heart: but, good Kate, mock me mercifully, the rather, gentle princess, because I love thee cruelly. If ever thou beest mine, Kate, as I have a saving faith within me tells me thou shalt, I get thee with scambling, and thou 200 must therefore needs prove a good soldier-breeder: shall not thou and I, between Saint Dennis and Saint George, compound a boy, half French, half English, that shall go to Constantinople, and take the Turk by the beard? Shall we not? What say'st thou, my fair flower-de-luce?

KATHARINE I do not know dat.

KING No; 'tis hereafter to know, but now to promise: do but now promise, Kate, you will endeavour for your French part of such a boy; and, for my English moiety, 210 take the word of a king and a bachelor. How answer you, la plus belle Katharine du monde, mon très cher et devin déesse?

KATHARINE Your majestee 'ave fause French enough to deceive de most sage demoiselle dat is en France.

KING Now fie upon my false French! By mine honour, in true English, I love thee, Kate; by which honour, I dare not swear thou lovest me, yet my blood begins to flatter me that thou dost; notwithstanding the poor and untempering effect of my visage. Now beshrew my 220 father's ambition! He was thinking of civil wars when he got me, therefore was I created with a stubborn outside, with an aspect of iron, that when I come to

woo ladies, I fright them: but in faith, Kate, the elder I
wax, the better I shall appear. My comfort is, that old
age, that ill layer up of beauty, can do no more spoil
upon my face. Thou hast me, if thou hast me, at the
worst; and thou shalt wear me, if thou wear me, better
and better: and therefore tell me, most fair Katharine,
will you have me? Put off your maiden blushes,   230
avouch the thoughts of your heart with the looks of
an empress, take me by the hand, and say 'Harry of
England, I am thine': which word thou shalt no
sooner bless mine ear withal, but I will tell thee aloud
'England is thine, Ireland is thine, France is thine, and
Henry Plantagenet is thine'; who, though I speak it
before his face, if he be not fellow with the best king,
thou shalt find the best king of good fellows. Come,
your answer in broken music; for thy voice is music,
and thy English broken: therefore, queen of all,   240
Katharine, break thy mind to me in broken English;
wilt thou have me?

KATHARINE Dat is as it sall please de roi mon père.

KING   Nay, it will please him well, Kate; it shall please him,
            Kate.

KATHARINE Den it sall also content me.

KING   Upon that I kiss your hand, and I call you my queen.

KATHARINE Laissez, mon seigneur, laissez, laissez: ma foi, je ne
            veux point que vous abaissiez votre grandeur en baisant
            la main d'une de votre seigneurie indigne serviteur;   250
            excusez-moi, je vous supplie, mon très-puissant
            seigneur.

KING   Then I will kiss your lips, Kate.

KATHARINE Les dames et demoiselles pour être baisées devant leur
            noces, il n'est pas la coutume de France.

KING   Madam my interpreter, what says she?

ALICE   Dat it is not be de fashon pour les ladies of France – I
            cannot tell vat is baiser en Anglish.

KING   To kiss.

ALICE   Your majestee entendre bettre que moi.   260

KING   It is not a fashion for the maids in France to kiss before
            they are married, would she say?

ALICE   Oui, vraiment.

KING   O Kate, nice customs curtsy to great kings. Dear Kate, you and I cannot be confined within the weak list of a country's fashion: we are the makers of manners, Kate; and the liberty that follows our places stops the mouth of all find-faults, as I will do yours, for upholding the nice fashion of your country, in denying me a kiss: therefore patiently, and yielding. [*kissing her*] You have 270 witchcraft in your lips, Kate: there is more eloquence in a sugar touch of them than in the tongues of the French council; and they should sooner persuade Harry of England than a general petition of monarchs. Here comes your father.

The FRENCH KING *and* QUEEN *return with* BURGUNDY, EXETER, WESTMORELAND, *and other French and English Lords*

BURGUNDY   God save your majesty! My royal cousin, teach you our princess English?

KING   I would have her learn, my fair cousin, how perfectly I love her, and that is good English.

BURGUNDY   Is she not apt?   280

KING   Our tongue is rough, coz, and my condition is not smooth: so that, having neither the voice nor the heart of flattery about me, I cannot so conjure up the spirit of love in her, that he will appear in his true likeness.

BURGUNDY   Pardon the frankness of my mirth, if I answer you for that. If you would conjure in her, you must make a circle: if conjure up love in her in his true likeness, he must appear naked, and blind. Can you blame her then, being a maid yet rosed over with the virgin crimson of modesty, if she deny the appearance of a 290 naked blind boy in her naked seeing self? It were, my lord, a hard condition for a maid to consign to.

KING   Yet they do wink and yield, as love is blind and enforces.

BURGUNDY   They are then excused, my lord, when they see not what they do.

KING   Then, good my lord, teach your cousin to consent winking.

BURGUNDY I will wink on her to consent, my lord, if you will
teach her to know my meaning: for maids, well sum- 300
mered and warm kept, are like flies at Bartholomew-
tide, blind, though they have their eyes, and then they
will endure handling, which before would not abide
looking on.

KING This moral ties me over to time, and a hot summer;
and so I shall catch the fly, your cousin, in the latter
end, and she must be blind too.

BURGUNDY As love is, my lord, before it loves.

KING It is so: and you may, some of you, thank love for my
blindness, who cannot see many a fair French city for 310
one fair French maid that stands in my way.

FR. KING Yes, my lord, you see them perspectively: the cities
turned into a maid; for they are all girdled with maiden
walls, that war hath never entered.

KING Shall Kate be my wife?

FR. KING So please you.

KING I am content, so the maiden cities you talk of may wait
on her: so the maid that stood in the way for my wish
shall show me the way to my will.

FR. KING We have consented to all terms of reason.   320

KING Is't so, my lords of England?

WEST'LAND The king hath granted every article:
His daughter first; and then in sequel all,
According to their firm proposéd natures.

EXETER Only he hath not yet subscribéd this:
Where your majesty demands that the King of France,
having any occasion to write for matter of grant, shall
name your highness in this form, and with this addition, in French: Notre très-cher fils Henri, Roi
d'Angleterre, Héritier de France: and thus in Latin; 330
Praeclarissimus filius noster Henricus, Rex Angliae, et
Haeres Franciae.

FR. KING Nor this I have not, brother, so denied,
But your request shall make me let it pass.

KING I pray you then, in love and dear alliance,
Let that one article rank with the rest,
And thereupon give me your daughter.

FR. KING	Take her, fair son, and from her blood raise up
	Issue to me, that the contending kingdoms
	Of France and England, whose very shores look pale 340
	With envy of each other's happiness,
	May cease their hatred; and this dear conjunction
	Plant neighbourhood and Christian-like accord
	In their sweet bosoms: that never war advance
	His bleeding sword 'twixt England and fair France.
ALL	Amen!
KING	Now welcome, Kate: and bear me witness all,
	That here I kiss her as my sovereign queen. ['*Flourish*'
ISABEL	God, the best maker of all marriages,
	Combine your hearts in one, your realms in one! 350
	As man and wife, being two, are one in love,
	So be there 'twixt your kingdoms such a spousal,
	That never may ill office, or fell jealousy,
	Which troubles oft the bed of blessèd marriage,
	Thrust in between the paction of these kingdoms,
	To make divorce of their incorporate league:
	That English may as French, French Englishmen,
	Receive each other. God speak this Amen!
ALL	Amen!
KING	Prepare we for our marriage: on which day, 360
	My Lord of Burgundy, we'll take your oath,
	And all the peers', for surety of our leagues.
	Then shall I swear to Kate, and you to me,
	And may our oaths well kept and prosp'rous be!

[*A trumpet sounds as they go*

EPILOGUE

'Enter CHORUS*'*

CHORUS   Thus far, with rough and all-unable pen,
          Our bending author hath pursued the story,
          In little room confining mighty men,
          Mangling by starts the full course of their glory.
          Small time: but, in that small, most greatly lived
          This star of England. Fortune made his sword;
          By which the world's best garden he achieved:
          And of it left his son imperial lord.
          Henry the Sixth, in infant bands crowned King
          Of France and England, did this king succeed: 10
          Whose state so many had the managing,
          That they lost France, and made his England bleed:
          Which oft our stage hath shown; and, for their sake,
          In your fair minds let this acceptance take.

                                                    [*Exit*

WORDSWORTH CLASSICS
OF WORLD LITERATURE

REQUESTS FOR INSPECTION COPIES   Lecturers wishing to obtain copies of Wordsworth Classics, Wordsworth Poetry Library or Wordsworth Classics of World Literature titles on inspection are invited to contact: Dennis Hart, Wordsworth Editions Ltd, Crib Street, Ware, Herts SG12 9ET; E-mail: dennis.hart@wordsworth-editions.com. Please quote the author, title and ISBN of the titles in which you are interested; together with your name, academic address, E-mail address, the course on which the books will be used and the expected enrolment.

Teachers wishing to inspect specific core titles for GCSE or A level courses are also invited to contact Wordsworth Editions at the above address.

Inspection copies are sent solely at the discretion of Wordsworth Editions Ltd.

APULEIUS
The Golden Ass

ARISTOTLE
The Nicomachean Ethics

MARCUS AURELIUS
Meditations

FRANCIS BACON
Essays

JAMES BOSWELL
The Life of Samuel Johnson
(UNABRIDGED)

JOHN BUNYAN
The Pilgrim's Progress

BALDESAR CASTIGLIONE
The Book of the Courtier

CATULLUS
Poems

CERVANTES
Don Quixote

CARL VON CLAUSEWITZ
On War
(ABRIDGED)

CONFUCIUS
The Analects

CAPTAIN JAMES COOK
The Voyages of Captain Cook

DANTE
The Inferno

CHARLES DARWIN
The Origin of Species
The Voyage of the Beagle

RENÉ DESCARTES
Key Philosophical Writings

FYODOR DOSTOEVSKY
The Devils

ERASMUS
Praise of Folly

SIGMUND FREUD
The Interpretation of Dreams

EDWARD GIBBON
*The Decline and Fall of the
Roman Empire*
(ABRIDGED)

GUSTAVE FLAUBERT
A Sentimental Journey

KAHLIL GIBRAN
The Prophet

JOHANN WOLFGANG
VON GOETHE
Faust

HERODOTUS
Histories

HOMER
The Iliad and The Odyssey

HORACE
The Odes

BEN JONSON
Volpone and Other Plays

KENKO
Essays in Idleness

WILLIAM LANGLAND
Piers Plowman

LAO TZU
Tao Te Ching

T. E. LAWRENCE
Seven Pillars of Wisdom